D0855420

GOSPEL
PERSPECTIVES

Studies of History and Tradition in the Four Gospels

Volume II

Edited by
R. T. France
and David Wenham

1981

JSOT Press

Copyright © 1981 JSOT Press

ISBN O 905774 31 O

Published by
JSOT Press
Department of Biblical Studies
The University of Sheffield
Sheffield S1O 2TN
England

Artwork by Roger Evans,
Sheffield University Printing Unit
Printed in Great Britain
by Redwood Burn Limited
Trowbridge & Esher
1981

Contents

PREFACE   5

THE PROBLEM OF THE GENRE OF THE GOSPELS: A CRITIQUE OF
C. H. TALBERT'S *WHAT IS A GOSPEL?*   9
D. E. Aune

SETTING 'THE QUEST FOR THE HISTORICAL JESUS' IN A BROADER
FRAMEWORK   61
R. J. Banks

HISTORICAL TRADITION IN THE FOURTH GOSPEL: AFTER DODD,
WHAT?   83
D. A. Carson

ANNOUNCEMENT IN *NAZARA*: AN ANALYSIS OF LUKE 4:16-21   147
Bruce Chilton

THE EMPTY TOMB OF JESUS   173
William Lane Craig

ON DISCERNING SEMITIC SOURCES IN LUKE 1-2   201
Stephen C. Farris

SCRIPTURE, TRADITION AND HISTORY IN THE INFANCY
NARRATIVES OF MATTHEW   239
R. T. France

JOHANNES UND MATTHÄUS - ZWIESPALT ODER VIERGESTALT DES
EVANGELIUMS?   267
Gerhard Maier

JOHN 21: TEST CASE FOR HISTORY AND REDACTION IN THE
RESURRECTION NARRATIVES   293
Grant R. Osborne

THE AUTHENTICITY OF THE PARABLES OF JESUS   329
Philip Barton Payne

PAUL AND THE SYNOPTIC APOCALYPSE   345
David Wenham

Preface

This volume, being a sequel to *Gospel Perspectives* I (1980), needs little explanation: like the first volume it is the fruit of the Gospels Research Project of Tyndale House in Cambridge, a project set up to look at the ever-important question of the historicity of the gospels; and our desire in this volume, as it was in the last, is to help 'provide answers to the questions of historicity which will stand up to serious academic scrutiny and will provide some help for those who are perplexed by scholarly disagreement'.

We explained in volume 1 that the essays in that volume were not a comprehensive study, but we expressed the hope that a fuller coverage would be achieved in future publications. We believe that volume 2 goes some way to fulfilling this hope, though there are important matters that have not been treated (e.g. the subject of miracles); and the need for continuing research is urgent. The Tyndale House Gospels Research Project is going to continue its work; but from now on our attention will be directed not to the question of historicity in general, but to more particular issues, such as that of gospel genre in relation to Jewish historiography.

How far have these two volumes taken us? First, there has been some useful discussion of method. Robert Stein in his study (in vol 1) has explained sympathetically and critically the various criteria for authenticity used by gospel scholars, but has reminded us of their limitations (especially when used negatively). Don Carson in his essay on historical tradition and the Fourth Gospel (vol 2) maintains that many Johannine scholars pay insufficient attention to questions of method and are as a result over-confident about doubtful conclusions. It is salutary to be reminded by both writers (a) of the danger of claiming more for the evidence than it properly allows - scholarly theorizing frequently goes far beyond the evidence -, and (b) of the influence of people's prior assumptions. No one can be free of such assumptions, but it is wise to be as aware and critical of them as possible. It does seem that much gospel study is conducted consciously or unconsciously within the framework of negative assumptions about the gospels' historicity - assumptions which deserve to be questioned on historical, literary and theological grounds and which may be blamed for some of the scholarly fog that surrounds the gospels.

A second important question discussed in our two volumes has been that of the nature of the gospel tradition. Some take the gospels as straightforward, historical accounts of Jesus' earthly life and ministry; others insist that they were not intended as historical reminiscences at all but as theological statements, and that they belong to Hellenistic or Jewish literary genres that were consciously and deliberately imaginative in their recounting of events. Several of our essays have touched on these questions. Grant Osborne (vol 2) has attempted to show that history and theology are complementary not contradictory in one chapter of that most theological gospel, John. David Aune (vol 2) has cautioned us against over-simple attempts to categorize the gospels as Hellenistic biography. Three essays have explored the relationship of the gospels to Jewish tradition: Bruce Chilton (vol 1) compares the gospels with the Jewish targums, an interesting approach, especially if it suggests that the church from very early on treated the Jesus tradition as the Jews treated Scripture; Peter Davids (vol 1) in his review of the work of Birger Gerhardsson and others argues that, although Gerhardsson may have overstated his case and although the gospel tradition has been exegetically expanded in the course of transmission, nevertheless the gospel material, especially the teaching of Jesus, was a tradition deliberately passed on to the disciples by Jesus and that the early church valued and made an effort to preserve that tradition; Rainer Riesner (vol 1) has approached the matter from a different angle by reminding us of how important memorization was in the life of ordinary Jewish people, not just for Jewish rabbis and their disciples. The upshot of these different reflexions is certainly to remind us that in the gospels we are dealing with first century and not twentieth century documents, but also that it is quite unwarranted to assume that the evangelists and their predecessors were incapable of or uninterested in preserving historical tradition.

A third and substantial ingredient in our discussions has been careful study of a wide range of gospel materials. Ultimately all general theories concerning the gospels must be put to the test in the 'real-life' situation of the text, and we have covered the infancy narratives (Dick France, vol 2; Stephen Farris, vol 2), the Nazareth sermon of Luke 4 (Bruce Chilton, vol 2), the parables (Philip Payne, vols 1 and 2), the ransom saying of Mark 10:45 (Sydney Page, vol 1), the eschatological discourse of Mark 13 par. (David Wenham, vol 2), the Johannine trial narrative (F. F. Bruce, vol 1), and the resurrection narratives (William Craig, vols 1 and 2; Grant Osborne, vol 2). We have also had broader studies of Mark (Dick France, vol 1), of Matthew and John (Gerhard Maier, vol 2), and of John (Don Carson, vol 2). There has been no uniformity in our approach, and we have only dipped into the problems and questions raised by the passages. But in different ways our essays have confirmed that the obvious theological interests of the evangelists have led them to preserve rather than to create historical tradition; repeatedly we have concluded that the evangelists, however much they may have coloured the picture themselves, were working with and controlled by sources and early traditions. We have also seen that some of the deep divisions presupposed by many modern scholars, e.g. between Paul and the evangelists or between John and the Synoptics, are not so deep after all, and that there are more similarities and connections between them than is often noted.

A fourth significant element in the two volumes is that they have pointed the way forward to some possibly valuable avenues for future research. Robert Banks' essay (vol 2) is notable in its plea for a broader perspective in gospel research; but other essays too, such as Bruce Chilton's on the Targums and David Aune's on the gospel genre, have opened up, without necessarily answering, questions which promise to increase our understanding of the nature of the gospel tradition.

To an extent this is true of our Project as a whole as represented in the two volumes. We cannot claim to have 'solved' many problems, nor even to have convinced each other by all our arguments; much work remains to be done. But we consider that the cumulative effect of our studies has been to show that serious historical and literary scholarship allows us to approach the gospels with the belief that they present an essentially historical account of the words and deeds of Jesus. As editors we are convinced that a recovery of that belief will prove liberating both in the scholarly enterprise, which has so often seemed locked in a straitjacket of rationalistic assumptions and arbitrary historical scepticism, and also within the church, which needs to hear, to see and to follow the Jesus of the gospels.

8

We are grateful to the Tyndale House Council for their sponsorship of the Research Project, to the participants in the Project (both authors and others), and to the JSOT Press for their cooperation in publishing *Gospel Perspectives* I and II.

R. T. FRANCE

DAVID WENHAM

Tyndale House, Cambridge

The Problem of the Genre of the Gospels:
A Critique of C. H. Talbert's What is a Gospel?

D. E. Aune,
Saint Xavier College,
Chicago, Illinois 60655.

I.   Introduction

One of the more significant trends in NT scholarship during the past decade has been the growing interest in the problem of the genre of NT literature/1/. Many recent studies have attempted to analyze and describe the generic types represented in the NT (gospel, history, letter, apocalypse), in light of comparable literary forms in Graeco-Roman and Israelite-Jewish literature/2/. While NT scholars have long recognized the generic affinities of the early Christian letter to Graeco-Roman letters, and of the Apocalypse of John to the apocalyptic literature of early Judaism, for two generations the *communis opinio* has been that the gospel form was the unique creation of early Christianity, without substantive parallel in the literature of Graeco-Roman paganism or early Judaism/3/.

The recent re-examination of the genre of the gospels is usually predicated on the notion that the gospels are not *sui generis*, but must be compared with other ancient literary types with which they have affinities in order that they may be properly understood and interpreted/4/. The primary purpose for determining the genre of the gospels, or any other piece of literature, is hermeneutical/5/. If the gospels are members of a particular literary genre, so the argument runs, they cannot be properly understood or interpreted unless that genre is recognized and its conventions understood/6/. According to E. D. Hirsch, 'All understanding of verbal meaning is necessarily genre-bound'/7/. While some literary critics espouse a synchronic approach to genre criticism, in which organization and structure are emphasized rather than time or place/8/, others (including NT scholars) insist on the necessity of diachronic, or historical, study of generic types in addition to a consideration of their internal and external form/9/. The complexity of the problem of determining the generic affiliation of the gospel form is dramatically exhibited by the wide variety of ancient literary types which

various scholars have regarded as paradigmatic for the gospel
form. Some have regarded the OT as the major source for the
patterns exhibited in the gospels, either in the stories and
sayings of Moses, or in the Elijah-Elisha cycle/10/. Others
have found the chief influence on the form and content of the
gospels to derive from early Judaism, either as a Christian
surrogate for the Passover haggadah or as a midrashic
interpretation of the life of Jesus structured in accordance
with the Jewish lectionary cycle or the festal cycle of
readings in ancient synagogues/11/. Those who find antecedents
for the gospel form in Graeco-Roman literature have suggested
various types of biography, particularly the lives of
philosophers, the tragedy (i.e., as a 'closet' drama not
intended for actual performance), the aretalogy (a narrative of
the miraculous deeds of a god or hero), the memoir, and the
Socratic dialogue (to name only a few of the many possibilities)
/12/. The diversity of these views suggests that scholars who
do not regard the gospel form as *sui generis* cannot agree on
the specific type of ancient literature with which the gospel
form has the closest affinity.

The current interest of NT scholars in genre is dependent
on work done by classical philologists and specialists in
Israelite-Jewish literature. In both areas, however, problems
of genre analysis exhibit great complexity. The NT scholar who
wishes to utilize the results of classical scholarship on the
question of genre, for example, soon finds himself embroiled in
problems with which he is ill-equipped to deal. Classical
scholars themselves have experienced difficulties in
identifying and analyzing the genres of many compositions from
Graeco-Roman antiquity. This difficulty is due in part to the
methodology employed. Two generations ago R. K. Hack discussed
the doctrine of literary forms in classical antiquity by
forcefully making three points/13/:   (1) The effect of ancient
poetic theory on actual composition has been greatly
overestimated (e.g. the theory of Horace in *Ars Poetica*
contradicts his practise).   (2) The 'doctrine of literary forms'
held by modern philologists emphasizes the supposed formal
features of a literary genre at the expense of idiosyncratic
features.   (3) The laws of genres are an expression in the
field of literature of the Platonic doctrine of ideas.

Ancient literature from the Hellenistic and Roman period
is, in fact, often very difficult to identify in terms of
strict literary forms/14/. In a chapter entitled "Die Kreuzung
der Gattungen" in the influential book *Studien zum Verständnis*

der römischen Literatur, Wilhelm Kroll discussed the phenomenon
of mixed genres as a characteristic of the late republican and
early imperial period in Roman literature/15/. The literary
epistle in particular provided the framework for the combination
of a number of genres/16/.

Determining the genre of many Graeco-Roman compositions
has proven to be a difficult task. One such generic problem is
presented by Petronius' *Satyricon*, which, according to P. G.
Walsh, 'is best regarded as a creative synthesis of Greek
fiction with Roman satire and mimic motifs'/17/. Classicists
have also had perennial problems with Plutarch's *Moralia*. With
regard to composition and structure, many of these essays have
been variously assessed as 'awkward,' 'incomplete,'
'unfinished,' 'written during his youth,' etc. Recent studies,
however, have discerned studied method in Plutarch's apparent
madness/18/. Many problems yet remain; what, for example, is
the genre of Plutarch's famous treatise *De Iside et Osiride?*
There are no close formal analogies to this composition in
Graeco-Roman literature. More relevant to the subject of this
essay are the problems involved in determining the genre of
Philostratos' *Vita Apollonii*. It has been variously regarded
as a biography, a novel, a 'Reiseroman,' and as a composite of
several genres/19/. One must be careful not to assume that the
Vita Apollonii is a typical example of Greek biography and to
base far-reaching conclusions on that doubtful assumption. If
I have conveyed the notion that a naive intrusion into the
world of classical philology is analogous to a blindfolded man
staggering through a minefield, then my caveat has been
successful.

Recently, Charles H. Talbert, in a slim volume entitled
What is a Gospel? The Genre of the Canonical Gospels
(Philadelphia: Fortress Press, 1977)/20/, has attempted to
buttress arguments advanced by earlier scholars, together with
his own work on the genre of Luke-Acts, by demonstrating that
the form of the canonical gospels is not a unique creation of
Mark and/or John, but that it exhibits the basic features of
ancient Graeco-Roman biography. In spite of the generally
positive tone of the reviews which have thusfar appeared, it is
my view that he has unwittingly misinterpreted the ancient
evidence to such an extent that his book is unusable in its
present state. I shall attempt to substantiate that rather
severe judgment in the following pages.

II.   The Major Theses of Talbert's *What is a Gospel?*

In Chapter 1, 'The Problem,' the author provides a brief
but incisive history of research into the question of the genre
of the gospels. For more than a generation the dominant view
has been that the gospels have no significant generic links with
ancient biography, but rather represent the narrative expansion
of the early Christian proclamation of Jesus. Talbert selects
Rudolf Bultmann as a major representative of this view and
summarizes the three 'foundation pillars' on which this view is
based: (1) The gospels are mythical in structure, while
Graeco-Roman biographies are not.   (2) The gospels are cult
legends, while Graeco-Roman biographies are not.   (3) The
gospels were produced by a community with a world-negating
attitude, while Graeco-Roman biographies were produced in
world-affirming settings. 'Implicit in these three arguments,'
claims Talbert, 'are the criteria assumed, by Bultmann and
others in the critical consensus, to be necessary for
establishing the genre of a document' (p. 6). After surveying
unsuccessful attempts to determine the genre of the gospels,
he concludes (p. 15):

> This volume shares the current dissatisfaction with the
> critical consensus that the canonical gospels are not
> biographies but are *sui generis*. Its purpose is to show
> that the canonical gospels do, in fact, belong to
> antiquity's genre of biography. It will accept Bultmann's
> assumed criteria for determining genre: there must be
> agreement in a conjunction of outer form (mythical
> structure), function (cultic), and attitude, if the
> canonical gospels are to be grouped with any known
> genre(s) in Mediterranean antiquity.

In Chapter 2, Talbert deals with the mythical structure of
the Synoptic Gospels, and in Chapter 3 with the mythical
structure of the Fourth Gospel; in both chapters it is his
purpose to 'show that certain ancient biographies, like the
canonical gospels, were ordered from a mythical point of view'
(p. 25). In addition to the basic categories 'gods' and 'men,'
there were also, between these two extremes, two additional
categories: (1) divine men, i.e., men who exhibited the
presence of the divine by a variety of means, and (2) men who,
at the end of their earthly lives, were taken up into heaven
and granted immortality and a status equal to the eternal gods.
In contrast to the eternal gods, deified men were designated
'immortals' (p. 26), and it is this category of divinity about

which Chapter 2 is structured. The typology of 'eternals' and
'immortals', according to Talbert, was at least as early as
Herodotos (5th cent. B.C.), and remained viable til the 3rd
cent. A.D. After a survey of the evidence, he concludes that
'Egyptian, Greek, Roman, and Jewish evidence points to the
belief in the existence of a certain category of deity, the
immortals, alongside the eternals' (p. 30). This mythology was
used of mythical and legendary figures of the remote past, and
eventually became attached to figures of the recent past,
particularly rulers and philosophers (p. 31). The myth of the
immortals became widely used in history, biography and satire.
Talbert summarizes the character of an immortal on p. 35:

> What is constitutive for the status of an immortal? The
> protagonist is first of all a mortal—though perhaps so
> extraordinary as to be regarded in some sense divine
> during his lifetime, but mortal nonetheless. At the end
> of his career, by the decree or act of some eternal, he is
> taken up into heaven, becomes immortal, and takes his place
> place in the pantheon of gods.

The ancient conception of the divine man, however, was
originally distinct from that of the immortal, though eventually
eventually the two notions merged (p. 36). Some early
Christians, suggests the author, thought of Christ in terms of
the myth of the immortals, a conclusion suggested by three
factors: (1) The Christology of Hellenistic-Jewish
Christianity conforms to the myth of the immortals with the
addition of an emphasis on the Parousia of Christ and his
unique Lordship. (2) Stories of Jesus' ascension, the empty
tomb (empty because of an ascension) and stories of
resurrection appearances function coherently within the
framework of the myth of the immortals. (3) The gospels are
structured by the myth of the immortals. The author concludes
(p. 42): 'The sweeping statement that Graeco-Roman biographies
were not mythical is inaccurate. The mythology of the
immortals was used by some as the frame for their story—as do
the synoptic gospels.'

In Chapter 3, Talbert considers the myth which controls
the use of the Jesus tradition in the Fourth Gospel, the myth
of the descending-ascending redeemer. He dismisses the gnostic
origin of the redeemer myth, and focuses on Jewish myths of the
descending-ascending redeemer. 'The early Christian myth of a
descending-ascending redeemer,' he claims, 'was taken over from
Hellenistic Judaism' (p. 77), and provided the basic structure
for the Fourth Gospel. Though Mark and John are generally

regarded as examples of the same genre, they use different
myths to structure their narratives.

The second pillar of Bultmann's view, according to Talbert,
is that the gospels had a cultic function while Graeco-Roman
biographies did not. The author takes up the subject of the
cultic function of Graeco-Roman biography in Chapter 4. 'Cult'
is defined as 'the worshiping community with its rites and
ceremonies' (p. 92, derived from Bultmann). After briefly
discussing Friedrich Leo's system of classifying ancient
biographies, Talbert presents what he regards as an alternative
classification based on the criterion of the function(s) of
ancient biographies in their 'social-intellectual-spiritual'
milieu (p. 93). On pp. 94-96, he presents a fivefold typology
of functions: Type A: Lives which function to provide a pattern
to emulate; Type B: Lives dispelling a false image of the
teacher and substituting a true one; Type C: Lives written to
discredit a teacher; Type D: Lives of philosophers indicating
where their true successors are found; Type E: Lives written to
validate or provide an interpretive key for a teacher's
doctrine. Talbert finds a striking similarity between Type B
lives and the gospels, since both were written to dispel a
false image and inculcate a new, more correct, one (p. 98).

Talbert then asks if didactic biographies (those divided
into the five types discussed above) had any connections with a
cult. He suggests three means for implying cultic functions:
(1) implications of the use of myth, (2) links between the life
of a teacher and his collected teachings, and (3) use of lists
of succession or narratives of succession. After discussing
the implications of the mythic structure of ancient biographies,
he concludes (p. 101):

> Given the view of myth espoused by the modern history of
> religions research, either these writings in their present
> form, or some earlier forms now expanded and utilized in
> these documents, were linked to communities founded by
> these hero figures who were the objects of the communities'
> devotion. That is, these didactic biographies which employ
> myth are either cult legends or expanded cult legends.

Following a discussion of ancient lives of teachers which are
linked with collections of their teachings, he concludes (p.
105):

> From what has been said about the Lives of both
> philosophers and rulers whose biographies are juxtaposed
> to their collected teaching or legislation, it is clear

that they were produced or preserved by religious or
semireligious communities and functioned on behalf of
their communities' religious or value objectives.   In
this very general sense, then, these biographies are cult
documents.

Finally, with regard to the use of succession lists appended
to lives of teachers, Talbert emphasizes the religious
character of ancient philosophical schools and the importance
of determining who the true successors of the Founder were.   In
this sense, then, such succession lists point to a cultic
setting; after comparing Luke-Acts to lives of ancient
teachers with succession lists, he concludes (p. 108):

Luke-Acts and those philosophical biographies with
succession lists/narratives arise out of a common milieu,
namely, communities in which there exists a struggle over
where the true tradition is to be found in the present.

Ancient biographies, he concludes, not only *could*, but *did* have
a cultic Sitz im Leben (p. 108).

Finally, in Chapter 5, Talbert discusses Bultmann's third
pillar, i.e., the fact that the eschatological perspective of
early Christianity, with its world-negating attitude, would
have demanded unique literary forms for its expression.   'In
order to say that the canonical gospels belong to any ancient
genre,' asserts Talbert, 'it would be necessary to show that in
this genre the attitude was world-negating just as in the
gospels' (p. 115).   He then poses some very important questions:
Would a gospel automatically have a unique genre simply because
it was an expansion of the Christian kerygma?   Since many
constituent forms in the gospels (parable, miracle story, etc.),
belong to ancient *Gattungen*, why cannot the gospels as a whole
have literary analogues (p. 116)?   Would a gospel produced by
Hellenistic Christians *necessarily* reflect a world-negating
mood?   Considering Paul's Corinthian opponents as examples,
Talbert suggests that such a gospel might well have a world-
affirming view.   Can an eschatological perspective use
non-eschatological genres with which to express itself?   Of
course!   Paul himself is a primary example, for he uses a
rhetorically sophisticated epistolary genre.   Talbert then
concludes (p. 118):

This data proves that Overbeck's thesis that an
eschatological consciousness was so world-negating that it
precluded the use of literary forms from the everyday
world is untenable.

Both Mark and Luke, contends Talbert, exhibit evidence which

suggests that they were written to prevent a misuse of the
Jesus traditions. 'The compositional principle followed by
these two Evangelists was that of inclusive reinterpretation.
A part with a different point of view was included but
reinterpreted by its inclusion in a larger whole' (p. 122).
The same holds true for the Fourth Gospel. After finding a
similar procedure and attitude in Graeco-Roman biography, he
concludes that the 'attitude of the canonical four is not at
all a world-negating one which prohibits Christian self-
expression in the literary forms of the profane world' (p. 127).
The preceding paragraphs represent an attempt to fairly and
extensively summarize the main points made by Talbert. Lengthy
quotations have been used to minimize the possibility of
distorting his position.

III. Preliminary Observations

Before discussing Talbert's main points in detail, there
are a number of important general issues which need to be
raised. First, while Talbert has chosen to refute the critical
consensus of NT scholarship as represented by Bultmann, the
real Goliath is K. L. Schmidt, whose 1923 article 'Die Stellung
der Evangelien in der allgemeinen Literaturgeschichte,' remains
the single most important and influential treatment of the view
that the gospels are the unique creation of early Christianity.
/21/ While Bultmann's discussion is brief and schematic,
Schmidt wrote eighty-four pages on the subject. It is Schmidt,
not Bultmann, who requires refutation if Talbert expects to
establish his thesis. Of the many important issues raised by
Schmidt, but not taken up by Talbert, three deserve mention
here: (1) The *anonymity* of the gospels is emphasized by
Schmidt in contrast to the various types of biographical
literature in the Graeco-Roman world; Xenophon, Arrian and
Philostratos, in contrast to the evangelists, are tangible,
specific authors (pp. 51, 54f., 58f.). Even in the *Vita
Apollonii* of Philostratos, the first person voice of the author
permeates the book (p. 82). (2) Schmidt regarded the gospels,
in contrast to Graeco-Roman biographies, as *Kleinliteratur* in
contrast to *Hochliteratur* (p. 76), a view with which ancient
literary critics would fully agree. By *Kleinliteratur*, Schmidt
means folk literature which exhibits universal characteristics
(p. 84): 'This type of biographical tradition to which we have
been led follows the same laws of transmission in all ages, in
all languages, in all cultures, races and creeds.' He
compares the gospels in great detail with the legends of the

saints, particularly St. Francis, the legends of the Hasidim,
and the German story of Dr. Faustus. (3) Schmidt did not, like
Talbert, lump the Synoptic Gospels together, but saw a
progressive 'literaturization' in Matthew and Luke when
compared with Mark (pp. 60-62).

A second feature of Talbert's book is the author's
failure to forge an alliance with Erhardt Güttgemanns' feisty
book, *Offene Fragen zur Formgeschichte des Evangeliums*, 2nd ed.
(München: Kaiser Verlag, 1971). This book constitutes a
frontal assault on the more cherished opinions of contemporary
NT scholarship from the perspective of modern studies in
sociology, linguistics, literary criticism and folkloristics.
The author strongly opposes Franz Overbeck's distinction
between *Hochliteratur* and *Kleinliteratur*, a dichotomy which has
been almost axiomatic for Form Critics since the First World
War. Talbert would have found many useful arguments in
Güttgemanns' book, including his discussion of 'Die fehlende
Analogie der jüdischen Apokalyptik' (pp. 97-100), where the
author points out that in early Judaism fervent eschatological
expectation was combined with the utilization of existing
literary genres.

A third feature of Talbert's book and one most disturbing
to classicists, is the fact that the author roams the length
and breadth of Graeco-Roman literature, almost exclusively
within the ambit of the *Loeb Classical Library* (numerous
translations from which are used but rarely credited), and
virtually unencumbered with the scholarly baggage of modern
classical philology. Like Geza Vermes and Michael Grant on
Jesus, Talbert has chosen not to familiarize himself with the
secondary scholarly literature on the subjects treated in his
book. While this guarantees a 'fresh' approach, it also
conjures up our image of a blindfolded man staggering across a
minefield. Many of the more useful resources for classical
studies are never used: modern commentaries on the various
writings to which the author refers, the scholia, collections of
inscriptions, editions of the fragments of the tragedians,
comedians, historians, presocratics, and such major reference
works as W. H. Roscher, *Ausführliches Lexikon der griechischen
und römischen Mythologie*, 6 vols. (Leipzig: B. G. Teubner,
1884-1937); Pauly-Wissowa's *Real-Encyclopädie der classischen
Altertumswissenschaft; Reallexikon für Antike und Christentum*,
etc. Further, Talbert tends to ignore much of the more
significant work in classical philology; he does refer to the

works of some eminent classicists (A. D. Nock, F. Leo, E. R.
Dodds, L. R. Farnell, M. Hadas, W. Jaeger, A. Momigliano, E.
Rohde, D. R. Stuart), but nearly always on relatively
insignificant issues. Where are Nilsson, Festugière, Burkert,
Guthrie, Pfister? The general failure to draw on the
achievements of modern classical philology is perhaps the main
reason for the many false assumptions, misinterpretations and
oversimplifications which permeate Talbert's book.

A fourth problem has to do with Talbert's assumption that
Bultmann's views on the nature of the gospels continue to
retain validity even though they were articulated more than
fifty years ago, and a great many developments in NT
scholarship have occurred since that time. Further, even
though Talbert thinks to accept Bultmann's implications of
what constitutes a genre, what Bultmann was really doing was
stating reasons why the gospels are *not* a literary genre in the
ordinary sense of that term. Can Talbert safely ignore the
altered perspective on the gospels introduced by the advent of
Redaktionsgeschichte? I think not.

Finally, when reading Talbert's book I found myself
harboring the suspicion that the ancient evidence was being
molded in such a way that the final product (primarily the
'myth of the immortals'), was predestined to bear an amazing
resemblance to the pattern of Luke-Acts: after thinking about
the issues raised in the book for the past two years, I am
convinced that this is precisely what has occurred.

IV. The 'Myth of the Immortals'

Between the two extremes of gods and men, there were,
according to Talbert, two intermediate categories, divine men
and immortals (i.e., mortals who became deified at the end of
their earthly careers). Both the canonical gospels, and
Graeco-Roman biographies, he claims, were structured by this
myth. Bultmann's contention that the gospels are mythical, but
ancient biographies are not is therefore refuted. Since there
was such an immense variation in ancient biography, Talbert's
basic contention is well-taken; 'myth' in the sense of
folkloristic themes and motifs did play a significant role in
the more popular ancient lives and those written after the
first century A.D. (the bulk of which are lost). But to use the
word *structure,* rather than *theme* or *motif,* is a basic error
which we must discuss at greater length below.

Talbert's 'myth of the immortals' is a serious oversimplification of ancient views on how mortals could become divine/22/. His use of the terms 'eternal' and 'immortal' to distinguish two types of god in the ancient world is his own, and not at all typical of the religious theories of ancient writers. In fact, *no ancient author uses the categories 'eternal'* (ἀίδιος) *and 'immortal'* (ἄφθαρτος, ἀθάνατος) *in both a consistent and exhaustive way to describe the traditional Greek Olympians on the one hand, and those, like Herakles, who were regarded as having achieved post-mortem immortality.* The reason is quite simple; for the Greeks ἀθάνατος and θεός were synonymous throughout antiquity/23/. Death and divinity were so mutually exclusive that a god who was mourned as dead (like Adonis; cf. Lucian *De Dea Syr. 6*) was always thought strange by the Greeks/24/. A great revolution in Greek religion had occurred when ἀθάνατος began to be applied to humans/25/.

The 'eternal'/'immortal' typology, claims Talbert, is at least as old as Herodotos; it is also found in Dionysios of Halicarnassos, Diodoros of Sicily, Plutarch and Philo. 'In Diodorus of Sicily,' he asserts, 'the typology is clearly articulated and applied to his narrative's contents' (p. 27). He then quotes the *LCL* translation of Diodoros 6.1, with a significant omission which I include in italics/26/:

Now concerning the gods, the ancients have transmitted to posterity two notions. They say that some are eternal [ἀίδιους] and immortal [ἀφθάρτους], *such as the sun, moon and the other stars of the heavens, as well as the winds and whatever has a similar nature, for the generation and permanence of this type is eternal* [ἀίδιον]. But they say that the other gods were earthly, but attained immortal [ἀθανάτου] honor and reputation because of their service to man, such as Herakles, Dionysos, Aristaios and many others like them.

This example of a 'clearly articulated' typology of 'eternal'/ 'immortal' gods does *not* contrast Olympians such as Zeus, Apollo, etc., with Herakles, Aristaios, etc., as Talbert would have the reader think, *but rather contrasts the eternally divine heavenly bodies with anthropomorphic deities, all of whom received divine honor through lives of service to man.* For the ancient Greeks, the cosmos itself was both eternal and divine, and the gods (whether Olympian or Chthonian) came into existence only after the ordering of the cosmos, as Hesiod relates in his *Theogony*. Further, Talbert seems unaware of the fact that Diodoros is a Euhemerist, i.e., one who believed that

the anthropomorphic deities worshipped by the Greeks were once
living kings. In the paragraph cited above from Diodoros, the
author is introducing one of several lengthy quotations from
Euhemeros; in fact, Diodoros is our chief source for the
fragments of Euhemeros which he preserves in 5. 41-46; 6.1 (F.
Jacoby, *FGrHist*, I, 300-313). The Olympians are conspicuous
by their absence in our quotation from Diodoros because he
wants to include them in the second category along with
Herakles, Dionysos and Aristaios. Further, Diodoros does *not*
say that immortality was bestowed on Herakles and the others
after death or at the conclusion of their lives as Talbert
implies. The reason is simply that Euhemeros and his spiritual
descendants contended that divine honors were paid to *living*
kings/27/. As we shall see below, Euhemeros (and his Roman
popularizer Quintus Ennius) provided the ideological basis for
the deification of the *diadochoi* of Alexander and eventually
for the Roman *princeps*.

     Talbert is quite correct, of course, in distinguishing a
category of divinity which the Greeks regarded as having once
been mortal, but who eventually received the post-mortem
status of immortals. He is very specific about this: 'I use
immortals here to refer to those humans who become deities by
virtue of their ascent to heaven at the end of their lives'
(p. 45, n. 10). However, we have already observed how
Euhemeros, followed by Diodoros, was actually referring to
humans who received honor as gods *during their lives*. While
the view that mortals could attain the post-mortem status of
gods was, as Talbert observes, 'at least as early as Herodotus';
(p. 26), one cannot read ascension into the deification process
where it is not mentioned any more than post-mortem
deification can be assumed when no specific mention is made of
that view. Talbert's myopic concern with only one mode of
deification in the Graeco-Roman world, i.e., post-mortem
ascension to heaven, appears to have been determined by the
model provided by Luke-Acts. He has reified one among many,
many ancient notions of how men could become gods, and in so
doing has distorted the ancient evidence.

     Gods and Heroes in Ancient Greek Religion
     Before developing a fuller typology of the ways in which
Greeks thought deification possible in myth, legend and history,
a general scheme of the Greek conception of gods and heroes
needs to be presented for the NT scholar who is, perforce,
a non-specialist in Graeco-Roman religions.

In addition to the heavenly bodies themselves, which the
Greeks regarded as eternal and divine though they accorded them
no cult, there were two general classes of deities,
distinguished primarily through the protocol of sacrifice. The
Olympian pantheon consists of Zeus as the head of a cluster of
major and minor deities, each of which had a complex history
prior to the systematization and harmonization of the divine
world represented by the Homeric epics and Hesiod. The
Chthonioi (χθόνιοι θεοί) were earth deities, many of whom were
aboriginal gods which the migrating Greeks encountered when
they arrived with an early version of the later Olympian
religion. Sky and earth religions subsequently blended, yet
always maintained a separate identity through distinctive
ritual protocol (cf. Plato *Leges* 828C), particularly in
sacrifice/28/. The Chthonioi consist not only of earth gods,
but also of heroes, i.e., minor deities who were thought to
have originated as mortal men. In contrast to other Chthonioi,
who were worshipped under local epithets throughout the Greek
world, the worship of heroes was limited to the site of their
tombs (with the important exception of Herakles), where they
were thought to continue to wield great power/29/. Similar
rituals for both Chthonioi and heroes resulted in a certain
amount of confusion between the two; some heroes were what
scholars have designated as 'faded gods¦' while some earth gods
appear to have originally been venerated as heroes/30/.

Some gods represented a unique blend of Chthonic and
Olympian forms of worship; these include Herakles, the
Dioskouroi (Kastor and Polydeukes), and Asklepios/31/. Even
Zeus Ouranios had a terrestrial aspect when venerated under the
epithet *Zeus Katachthonios* (*Iliad* i. 457; Hesiod *Op*. 465). The
worship of ancestors very probably preceded the cult of heroes,
since the deification of deceased ancestors supplies the
presuppositions which make the cult of heroes comprehensible
/32/. Heroes were generally regarded as offspring of a mortal
woman and a god, far less commonly a mortal man and a goddess.
They are therefore designated ἡμίθεοι, or 'demigods.' Nearly
all the heroes of Greek myth have a divine parent, a typically
Greek way of accounting for exceptional beauty, strength,
bravery, success, and so on. Modern scholarship's conception
of the 'divine man' is an attempt to deal systematically with a
characteristically Greek way of conceptualizing the relations
between the divine and human worlds.

The two basic configurations of Greek religion, Olympian
and Chthonian, engendered two radically different attitudes and
practises regarding the relationship between gods and men. In
Homeric religion, the oldest and most definitive statement of
Olympian religion (with only few and meager glimpses of
Chthonian cults), gods and men are separated by an unbridgeable
gulf. Gods are immortals; men are mortals. Any attempt on the
part of men to bridge the gulf is an act of *hybris*, which must
result in dismal failure if not utter destruction/33/. Man has
nothing divine in him, and there is no notion of individual
immortality/34/. In Chthonic religion, however, a very close
relationship, even assimilation, was possible between gods and
men. This is evident in the oldest Greek Chthonic cult, the
Eleusinian Mysteries of Demeter and Persephone, the experience
of which guaranteed a blissful afterlife to the initiant. Like
the Eleusinian Mysteries, Orphism and Pythagoreanism (if the
two are not identical), viewed the soul as an entity separable
from the body/35/. Since immortality had been an exclusive
prerogative of the gods, the growing belief in the immortality
of the soul represents the democratization of divinity.
According to Guthrie, 'It follows that to believe the soul to be
immortal is to believe it to be divine. If man is immortal,
then he is god'/36/. Epigraphical evidence supports the view
that the hope of life beyond the grave, i.e., immortality, was
an uncommon expectation until the Hellenistic and Roman period
/37/. The universal human dissatisfaction with the
inevitability of death resonates through the Greek myths, where
topics of life and death, and particularly the motif of
attempts to conquer death or attain immortality, occur
frequently/38/.

Modes of Deification in Greek Myth
Let us begin our discussion of ancient Greek notions of
deification with a quotation from Pausanias, the mid-second
century A.D. traveler and geographer (viii. 2. 4-5: *LCL*
trans.):
> For the men of those days, because of their righteousness
> and piety, were guests of the gods, eating at the same
> board; the good were openly honoured by the gods, and
> sinners were openly visited with their wrath. Nay in
> those days men were changed to gods [θεοὶ τότε ἐγύνοντο ἐξ
> ἀνθρώπων], who down to the present day have honours paid
> to them--Aristaeus, Britomartis of Crete, Heracles the
> son of Alcmena, Amphiaraus the son of Oicles, and
> besides these Polydeuces and Castor. So one might

believe that Lycaon was turned into a beast, and Niobe,
the daughter of Tantalus, into a stone. But at the
present time, when sin has grown to such a height and has
been spreading over every land and every city, no longer
do men turn into gods, except in the flattering words
addressed to despots, and the wrath of the gods is
reserved until the sinners have departed into the next
world.

Here the basic categories are gods (i.e., immortals), and
mortals-become-gods. Pausanias accepts these categories, not
because they embody some abstract principle, but because he
knows of many exceptions to the 'rule' that an unbridgeable
gulf is fixed between mortality and immortality. Pausanias is
struck by the fact that this gulf had been bridged *in the
distant past* by various individuals. Now, however, men can no
longer become gods; Hellenistic and Roman ruler worship is mere
flattery. Though Pausanias' list of mortals-become-mortals is
short (elsewhere he mentions others whom he could well have
included on this list), it is clear that no two instances of
ektheosis or *apotheosis* occurred in quite the same manner.

In the following paragraphs I propose to survey many of
the ways whereby the ancient Greeks thought that the wall
between mortal and immortal, man and god, could be breached.
The deification of mortals was, throughout Graeco-Roman
antiquity, an exception to the general rule that immortality is
quite beyond the grasp of mortals; yet the gods may, in certain
circumstances, grant the gift of immortality (and so divinity)
to their favorites/39/.

Herakles as the Paradigmatic Mortal-Become-Immortal
Even earlier than Herodotos there is a famous passage in
Odyssey xi. 601-4, in the midst of the *Nekyia*, in which
Odysseus describes Herakles in Hades/40/:

After him [Sisyphos] I was aware of powerful Herakles; his
image [εἴδωλον], that is, but he himself among the
immortal gods [ἀθανάτοισι θεοῖσι] enjoys their
festivals, married to sweet-stepping Hebe, child of great
Zeus and Hera of the golden sandals.

Here the interpolator has attempted, without great success, to
blend two contradictory traditions about Herakles, one which
sees him as a hero, and the other a god/41/. The origin of
these two traditions is almost certainly the result of two
distinct types of ritual protocol associated with his worship.
This view is found in Pausanias (ii. 10. 1), but is also (as

Talbert notes) found in Herodotos ii. 44 (*LCL* trans.):
> And further: those Greeks, I think, are most in the right,
> who have established and practise two worships of
> Heracles, sacrificing [θύουσι] to one Heracles as to an
> immortal [ἀθανάτῳ], and calling him the Olympian, but to
> the other bringing offerings [ἐναγίζουσι] as to a dead
> hero.

The sacrificial terminology is important, for the Greeks used a
distinctive ritual procedure in sacrificing to the Olympians on
the one hand and the Chthonioi and heroes on the other (see
above, note 28). In some localities Herakles was honored as a
hero, in others as a god. In the earliest extant Greek poetry,
Homer and Hesiod, a complex conflation and harmonization of
many originally discrete religious and mythological traditions
had already been accomplished. Pindar, an older contemporary
of Herodotos, reflects this conflation of cultic traditions
also when he refers to Herakles as ἥρως θεός, i.e., as a 'hero-
god' (*N*. 3. 22), i.e., 'a hero who has become a god in reward
for his sufferings and prowess'/42/.

Early tradition held that Herakles had died (*Iliad* viii.
117-19), a view contradictory to the Greek notion of gods as
immortals if Herakles were originally a god. The scholiast is
well aware of the problem: 'Some affirm that Homer was
unaware that Herakles was apotheosized since he says that he
died. Yet saying that he did not escape death does not
indicate ignorance of his deification'/43/. Pfister was
doubtless right when he theorized that rapture legends
('Entrückungslegende') were a mythical way of rationalizing
cultic offerings of both an Olympian and Chthonian type for one
and the same individual/44/. While the translation of
Herakles to Olympos is presupposed in the ancient traditions we
have surveyed, the juxtaposition of that translation with his
self-immolation on a pyre on Mt. Oita in Trachis is probably a
later development. In Sophokles *Trach*. 1191-1278, there is no
trace of the apotheosis legend; it is present, however, in
Euripides *Heracl*. 910-16/45/. According to Diodoros iv. 38. 5,
when Herakles' companions found none of his bones on the pyre,
they inferred that he had joined the gods; henceforth they
sacrificed to him as a hero, while the Athenians were
reportedly the first to honor him as a god (iv. 39. 1). In the
handbook of Greek myths summarized by Apollodoros (1st cent.
A.D.), there is a succinct, though fully developed version of
Herakles' apotheosis (ii. 7. 7)/46/: 'While the pyre was
burning a cloud is said to have enveloped Heracles and to have

raised him up to heaven with a crash of thunder. Thenceforth
he was immortal.'   Lucian *Herm*. 7 regards the fire used in
Herakles' deification as a means of purging the mortal element
so that the divine portion may ascend to the gods in a state of
purity. Apotheosis through fiery immolation occurs with fair
frequency in Greek myths/47/.

Herakles is the earliest and most popular of those heroes
thought to have attained the status of Olympians, and became
the pattern for others. Yet it was certainly not the only
pattern, as Talbert implies. Further, it is not insignificant
that *there is nothing in Graeco-Roman literature resembling a
'biography' of Herakles*. Though many episodes of his life and
adventures were recounted, expanded and embellished by popular
storytellers and literary artists, no one thought to assemble
the whole into a 'biography,' with the partial exception of the
late mythographers (such as Apollodoros) who attempted to
synthesize all major stories told about various gods and
heroes. Pfister was so impressed with the similarities between
the life of Herakles and the gospel accounts of Jesus that he
regarded the latter as patterned on the former/48/.

Deification through Descent to the Underworld
If the pattern of Herakles as the archetypal hero who was
apotheosized through death to join the company of the gods on
Olympus was influential, another pattern, quite the reverse,
was also very popular. Legends of the descent (κατάβασις) of a
mortal (usually a hero) to the underworld could be accompanied
by transformation to the status of a Chthonic deity. One of
the more notable instances of deification through descent is
the case of the epic hero Amphiaraos/49/. Whether an original
fertility divinity who had 'faded' to heroic status, or
originally an epic hero promoted to divine status, his story is
told succinctly by Apollodoros (iii. 6. 8):
> Amphiaraos fled along the river Ismeneos, and before he
> could be wounded from behind by Periklymenos, Zeus cleft
> the earth by throwing a thunderbolt, and he with his
> chariot and his chariot driver Baton (or Elato, according
> to others), disappeared, and Zeus made him immortal.
In this legend, appearing first in Pindar, the *death* of the hero
is never mentioned, for the assumption is that he never
experienced death but rather became one of the μάκαρες
ὑποχθόνιοι/50/. Both Euripides (*Suppl*. 925-27) and Sophokles
(*El*. 838-41) emphasize the fact that Amphiaraos was swallowed
up into the earth *alive*. Trophonios is another example of a

hero whom the earth had swallowed up (Pausanias ix. 37. 7), and
it was in consequence of this event that he became a popular
oracular deity/51/. Trophonios, as his name suggests, was in
all probability a local fertility spirit who later 'faded' into
a hero who experienced deification in the underworld.
Pausanias describes the elaborate procedure used to consult
Trophonios in ix. 39. 1-14, and explicitly designates him as a
mortal who became a god (i. 34. 2).

   Deification through Transport to an Earthly Paradise
   Another mode of deification which did not involve physical
death is exemplified in the special provision made for
Menelaos, the hero of the Trojan cycle. In *Odyssey* iv. 561-68
(trans. Lattimore), Proteus prophesies the fate of Menelaos:
   But for you, Menelaos, O fostered of Zeus, it is not the
         gods' will
   that you shall die and go to your end in horse-pasturing
         Argos,
   but the immortals will convoy you to the Elysian Field,
         and the limits of the earth, where fair-haired
         Rhadamanthys
   is, and where there is made the easiest life for mortals,
   for there is no snow, nor much winter there, nor is there
         ever
   rain, but always the stream of the Ocean sends up breezes
   of the West Wind blowing briskly for the refreshment of
         mortals.
Here the paradise to be eternally enjoyed by Menelaos is
earthly and he becomes an immortal simply by being transported
to that region never having experienced death or ageing/52/.
In Hesiod's description of the Ages of Man, the fourth age,
somewhat awkwardly inserted among the others, is that of the
Heroes or ἡμίθεοι, some of whom were allowed to live in
perpetual bliss at the edge of the world on the Islands of the
Blessed Ones (μακάρων νῆσοι) under the beneficent rule of
Kronos (Hesiod *Op.* 156-69). Here μάκαρες is a poetic term for
the gods/53/, and the Islands of the Blessed Ones provide a
fitting environment for mortals to feast with the gods
forever, thereby becoming immortal and ageless themselves/54/.
Pindar also has occasion to mention these Islands with their
paradisiacal conditions; there Peleus, Cadmus and Achilles
dwell (*O.* ii. 55-80), as does Semele (*O.* ii. 26f.). Pindar
hints that Theron, a contemporary, may also enjoy that blissful
life (iii. 36ff.)/55/.

Deification through a Special Diet
     Greeks cherished the idea that one route to immortality
lay in partaking of the almost inaccessible food of the gods,
nectar and ambrosia/56/. The nymph Kalypso intended to make
Odysseus immortal by a combination of nectar and ambrosia
interspersed with heavy doses of divine affection (*Odyssey*
v. 135f.; vii. 255-58; xxiii. 333-37). In *Odyssey* v. 135f
Kalypso says to Hermes, 'I gave him [Odysseus] my love and
cherished him, and I had hopes also that I could make him
immortal [ἀθάνατον] and all his days to be endless.' At their
parting meal, Kalypso carefully separates her own divine fare
from that which she serves Odysseus. Tantalos is another
mortal whom the gods made immortal (ἄφθιτος) with ambrosia and
nectar (Pindar *O*. i. 52-64) yet because he stole the divine
food to share with other men, he was made to endure eternal
punishment. Another variant of what Mrs. Vermeule has called
the 'principle that you are what you eat'/57/, is the story of
Glaukos of Anthedon who, upon eating a particular type of grass,
turned into a sea deity with the ability to foretell the
future (Pausanias ix. 22. 6).

Deification through Fiery Purgation
     By the Hellenistic period it was widely thought that
mortals consisted of two separable components, body and soul.
The former was thoroughly mortal and the latter immortal, or at
least *potentially* immortal. In post-mortem ascension myths, as
we have already noted, it was often the soul which was thought
to ascend to the heavens unencumbered by a mortal body. In the
case of heroes like Herakles, the final destination could be
Olympos; in the case of others it could be to take their place
among the stars (Aristophanes *Pax* 832ff.). For Herakles and
Empedokles, a funeral pyre and a volcanic abyss respectively,
were thought to have contributed to final separation and
purification of the apotheosized soul. In a Greek mythic motif
which I will facetiously designate *apotheosis interrupta*,
various attempts are made, usually by a goddess, to burn away
the mortal portions of an infant, only to be prevented from
completing the process by a terrified parent. Demeter is said
to have tried making Demophoon immortal and ageless by burning
away his mortality, when Metaneira (the mother), accidentally
witnessed the frightful sight and interrupted the procedure
(*Hymn to Demeter* 231-74; Ovid *Fasti* iv. 555-56; Apollodoros i.
5. 1-2). In a similar account, probably dependent on the
Demeter myth, Plutarch relates how Isis (mourning the death of
Osiris), tried to make the child of the queen of Byblos

immortal only to be prevented by the frightened mother (*De Is.
et Os*. 16, 357C)/58/. The same motif is used to describe how
Thetis tried to immortalize Achilles with fire and ambrosia,
but was interrupted by Peleus (Apollonios Rhod. iv. 864-79;
Apollodoros iii. 6).

Deification through Seizure and Translation

The gods had the power requisite to grant certain mortals
the gift of immortality, a power which they used very
selectively. One of the major motivations for deifying certain
mortals was love, heterosexual or homosexual. Ganymede, the
most attractive of mortal men, was said to have been caught up
by the gods to be the cup bearer for Zeus eternally (*Iliad* xx.
232-35; Pindar *O*. i. 43-45). The scholiast on *Iliad* xx. 234
insists that it was 'not because of sexual passion [ἔρωτα]
that Ganymede was seized, but (he was seized) by the gods that
he might pour wine for Zeus because of his beauty'/59/. While
this may be true for Homer (though intimations of homosexual
relationships seem to be suppressed in the *Iliad*; cf. the
relationship between Achilles and Patroklos), but erotic
overtones quickly became incorporated into the legend/60/. The
story is told at length in the *Hymn to Aphrodite* 202-217, where
the stated purpose of the seizure was 'that he might be
immortal [ἀθάνατος] and unageing [ἀγήρως] like the gods' (line
214). Tithonos was also made a god (ἔθηκεν δαίμονα)/61/, at the
request of the goddess Eos. In her request to Zeus, however,
she neglected to specify agelessness in addition to immortality;
in consequence she removed Tithonos to the edge of the earth
where he aged, though could not die/62/. Pelops too, in a tale
probably invented by Pindar, was carried off by Poseidon for
amorous reasons just as Ganymede was later seized by Zeus
(Pindar *O*. i. 35-51). Thetis, in a speech to Peleus in
Euripides *Andr*. 1254-56, tells him of her intentions to deify
him to keep him from decay and death. Athena is said to have
made Diomedes a god (ἔθηκε θεόν), though, given her masculine
personality, it can hardly have been for amorous reasons
(Pindar *O*. x. 7)/63/. Phaëthon, a man like the gods (θεοῖς
ἐπιείκελον), was seized by Aphrodite and made a divine spirit
(δαίμονα δῖον), according to Hesiod *Theog*. 987-91. Similarly,
Ariadne, the spouse of Dionysos, was made immortal and unageing
(Hesiod *Theog*. 947-49).

These myths, and many more could be mentioned, hinge on the
'love is stronger than death' theme, and almost all of them have
an emphasis on the seizure motif (ἁρπάζειν, ἀνερείπεσθαι). In

these stories the experience of *ektheosis* or *apotheosis* occurs
in the prime of life. Since physical beauty was a Greek
counterpart to physical prowess (cf. Hektor and Paris), many of
these mortals were never considered heroes, nor did they ever
have a cult devoted to their worship/64/.

Distinctive Deification Legends

Not all Greek *apotheosis* traditions fit the patterns
discussed above; two interesting exceptions are the Dioskouroi
and Empedokles, the former completely mythical and the latter a
historical figure shrouded with legend. The Dioskouroi ('sons
of Zeus'), Kastor and Polydeukes, were brothers of Helen;
according to the *Iliad* (iii. 237-44), they had died/65/. Yet
in *Odyssey* xi. 300-304 (trans. Lattimore), we read: 'The life-
giving earth holds both of them, yet they are still living, and
even underneath the earth, enjoying the honor of Zeus, they
live still every other day; on the next day they are dead, but
they are given honor even as gods are.' Originally regarded as
sons of Tyndareos and Leda, Polydeukes came to be regarded as a
son of Zeus, while Kastor was thought the son of Tyndareos
(Pindar *N.* x. 80-90). According to Pindar, Zeus gave Polydeukes
the option of sharing his immortality with the deceased Kastor
by living half his time under the earth and half on Olympos.
In the late summary by Apollodoros (iii. 11. 2; trans. Simpson):
'Zeus struck Idas down with a thunderbolt and carried Pollux to
heaven. Since Castor was dead, Pollux refused immortality and
so Zeus granted that they live on alternate days with the gods
and with the dead.' The Dioskouroi were associated with the
stars, and the presence of stars on certain occasions was
regarded as an epiphany of the Dioskouroi (Diodoros iv. 43.
1-2). Pausanias knew the traditional tomb of Kastor (iii. 13.
1), and notes that they were not considered gods until forty
years after their fight with Idas and Lynkeos.

Empedokles, to whom Talbert refers on more than one
occasion, is a figure whose apotheosis is associated with
incineration (Diogenes Laertius viii. 69), or simply with his
disappearance while dining with friends (viii. 68). As Dodds
has observed, Empedokles contributed to his own legend through
his famous 'I am a god' saying preserved by Diogenes Laertius
(viii. 62, 66/66/: ἐγὼ δ' ὑμῖν θεὸς ἄμβροτος, οὐκέτι θνητὸς
πωλεῦμαι μετὰ πᾶσι τετιμένος, ὥσπερ ἔοικα, ταινίαις τε
περίστεπτος στέφεσίν τε θαλείοις). This statement, however, *is
not a personal claim to divinity*, as N. van der Ben and others
have conclusively demonstrated/67/. Van der Ben suggests the

following periphrastic translation to carry the sense of
Empedokles' statement: 'I am, you must know, while now I am
travelling about, honoured among all men as an immortal god,
(as if I were) no longer mortal, and indeed a god is exactly
what I look like, crowned as I am with fillets and rich
garlands.' Had Empedokles claimed to be a god, he would indeed
have been an erratic boulder on the terrain of Greek religious
beliefs. Menekrates the Syracusan physician did claim to be
Zeus, and even dressed the part, yet he was obviously suffering
from a mental disorder/68/.

Hellenistic and Roman Ruler Worship
Euhemeros of Messene, at the end of the 4th cent. B.C.,
wrote an influential volume entitled Ἱερὰ ἀναγραφή, or
Sacred Treatise, in which he proposed (on the basis of supposed
archaeological evidence) that those now reverenced as gods were
once great kings who had been honored as gods by their people
because of their great benefactions. Euhemeros thus provided
an ideological basis on which the Hellenistic notion of divine
kingship could be erected. Ruler cults were based on two
widely shared views, that the gods of popular worship were
actually men deified by a grateful humanity, and that the soul
of an outstanding person was in some sense divine. The
deification of dead and living rulers in the Graeco-Roman
world is important for our discussion since it represents the
application of mythic motifs to persons of the recent past or
present; unaccountably this subject is almost completely
ignored by Talbert. For citizens of the ancient world,
particularly in the first century A.D., testimonies to ruler
worship were ubiquitous: coins, temples, processions,
inscriptions, festivals, iconography and proclamations bore
witness to the conviction that men could become gods/69/.

It was scarcely coincidental that Euhemeros was propounding
his views at the same time that Hellenistic kings were claiming
divine honors for themselves and their predecessors. The
Ionian cities of Asia Minor had proclaimed the divinity of
Alexander when he liberated them during his campaign against
Darius. Of the mainland Greeks, only the League of Corinth
voted him divine honors (324 B.C.). Shortly after Alexander's
death, Ptolemy I founded the cult of Alexander in 322 B.C., in
an apparent attempt to secure his own new dynasty. The
Athenians voted divine honors to Antigonos and Demetrios
Poliorketes in 307 B.C. Demetrios then moved into the
Parthenon and had his mistress worshipped as Aphrodite. In

280 B.C. Ptolemy Philadelphos founded a cult honoring Ptolemy
Soter and Berenice, his parents, as 'savior gods,' and ca. 270
founded a cult declaring his own divinity and prescribing
divine honors for both himself and his wife Arsinoë/70/. After
the peace between Antiochos II and Ptolemy in 255, the former
appropriated the title *theos*. Antiochos III, however, was the
first Seleucid to attempt an empire-wide cult of the ruler.
Divine honors claimed by the Hellenistic kings were usually
linked in cult to traditional gods such as Zeus or Apollo.

    The practise of paying divine honors to individuals by
Hellenistic cities, including the establishment of priests,
sacrifices, temples, festivals, processions and cult epithets,
was motivated by gratitude/71/. This motivation is evident in
the reaction of many Greek cities to their 'liberation' by
Roman generals. T. Quinctius Flamininus, the victor over
Philip in the Second Macedonian war, was hailed as *soter*, and
honored with the other gods after proclaiming the freedom of
the Greeks at the Isthmian games of 196 B.C. (Plutarch *Flam.*
10). Chalcedon voted Flamininus divine honors as well, linking
him cultically with both Herakles and Apollo, a precedent
followed by other Greek cities (Plutarch *Flam.* 16f.). The
notion of deification for merit, experienced by Roman field
commanders in the East, was brought home to Rome through
Quintus Ennius' famous *Euhemerus*, an adaptation of Euhemeros'
Sacred Treatise, written two generations earlier. Ennius'
reduction of Roman deities to the status of men-honored-as-gods
elicited no negative reaction from the Romans, even though
their principal deity, Jupiter Optimus Maximus, was
demythologized.

    In 42 B.C., the triumvirs put a bill through the Senate
deifying Julius Caesar, a move with which the general populace
of Rome agreed (Suetonius *Div. Iul.* 88). A temple was
dedicated to Caesar in 29 B.C. After 40 B.C. Octavian was
designated *divi filius*, i.e., 'son of god,' or son of the
deified Julius. To this time the terms *deus* and *divus* had been
roughly synonymous; henceforth *divus* began to connote a 'man-
become-god.' Shortly after the death of Octavian, on 17
September 14 A.D., the Senate decreed that he, as *Divus
Augustus*, was to be enrolled among the gods of the state.
Correspondingly, Tiberius was designated *divi filius* as the
adopted son and successor of the deified Augustus. At the
funeral of Augustus, an eagle was released near the pyre
signifying that the soul of the imperator was being carried to

heaven (Dio lxvi. 43. 2). Numerius Atticus swore that he had
seen Augustus ascending to heaven, just as Proculus Julius (an
ancestor of the Julian clan) claimed to have witnessed the
apotheosis of the deified Romulus/72/. Romulus had
traditionally been identified with the god Quirinius, and this
facilitated the notion of apotheosis when applied to the later
emperors. The tradition of the apotheosis of the deceased
emperor, celebrated on coins, in art and poetry, was linked to
the funerary ritual described by Herodian, commenting on the
ritual surrounding Severus' deification in A.D. 211 (iv. 2.
10f. *LCL* trans.):

> After this part of the ceremony the heir to the principate
> takes a torch and puts it to the built-up pyre, while
> everyone else lights the fire all round. The whole
> structure easily catches fire and burns without difficulty
> because of the large amount of dry wood and aromatic
> spices which are piled high inside. Then from the highest
> and topmost storey an eagle is released, as if from a
> battlement, and soars up into the sky with the flames,
> taking the soul of the emperor from earth to heaven, the
> Romans believe. After that he is worshipped with the rest
> of the gods.

The body of the emperor, however, had previously been interred,
and only a wax figure is cremated (Herodian iv. 2. 1-2).
Post-mortem apotheosis became an integral feature of the
imperial funerary ritual, with certain notorious exceptions.
Domitian had claimed, during his lifetime, the status of
dominus et deus (Suetonius *Dom*. 13. 4; Dio lxvii. 5. 7); after
his death he was denied deification. From the first century
B.C. on, the prominent Roman patrician families went to great
lengths to establish genealogies going back to various gods.
Consequently, divine descent coupled with post-mortem
apotheosis became two of the more common ways in which imperial
rule was absolutized.

Talbert was able to claim an Egyptian provenance for his
'myth of the immortals' (pp. 28ff.), only by misinterpreting
the evidence. However, in view of Diodoros' account of the
feats of Osiris which eventuated in his deification as a
benefactor of man (i. 11-23), we must consider the extent to
which Diodoros' views cohere with native Egyptian ideas of
divine kingship. In Diodoros i. 14-21, containing the most
extensive account of the adventures of Osiris-Dionysos found in
ancient literature, we have what many scholars regard as a
thoroughly Greek account of Osiris as civilizer and conqueror

based on the *interpretatio Graeca* of Dionysos. Osiris'
adventures are briefly mentioned by Plutarch, who provides a
much more detailed account of the myth of the death,
dismemberment and quest for Osiris and his succession by Horus
than any other ancient author (*De Is. et Os*. 12-19, 355D-358E).
The brief narrative in Plutarch and the more elaborate one in
Diodoros of Osiris as civilizer and conqueror appear to be
based on native Egyptian stories, and are not simply the
imposition of legends about Dionysos superimposed on Osiris
/73/. That raises the question of the propriety of a
Euhemerist interpretation of native Egyptian kingship and its
successor, the Ptolemaic dynasty/74/. The basic mythic
pattern of Egyptian kingship was that the pharaoh became, upon
his coronation, the incarnate god Horus, successor to the
throne of his predecessor, the murdered Osiris; the dead ruler
had become Osiris/75/. During his reign, the monarch was
regarded as 'Son of Re' (the sun god, variously designated Re,
Khepi, Amun), and though his rule was regarded as imaging the
rule of Re, the king was never regarded as Re incarnate/76/.
Ultimately, every Egyptian in death expected to be identified
with Osiris, the dead king/77/. Yet the fact that the gods
have an earthly existence is not an argument favoring
Euhemerism, for, according to Hani, 'these divine biographies
occur in mythological time and serve only to facilitate the
personality of the gods in an anthropomorphic form, but without
implying an actual historical dimension'/78/.

Ptolemaic divine kingship differed radically from the
native Egyptian kingship ideology. Hani captures the
difference with this observation/79/: 'Egyptian thought is
theocentric, while Greek thought, throughout the Hellenistic
and Roman period, is decidedly anthropocentric.' Therefore the
idea of a *descent* to earth in the incarnation of Horus as
pharaoh, together with the death of the king as the return and
reunion with his father Re *is thoroughly Egyptian*. The view
reflected by the anti-euhemerist Plutarch (*De Is. et Os*. 21-23,
359D-360B) accurately reflects native Egyptian thought/80/.
Plutarch's daimonological theory encourages the reinterpretation
of the story of the deification of Osiris, not as the
elevation of a mortal to immortal status (indeed, he is
offended by those who claim divine honors and those who
attributed divinity to mortals (*De Is. et Os*. 24, 360B-D), but
as an ontological promotion from daimon to god. This is
reflected in *De Is. et Os*. 27, 361E (*LCL* trans.):

> She [Isis] herself and Osiris, translated [μεταβαλόντες]
> for their virtues [δι' ἀρετήν] into gods, as were
> Heracles and Dionysus later, not incongruously enjoy
> double honours, both those of gods and those of daimons,
> and their powers extend everywhere, but are greatest in
> the regions above the earth and beneath the earth.

This coheres with Plutarch's general theory of post-mortem
promotion (or demotion) of the *daimones* of individuals to a
higher state of existence on the moon (*De fac.* 29f., 943A-
945D).

Deification Motifs in Graeco-Roman Folklore and Literature
     The numerous examples discussed of various modes of
ektheosis or *apotheosis* in Graeco-Roman myth and cult
indicates that Talbert's typology of 'eternals'/'immortals' is
a drastic reduction in the ways ancients believed mortals could
obtain immortal status. Most of the examples of deification we
have presented are not drawn from Graeco-Roman *biographies*, but
from episodes originating in Graeco-Roman *folklore* in which the
deification motif is prominent. To be sure, some 'biographies'
such as Diogenes Laertius' account of Empedokles and the *Vita
Apollonii* of Philostratos (both from the 3rd cent. A.D.), do
include a variety of deification motifs as a way of framing the
life of a 'divine man,' yet these motifs must be viewed as the
intrusion of folklore elements into biographical conventions
*rather than as an acceptable structure for Graeco-Roman
biography*. The predominantly rationalistic perspective of
ancient authors underwent profound changes after the first
century A.D. Just as magic was domesticated by the Neoplatonic
philosophers, so other forms of superstition invaded literature
and rhetoric. Lucian of Samosata vainly tried to stem the tide,
but with little effect. Therefore, when Talbert tries to argue
that some characteristic features of late biography are really
much earlier than the third or second cent. A.D. (p. 43), he
fails to take into account the revolution which occurred in the
first and early second centuries.

     Deification, regardless of its specific form, functioned
in at least three ways in Graeco-Roman myth: (1) It
rationalized and harmonized the conflicting evidence that some
beings were worshipped as heroes in some places and as gods in
others. (2) It accounted for exceptional qualities present in
certain mortals by regarding their lives as scenes of divine
activity either in terms of the kaleidoscopic 'divine man'
conception or deification motifs. (3) Deified mortals provided

paradigms of hope in the face of the apparent inevitability of
death. Apotheosis, whether experienced during life or as a
post-mortem transformation, was but one of many related Greek
folklore motifs. Birth caused by a divine parent, heroic
deeds, the utterance of great wisdom, the performance of
astonishing feats, are all common motifs in Greek myth and
legend which attempt to account for the exceptional, the
superior and the beneficent achievements of mortals by placing
them in a special relation to the divine world. Unfortunately,
Greek myth and folklore underwent the process of
'literaturization' and, with few exceptions, have been lost to
prosperity. Occasionally Apollodoros may be suspected of
including oral variants into his compendium of Greek mythology,
and Pausanias is particularly rich in preserving many local
variants of Greek myths and legends/82/. The deification
motifs discussed above were used in folktale and popular
literature to *transcendentalize* the hero of the tale. Such
motifs may be used episodically (as in the many anecdotes
preserved by Pausanias), or they may be used to their fullest
extent in providing a scenario for the entire life of the hero,
from birth (or even before), to death and beyond.

Many attempts have been made to discover the structural
pattern of hero cycles/83/, yet research into this area has
just begun/84/. J. G. von Hahn suggested a list of sixteen
events constitutive of Aryan folktales, a particular type of
which he designated the 'Arische Aussetzungs- und Rückkehr-
Formel,' i.e., the 'Aryan Expulsion and Return Formula'/85/:
(1) hero is of illegitimate birth, (2) mother is the princess
of the country, (3) father is a god or foreigner, (4) signs
warn of his ascendance, (5) for this he is abandoned, (6) he is
suckled by animals, (7) he is raised by a shepherd, (8) he is a
spirited youth, (9) he seeks service in a foreign land, (10) he
returns victorious, (11) he slays his original persecutors and
accedes to the rule, freeing his mother, (12) he founds cities,
(13) the manner of his death is unusual, (14) he is reviled
because of incest and dies young, (15) he dies by an act of
revenge at the hands of an insulted servant, (16) he murders
his younger brother. Similarly, Lord Raglan proposed twenty-
two elements which he saw as the basic structure of hero
stories/86/. Like von Hahn, Raglan's study is of interest
because of its emphasis on heroes of Graeco-Roman myth and
legend. Comparing various hero cycles against his list of
twenty-two elements, Raglan found the following number of
correspondences: Oidipous (22), Theseus (20), Romulus (18),

Herakles (17), Perseus (18), Jason (15), Bellerophon (16),
Pelops (13), Asklepios (12), Dionysos (19), Apollo (11), Zeus
(15), Joseph (12), Moses (20), Elijah (9), Watu Gunung (18),
Nyikang (14), Siegfried (11), Arthur (19), Llew Llawgyffes
(17). To be sure, deification notifs are not part of these
morphological analyses, yet that omission is due to the fact
that such motifs were *optional elements* in hero cycles. More
recent analyses of the structure of hero tales include the work
of Vladimir Propp, the Russian formalist, and Jan de Vries'
morphology of hero stories in terms of ten elements/87/. The
recurring patterns in hero stories, patterns also evident in
the Synoptic Gospels, are certainly not fortuitous; these
appears to be a principle at work which Martin Dibelius has
labeled the 'law of biographical analogy'/88/. Though some
scholars claim universality for such structural patterns, it is
more prudent to extend such claims only to particular cultures
during certain periods in their history. In Graeco-Roman myth,
divine man motifs and deification motifs occur with greater
frequency than in other cultures and in other periods. I must
make it quite clear that my purpose is not to claim that the
gospels exhibit a thoroughly mythical structure, but rather to
suggest that the retelling of the life stories of certain
select individuals (culture heroes, etc.), appears to undergo a
stereotypical patterning process with the result that the
'heroization' of the narrative gives the hero's life
paradigmatic significance. For early Christians there is no
question but what the narrative of the words and deeds of
Jesus was given paradigmatic status to the exclusion of all
other models.

The older distinction between *Hochliteratur* and
Kleinliteratur is made on the basis of ideal types; in reality
only a hazy border separated the two conceptions. Literary
traditions in the Graeco-Roman world, like any society with a
rigid social structure, had an approximate correlation with the
social status of its originators. To regard 'biography' as a
monolithic literary form (despite the proposal of five
functional types), is a major methodological error of Talbert,
but to ignore the confluence of 'biography,' 'romance' and even
'aretalogy' in the legendary lives of Alexander or the *Vita
Apollonii* of Philostratos only compounds that error. To claim
that the gospels share the genre of Graeco-Roman biography,
particularly the lives of the philosophers, and to include
under the rubric 'biography' all that Talbert does, is to
empty the hermeneutical significance of the comparison of all
meaning.

V.   The Cultic Function of Graeco-Roman Biography

One aspect of the uniqueness of the gospel form, according
to Bultmann, is its cultic function.   To refute this notion,
Talbert tries to demonstrate the cultic function of Graeco-
Roman biography.   K. L. Schmidt also readily designates the
gospels as 'cult legends'/89/.   The passion narrative in
particular, he claims, goes back to no literary form, but to
living, popular cultic tradition/90/.   Yet for Schmidt, the
gospels are cult legends *only because they are products of the
activity of the anonymous community*/91/.   'Cult legend' and
individual authorship are for him mutually exclusive entities
/92/.   He contends that the gospels arose out of the
worshipping church as anonymous products.   Nowhere in his book
does Talbert betray an awareness of the antinomy felt by
Schmidt and Bultmann between cult legend and community
production versus creative, self-conscious authorship.

*The Cultic Function of the Gospels: Formgeschichte vs.
Redaktionsgeschichte*
Both R. Bultmann and K. L. Schmidt regarded the gospels as
'cult legends;' here is how Bultmann defined the gospels/93/:
> But their own specific characteristic, a creation of Mark,
> can be understood only from the *character of the Christian
> kerygma*, whose expansion and illustration the gospels had
> to serve. . . . The Christ who is preached is not the
> historic Jesus, but the Christ of the faith and the cult.
> Hence in the foreground of the preaching of Christ stands
> the death and resurrection of Jesus Christ as the saving
> acts which are known by faith and become effective for the
> believer in Baptism and Lord's Supper.   Thus the kerygma
> of Christ is cultic legend and the *Gospels are expanded
> cult legends*.
C. H. Dodd, in his own way, emphasized the kerygmatic character
of the gospels, yet with this he included an emphasis on the
essential historicity of the Markan outline of Jesus' life/94/.

Recent research has discovered several problems surrounding
the assumption that the gospels are cult legends.   The method
of *Redaktionsgeschichte* has implicitly rejected the idea that
the gospel form is the literary expression of cult legend.
Emphasis on the gospel authors as self-conscious writers with a
theological program contradicts the view fostered by Form
Criticism of the evangelists as editors and compilers/95/.
Erhardt Güttgemanns has thoroughly exposed and criticized this

contradiction/96/. Both Bultmann and Dibelius regarded the various oral forms reflected in the gospels as dependent on patterns found in Graeco-Roman culture; Martin Albertz, on the other hand, regarded the OT as the primary source of Synoptic patterns of composition. Form criticism, however, saw no parallel to the gospel form as a whole in ancient literature.

While it is probable that some of the *constituent traditions* out of which the gospels were fashioned had a cultic function (i.e., the Lord's Prayer was doubtless used in communal liturgies; the Last Supper narrative was repeated in eucharistic settings; parables and sayings of Jesus were used in homilies, etc.), the final product was the work, not of mere collectors and editors, but of self-conscious authors with literary pretensions. However, the gospels *qua* gospels, according to this view, are not cult legends, for only their constituent traditions functioned in this way. In order to defend a cultic function for the gospels, then, Talbert cannot use the method of *genre criticism*, but rather *source criticism* or *form criticism*. If the gospels in their present form are to be regarded as 'cult legends,' then that function must be determined by redaction criticism. The outlook for that possibility is very bleak.

In considering the relation between the gospel form and the cult, there are three possible options: (1) The gospel form arose from a cultic setting, possibly as the kerygma of the early Christians. (2) The gospels were expressly designed for use within a cultic setting, using an appropriate liturgical genre. (3) The gospels, though they eventually occupied a central role in the Christian cult, were not originally and expressly intended for that function. Many scholars have suggested that the NT letters, even the Apocalypse, were structured consciously to fit oral presentation or reading in the setting of worship/97/. In the case of the gospels, however, there do not appear to be formal indications, comparable to the supposed liturgical allusions at the end of some NT letters and the Apocalypse, which might suggest a liturgical destination. On the other hand, several scholars have argued that Mark and Matthew are structured in accordance with a lectionary pattern derived from Judaism/98/. Such theories, however, have not proved persuasive.

Talbert's Typology of Didactic Biography
Scholarly dissatisfaction with Friedrich Leo's descriptive
classification of Graeco-Roman biography has motivated Talbert
to propose an alternate method of classification based on the
'function(s) of the writings in their social-intellectual-
spiritual milieu' (p. 93). Graeco-Roman biographies are either
didactic (the example of the principal figure is to be emulated
or shunned), or non-didactic; all didactic biographies have a
propagandistic function (p. 93). Talbert distinguishes five
types of didactic lives: (1) Type A: lives providing a pattern
for emulation, (2) Type B: lives dispelling a false image and
replacing it with a true one, (3) Type C: lives written to
discredit the individual, (4) Type D: lives written to show
where the authentic tradition is now available, and (5) Type E:
lives written to validate or provide the interpretive key to
the teacher's doctrine (pp. 94-98). While Types D and E are
dubious distinctions, it cannot be doubted that many ancient
biographies functioned in the ways categorized in the first
three types. Talbert has made a potentially important
contribution to this aspect of the discussion.

However, in view of the enormous literature on the subject
of ancient biography, it is bold for Talbert to strike off on
his own in proposing a new typology of Graeco-Roman biography.
His typology is not an improvement of Leo's formally
descriptive classification, but a completely different, and
less formalistic way of typing ancient biographies. Leo's
system of classification is basically a way of distinguishing
sub-genres within Graeco-Roman biography; Talbert's typology
does nothing in this regard since it avoids formal literary
criteria. Further, Leo's system has received many
modifications, amplifications and criticisms in the scholarly
literature, some of which might have proven helpful to Talbert.
In Wolf Steidle's discussion 'Zur Formgeschichte von Suetons
Caesares,' for instance, the author makes some important
improvements in Leo's system by emphasizing the influence of
historical writing on Suetonius, and by showing a pattern of
precedents in Suetonius' biographical-dynastic interests, a
pattern found in Plutarch's biographies as well as in Diogenes
Laertius/99/.

Talbert discusses his typology of five functions of
didactic biography in the chapter dealing with the cultic
function of Graeco-Roman biography, though the two have very

little in common. Though he begins by dealing with the
functions of didactic biographies in their 'social-
intellectual-spiritual milieu' (p. 93), he slides into the
claim that 'This proposed alternative method of classification
of ancient biographies according to their *social functions* has
yielded substantial results' (p. 97, my italics). However,
the five functions distinguished by Talbert are not *social
functions* (since we do not know nor can we reconstruct the
social setting for the vast majority of such biographies), but
rather *rhetorical functions*. For example, it may well be that
Philostratos' hostility toward Moiragenes (the author of an
earlier biography of Apollonios of Tyana) was based primarily on
the fact that Moiragenes' life of Apollonios was the standard
work on the subject which Philostratos was attempting to replace
with his own/100/. Again, one of the distinctive features of
the historical *prooimion* of Luke's gospel is the fact that it
does not denigrate the work of his predecessors. A careful
distinction must be made between various rhetorical *topoi* and
the literary function of ancient literature.

The Cultic Function of Graeco-Roman Biographies
Professor Talbert defines 'cult,' quite acceptably, as 'the
worshiping community with its rites and ceremonies' (p. 92). He
then observes: 'The issue at hand is essentially this: do any
Graeco-Roman biographies arise out of, presuppose, or function
in the interests of religious/worshiping communities?' (p. 92).
In effect, he has so broadened the notion of 'cult legend'
espoused by Schmidt and Bultmann that any tangentially
religious connection can merit the designation 'cultic.'

Talbert advances three arguments to demonstrate the cultic
function of some Graeco-Roman biographies. First, since myth
functions as a paradigmatic model for the present life of man,
the author claims, Graeco-Roman communities needed mythological
accounts of their founders. After referring to Porphyry's *Vita
Pythagorae*, Diogenes Laertius' treatment of Empedokles, and the
Vita Apollonii of Philostratos, Talbert observes (p. 101;
italics added):

> Given the view of myth espoused by the modern history of
> religions research, either these writings in their present
> form, *or some earlier forms now expanded and utilized in
> these documents*, were linked to communities founded by
> these hero figures who were the objects of the communities'
> devotion. That is, these didactic biographies which employ
> myth are either cult legends or expanded cult legends.

Again, Talbert *assumes* a connection between legendary biography and the community which regarded that figure as a divine man or a god; *Talbert never demonstrates such a connection.* Further, in the last citation, he wavers between *genre criticism* and *source* or *form criticism.* Even if it could be decisively proven that earlier elements of Graeco-Roman biographies had a cultic function, that would be irrelevant for the determination of the genre of those biographies in their present form. Talbert assumes a connection between the Alexander cult in Egypt and Pseudo-Callisthenes' *Life of Alexander,* which he claims 'is doubtless an expanded form of the cult legend shaped so as to protect the ruler from attack and to present a true picture of him' (p. 102). Talbert cannot be permitted to assume what he should have attempted to prove. The most recent work on Pythagoreanism and Neo-Pythagoreanism, for example, persuasively demonstrates that despite the immense quantity of Pythagorean literature which was written and circulated during the Hellenistic and Roman periods, *there were no Pythagorean communities*/101/. In another connection, A. J. Malherbe has observed that 'it is too facile to view literature as the product of communities'/102/. Specifically, he refers to the Cynic letters which he and his students have edited and translated/103/:

> Groups that did not constitute organized communities are known to have produced bodies of literature reflecting their concerns. An example of this is the Cynic letters from the early Empire. Not real letters, these fictitious documents, purportedly written by the ancient heroes of the sect, are propaganda pieces; they are of major importance because they tell us what was considered important by the Cynics themselves and alert us to the diversity of views they held. But to what degree Cynics can be said to have constituted communities depends on how one defines *community.* It is unlikely that the highly individualistic Cynics had organized communities. They showed a certain community of interests, which is reflected in their writings; but this did not lead to the formation of social communities.

The cultic function, or indeed any social function, of ancient literature must be demonstrated, not assumed.

Second, Talbert argues that the link between the life of a teacher or legislator and his collected teachings or laws provides a clue for the cultic setting and function of the biography. Again, he fails to demonstrate a firm connection

between such lives and the communities which supposedly
produced or preserved them (cf. p. 105).

Finally, Talbert argues that succession lists or
narratives suggest the cultic function of certain ancient
lives/104/. He claims that 'wherever one finds a biography of
a philosopher that contains a succession list or narrative,
behind it stands a philosophical school with its debate over
the true followers of the founder' (p. 106). In the next
sentence he claims that even in neutral literary texts (e.g.
Diogenes Laertius) one is entitled to *infer* that such materials
arose in school controversies. That succession lists and
narratives *could* function in an apologetic manner cannot be
doubted, yet the originators of the literary genre διαδοχαί,
Antisthenes of Rhodes and Sotion of Alexandria (both 2nd cent.
B.C.), appear to have had no such motivation. A careful
reading of the *prooimion* of Diogenes Laertius does not
encourage Professor Talbert's view.

Conclusions

The case for the cultic function of Graeco-Roman biography
advocated by Professor Talbert is based almost entirely on
inference and speculation, not on hard evidence. Furthermore,
such biographies cannot be regarded as 'cult legends' in the
same sense that Schmidt and Bultmann viewed the canonical
gospels as 'cult legends.' If we wish examples of cult legends
from the Graeco-Roman world, we should consider the myth of
Demeter and Persephone (in the Homeric *Hymn to Demeter*), which
was probably part of the δρώμενα of the Eleusinian Mysteries
/105/, just as the story of the adventures of Osiris and Isis
preserved by Plutarch in *De. Is. et Os.* was probably the cult
legend of a Graeco-Egyptian mystery religion/106/. The thesis
of the cultic function of Graeco-Roman biographies remains
unproven.

VI.   Summary Judgment of Talbert's Theses

Throughout the foregoing discussion, we have found a great
deal to criticize in Talbert's attempt to overthrow the first
two 'pillars' of Bultmann's view that the gospels represent a
unique genre in the history of ancient literature. The
fundamental character of our criticisms invalidates many of the
more important arguments presented by Talbert. Yet there
remain two important features of his proposal which have not
yet been discussed. The first is his response to Bultmann's

third 'pillar,' and the second is his attempt to locate the
'descending-ascending redeemer myth' (which he sees as basic to
the structure of the Fourth Gospel) in early Judaism.

In discussing Bultmann's third 'pillar,' Talbert breaks
his usual pattern of argumentation. He thoroughly rejects the
view that the gospels constitute a unique genre because the
eschatological stance of early Christianity, with its negative
view of the world, resulted in an implicit rejection of the
world's literary modes of expression. Talbert is quite right
to reject this view, originally propounded by Franz Overbeck.
However, he fails to call attention to one of the strongest
arguments against that theory, namely the 'missing analogy from
Jewish apocalyptic'/107/. Early Jewish apocalypticism, which
also adopted a strongly negative stance toward the world
coupled with imminent eschatological expectation, chose to
express itself literarily in the traditional genre 'apocalypse.'

The location of a 'descending-ascending redeemer myth' in
early Judaism, rather than in Gnosticism or Graeco-Roman
paganism, constitutes a major emphasis of Talbert's book, since
he regards it as a neglected issue which is fundamental for
understanding the mythical structure of the Fourth Gospel
(pp. 53-89). Though space does not permit detailed discussion,
I should like to make three observations: (1) The *structure* of
the Fourth Gospel should not be confused with the presence of a
particular *motif*, in this case the motif of the 'descending-
ascending redeemer.' (2) Talbert's discussion of the
'descending-ascending redeemer' motif in the OT and early
Judaism is important and suggestive and merits refinement and
elaboration. (3) The author turns too quickly away from
Graeco-Roman traditions of descending-ascending divinities.
From the *Iliad* and *Odyssey* to the *Bacchae* of Euripides and
beyond, the gods of the Greeks are constantly thought of as
involved in the activities of men through direct and personal
intervention. In a very interesting and suggestive fragment of
Empedokles we find echoes of this conception/108/: 'deities
[δαίμονες] whose lot is to live a long time, that they, during
a thrice countless number of seasons, must wander away from the
blessed ones, becoming throughout that period all manner of
mortal beings who change one for another life's painful paths.'

A careful and critical appraisal, then, of the theses
advanced by Professor Talbert must conclude that his arguments
are flawed, the evidence adduced is frequently unable to bear

the weight given it, and his proposal that the gospels share
the genre of Graeco-Roman biography falls embarrassingly short
of demonstration.

VII. The Problem of the Gospel Genre

At this point in the history of NT research, it does not
appear that a satisfying solution to the problem of the genre of
the gospels can be proposed which could overturn the critical
consensus that the gospels are unique. A great deal of work
must be done before such a solution can be proposed, and the
effectiveness of that work depends on the relevance of the
questions posed by scholars. While the issues discussed in the
following paragraphs do not represent a programmatic attempt to
define the parameters of the problem, they are nevertheless
critical issues which must be carefully dealt with by concerned
scholarship.

The Anonymity of the Gospels
NT scholars are generally agreed that the four canonical
gospels share the same literary genre/109/. One of the formal
features shared by each of the gospels is *anonymity*. The
present superscriptions were probably affixed early in the 2nd
cent. A.D./110/. The homogeneity of form in the superscriptions
suggests that they were affixed to each of the gospels only
after they had been assembled into a fourfold collection (ca.
A.D. 125). Whether or not those who originally circulated the
gospels knew the identity of the authors, or whether or not
they are 'accidentally' anonymous are issues which can be
debated; the fact remains, however, that in their present form
(apart from the superscriptions), they are *anonymous*. The
anonymous character of the gospels may be contrasted with
Graeco-Roman biographies, for with few exceptions, *all ancient
biographies of the Graeco-Roman world were written in the names
of real or fictitious/pseudonymous authors*. While Mark and
Matthew are composed entirely in the third person, the first
person appears briefly in the *prooimiai* of Luke (1:1-4) and
John (1:14,16). The tenacity of the formal feature of
anonymity is exhibited in Luke. Though he used some of the
forms and methods of Hellenistic historians, yet he does not
violate the convention of anonymity. No proposed solution to
the genre of the gospels can avoid this issue, though it is not
mentioned by Talbert. It is of course true that the *Life of
Aesop*, emanating from 1st cent. A.D. Egypt, was anonymous, as
was the famous Alexander romance which was popular during the

middle ages/111/. Yet the relationship of this popular
literature to the gospels and other Graeco-Roman literature
remains to be explored.

The Literaturization of the Gospels

Though the gospels share the same genre, they exhibit a
relatively wide variety of form and structure. Assuming the
validity of the theory of Markan priority, Matthew and Luke
exhibit a literary movement which I would designate as
'literaturization'/112/. That is, they augment and alter Mark
in the direction of an increasing literary sophistication and
respectability. Greater conformity to ancient biographical and
historical conventions is found, for example, in the inclusion
of both narratives and genealogies in Matthew and Luke as well
as by the fact that Luke frames his gospel with a historical
prooimion and an ascension narrative/113/.

The addition of superscriptions, with their explicit claim
of authorship, constitute a significant stage in the external
process of literaturization. Since ancient biographies were
rarely, if ever, anonymous, attributions of authorship would
place the gospels in greater conformity to Graeco-Roman
literary conventions. Another external indication of the
process of literaturization involves the style with which the
gospels were copied on papyrus. Though few papyri containing
portions of the gospels can be dated with any confidence to the
2nd cent. A.D., those which can exhibit 'quasi-literary'
stylistic features, such as spacing, use of the iota adscript,
paragraph marks, etc.; palaeographers customarily distinguish
between documentary hands and calligraphic or literary hands
/114/.

Further, some of the fragments of Papias (Eusebius *Hist.
eccl.* iii. 39. 14-16) suggest that Papias was attempting to
defend the literary character of the Gospel of Mark against
unknown critics/115/. Papias does exhibit a familiarity with
technical rhetorical terms and conventions, and was apparently
embarrassed by the sub-literary features of Mark/116/.
Similarly, Justin's famous attempt to classify the gospels as
ἀπομνημονεύματα, or 'memoirs' of the apostles was another effort
to associate the gospels with a widely respected literary type
/117/. This evidence combines to suggest that the process of
literaturization was necessitated by the perceived sub-literary
character of the Gospel of Mark. The literaturization of Mark
and, to a lesser extent, of Matthew and Luke, would have been
superfluous had the Synoptic Gospels conformed recognizably to

conventions of ancient literature.

Constituent Literary Forms and 'Mixed Genres'

A fascinating, yet problematic, development in the history
of literature during the Hellenistic and Roman periods is the
emergence of various 'new' genres through the transformation of
earlier forms and their recombination in novel ways. The genre
of the gospels is a problematic issue not dissimilar from the
generic character of the *Vita Apollonii* of Philostratos, the
Satyricon of Petronius, and the *De Iside et Osiride* of Plutarch.
Yet the notion of 'mixed genres,' which some have applied to
this type of literature is infelicitous, since it reflects a
historical approach to genres which regards earlier forms as
somehow *normative*/118/. In many types of Graeco-Roman
literature, including the NT, there is often a tension evident
between constituent literary forms (the part), and the total
composition. To regard a 'new' composition as merely a mixture
of earlier genres destroys the possibility of viewing the
composition in its totality as an entity greater than the mere
sum of its parts. On the other hand, to ignore the particular
literary history and conventions of the constituent literary
forms impedes our understanding of the part. The literary
genre apocalypse, for example, is often described through a
serial description of its salient features; yet such lists do
not deal satisfactorily with the question of the genre of the
total composition/119/. Similarly, one may describe the
constituent forms of the gospels without touching the
important issue of the genre of the whole/120/.

The understanding and analysis of the constituent *literary
forms and patterns of compositions* in the gospels, remains in
its beginning stages. Form criticism, certainly, has exhibited
concern for forms which had a pre-literary history, yet since
the classical works of Bultmann and Dibelius, few studies have
advanced our knowledge of any of these forms in appropriate
detail/121/. Yet in the wake of the many suggestive studies by
Jacob Neusner and his students, the NT scholar now possesses a
means for comparing the literary forms of the gospels with
those of rabbinic literature impossible just a decade ago/122/.
While the same claim cannot be made for Graeco-Roman literature
literature, isolated studies, such as those of C. H. Dodd on
the dialogue form in the gospels and H. D. Betz on the
literary genre of the Sermon on the Mount, have pointed the way
in which research must go if the constituent literary elements
of the gospels are to be understood correctly/123/.

The Language and Style of the Gospels
With few exceptions, the literary heritage of the Graeco-
Roman world reflects the culture, values and tastes of the
upper classes. In that highly structured elitist society,
there was a correlation between 'social level and literary
culture'/124/. Though the style of early Christian literature
is one of the more seriously neglected aspects of NT
scholarship/125/, it is clear that the style of Mark is quite
different from that of Graeco-Roman *Hochliteratur*/126/.
Various studies have suggested that the Greek of the NT,
including that of the gospels, is not that of the papyri (as
Deissmann insisted), but rather a kind of language reflecting
minority group status/127/. Though our knowledge of the Greek
style of some of the Hellenistic authors has been revised/128/,
the literary level of Mark is still far below that of ancient
literary standards. A consideration of the cultural
significance of the language and style of the Synoptic Gospels
must inform any serious discussion of the problem of the genre
of the gospels.

Formal Parallels, Material Differences
Comparative religion and literature are disciplines which
make it their business to reflect on the significance of
parallel phenomena in two or more religious systems or corpora
of literature. NT scholars are compelled to dabble in both
enterprises. Twin dangers beset such comparative studies,
however; there is the danger of regarding the unique as
inherently better, and the danger of parallelomania. The NT
scholar must be sensitive to both the similarities and the
differences of NT literature on the one hand, and Graeco-Roman
and/or Israelite-Jewish literature on the other. Ancient
Israel, for example, knew ascension or translation traditions
in connection with the figures Enoch and Elijah; yet the notion
of deification is absolutely irrelevant for understanding those
traditions.

Professor Talbert often glosses over the differences
between various motifs with apparent parallels in the gospels
in favor of focusing on the similarities. First, Talbert often
reflects on how the 'average Mediterranean man-on-the-street'
(p. 39), would have understood the gospels. Apart from the
question of whether such persons existed, the important issue
is rather *how did the evangelists intend their compositions to
be understood?* Second, the notion of deification is totally
alien to the Synoptic Gospels. The ascension tradition of
Luke-Acts, while it has external similarities with Graeco-Roman

conceptions of *ascensio*, has two important material differences:
(1) The ascension tradition, found only in Luke-Acts, does not
change the *status* of Jesus, only his *location* and *mode of
presence*.   (2) The ascension tradition is intimately connected
with the resurrection tradition, and it is through the latter
that the *status* of Jesus is changed. Talbert's silence on the
subject of resurrection traditions is doubtless because no
parallel to them is found in Graeco-Roman biography. Third,
the absence of the material remains of Jesus in the empty tomb
narratives and his various appearances to friends and disciples
are not evidence of deification; rather, they function to
corroborate the reality of the resurrection. Further, Talbert
has neglected to observe that the physical disappearance of a
hero is one way in which traditions of his translation or
deification may be implicitly denied/129/. Fourth, the view
that a virtuous life exhibited by both the words and deeds of
the hero, and which is ultimately rewarded by apotheosis, is a
concept foreign to the Synoptic Gospels. While I have no
desire to deny that the life of Jesus portrayed in the gospels
is virtuous, it does not appear that the ethical superiority of
Jesus was a major concern of the evangelists. Rather, his
words and deeds provide dramatic evidence of the breaking in of
the reign of God. Further, the resurrection is never viewed as
the consequence of the moral achievement of Jesus, but rather
as the predestined vindication of his implicit claim to
messianic status.

VIII. Conclusions

The genre of the gospels is a literary, not a theological
problem. The present critical consensus that the gospels
constitute a unique genre in the history of literature is often
tied to the theologoumenon which equated uniqueness with truth.
In fact, 'new' genres were constantly emerging during the
Graeco-Roman period, if by 'new' we mean a recombination of
earlier forms and genres into novel configurations. Analogous
phenomena are also found in Hellenistic and Roman art and
architecture. Professor Talbert's thesis that the gospels
belong to the general category of Graeco-Roman biographical
literature is beset with difficulties. Many of these could
have been avoided had the author approached the ancient
literature more knowledgeably with a different and more
appropriate set of questions. Before the genre of the gospels
can be satisfactorily resolved, many of the issues raised in
the last part of our discussion must be faced and answered.

Notes

/1/ M. Gerhart, 'Generic Studies: Their Renewed Importance in Religious and Literary Interpretation,' *JAAR*, 45 (1977), 309-325.

/2/ Recent studies on the epistolary genre are succinctly reviewed by N. A. Dahl, 'Letter,' *IDB Supplement*, pp. 538-41. More recent studies include the innovative analysis of the form of Galatians in H. D. Betz, *Galatians* (Philadelphia: Fortress, 1979), pp. 14-25, and A. J. Malherbe, 'Ancient Epistolary Theorists,' *Ohio Journal of Religious Studies*, 5 (1977), 3-77. On the genre of Acts, see C. K. Barrett, *Luke the Historian in Recent Study*, rev. ed. (Philadelphia: Fortress, 1970), pp. 9-15; W. C. Robinson, Jr., 'Acts, Genre,' *IDB Supplement*, pp. 6f.; M. Hengel, *Acts and the History of Earliest Christianity* (Philadelphia: Fortress, 1979), pp. 3-34. For the Apocalypse of John, see P. D. Hanson, 'Apocalypse, Genre,' *IDB Supplement*, pp. 27f.; J. J. Collins, 'Pseudonymity, Historical Reviews and the Genre of the Revelation of John,' *CBQ*, 39 (1977), 329-43; *idem*, 'Apocalypse: Towards the Morphology of a Genre,' *SBL 1977 Seminar Papers*, ed. P. J. Achtemeier (Missoula: Scholars Press, 1977), pp. 359-70. Collins also edited *Semeia*, 14 (1979), which focused on the topic 'Apocalypse: The Morphology of a Genre,' and included survey articles on the genre of early Jewish, early Christian, Gnostic, Graeco-Roman, Rabbinic and Persian apocalypses.

/3/ The case for the uniqueness of the gospel genre is succinctly presented by W. G. Kümmel, *Introduction to the New Testament*, rev. ed. (Nashville: Abingdon, 1975), p. 37; for a more literary perspective see E. Auerbach, *Mimesis* (Princeton: Princeton University Press, 1953), pp. 40-49. The thesis of the uniqueness of the gospel genre is stated carefully though uncompromisingly by O. Cullmann, 'Das Urchristentum und die Kultur,' *Vorträge und Aufsätze: 1925-1962* (Tübingen: Mohr; Zürich: Zwingli Verlag, 1966), p. 496.

/4/ An excellent review of the literature is found in R. H. Gundry, 'Recent Investigations into the Literary Genre "Gospel,"' *New Dimensions in New Testament Study*, ed. R. Longenecker and M. C. Tenney (Grand Rapids: Zondervan, 1974), pp. 97-114.

/5/ N. Frye, *Anatomy of Criticism* (Princeton: Princeton University Press, 1957), pp. 247f.

/6/ E. D. Hirsch, *Validity in Interpretation* (New Haven: Yale University Press, 1967), p. 86.

/7/ *Ibid.*, p. 78.

/8/ R. Wellek and A. Warren, *Theory of Literature*, 3rd ed.
(New York and London: Harcourt Brace Jovanovich, 1977), p. 226.
Categorizing the gospels as 'dramatic history,' R. Frye moves
easily from the first cent. A.D. to Shakespearean tragedy of
seventeenth cent. England in 'A Literary Perspective for the
Criticism of the Gospels,' *Jesus and Man's Hope* (Pittsburgh:
Pittsburgh Theological Seminary, 1971), II, 193-211.
/9/ This is the emphasis of Hirsch (note /6/), pp. 102-111.
/10/ On Moses' stories and sayings: D. A. Baker, 'Form and
the Gospels,' *Downside Review*, 88 (1970), 14-26; M. G. Kline,
'The Old Testament Origins of the Gospel Genre,' *WJT*, 38 (1975),
1-27.   On the Elijah-Elisha cycle: R. E. Brown, 'Jesus and
Elisha,' *Perspective*, 12 (1971), 85-104.
/11/ On Mark as Christian Passover haggadah: J. Bowman, *The
Gospel of Mark: The New Christian Jewish Passover Haggadah*
(Leiden: Brill, 1965); on the lectionary structure of the
gospels, i.e., as a liturgical genre, see A. Guilding, *The
Fourth Gospel and Jewish Worship* (Oxford: the University Press,
1960); P. Carrington, *The Primitive Christian Calendar: A Study
in the Making of the Markan Gospel* (Cambridge: The University
Press, 1952); M. D. Goulder, *Midrash and Lection in Matthew*
(London: SPCK, 1974); *idem, The Evangelist's Calendar: A
Lectionary Explanation of the Development of Scripture* (London:
SPCK, 1978).   For critiques of Guilding and/or Carrington, see
W. D. Davies, 'Reflections on Archbishop Carrington's "The
Primitive Christian Calendar,"' *Christian Origins and Judaism*
(Philadelphia: Westminster, 1962); L. Morris, *The New
Testament and the Jewish Lectionaries* (London: Tyndale Press,
1964).
/12/ On Graeco-Roman biography: C. W. Votaw, *The Gospels and
Contemporary Biographies in the Greco-Roman World* (Philadelphia:
Fortress, 1970); C. H. Talbert, *Literary Patterns, Theological
Themes and the Genre of Luke-Acts* (Missoula: Scholars Press,
1974); D. Georgi, 'The Records of Jesus in the Light of Ancient
Accounts of Revered Men,' *SBL, 1972 Seminar Papers* (Missoula:
Scholars Press, 1972), II, 527-42.   On tragedy: G. Bilezikian,
*The Liberated Gospel: A Comparison of the Gospel of Mark and
Greek Tragedy* (Grand Rapids: Baker, 1977), with references to
other studies.   On memoir: T. Zahn, *Geschichte des
Neutestamentlichen Kanons*, I (Erlangen and Leipzig: A.
Deichert, 1889), 463-76.   On aretalogy: M. Hadas and M. Smith,
Heroes and Gods: Spiritual Biographies in Antiquity (New York:
Harper, 1965); M. Smith, 'Prolegomena to a Discussion of
Aretalogies, Divine Men, the Gospels and Jesus,' *JBL*, 90 (1971),
74-99.   On the Socratic dialogue: D. L. Barr, *Toward a*

*Definition of the Gospel Genre: A Generic Analysis and
Comparison of the Synoptic Gospels and the Socratic Dialogues
by Means of Aristotle's Theory of Tragedy*, Ph.D. Dissertation
(Florida State University, 1974).

/13/ R. K. Hack, 'The Doctrine of Literary Forms,' *Harvard
Studies in Classical Philology*, 27 (1916), 1-65; many of Hack's
points are emphasized anew in W. Allen, *et al.*, 'Horace's First
Book of *Epistles* as Letters,' *Classical Journal*, 68 (1972-73),
119-133.

/14/ Allen, *op. cit.*, p. 119.

/15/ (Stuttgart: J. B. Metzler, 1924), pp. 202-224.

/16/ *Ibid.*, pp. 216-19. For a more recent discussion of this
phenomenon, see H. W. Traub, 'Pliny's Treatment of History in
Epistolary Form,' *TAPA*, 86 (1955), 213-32.

/17/ P. G. Walsh, *The Roman Novel: The 'Satyricon' of Petronius
and the 'Metamorphoses' of Apuleius* (Cambridge: The University
Press, 1970), p. 7. For a less guarded assessment of
Petronius' uniqueness, see A. Scobie, 'Aspects of the Ancient
Romance and Its Heritage,' *Beiträge zur klassischen Philologie*,
Heft 30 (Meisenheim: Verlag Anton Main, 1969), p. 83.

/18/ See the structural analyses of the *Moralia* included in
H. D. Betz, ed., *Plutarch's Ethical Writings and Early
Christian Literature* (Leiden: Brill, 1978).

/19/ Friedrich Leo thought the *Vita Apollonii* an example of
peripatetic biography (*Die griechisch-römische Biographie
nach Ihrer litterarischen Form* [Leipzig: Teubner, 1901], p. 262).
E. Meyer, 'Apollonios von Tyana und die Biographie des
Philostratos,' *Hermes*, 52 (1917), 371-424, regarded it as a
'Reiseroman.' The view that it is a novel or romance is more
recently espoused by E. L. Bowie, 'Apollonius of Tyana:
Tradition and Reality,' *Aufstieg und Niedergang der römischen
Welt*, Part II, Vol. 16/2 (Berlin and New York: W. de Gruyter,
1978), pp. 1664f. The view that the *Vita Apollonii* is a
mixture of genres is presented by G. Petzke, *Die Traditionen
über Apollonius von Tyana und das Neue Testament* (Leiden:
Brill, 1970), p. 60.

/20/ Chapter 2 appeared earlier as 'The Concept of Immortals in
Mediterranean Antiquity,' *JBL*, 94 (1975) 419-36. Chapter 3
appeared earlier as 'The Myth of a Descending-Ascending
Redeemer in Mediterranean Antiquity,' *NTS*, 22 (1976), 418-40.
Much of what appeared subsequently in the book was repeated in
'Biographies of Philosophers and Rulers as Instruments of
Religious Propaganda in Mediterranean Antiquity,' *Aufstieg und
Niedergang der römischen Welt*, Part I, Vol. 16/2 (Berlin and
New York: W. de Gruyter, 1978), pp. 1619-1651.

/21/ In, *Eucharisterion: Studien zur Religion und Literatur des Alten und Neuen Testaments,* ed. H. Schmidt, 2 vols. (Göttingen: Vandenhoeck & Ruprecht, 1923), II, 50-134.

/22/ The complexity of this subject is evident in D. Roloff, *Gottähnlichkeit, Vergöttlichung und Erhöhung zu seligem Leben: Untersuchungen zur Herkunft der platonischen Angleichung an Gott* (Berlin: W. de Gruyter, 1970). A catalogue of various historical and/or mythical persons of whom tales of heroization or divinization are told in antiquity (consisting of some 14 classifications) is found in L. Cerfaux and J. Tondriau, *Le culte des souverains dans la civilisation Gréco-Romaine* (Paris: and Tournai: Desclée & Co., 1957), pp. 457-80. The notion of *ascensio* in Roman ruler worship and early Christianity is discussed with references to numismatic and artistic evidence in Sr. Dominique Cuss, F.C.J., *Imperial Cult and Honorary Terms in the New Testament* (Fribourg: The University Press, 1974), pp. 113-34. Rohde's work (note /23/) is also essential.

/23/ E. Rohde, *Psyche: The Cult of Souls and Belief in Immortality among the Greeks,* 2 vols. (New York: Harper & Row, 1966), I, 115f.; W. K. C. Guthrie, *The Greeks and Their Gods* (Boston: Beacon Press, 1950), p. 239.

/24/ W. Burkert, *Griechische Religion der archäischen und klassischen Epoche* (Stuttgart: Kohlhammer, 1977), p. 309.

/25/ *Ibid.,* p. 446.

/26/ Translated by the author, as are all other texts for which a particular translation is not cited.

/27/ A common misconception of Euhemerism is that it viewed the gods as *dead* kings or benefactors, whereas Euhemeros thought that they were honored as divine while living; cf. Diodoros vi. 1. 10 and J. Fontenrose, *The Ritual Theory of Myth* (Berkeley: University of California Press, 1971), pp. 20f.

/28/ A. D. Nock, 'The Cult of Heroes,' *HTR,* 37 (1944), 141ff.; W. K. C. Guthrie, *op. cit.,* pp. 220-22; W. Burkert, *op. cit.,* pp. 306f.; E. Rohde, *op. cit.,* I, 116f.

/29/ The main work on this is F. Pfister, *Der Reliquienkult im Altertum* (Giessen: Töpelmann, 1909-1912).

/30/ For a fuller discussion of these issues, see (in addition to Pfister, note /29/), L. R. Farnell, *Greek Hero Cults and Ideas of Immortality* (Oxford: Clarendon Press, 1921), esp. pp. 19-70; W. K. C. Guthrie, *op. cit.,* pp. 217-53; M. Nilsson, *Geschichte der griechischen Religion,* I, 3rd ed. (München: C. H. Beck, 1967), pp. 184-91; W. Burkert, *op. cit.,* pp. 293-319.

/31/ W. Burkert, *op. cit.,* pp. 319-30; W. K. C. Guthrie, *op. cit.,* pp. 235-53.

/32/ The cult of heroes probably originated in the grave cult
of Mycenean Greece (M. Nilsson, *op. cit.*, I, 378-84), though
see the more cautious remarks of B. C. Dietrich, *The Origins of
Greek Religion* (Berlin and New York: W. de Gruyter, 1974), pp.
160-66. Various types of Greek worship are listed in Plato
Leges 717A. One of the most influential accounts of the origins
of Greek religion in ancestor worship to hero worship to
Olympian religion is the remarkable book by N. D. Fustel de
Coulanges, *The Ancient City* (Baltimore: Johns Hopkins, 1980).
/33/ This is also the view of Pindar; cf. C. M. Bowra, *Pindar*
(Oxford: Clarendon Press, 1964), pp. 189-90.
/34/ E. Ehnmark, 'Some Remarks on the Idea of Immortality in
Greek Religion,' *Eranos*, 46 (1948), pp. 7f. No one has better
captured the contradictory Greek attitudes toward relations
between gods and men than W. K. C. Guthrie, *op. cit.*, pp. 113-
27, 254-306.
/35/ E. Ehnmark, *op. cit.*, p. 11; W. K. C. Guthrie, *op. cit.*,
p. 284; W. Jaeger, 'The Greek Ideas of Immortality,' *HTR*, 52
(1959), 139.
/36/ W. K. C. Guthrie, *op. cit.*, p. 115.
/37/ R. Lattimore, *Themes in Greek and Latin Epitaphs* (Urbana:
University of Illinois Press, 1963), pp. 21-86.
/38/ G. S. Kirk, *Myth: Its Meaning & Functions in Ancient &
Other Cultures* (London: Cambridge University Press, 1970),
pp. 192-205.
/39/ E. Rohde, *op. cit.*, I, 57; D. Roloff, *op. cit.*, p. 83.
/40/ Translation of R. Lattimore, with some rearrangements to
reflect the original Hexameter lines. The *Nekyia* is widely
regarded as a later interpolation into the *Odyssey* made no
later than the 6th cent. B.C. Aristarchos the Alexandrian
grammarian and Homeric scholar regarded lines 568-627 in
particular as spurious, and the scholiast views lines 602-4 as
an insertion by Onomakritos. The tradition of Herakles'
deification is also found in Hesiod *Theog.* 950-55; Pindar *N.* 1.
71f.; 10. 16f.; *I.* 4. 55-60.
/41/ W. K. C. Guthrie, *op. cit.*, p. 237.
/42/ C. M. Bowra, *op. cit.*, p. 46.
/43/ W. Dindorf, *Scholia Graeca in Homeri Iliadem* (Oxford:
Clarendon Press, 1875), II, 153.
/44/ F. Pfister, *op. cit.*, p. 481; he discusses 'Götterkult und
Entrückungslegende' on pp. 480-88.
/45/ Herakles' fiery apotheosis mentioned in Ovid *Metam.* ix.
229-78; Seneca *Herc. Oet.* 1483ff.; Hyginus *Fab.* 36.
/46/ Translated by M. Simpson, *Gods and Heroes of the Greeks:
The 'Library' of Apollodorus* (Amherst: University of

Massachusetts Press, 1976), p. 107; references in ancient
sources to the deification of Herakles are collected in D.
Roloff, op. cit., p. 88.
/47/ J. G. Frazer links the legendary death of Herakles, the
historical death of Hamilcar, the self-immolation of
Peregrinus (Lucian Peregr. 25), and the story of Empedokles'
leap into the crater of Mt. Etna to prove that he had become a
god (Diogenes Laertius viii. 69), and claims that 'all combine
to indicate that to be burnt alive was regarded as a solemn
sacrifice, nay, more than that, as an apotheosis which raised
the victim to the rank of a god' (The Golden Bough: A Study in
Magic and Religion, 3rd ed. [New York: Macmillan, 1935], V,
179f.
/48/ Pfister's proposal was rebutted by H. J. Rose, 'Herakles
and the Gospels,' HTR, 31 (1938), 113-42.
/49/ On deification through descent to the underworld, see E.
Rohde, op. cit., I, 88-114; D. Roloff, op. cit., pp. 91-93.
For a complete survey of legends surrounding Amphiaraos, see W.
H. Roscher, Ausführliches Lexikon der griechischen und
römischen Mythologie, I, 293-303.
/50/ Pindar N. ix. 24-27; x. 8-9; Diodoros iv. 65. 8;
Pausanias i. 34. 2.
/51/ See discussion in W. K. C. Guthrie, op. cit., pp. 223-31.
/52/ On translation to the Islands of the Blessed, see E.
Rohde, op. cit., I, 55-87; D. Roloff, op. cit., pp. 93-101.
/53/ M. L. West, Hesiod, Works and Days (Oxford: Clarendon
Press, 1978), p. 193.
/54/ Greek myths frequently mention the feasting together of
men and gods until some heinous deed interrupted their
fellowship; cf. Hesiod Theog. 535-37, and the discussion in M.
L. West, Hesiod, Theogony (Oxford: Clarendon Press, 1966), ad.
loc. Several types of Greek sacrifice involve the idea of
sharing food with the gods; cf. D. Gill, 'Trapezomata: A
Neglected Aspect of Greek Sacrifice,' HTR, 67 (1974), 117-37.
/55/ C. M. Bowra, op. cit., p. 189.
/56/ E. Vermeule, Aspects of Death in Early Greek Art and
Poetry (Berkeley: University of California Press, 1979), pp.
130-33.
/57/ Ibid., p. 131.
/58/ This dependence is based on the interpretatio Graeca, at
least as early as Herodotus, that Isis ≠ Demeter.
/59/ W. Dindorf, op. cit., II, 202.
/60/ K. J. Dover, Greek Homosexuality (Cambridge: Harvard
University Press, 1978), pp. 196f. and plates R348, R829, R833.
/61/ θεός and δαίμων are synonyms, not explicitly distinguished

until the 5th cent. (M. L. West, *Hesiod, Works and Days*, p.
182).   N. van der Ben suggests that δαίμων was used of a θεός
in relation to human beings (*The Proem of Empedocles' Peri
Physios* [Amsterdam: B. R. Grüner, 1975], p. 133).
/62/ Theognis *Eleg.* ii. 1374f.; *Hymn to Aphrodite* 218-38.
/63/ S. B. Pomeroy, *Goddesses, Whores, Wives and Slaves: Women
in Classical Antiquity* (New York: Schocken, 1975), pp. 4f.
/64/ Against D. Roloff, *op. cit.*, p. 127, who, for some
unknown reason, considers Ganymedes under the category of hero.
/65/ On the Dioskouroi, see Roscher, *Ausführliches Lexikon*,
I, 1162-63 for full particulars.
/66/ E. R. Dodds, *The Greeks and the Irrational* (Berkeley:
University of California Press, 1951), p. 145; the fragment is
found in H. Diels and W. Kranz, *Die Fragmente der Vorsokratiker*,
8th ed. (Berlin: Weidmann, 1956), I, pp. 354f.
/67/ N. van der Ben, *op. cit.*, pp. 22-25.
/68/ O. Weinreich, 'Menekrates Zeus und Salmoneus:
Religionsgeschichtliche Studien zur Psychopathologie des
Gottmenschtums in Antike und Neuzeit,' *Religionsgeschichtliche
Studien* (Darmstadt: Wiss. Buchgesellschaft, 1968), pp. 299-434.
/69/ Statements made in the following paragraphs are dependent
on the following sources: A. D. Nock, 'Ruler-Worship and
Syncretism,' *Essays on Religion and the Ancient World*
(Cambridge: Harvard University Press, 1972), II; W. W. Tarn,
Hellenistic Civilization, 3rd ed. by G. T. Griffith
(Cleveland: and New York: World, 1961), pp. 49-55; L. Cerfaux
and J. Tondriau, *Le culte des souverains dans la civilisation
gréco-romaine* (Paris and Tournai: Desclée, 1957); C. Habicht,
Gottmenschentum und griechische Städte (München: Beck, 1956).
/70/ Arsinoë died 9 July 270, and was deified upon death
(cf. Callimachos *frag.* 228).   She was predeceased by a younger
sister Philotera, who had already been honored as a goddess
(*frag.* 228, line 52).   In Callimachos *Del.* 165, Ptolemy II is
specifically designated θεός.
/71/ C. Habicht, *op. cit.*, pp. 164f.
/72/ The legendary testimony of Julius Proculus, which probably
does not antedate the first cent. B.C., functioned more to
legitimate the ancient origin of the Julian clan than to affirm
the apotheosis of the deified Romulus; cf. G. Dumezil, *Archaic
Roman Religion* (Chicago: The University of Chicago Press,
1970), I, 248f.
/73/ J. Hani, *La religion égyptienne dans la pensée de
Plutarque* (Paris: Société d'Édition 'Les Belles Lettres,' 1976),
pp. 42-47.
/74/ Discussed in detail in J. Hani, *op. cit.*, pp. 131-40.

/75/ H. Frankfort, *Kingship and the Gods* (Chicago: The University of Chicago Press, 1948), pp. 110f.

/76/ *Ibid.*, pp. 149f.

/77/ *Ibid.*, pp. 207f.

/78/ J. Hani, *op. cit.*, p. 139.

/79/ *Ibid.*, p. 138.

/80/ J. G. Griffiths, *Plutarch's De Iside et Osiride* (Cardiff: University of Wales Press, 1970), p. 371.

/81/ Translation slightly revised. On Plutarch's notion of ontological promotion from daimon to god, see G. Soury, *La démonologie de Plutarque* (Paris: Société d'Édition 'Les Belles Lettres,' 1942), p. 111.

/82/ By 'folklore' is meant oral traditions with stereotyped style and structure, dissociated from specific originators and existing in many variants; cf. J. H. Brunvand, *Folklore: A Study and Research Guide* (New York: St. Martin's Press, 1976), p. 2.

/83/ For a review of research on this subject, see Archer Taylor, 'The Biographical Pattern in Traditional Narrative,' *Journal of the Folklore Institute*, I (1964), 114-29.

/84/ A. Taylor, *op. cit.*, p. 129.

/85/ J. G. von Hahn, *Sagwissenschaftliche Studien* (Jena: F. Mauke, 1876), see chart between pp. 340-41.

/86/ Lord Raglan, *The Hero: A Study in Tradition, Myth and Drama* (New York: Vintage Books, 1956), pp. 173-85.

/87/ V. Propp. *The Morphology of the Folktale*, 2nd ed. (Austin: University of Texas Press, 1968); J. de Vries, *Heroic Song and Heroic Legend* (London: Oxford University Press, 1963).

/88/ M. Dibelius, *Die Formgeschichte des Evangeliums*, 6th ed. (Tübingen: J. C. B. Mohr, 1971), p. 106.

/89/ K. L. Schmidt, *op. cit.*, pp. 76, 114-24.

/90/ *Ibid.*, p. 78.

/91/ *Ibid.*, p. 100.

/92/ *Ibid.*, p. 117.

/93/ R. Bultmann, *The History of the Synoptic Tradition* (New York and Evanston: Harper & Row, 1963), pp. 370f.

/94/ C. H. Dodd, 'The Framework of the Gospel Narrative,' *New Testament Studies* (Manchester: The University Press, 1953), pp. 1-11. Dodd's view has provoked a good deal of debate; it has been rejected by D. E. Nineham, 'The Order of Events in St. Mark's Gospel—An Examination of Dr. Dodd's Hypothesis,' *Studies in the Gospels*, ed. D. E. Nineham (Oxford: Blackwell, 1957), pp. 223-39.

/95/ N. Perrin, 'The Evangelist as Author: Reflections on Method in the Study and Interpretation of the Synoptic Gospels and Acts," *Biblical Research*, 17 (1972), 5-18.

/96/ E. Güttgemanns, *Offene Fragen zur Formgeschichte des
Evangeliums: Eine methodologische Skizze der Grundlagenproblem-
atik der Form- und Redaktionsgeschichte* (München: Kaiser,
1971).
/97/ For Pauline letter-endings, see H. Lietzmann, *Mass and
Lord's Supper* (Leiden: Brill, 1955-79), p. 186; K.-M. Hofmann,
Philema Hagion (Gütersloh: Bertelsmann, 1938), pp. 23-26; R.
Seeberg, 'Kuss und Kanon,' *Aus Religion und Geschichte:
Gesammelte Aufsätze und Vorträge* (Leipzig: A. Deichert, 1906),
I, 118-22. For the ending of the Apocalypse, see G. Bornkamm,
'The Anathema in the Early Christian Lord's Supper Liturgy,'
Early Christian Experience (New York: Harper & Row, 1969), pp.
169-79. The hypothetical nature of these suggestions is
emphasized in H. Gamble, Jr., *The Textual History of the Letter
to the Romans* (Grand Rapids: Eerdmans, 1977), pp. 75-76.
/98/ See above, note 11.
/99/ W. Steidle, *Sueton und die Antike Biographie* (München:
C. H. Beck, 1951), pp. 126-77.
/100/ E. L. Bowie, *op. cit.*, pp. 1673-79.
/101/ W. Burkert, 'Hellenistische Pseudopythagorica,'
Philologus, 105 (1961), 234: 'Es gibt in hellenistischer Zeit
eine ganze Flut pythagoreischen Schrifttums, aber es gibt keine
Pythagoreer.' The problem of the continuity of Pythagorean
tradition is dealt with by Burkert on pp. 226-46; see also his
*Weisheit und Wissenschaft: Studien zu Pythagoras, Philolaos und
Platon* (Nürnberg: H. Carl, 1962). The only real evidence for a
Pythagorean community in the Hellenistic and Roman periods is
the theory of J. Carcopino that an underground basilica
discovered in 1917 near the Porta Maggiore in Rome was the
meeting place for a Pythagorean society (*La Basilique
pythagoricienne de la Porte Majeure* [Paris: L'Artisan du Livre,
1926]). Carcopino's view appears to be accepted by A. D. Nock,
Conversion (London: Oxford University Press, 1933), p. 168,
though it is disputed by U. von Wilamowitz-Moellendorff, *Der
Glaube der Hellenen* (Berlin: Weidmann, 1931-32), II, 438f. For
difficulties with Carcopino's view, see Burkert, 'Hellenistische
Pseudopythagorica,' pp. 226ff.
/102/ A. J. Malherbe, *Social Aspects of Early Christianity*
(Baton Rouge: Louisiana State Univ. Press, 1977), p. 13.
/103/ *Ibid.*, pp. 13f. See also A. J. Malherbe (ed.), *The Cynic
Epistles: A Study Edition* (Missoula: Scholars Press, 1977).
/104/ C. H. Talbert, *What Is a Gospel?*, pp. 102-5; the
quotation is from p. 105.
/105/ G. E. Mylonas, *Eleusis and the Eleusinian Mysteries*
(Princeton: Princeton University Press, 1961), pp. 261-72. For

a potentially significant qualification to rash associations of
particular myths with particular rituals, see W. Burkert,
Structure and History in Greek Mythology and Ritual (Berkeley:
The University of California Press, 1979), pp. 99-122.

/106/ G. Nagel, 'The "Mysteries" of Osiris in Ancient Egypt,'
The Mysteries: Papers from the Eranos Yearbooks, ed. J.
Campbell (Princeton: Princeton University Press, 1955), II,
119-34; J. G. Griffiths, *op. cit.*, pp. 42f.

/107/ E. Güttgemanns, *op. cit.*, pp. 97-100.

/108/ Frag. 115 in H. Diels and W. Kranz, *Die Fragmente der
Vorsokratiker*, I, 356-58; the translation is by N. van der Ben,
op. cit., p. 107.

/109/ That Mark alone merited the generic designation 'gospel'
was the idiosyncratic view of N. Perrin, 'The Literary
Gattung "Gospel'--Some Observations,' *ExpT*, 82 (1970), 4-7. He
held that the central characteristic of the gospel form is that
past and future flow together in the narrative, though the form
of a past narrative is retained; Matthew and Luke both
departed from this. The uniqueness of Mark over against
Matthew and Luke is also emphasized by G. Petzke, *op. cit.*,
p. 62.

/110/ N. B. Stonehouse, *Origins of the Synoptic Gospels* (Grand
Rapids: Eerdmans, 1963), pp. 15-18.

/111/ B. E. Perry, *Aesopica: A Series of Texts Relating to
Aesop* (Urbana: University of Illinois Press, 1952). A. Ausfeld,
Der griechische Alexanderroman (Leipzig: Teubner, 1907); R.
Merkelbach, *Die Quellen des griechischen Alexanderromans*
(München: C. H. Beck, 1954); Friedrich Pfister, *Der
Alexanderroman mit einer Auswahl aus den verwandten Texten*
(Meisenheim am Glan: Verlag Anton Hain, 1978).

/112/ I had originally adapted this term from G. A. Kennedy,
Classical Rhetoric (Chapel Hill: University of North Carolina
Press, 1980), p. 5, where the Italian word *letteraturizzazione*
is used to describe the transformations in rhetoric from
discourse to literature, oral to written. Later I found the
phrase 'der Prozess der Evangelien-Literarisierung' in K. L.
Schmidt, 'Die Stellung der Evangelien,' p. 59.

/113/ The best discussion of this process is still that of J.
Weiss, *Das älteste Evangelium* (Göttingen: Vandenhoeck &
Ruprecht, 1903), pp. 11-22.

/114/ C. H. Roberts, *Manuscript, Society and Belief in Early
Christian Egypt* (London: Oxford University Press, 1979), pp.
14-15, 21, 24.

/115/ J. Kürzinger, 'Das Papiaszeugnis und die Erstgestalt
des Matthäusevangeliums,' *BZ*, 4 (1960), 19-38, esp. 23-25.

/116/ J. Munck, 'Presbyters and Disciples of the Lord in
Papias,' *HTR*, 52 (1959), 230; W. R. Schoedel, *Polycarp,
Martyrdom of Polycarp, Fragments of Papias*, Vol. 5 of *The
Apostolic Fathers*, ed. R. M. Grant (New York: Harper & Row,
1967), pp. 100f.; D. E. Aune, 'Septem Sapientium Convivium,'
Plutarch's Ethical Writings and the New Testament, ed. H. D.
Betz (Leiden: Brill, 1978), pp. 80-82.
/117/ Justin *I Apol.* 66. 3; *Dial.* 106; other references are
found in T. Zahn, *op. cit.*, I, 475, n. 1.   Zahn's view that
the gospels conformed to the genre of memoir literature was
critiqued and rejected by K. L. Schmidt, 'Die Stellung des
Evangeliums,' pp. 54-59, primarily because Schmidt thought that
memoir literature was always written with the frequent use of
the first person, a view shared by J. Weiss, *Das älteste
Evangelium*, pp. 6-11. Zahn's view needs reassessment, however,
for in the 2nd cent. A.D. rhetorician Hermogenes *Prog.*, the
ἀπομνημόνευμα is not described as using the first person.
/118/ E. D. Hirsch, *op. cit.*, p. 106.
/119/ H. D. Betz, 'On the Problem of the Religio-Historical
Understanding of Apocalypticism,' *Journal for Theology and the
Church*, 6 (1969), 135f.
/120/ See J. A. Baird, 'Genre Analysis as a Method of
Historical Criticism,' *SBL Proceedings, 1972* (Missoula:
Scholars Press, 1972), II, 385-411, in which the author names
twelve different genres found in the gospels, first concluding
that the gospels represent a literary composite (p. 400), and
then concluding that they are unique in ancient literature.
/121/ A notable exception is A. J. Hultgren, *Jesus and His
Adversaries: The Form and Function of the Conflict Stories in
the Synoptic Tradition* (Minneapolis: Augsburg, 1979).
/122/ J. Neusner, *The Rabbinic Traditions about the Pharisees
Before 70*, 3 vols. (Leiden: Brill, 1971); *idem, Early Rabbinic
Judaism* (Leiden: Brill, 1975), pp. 73-136. An overview of
Neusner's research and perspectives may be found in *Method and
Meaning in Ancient Judaism* (Missoula: Scholars Press, 1979).
/123/ C. H. Dodd, 'The Dialogue Form in the Gospels,' *BJRL*, 37
(1954-55); H. D. Betz, 'The Sermon on the Mount: Its Literary
Genre and Function,' *JR*, 59 (1979), 285-97.
/124/ This is the chapter title of A. J. Malherbe, *Social
Aspects of Early Christianity*, pp. 29-59.
/125/ Evident in all major grammars of NT Greek.
/126/ N. Turner, *Style*, Vol. 4 of *A Grammar of New Testament
Greek*, by J. H. Moulton (Edinburgh: T. & T. Clark, 1976), p. 27.
/127/ A. D. Nock, 'The Vocabulary of the New Testament,' *JBL*,
52 (1933), 135.

/128/ Particularly significant in this regard are the works of
Jonal Palm, *Über Sprache und Stil des Diodoros von Sizilien:
Ein Beitrag zur Beleuchtung der hellenistischen Prosa* (Lund:
Gleerup, 1955), and Ove Strid, *Über Sprache und Stil des
Periegeten Pausanias* (Uppsala: Almqvist & Wiksell, 1976).
/129/ Strabo does this to the story of Amphiaraos in ix. 2. 11.

Setting 'The Quest for the Historical Jesus' in a Broader Framework

R. J. Banks,
History Department, SGS,
Australian National University,
Canberra.

Despite Schweitzer's strictures, there has been an unbroken interest in the 'quest for the historical Jesus' in Anglo-Saxon circles, while the return of concern among German scholars, first heralded in Ernst Käsemann's well-known essay/1/, has now proceeded for more than twenty-five years. Research during the time since Schweitzer wrote has certainly vindicated the possibility of reaching back through the evangelists' redactions and oral tradition to the sayings and actions of Jesus, even if considerable disagreement exists over the way these are reconstructed. The range, nature and distinctiveness of Jesus' words and deeds all remain the subject of continuing debate, with conflicting attitudes being expressed about the extent to which his original message and activity can be recovered, the character and significance of his mission, and the degree of individuality it possessed in the light of contemporary Jewish parallels.

This being the case, it is not surprising that a number of scholars have had second thoughts about the legitimacy of the methods employed in the 'new' quest. Consequently some serious reservations have been expressed about the assumptions underlying much redactional, form and even source critical study of the Gospels/2/, about the validity and application of criteria of authenticity used to distinguish the authentic words of Jesus/3/, and, more fundamentally still, about the adequacy of the hermeneutical principles inherent in historico-critical research generally/4/. The queries raised by these writers, and the proposals they put forward to deal with them, merit serious attention if historico-critical study of the Gospels is to advance beyond its present limits and polarities.

In this paper, however, I wish to raise some questions about a different facet of the historical Jesus question.

These do not spring from a reconsideration of the scope,
character and singularity of Jesus' mission. Nor do they begin
with a reappraisal of the criteria of authenticity employed in
such an investigation or with a fundamental questioning of the
underlying hermeneutical approach involved. They concern,
rather, exploration of the context in which Jesus' mission was
conducted and its reconstruction through the assistance of both
existing historico-critical methods and additional approaches.
This is the 'broader framework' to which my title applies. I
want to suggest that because concentration on the former
issues has generally not been accompanied by a sufficient
concern for the latter, study of the historical Jesus has
frequently been conducted within too narrow a horizon. Also,
that this restriction of vision has resulted not only in a
less comprehensive understanding of Jesus' teaching and
practice but necessarily in a certain distortion of it as well.

The questions I wish to put are these:

(i)   in our pursuit of the words and works of the historical
        Jesus, should we not attempt to set Jesus more firmly
        in his actual *social and cultural milieu* than at
        present we tend to do?

(ii)   in relating Jesus to various first-century religious
        traditions and groups, do we not need to extend our
        comparisons more systematically to the surrounding
        popular attitudes and ethical traditions of his time?

(iii)   in utilising the methods developed through historico-
        critical study of the Gospels, ought we not to supplement
        and hopefully sharpen these by approaching the
        materials along *psychological and sociological lines*
        of enquiry?

Although there are genuine difficulties involved in following
each of these through, and real limits to what can be gained
from them, they could contribute to a fuller, more accurate,
presentation of Jesus' ministry than we have so far attained
and so also to a clearer understanding of Jesus himself. In
raising these questions, I do not wish to give the impression
that research along these lines has been altogether ignored in
the past, and that it is completely lacking in work on the
Gospels today. One only has to mention the names of Deissmann
and Jeremias in this connection, and the newer investigations of

such scholars as Theissen and Meeks.   But such works are far
from representative of research on the Gospels as a whole and
have not always received the attention they deserve.   So then,
some resources for this task already lie to hand in work
completed but not yet sufficiently integrated into historical
Jesus research.   Other resources await future investigation and,
in what follows, I have given some suggestions as to the sorts
of areas that might be fruitfully explored.

1.   The Social and Cultural Milieu

With few exceptions, scholars involved in the quest have
shown little interest in the 'everyday world' in which Jesus
lived.   Discussions of his sayings and actions have tended to
concentrate on the figure of Jesus himself and on the content
of the words or works under consideration.   For the rest,
attention is mainly devoted to the leading figures around him
(e.g., Peter), significant groups in society (e.g., Pharisees
and Sadducees)/5/, major religious institutions (e.g.,
synagogues), or more broadly to the legal and political
framework with which he came in conflict/6/.   But there has
been little attempt to reconstruct the everyday world in which
Jesus moved, the ordinary life of people and places in which
much of his ministry occurred, the general social and cultural
setting of early first-century Palestine.   There is a tendency
to forget that much of Jesus' activity - particularly in
Galilee but partially also in Jerusalem - takes place within
just such a context.

Consequently, in so many scholarly presentations, Jesus
rarely comes to life as a fully human person moving amongst
common people in actual first-century locations.   There is what
might be called a partially docetic element in a great deal of
scholarly writing about Jesus - conservative as well as more
critical or radical - with the result that Jesus becomes at
times something of a theological construct, and his encounters
with others a sort of dramatic affair abstracted from the kind
of 'reality' which we daily experience in the world.   This is
not to say that the Jesus who emerges in such treatments
altogether lacks a genuinely human character, nor that his
encounters with others fail to possess a decidedly
interpersonal quality.   But it is the concrete social matrix in
which he appears and such confrontations take place that is so
often absent.   Correspondingly, there is a failure to see how
this might have influenced the particular texture of the

encounter that the Gospels record/7/.

Of course, there are real problems in what I am suggesting.
In the first place, the Gospels are not in any strict sense
biographical accounts of the life of Jesus but rather
kerygmatic compositions designed for the needs of their
readers, based on oral traditions preserved in a variety of
literary forms and transmitted for a variety of different
reasons. Although, in my view, one of the main intentions of
the evangelists was the portrayal of what Jesus actually
said or did on various occasions, they are not primarily
interested in passing on the sorts of details from which a
reconstruction of Jesus' everyday social and cultural context
might be fashioned. This is not to say that such details do
not survive in their records, material that is all the more
valuable because of its 'accidental' rather than conscious
preservation. In the second place, even where we possess such
data we do not always have sufficient correlative evidence to
prove that these details reflected the conditions of Jesus' own
lifetime. Where they do exist, they may instead reflect the
conditions of those who transmitted the oral traditions or of
those who later received their written formulation/8/.

For some, these problems are virtually insuperable, so
that any attempt to build up a picture of everyday social and
cultural life is ruled out from the start. But for others this
is not the case. So we have various investigations of the
economic and social life of Jerusalem and, less extensively,
of Galilee/9/. Also, an interest in legal provisions which
pervaded various aspects of daily life/10/. There are, too, a
small number of contributions to our understanding of the more
general social and cultural climate of the time/11/. Although
all such works draw heavily on extra-biblical literary
inscriptional and other archaeological sources for the
information they contain, they also in varying degrees show
that, behind the various layers in the Gospels, references to
the everyday world of Jesus' time do exist. These references
are sometimes preserved in purely incidental remarks, are
sometimes caught up into parables, riddles and maxims, and
sometimes form part of the narrative core of various stories
about Jesus. While we must always check whether such details
were added at a later stage in the process of transmission
(either as embellishments to lend greater credence to the
accounts or as reflections of circumstances which in later
times were being addressed), work so far undertaken reinforces

the view that genuine echoes of life in Jesus' period have
survived in the literature.   Since we also have evidence
relevant to this from other Jewish sources of a contemporary
or near-contemporary character, e.g., Josephus' writings,
epigraphical materials of various kinds, and archaeological
finds (together with such contemporary sources as the
Roll of Fasts and such later sources as the Mishnah, which has
too long dominated study of many of these questions), the
details found in the Gospels may be checked against such
information and complemented by it.

In view of such contributions as the ones mentioned above,
it could be asked why I have suggested there is a lack of
interest in Jesus' social and cultural milieu.   For the
following three reasons.   Firstly, broader reconstructions of,
more limited investigations into, and detailed commentaries
upon Jesus' teaching and activity still sometimes fail to
mobilise these findings and use them in any creative fashion.
Secondly, such contributions have also failed to produce many
imitators: indeed, it is interesting to note how frequently
interest in these questions comes from ancient historians,
orientalists and the like rather than from New Testament
scholars as such.   (Some of the latter still suffer from the
influence of existential, or from certain kinds of evangelical,
theology here, with their concentration on the individual at
the expense of the social dimension).   While interest in the
social world of the early Christians has been a growing
preoccupation in American scholarship, it has tended to
concentrate on the early church rather than on Jesus' ministry,
and on the Graeco-Roman background rather than the Jewish/12/.
Thirdly, although much valuable work has been done, more
remains to be investigated, some of it of particular
significance for our understanding of the ministry of Jesus.

So far as materials for this are concerned we have, inter
alia, the recent archaeological discoveries round the Temple
Mount in Jerusalem and the prospect of continuing study of
texts from gravestones and ostraca/13/.   There are also
details in the Gospels which have still not been sufficiently
exploited/14/.   Even the well-worked through materials in
Josephus will yield further information if approached with new
questions in mind and from new perspectives/15/.   Turning to
possible topics for investigation, there are several areas
which require more detailed attention than they have received
up to this point.   For example, both Josephus and Luke

contain information about the activities of women in first-
century Jewish society, material that still awaits systematic
exploration. As well, the parables in the Gospels have more
light to throw on the position and function of servants, slaves
and labourers in Jewish society at this time than previous work
on this question would suggest. The identity of the 'poor' in
the Gospels, and Jesus' relationship to them - so central a
theme in liberation theology today - also requires more careful
and precise consideration/16/. Then there is the question of
the social level of the people Jesus most frequently moved
amongst in his travels through Galilee, neighbouring regions and
Jerusalem. Attention to such matters, when supplemented by the
information already available to us about economic, legal,
social and cultural conditions prevailing at this time, would
enable us not only to widen our understanding of Jewish society
in general during this period, but give a sharper focus to our
picture of Jesus himself in his contact with it.

2. Popular Attitudes and Ethical Traditions

A great deal of attention in past, and recent, work on the
Gospels has sought to clarify Jesus' attitude to the various
religious groups of his day. The discovery of the Dead Sea
Scrolls extended the range of movements with which Jesus could
be brought into comparison, and has led to new investigations
of his teaching, practice and fate, as well as of many other
details in the Gospels/17/. During this period, the
increasing engagement of such Jewish scholars as David Flusser,
Geza Vermes, David Daube and Jacob Neusner with first-century
literature has also widened our study of the main Jewish
parties in the first century and profited our understanding of
many other aspects of the Gospels/18/. As well, investigation
of the world of the Zealots and their predecessors by a number
of different scholars has led to a clearer understanding of
their place in first-century Jewish life and of the far-ranging
dissimilarities between Jesus' mission and theirs/19/. All
this has helped to fill out our knowledge of the religious
climate in which Jesus' ministry was exercised and given us a
greater sensitivity to some of the issues with which he was
dealing.

But perhaps we have defined Jesus' religious environment
too narrowly, for there were other groups in society with whom
he should be brought into contact if a more complete picture of
his activities and contribution is to be gained. As I have

already indicated, a considerable amount of Jesus' time was
spent with people from ordinary walks of life. Encounters with
such groups as the Pharisees and Sadducees, and perhaps with
individuals sympathetic to 'Zealot' ideals (the term is
probably anachronistic for Jesus' own time), he certainly had
/20/. But these are matched, possibly outnumbered, by his broad
range of contacts with people living to a greater or lesser
extent on the margins of well-defined Jewish religious society.
It is precisely these people whose attitudes have received so
little scholarly attention.

They do not, of course, form one homogeneous group. There
is the devout piety of various figures in the early chapters of
Luke. There is the practical commitment of different people
whom Jesus encounters in synagogues and in his travels. There
is the more sceptical and, at times, demon-possessed attitudes
expressed by some in town and countryside. And there are many
other variations in between. This makes it difficult to deal
with this diverse group of people in the same way as with the
more clearly defined religious groups in society. Even there,
however, it should be more seriously asked whether such groups
as the Pharisees, Sadducees and Essenes were as uniform as we
assume. Certainly the existence of different emphases, even
schools, within their movements has always been recognised. But
it is possible that such designations as Pharisees, Sadducees,
Essenes, etc. are analogous less to denominational terms like
Methodist, Anglican, Brethren, etc., than to others denoting
tendencies of a much broader nature, e.g., evangelical, liberal,
charismatic, our sources having partly simplified or
standardised what was once a more fluid religious situation.

The attitudes of those who did not belong to a particular
religious outlook do occasionally come to expression in the
Gospels. For the most part this takes place incidentally, or
indirectly in parables, but here and there it does so in a more
explicit fashion. And in addition to the material in the
Gospels we have scattered remarks in Josephus' writings and
later rabbinic sources, as well as in apocalyptic literature,
which throw further light on such attitudes. The first
detailed enquiry for many years into one section of this wider
group, the so-called 'Am-Ha-Aretz', has just appeared, but the
range of people of which I am thinking is far broader than that
included in this category/21/. (Indeed, the 'Am-Ha-Aretz' were
another relatively well-defined religious group in society
alongside those that have been mentioned above.) It may still

be too early to write an account of the 'popular religion' of
Jesus' day. But there are some modest contributions to be
made which could open up new aspects of this subject in a
fruitful way and gather material that could be utilised in
discussions of the historical Jesus.

Yet we need to be working on a much broader front as well,
for Jesus should be viewed within a larger context than that
provided by the Jewish groups of his day, whether well-defined
or not. From the viewpoint of the history of ideas, Jesus has
his context in what is generally designated as 'the Western
intellectual tradition', which has its roots not only in the
Jewish and Christian, but also Roman and Greek outlook on life.
Setting Jesus against this wider background used to be
characteristic of that 'discredited liberalism' which post-
World War dialectical theology called into question/22/. But
behind the isolation of Jesus from the broader cultural
environment in which he lived, lies that longstanding divorce
between biblical and classical studies/23/, biblical studies
and ancient history/24/, and biblical ethics and moral
philosophy/25/, which has become virtually taken-for-granted
in an increasingly specialised age, and largely
institutionalised in teaching departments and professional
organisations of scholars. Only occasionally are the academic
barriers between these different fields broken, and even rarer
is the attempt to identify Jesus' exact contribution within
their wider perspective/26/.

Admittedly the Hellenistic background to titles used of or
by Jesus, and to his charismatic and miraculous activities, has
recently again come in for serious examination, and such
studies are producing helpful materials for comparison/27/. To
some extent also, the basis for a comparative examination of
Jesus' teaching is being provided by investigations of the
similarities between the utterances of significant Greek
thinkers and the New Testament writers/28/. In the past it has
almost always been Paul who has been brought into comparison
with such figures: this is understandable in view of his
background, approach and interests, but it is a pity that more
general comparisons with the attitude of Jesus have been
neglected. For Jesus does have a central place in the Western
cultural tradition, even if biblical scholars, ancient
historians and historians of moral philosophy rarely set his
distinctive contribution within that broader framework. And
there are many facets of Jesus' teaching and life that can only

be fully revealed for what they are by being set in such a
context. Quite apart from this, one of the real dangers
associated with the current quest for the historical Jesus is
that the results achieved will be closeted within the province
of biblical studies and limited to an essentially religious
audience, rather than making their appropriate contribution to
related academic disciplines and having their deserved impact
upon a wider audience. This can only be overcome, however, if
we encourage at least some of those embarking on research in
the Gospels, as well as others already involved in it, to
develop a broader understanding of the ancient world in which
Jesus emerged and of his unique contribution to that cultural
tradition by which we are all, Christian or otherwise, still
so strongly influenced.

3. Psychological and Sociological Lines of Enquiry

Alongside the refinement of historico-critical methods,
the last century has seen the development of other
disciplinary approaches which historians are increasingly
using in their investigations. I am thinking here
particularly of the application of psychological and
sociological methods to the study of previous figures and
epochs. In the past, various psychological interpretations of
Jesus have been attempted but did not manage to produce any
persuasive accounts of his character/29/. Certainly there are
great difficulties attending such an approach. Psychological
methods of enquiry have not, and by their nature cannot, attain
the degree of precision that has often been claimed for them,
and all too often such methods are employed in an arbitrary
fashion instead of supplementing other critical methods. The
strongly kerygmatic orientation and largely fragmentary nature
of the Gospel accounts also makes it unlikely that a psycho-
historical account could significantly further our
understanding of the historical Jesus.

Even so, while it may not be possible to penetrate very
far into Jesus' own psychological development, it is not beyond
our capacity to explore other interesting matters. For
example, the sorts of motives he appealed to in his teaching,
the kinds of responses he was seeking to elicit, the
expectations of various people that he had, the types of
reactions he provoked, and so on/30/. This kind of enquiry
has too often been pushed to the margins of New Testament
study and left to the so-called 'pastoral' or 'practical'

theologians, who are not always exegetically equipped for the
task. To some extent, of course, clarity on these issues can
only be gained when we know the character of the audiences whom
Jesus was addressing. Despite the large degree of scepticism
that has surrounded the possibility of identifying the exact
groups who heard Jesus, there are now grounds for more
confidence in what has been designated 'audience-criticism' of
the Gospels/31/.

We need not be so sceptical about the application of
sociological methods of enquiry and categories of explanation to
these documents. The value of such an approach to the Old
Testament was long ago demonstrated in Max Weber's celebrated
study of Judaism/32/, and its fruitfulness for early Christian
attitudes was exemplified in Ernst Troeltsch's famous work on
the social teaching of the Christian churches/33/.
Unfortunately both these seminal works have found few
successors, particularly within New Testament studies/34/.
Sociological tendencies in the work of Adolf Deissmann and
Martin Dibelius were forced further into the background through
the ascendancy of Rudolf Bultmann/35/. While in his work
sociological interest was not altogether lacking, it was
concentrated only on the context in which the oral tradition
was formed.

More recently, however, particularly in the writings of
Gerd Theissen, a renewed interest in the value of sociological
perspectives for study of the Gospels has begun to emerge/36/.
This is now starting to attract a good deal of attention,
though only a beginning in the way of substantive contributions
has yet been made. Such endeavours face a similar temptation
to that involved in the earlier, too enthusiastic, application
of psychological categories to the figure of Jesus, i.e., the
danger of sociologising him in as unconvincing and as
illegitimate a way as writers of that generation succeeded in
psychologising him. The reality of these dangers may already
be seen in some conceptually too hasty and historically ill-
fitting uses of sociological frames of reference to illuminate
Jesus' person and work/37/. But this should not deter us from
making the attempt to understand Jesus and his background with
the aid of such methods. As Theissen's work shows, despite its
lack of interest in Jesus himself, this kind of approach can
throw light in all sorts of ways on various aspects of the
mission he initiated, e.g., analysis of the roles of the chief
agents within it and the social attitudes that went with them,

identification of economic, geographical, political and
cultural factors affecting the movement Jesus began, and
exploration of the diverse effects it had on the society
around it.

In sociological enquiry generally, considerable energy
has been devoted to understanding the nature of apocalyptic
movements, charismatic authority, social stratification,
primary group structures and kinship patterns, etc., all of
which are relevant to study of the Gospels. Bearing this in
mind the renewal of interest in the apocalyptic horizon in
Jesus' thought, and recent emphasis on the charismatic rather
than rabbinic nature of his relationship with his disciples
/38/, would both benefit from the application of a sociological
perspective, in much the same way as Theissen has thrown light
on the socio-economic and eschatological dimensions present in
the wandering charismatic lifestyle of Jesus' disciples/39/,
and F. Belo has sought to illuminate the socio-historical and
sociological environment surrounding Jesus in Mark's Gospel
/40/.   In view of H. Kippenberg's discussion of class structure
in Jewish society, the social status of the disciples, and the
social dynamics and structure of the disciple group itself,
would gain from closer attention/41/.

In all this, the temptation to simply fit the biblical
data into previously defined sociological categories must be
kept in mind.   The distinctiveness of Jesus and his mission
should alert us to the possibility that the categories
themselves may need to be revised in order to catch the
novelty of the matters with which they are dealing.   H. J.
Schütz's book on the Pauline approach to authority, drawing as
it does on the contribution of Weber and others at the same
time as it criticises and recasts them, is an excellent model
in this regard, even though it is unlikely to have said the
last word on the subject/42/.   So there is much to be said for
a more stringently sociological approach to the data in the
Gospels.   As a result, not only will the context in which
Jesus worked be illumined, as well as his relationship with
those involved in that mission, but also certain aspects of
Jesus himself.

I have been arguing in this paper for a broadening of the
way in which we presently conceive the task of investigating
the historical Jesus. While this concentrates attention on the
context in which Jesus lived rather than on Jesus himself, it
would indirectly cast light on the figure of Jesus as well.
Some of the resources for this, I have suggested, already lie at
hand, but it is necessary for them to be drawn more explicitly
into presentations of Jesus and his mission, whether these take
a systematic form, deal only with aspects of the whole, or
emerge out of commentaries on individual Gospels. Others still
remain to be explored: here various possibilities have been
mentioned which could produce material for integration into our
portrait of Jesus. In carrying out this work there is much to
be said for its being conducted, not as an individual exercise,
but within the framework of an association of scholars from
different disciplines and backgrounds who are willing to work
together for the accomplishment of specific objectives. While
the colloquia of the Corpus Hellenisticum Novi Testamenti and
seminars of the Society for Biblical Literature, and now
Society for New Testament Studies, on 'the Social World of
Early Christianity', provide models for this, more local or
regional groups could also be formed with similar aims. The
consequence of such research would, I believe, be a Jesus more
firmly located in his immediate social and historical context,
more broadly related to the popular attitudes and ethical
ideals of his times and more precisely understood at a
psychological and sociological level.

Some possibilities can be drawn from each of the three
areas I have mentioned. An investigation of the already
existing relationships between members of the early Christian
movement would show that, despite Jesus' warnings about its
divisive effects within families, it was in some respects a
strongly familial and 'natural' affair. The precursor of the
movement, John the Baptist, its central figure, Jesus himself,
and the one who gained most prominence in the Jerusalem church,
James, were all related. Within the disciple group itself
there were two sets of brothers, Simon and Andrew, John and
James, all of whom also came from the same area and worked in
the same trade. Another disciple, Philip, was already probably
known to them, for he came from the same town and it was he who
brought a friend, Nathanael, into contact with Jesus. This
suggests that at least half the disciple group previously had
connections of one sort or another prior to their call by Jesus,
not to speak of the presence of other members of their families,

e.g., the mothers of James and John and of James the Less, in
the wider group following Jesus. Demonstration of these, and
perhaps other, interconnections would not only illuminate the
character of the movement in a way that has not been
sufficiently explored but should also reinforce and extend the
basic historical credibility of the narratives dealing with the
composition of the disciple band.

Among Jesus' many actions, his welcoming attitude towards
children, and positive references to them, have often
attracted comment. It seems clear from the way in which the
narrative is introduced, viz., the disciples' assumption that
the women bringing the children should be discouraged, that a
different attitude generally prevailed even in Jewish circles
for all the position occupied by children within them. But
when Jesus' remarks and actions are set within the wider
Graeco-Roman approach to children, their distinctiveness
becomes even more marked. With the spread of Christianity this
led, in time, to a genuine revolution in social attitudes in
this area. Jesus' contribution at this point in the Western
ethical tradition has not been sufficiently appreciated by
those who have recounted its development./43/ Correspondingly, New
Testament scholars' subordination of Jesus' concern for
children to a preoccupation with the relevance or otherwise of
these accounts for early Christian baptismal practice, has also
tended to miss their real significance. In any case, we cannot
see the historical uniqueness and influence of the attitude for
what it was unless it is viewed from a broader perspective as
well as in its more native Jewish setting.

A greater integration of Jesus' itinerant lifestyle and
ethical teaching would also, I suspect, tell us a good deal
more about the source of that teaching and the important part
played by his own experience in its formation. Gerd Theissen
has already shown that the wandering lifestyle of the
disciples explains, in significant part at least, some of the
attitudes to which they gave expression. May it not also be
true that many of Jesus' injunctions, e.g., about sitting
lightly to material possessions and not being anxious for what
tomorrow might bring, as well as some of his illustrations,
the so-called 'good samaritan' to name just one, spring
directly from his own itinerant way of life. This would
suggest that much of the teaching on such matters did not drop
as it were, fully-formed into his own consciousness as he
sought God's will in prayer and meditation, but emerged

through his involvement in his day-to-day activities with all
their temptations, challenges and possibilities. As well as
throwing new light on his words and tying them more firmly
into his experience, this demonstration of their coherence with
his life would strengthen the grounds for their authenticity,
or support it where it came under attack.

Yet a caution must again be sounded here, as it was at the
beginning of this paper and has been throughout. For the
particular nature of the biblical sources with which we have to
deal, and the relatively small amount that they and extra-
biblical materials contain means that, when all is said and
done, only a limited amount of assistance in each of the areas
I have designated will be forthcoming. And I do not wish to
overlook the need for re-evaluation at a methodological and
hermeneutical level of the historico-critical approach, for
that could well lead us into a clearer understanding of the
historical Jesus as well. For that reason, I would not wish to
make any ambitious or exclusive claims for the sort of study I
have been encouraging. The results, at their best, will be of
a quite modest kind. But even if we make only marginal gains
in our understanding of the historical Jesus, extending our
understanding a little here and revising our understanding a
little there, the exercise will have been a valuable one if in
any way at all it has brought the figure of Jesus more
historically, and therefore more vitally, to life.

Notes

/1/ E. Käsemann, 'Das Problem des historischen Jesus', *ZThK* 51
(1954) 125-153, though one should not forget such works as E.
Stauffer, *Jesus and his Story* (London: SCM, 1960). Among
Anglo-Saxon scholars, T. W. Manson, 'The Life of Jesus: Some
Tendencies in Present-Day Research', *The Background of the New
Testament and its Eschatology: Studies in Honour of C. H.
Dodd* (eds. W. D. Davies and D. Daube; Cambridge: Cambridge
University, 1956) 211-222 and more recently in C. H. Dodd, *The
Founder of Christianity* (London: MacMillan, 1970) should not be
overlooked.
/2/ On redaction-criticism see, inter alia, M. Hooker, 'In His
Own Image', *What About the New Testament?* (eds. M. Hooker and
C. Hickling; London: SCM, 1975) 28-44; on form-criticism G.
Stanton, 'Form Criticism Revisited', ibid., 13-27 and on

source-criticism J. M. Rist, *On the Independence of Matthew and Mark* (Cambridge: Cambridge University, 1978).   See also more extensively E. Güttgemans, *Offene Fragen zur Formgeschichte des Evangeliums. Eine methodologische Skizze der Grundproblematik der Form- und Redaktionsgeschichte* (München: Kaiser, 1970) esp. ch. 3, 44-68.

/3/ So, for example, D. G. Calvert, 'An Examination of the Criteria for Distinguishing the Authentic Words of Jesus', *NTS* 16 (1971-2) 209-213 and R. G. Barbour, *Traditio-Historical Criticism of the Gospels: Some Comments on Current Methods* (London: SPCK, 1972).   Also R. H. Stein, 'The "Criteria" for Authenticity', *Gospel Perspectives: Studies of History and Tradition in the Four Gospels*, Vol. I, ed. R. T. France and David Wenham (Sheffield: JSOT Press, 1980), 225-263.

/4/ So P. Carnley, 'The Poverty of Historical Criticism', *Christ, Faith and History* (eds. S. W. Sykes and J. Clayton, Cambridge: Cambridge University, 1972) 165-189 but most perceptively P. Stuhlmacher, *Schriftauslegung auf dem Wege zur biblischen Theologie* (Göttingen: Vanderhoeck & Ruprecht, 1975). Another who has addressed himself to this issue is G. Maier, *Das Ende der historischkritischen Methode*, Brockhaus: Wuppertal, 1975), but the unsatisfactory nature of his solution - which is virtually to do away with historico-critical methods altogether - is rightly criticised by P. Stuhlmacher, ibid., 103-108.   Relevant here also is the concluding chapter of G. W. Hughes, *Hebrews and Hermeneutics* (Cambridge: Cambridge University, 1979) 101-136.

/5/ For Peter, see (ed.), R. E. Brown, K. P. Donfried and J. Reumann, *Peter in the New Testament* (Minneapolis: Augsburg, 1975), and O. Karrer, *Peter and the Church: An Examination of Cullmann's Thesis* (New York: Herder, 1963).   On the Pharisaic and Sadducaean groups, the most important recent contributions have been made by J. Neusner, *The Rabbinic Traditions about the Pharisees before 70 A.D.* (Leiden: Brill, 1971), and J. Le Moyne, *Les Sadducéens* (Gabalda: Paris, 1972).   On the synagogue see K. Hruby, *Die Synagogue: Geschichtliche Entwicklung einer Institution* (Zürich: Theologischer, 1971), as well as (ed.) J. Gutmann, *The Synagogue: Studies in Origins, Architecture and Archaeology* (New York: Ktav, 1974).   See also the various articles on the main Jewish parties and the synagogue in (ed.) H. Temporini und W. Haase, *Aufstieg und Niedergang der römischen Welt*, Bd. II 19, 1 und 2 (Berlin: de Gruyter, 1979).

/6/ On the broader political situation, we have now both the more general discussion of M. Grant, *The Jews in the Roman World* (London: Weidenfeld & Nicholson, 1973) and the excellent

detailed treatment of E. M. Smallwood, *The Jews Under Roman
Rule* (Leiden: Brill, 1977), while on the most important
political figures in the Gospels there are the books of S.
Sandmel, *Herod: Profile of a Tyrant* (Philadelphia: Lippincott,
1967): A. Schalit, *König Herodes* (Berlin: de Gruyter, 1969) and
H. Hoehner, *Herod Antipas* (Cambridge: Cambridge University,
1972). But see now as well the relevant articles in (ed.) H.
Temporini und W. Haase, *Aufstieg und Niedergang*, Bd. II 8
(Berlin: de Gruyter, 1977). (On this topic see also the books
listed in Note 11 following.) The question of Jewish legal
powers during the Roman period continues to be much discussed,
especially in respect to Jesus' arrest and trial. Most
comprehensive here from a history-of-exegesis and
bibliographical point of view is D. Catchpole, *The Trial of
Jesus: A Study in the Gospels and Jewish Historiography from
1770 to the Present Day* (Leiden: Brill, 1971), though other
works, chiefly of a more popular nature, have appeared since.
/7/ In a sense, criticism of many contemporary representations
of Jesus and his relations with others is analogous to the
Marxian critique of Feuerbach's account of 'man' for its
failure to stress the concrete social framework in which human
life is lived and specific social forces by which it is
affected.
/8/ See here, for example, with its detailed investigation of
the context in which Q was preserved, P. Hoffmann, *Studien zur
Theologie der Logienquelle* (Münster: Aschendorff, 1972), esp.
312ff, and S. Schulz, *Q: Die Spruchquelle der Evangelisten*
(Zürich: Theologischer, 1972), as well as, for its exploration of
the community bound up with Mark's Gospel, H. C. Kee, *Community
in the New Age* (London: SCM, 1977). Many other examples could
be cited: see further the works listed in K. Berger, *Exegese des
Neuen Testaments* (Heidelberg: Quelle und Meyer, 1977) 226-227,
and that author's own following discussion.
/9/ J. Jeremias, *Jerusalem in the Time of Jesus: An
Investigation into Social and Economic Conditions during the New
Testament Period* (London: SCM, 1969); A. N. Sherwin-White, 'The
Galilean Narrative and the Graeco-Roman World', *Roman Society
and Roman Law in the New Testament* (Oxford: Clarendon, 1963)
120-143. Older writings such as F. C. Grant, *Economic
Background of the Gospels* (London: Oxford University, 1926) and
more detailed investigations such as D. Sperber, 'Costs of
Living in Roman Palestine', *JESHO*, 8 (1965) 248-271, are also
relevant here. More recently, however, we have the excellent
summary of the evidence provided in *The Herodian Period* (The
World History of the Jewish People, Vol. 7; ed. Michael

Avi-Yonah; New York: Rutgers, 1975) esp. the chapter by J.
Klausner on 'The Economy of Judaea in the Period of the 2nd
Temple', 180-206, and various articles on social and economic
aspects of Eastern Mediterranean life in (ed.) H.
Temporini und W. Haase, *Aufstieg und Niedergang*, Bd. II 8.
On all this see, too, the magisterial work of G. Dalman,
Arbeit und Sitte im Palästina (5 vols.; Gütersloh: Bertelmann,
1928-42).

/10/ See especially here, J. D. M. Derrett, *Law in the New
Testament* (London: Dartman, Longman & Todd, 1970) and
subsequent articles, and the earlier contribution of D. Daube,
The New Testament and Rabbinic Judaism (London: Athlone,
1956).

/11/ In, for example, such works as *The Jewish People in the
First Century* (eds. S. Safrai and M. Stern; Assen: van Gorcum,
I, 1974; II, 1976), especially the second volume, and in the
slowly appearing revision of E. Schürer, *The History of the
Jewish People in the Age of Jesus Christ* (eds. G. Vermes and
F. Millar; Edinburgh: T. & T. Clark, I, 1973). See too S.
Sandmel, *Judaism and Christian Beginnings*, 2 vols. (New York:
Oxford University Press, 1979). As a general background to all
such attempts, we must note the scrupulous studies of M.
Hengel, *Judaism and Hellenism* (London: SCM, 1966) and
Judentum, Griechen und Barbaren (Stuttgart: Katholisches
Bibelwerk, 1976). At a different level, see now as well the
useful compendium of materials in *Greek and Latin Authors on
Jews and Judaism* (ed. M. Stern; Jerusalem: Israel Academy of
Science and Religion, 1974), and various related articles in
(ed.) H. Temporini und W. Haase, *Aufstieg und Niedergang* Bd. II
19, 2.

/12/ Much of this work has been carried out within the
framework of the Society for Biblical Literature and some of it
has found its way into published reports of its Seminars. See
also the helpful survey provided by A. J. Malherbe, *Social
Aspects of Early Christianity* (Baton Rouge: Louisiana State
University, 1977). Also the anthology compiled by (ed.) W.
Meeks, *Zur Soziologie des Urchristentums* (München: Chr. Kaiser,
1979).

/13/ On these see especially the series of articles, past and
present, in *Qadmoniot*, some of which are summarised in
Jerusalem Revealed: Archaeology of the Holy City, 1968-1974
(Jerusalem: Israel Exploration Society, 1975). The fuller
'Preliminary Reports' of the various seasons' discoveries are
only slowly appearing, though see now B. Mazar, *The Mountain of
the Lord: Excavations in Jerusalem* (New York: Doubleday,

1975), for a survey of many of the findings.

/14/ A good illustration of the way in which the parables can
be used to illumine daily life, achieved interestingly enough
by one who has had a close acquaintance with peasant life in
modern Israel, may be found in K. E. Bailey, *Poet and Peasant:
A Literary Cultural Approach to the Parables in Luke* (Grand
Rapids: Eerdmans, 1976). In this book the author also lists
and critically evaluates earlier approaches of this kind,
e.g., that of E. F. F. Bishop, *Jesus of Palestine: the Local
Background to the Gospel Documents* (London: Lutterworth, 1955).
Relevant here too are portions of J. Jeremias, *The Parables of
Jesus* (London: SCM, 1963).

/15/ But I am thinking here of more thematic investigations of
their contents. As, for example, in P. W. Barnett, *The Jewish
Eschatological Prophets AD 40-70 in their Theological and
Political Setting* (Dissertation: London, 1977).

/16/ This subject was opened up again in a serious way by
H. J. Degenhardt, *Lukas. Evangelist der Armen* (Stuttgart:
Katholisches Bibelwerk, 1965), L. Schottroff-W. Stegemann,
Jesus von Nazareth - Hoffnung der Armen (Stuttgart: Kohlhammer,
1978), and D. Seccombe, *The Poor and Possessions
in Luke-Acts*, (Dissertation: Cambridge, 1978); and an
interesting approach to the identity of the poor in Jesus'
environment is at present being worked out by R. Guelich in his
forthcoming commentary on the Sermon on the Mount.

/17/ Most recently on the Scrolls we have G. Vermes, *The Dead
Sea Scrolls: Qumran in Perspective* (London: Collins, 1977).

/18/ Thinking of the Gospels, and of Jesus in particular, see
especially D. Flusser, *Jesus* (Herder: New York, 1969), and G.
Vermes, *Jesus the Jew* (London: Collins, 1973). But, of course,
these and other Jewish scholars have made many additional
contributions whose findings are relevant to the question we
are discussing.

/19/ In particular we have the newly revised edition of the
magisterial work by M. Hengel, *Die Zeloten: Untersuchung zur
jüdischen Freiheitsbewegung in der Zeit von Herodes I bis 70 n.
Chr.* (2nd ed.; Leiden: Brill, 1976). Among others, there are
the discussions of Y. Yadin, *Masada: Herod's Fortress and the
Zealots' Last Stand* (London: Weidenfeld & Nicholson, 1966),
and H. P. Kingdon, 'Who were the Zealots and their Leaders in
A.D.66?', *NTS* 17 (1970) 68-72; 'The Origins of the Zealots',
NTS 19 (1972) 74-78, as well as M. Smith, 'Zealots and
Sicarii: their origins and relations', *HTR* 64 (1971) 1-19.

/20/ A fresh treatment of this subject may be found in G.
Baumbach, *Jesus von Nazareth im Lichte der jüdischen
Gruppenbildung* (Berlin: Evangelischer Verlagsanstalt, 1971).

/21/ I am thinking of A. Oppenheimer, *The 'Am-Ha-Aretz'*: *A Study of the Social History of the Jewish People in the Hellenistic-Roman Period*, (Leiden: Brill, 1977). Relevant here too is the study of Galilean religion in S. Freyne, *Galilee from Alexander the Great to Hadrian 323 B.C.E. to 135 C.E. A Study in Second Temple Judaism* (Wilmington: Notre Dame, 1980).

/22/ Consider, for example, the older works of T. R. Glover, *The Influence of Christ in the Ancient World* (Cambridge: Cambridge University, 1929) and, though less focussed on Jesus himself, S. J. Case, *The Social Triumph of the Ancient Church* (London: Allen and Unwin, 1934).

/23/ On this see also F. F. Bruce, 'The New Testament and Classical Studies', *NTS* 22 (1975) 52-72.

/24/ An exception here is the historian Michael Grant with his recent books on *Paul* (London: Weidenfeld & Nicholson, 1976) and *Jesus* (London: Weidenfeld & Nicholson, 1977). In relation to Paul, the point I am making here is also eloquently argued by E. A. Judge, 'St. Paul and Classical Society', *JAC* 15 (1972) 19-36.

/25/ A rare exception to this in English scholarship, though it contains many inadequacies, is A. Flew, *A Short History of Ethics* (London: Routledge and Kegan Paul, 1967) 110-120.

/26/ One who has consistently attempted to break such barriers is A. Dihle, but his works do not appear to have made much impact in New Testament circles. See, for example, *Die Goldene Regel. Eine Einführung in die Geschichte der antiken und frühchristlichen Vulgärethik* (Göttingen: Vandenhoeck & Ruprecht, 1962): *Der Kanon der zwei Tugenden* (Köln: Westdeutscher, 1968); 'Greek and Christian Concepts of Justice' (The Center for Hermeneutical Study in Hellenistic and Modern Culture: *Colloquy* 10, 1974), and his forthcoming Sather lectures. One explicit attempt to place Jesus within the developing Greek tradition is in J. D. P. Bolton's *Glory, Jest and Riddle* (London: Duckworth, 1973), which sees Jesus' understanding of man as the culmination and, in part, negation of the non-biblical anthropological outlook. For an earlier, more general, treatment, see W. F. Albright, *From the Stone Age to Christianity* (Baltimore: John Hopkins, 1940), the closing section.

/27/ One thinks here, for example, of such works as M. Hengel, *The Son of God* (London: SCM, 1976); D. L. Tiede, *The Charismatic Figure as Miracle Worker* (Missoula: SBL, 1972); J. M. Hull, *Hellenistic Magic and the Synoptic Tradition* (London: SCM, 1974); M. Smith, *Jesus the Magician* (New York: Harper & Row, 1978), and various other items published through the Center for Hermeneutical Study in Hellenistic and Modern Culture mentioned above. Consult as well now the closing articles in (ed.) H. Temporini and W. Haase, *Aufstieg und*

Niedergang, Bd. II, 23 (1979).

/28/ Unfortunately the ancient authors considered mostly post-
date Jesus himself. But see H. D. Betz, *Lukian von Samosata
und das Neue Testament* (Berlin: Akademie, 1961); G. Mussies,
Dio Chrysostom and the New Testament (Leiden: Brill, 1972); P.
van der Horst, 'Musonius Rufus and the New Testament', *NovT* 16
(1974) 306-315; (ed.) H. D. Betz, *Plutarch's Ethical Writings
and Early Christianity* (Leiden: Brill, 1978).

/29/ See, for example, the critique of some earlier
psychological - more strictly pathological! - interpretations
of Jesus in A. Schweitzer, *The Psychiatric Study of Jesus:
Exposition and Criticism* (Boston: Beacon, 1948).

/30/ Some pointers in this direction are provided by G.
Theissen, *The First Followers of Jesus* (London: SCM, 1978), 99-
110, who utilises insights derived from the psychoanalytic
hermeneutics discussed in (ed.) Y. Spiegel, *Psychoanalytische
Interpretationen biblischer Texte* (München: Kaiser, 1972).
Personally I would not wish this kind of investigation to be
tied too closely to psychoanalytic, as compared with other
psychological, approaches. A more general plea for the
broadening of exegesis to take psychological considerations into
account is made by W. Wink, *The Bible in Human Transformation*
(Philadelphia: Fortress, 1973).

/31/ A start has been made here by J. D. M. Derrett, *Jesus'
Audience: The Social and Psychological Environment in which He
Worked* (London: SPCK, 1973), while the case, and some of the
methodology, for taking this factor into account was presented
persuasively earlier by J. A. Baird, *Audience-Criticism and the
Historical Jesus* (Philadelphia: Westminster, 1969). More generally here see also E. Trocmé, *Jesus and His Contemporaries* (London:
/32/ M. Weber, *Ancient Judaism*, (Glencoe: Free Press, 1952). SCM,1973).

/33/ E. Troeltsch, *The Social Teaching of the Christian
Churches* (2 vols.; London: Allen & Unwin, 1931).

/34/ In their sociological orientation, that is, not their
concern with social attitudes in themselves. On the latter,
see further E. Lohmeyer, *Soziale Fragen im Urchristentum*
(Darmstadt: Wissenschaftliche Buchgesellschaft, 1973); S. J.
Case, *The Social Origins of Christianity* (Chicago: University
of Chicago, 1923); C. J. Cadoux, *The Early Church and the
World* (Edinburgh: T. & T. Clark, 1955); P. Alfaric, *Die
sozialen Ursprünge des Christentums* (Wissenschaftliche
Buchgesellschaft: Darmstadt, 1963) J. Leipoldt, *Der soziale
Gedanken in der altchristlichen Kirche* (Leipzig: Köhler und
Amelang, 1952). A list of works of a more general kind arguing
the case for a sociological approach to religious writings may

be found in the book, earlier mentioned, by K. Berger, *Exegese* (1977) 218.

/35/   Further on this point see the remarks of D. Gewalt, 'Neutestamentliche Exegese und Soziologie', *Ev.Th.* 31 (1971) 87-99.

/36/   Apart from the work of Theissen already cited, see his articles 'Theoretische Probleme religionssoziologischer Forschung und die Analyse des Urchristentums', *NZST* 16 (1974) 35-56, and 'Die soziologische Auswertung religiöser Überlieferungen', *Kairos*, 17 (1975) 284-299, and those referred to below in Note 39. As well there is J. Gager, 'The Gospels and Jesus: Some Doubts about Method', *JR* 54 (1974) 244-272, and now E. Stevenson, 'Sociological Insights into the Early Church', *ExpTim* 90, 10 (1979) 300-304.

/37/   Though its intentions are sound, there are real weaknesses in Gager's approach, as exemplified in his book *Kingdom and Community: The Social World of Early Christianity* (Englewood Cliffs: Prentice Hall, 1975).

/38/   See, inter alia, M. Hengel, *Nachfolge und Charisma: Eine exegetisch-redaktionsgeschichtliche Studie zu Mt. 8.21f. und Jesus Ruf in die Nachfolge* (Berlin: Topelmann, 1968); J. D. G. Dunn, *Jesus and the Spirit: A Study of the Religious and Charismatic Experience of Jesus and the First Christians as Reflected in the New Testament* (London: SCM, 1975).   On apocalyptic, see S. R. Isenberg, 'Millenarism in Graeco-Roman Palestine', *Religion* 4 (1974), 26-46, and B. W. Kovacs, 'Contributions of Sociology to the Study of the Development of Apocalypticism: A Theoretical Survey', A Paper of the Consultation on the Social World of Ancient Israel of the *SBL*, Annual Meeting, St. Louis, Missouri, 1976, 1-32.

/39/   In his 'Wanderradikalismus. Literatursoziologie der Überlieferung von Worten Jesu im Urchristentum', *ZTK* 70 (1973) 245-271 and 'Wir haben alles verlassen' (Mk. 10, 28). Nachfolge und soziale Entwurzelung in der jüdisch-palästinischen Gesellschaft des 1 Jahrhunderts n.Chr.', *NovT* 19 (1977) 161-196.

/40/   F. Belo, *Lecture matérialiste de l'évangile de Marc* (Paris: Cerf, 1974), which makes considerable use of Marxian categories in approaching and exegeting the text.   Also on Mark's Gospel from this perspective, though containing a more general discussion as well, there is M. Clévenot, *Approches matérialistes de la Bible* (Paris: Cerf, 1976).

/41/   See H. G. Kippenberg, *Religion und Klassenbildung in antiken Judäa.   Eine religionssoziologische Studie zum Verhältnis von Tradition und gesellschaftlicher Entwicklung*

(Göttingen: Vanderhoeck und Ruprecht, 1978). Also H.
Kreissig, *Die soziale Zusammenhänge des jüdäischen Krieges:
Klassen und Klassenkampf in Palästina des I. Jahrhunderts*
(Berlin: Akademie, 1970). An earlier work which began to
explore seriously the social status of some of the disciples was
W. Wuellner, *The Meaning of 'Fishers of Men'* (Philadelphia:
Westminster, 1967).
/42/ H. J. Schütz, 'Charisma and Social Reality in Primitive
Christianity', 54 (1974) 51-70, and *Paul and the Anatomy of
Apostolic Authority* (Cambridge: Cambridge University, 1975).
/43/ It has taken a Marxist to remind us of this. See M.
Machovec, *A Marxist Looks at Jesus* (London: Dartman, Longman &
Todd, 1976) 99-104, certainly the most satisfactory treatment
of Jesus ever to come out of Marxist circles. One only has to
put it alongside K. Kautsky, *The Foundations of Christianity*
(New York: International, 1925), to see the advance that has
been made.

* This article is based on a paper read at the 1977 meeting of
The Tyndale New Testament Conference, and was completed in
mid-1979 with a further bibliographical revision in mid-1980.

Historical Tradition in the Fourth Gospel:
After Dodd, What?

D. A. Carson
Trinity Evangelical Divinity School
2045 Half Day Road
Deerfield, Il 60015
U.S.A.

I

Many recent writers have shown us that there is good reason for regarding this or that story in John as authentic. C. H. Dodd in his great work, *Historical Tradition and (sic) the Fourth Gospel*, has carried out a systematic examination as a result of which he concludes that behind this Gospel there lies a very ancient tradition, quite independent of that embodied in the Synoptic Gospels. It is difficult to go through such a sustained examination and still regard John as having little concern for history. The fact is that John is concerned with historical information.

So writes Leon Morris. /1/ With this statement, we may profitably compare a recently published judgment by Robert Morgan, who writes: 'Just as gospel criticism finds in the Fourth Gospel a source whose historical value cannot be compared with that of the Synoptics, so too Acts and the authentic epistles are of quite unequal value for a knowledge of Paul.'/2/

One may argue with both of these statements. Morgan's comparison is not very apt: the pauline epistles stand in relation to Acts as primary source to secondary source, whereas neither the fourth gospel nor the synoptics purport to be more than a secondary source for the life, ministry, passion and resurrection of Jesus. For his part, Morris jumps rather quickly from the independence of the tradition in the fourth gospel to the historical trustworthiness of that tradition. Yet the two statements, placed side by side, neatly reveal the simple fact that there is little consensus among johannine scholars as to the historical reliability of John's gospel.

The statement by Morris reflects something else. It is

typical of a fairly broad consensus that attributes to Dodd's
Historical Tradition in the Fourth Gospel (hereafter *HTFG*) a
turning point in the history of johannine criticism.   There is
some truth to this assessment, if only because the size of the
work and its meticulous scholarship, coupled with Dodd's elegant
understated prose, commanded massive respect even where it did
not gain universal agreement.   In any case, Dodd's work
provides an excellent starting-point for anyone who wishes to
ask historical questions of John's gospel.

      To begin with Dodd is not to ignore the contributions of
earlier generations.   It is well known that at various times
during the last two centuries, John has been thought to be more
historically reliable than the synoptics, because he recounts
fewer miracles, no exorcisms, and contains more propositional
teaching.   Conversely, at other times John has been assessed as
virtually useless, historically speaking, when compared with the
synoptics.   Nor has this debate been purely diachronic: a
little hunting turns up representatives on both extremes in
almost every decade of the last two hundred years.   Interest in
the subject was not waning when Dodd wrote: three years before
HTFG, A. J. B. Higgins published his little monograph, *The
Historicity of the Fourth Gospel*. /3/ About the same time,
before Dodd's work put in an appearance, several essays
appeared on the subject. /4/

      But *HTFG* is more than just one more entry on a list; and
for that reason it still merits close attention.   In the course
of his work, Dodd does not so much assess the historical
reliability of this little snippet or that (some exceptions will
be considered later), as assess the historical reliability of
the underlying traditions.   He is not an R. D. Potter, /5/
demonstrating the historicity of this or that topographical
detail by appeal to archaeology, however useful such work may
be;   rather, he is to the fourth gospel something of what J.
Jeremias is to the synoptic gospels. /6/ No matter how
meticulous the detail of the picture Dodd paints, he paints on a
grand scale; and adequate response requires similar detail and
similar scope.

      This paper lays claim to no such magnificent pretensions.
Its contours are far humbler.   It does not even attempt a
detailed catalogue of positions adopted since Dodd, although it
interacts with some of them.   Rather, after dealing with
several preliminary matters, it offers a few reflexions on some

methodological problems involved in probing the historicity of
the fourth gospel.   These reflexions arise out of a close
reading of Dodd and of much other recent literature on the
subject, and thereby stand in Dodd's shadow.   But they are
largely methodological in nature, exploratory in intent.

It may be helpful first of all to summarize the argument of
HTFG, if for no other reason than that it has become such a
standard work that although everyone knows about it, and many
cite it, and some dip into it--few read it.

II

HTFG is, of course, Dodd's second major work on the Gospel
of John.   To the end of his first work, *The Interpretation of
the Fourth Gospel* /7/ (hereafter *IFG*), Dodd appends a brief
chapter entitled, 'Some Considerations Upon the Historical
Aspect of the Fourth Gospel.'   This chapter sets forth in brief
what is expanded at length in *HTFG*.   Already in *IFG*, Dodd
writes both that he regards 'the Fourth Gospel as being in its
essential character a theological work, rather than a history,'
and also that 'it is important for the evangelist that what he
narrates happened.' /8/   At the same time, Dodd assumes (his
word) that although the evangelist intended to record that
which happened, he nevertheless felt free 'to modify the factual
record in order to bring out the meaning.' /9/   I shall have
more to say about this remarkable pair of positions a little
farther on;   but certainly Dodd follows these convictions in
writing *HTFG*.

In *HTFG*, Dodd adopts a method which springs from the
seminal work of P. Gardner-Smith.   In 1938, Gardner-Smith
published his little book, *Saint John and the Synoptic Gospels*.
/10/   There he argues that John is not demonstrably dependent
upon the synoptic gospels at any point, and therefore represents
an independent stream of tradition.   Where reasonably close
parallels do occur, they are better accounted for by theorizing
about cross-fertilized oral traditions than by appeal to direct
literary dependence.

Dodd approaches the question of historical tradition by
examining the fourth gospel's relationship to the synoptics.
Essentially *HTFG* is a detailed (one might almost say,
microscopic) examination of that relationship.   The book is
divided into two unequal parts: 'The Narrative' and 'The

Sayings.' The former, which comprises three quarters of the work, is divided into three sections, which successively focus on the passion narrative, the ministry, and John the Baptist and the disciples. In other words, the order of the work flows from passages with closest approximation to synoptic gospel material to passages with least approximation to such material.

In each chapter, Dodd concludes that the fourth gospel is not dependent in a literary way on any one of the synoptic gospels. Clearly there is a large distinction to be made between the literary dependence or independence of a passage and its historical worth. But what Dodd argues is that where the fourth gospel is close to the synoptics, it constitutes powerful *independent* evidence for a common dependence upon pre-canonical (and presumably oral) /11/ tradition; and where the fourth gospel stands at some distance removed from the synoptics, it very often shows signs of passing on solid tradition, inasmuch as that tradition is rarely tangled up with johannine themes and therefore to be distrusted. Indeed, in not a few instances Dodd argues that the tradition reflected in John is more primitive and more reliable than the synoptic tradition of the same event or utterance. One prominent example of the latter is the johannine dating of the crucifixion.

Such an approach is therefore in the first instance an inquiry into questions of literary dependence, not into questions of historicity *per se*. Because Dodd has so high a regard for pre-canonical tradition, however, he repeatedly turns the literary inquiry into historical considerations. Moreover, his work is rich in asides which affirm the historicity of this or that detail, although it boasts an almost equal number of asides which deny the historicity of some other detail.

It remains to provide some quotations from Dodd's work. Dodd reveals his own estimate of the importance of his method-- *viz.* examining literary dependence in order to get at the traditional material (by which Dodd normally means 'historical material') in the fourth gospel—when he writes:

> Such examples allow of no positive inference, but they may
> rightly serve as warning against a hasty assumption that
> nothing in the Fourth Gospel which cannot be corroborated
> from the Synoptics has any claim to be regarded as part of

the early tradition of the sayings of Jesus.   That
tradition was probably more manifold than we are apt to
suppose, and the fact that a substantial element in the
Johannine report of the teaching can be traced with great
probability to traditional sources suggests that he was
more dependent on information received than might appear,
although he has developed it in new and original ways.
*But I do not at present see any way of identifying further
traditional material in the Fourth Gospel, where comparison
with the other Gospels fails us, without giving undue
weight to subjective impressions.* /12/

At the beginning of *HTFG,* when Dodd is setting forth the
nature of his research, especially with reference to the passion
narrative where parallels between the fourth gospel and the
synoptics tend to be closer than they are elsewhere, Dodd says
something similar:

This survey in itself justifies the inference that so
striking a measure of agreement among the four gospels
permits only two alternative ways of explaining the facts:
either there is literary interdependence among the four--a
theory which almost invariably takes the form of
dependence of John on one or more of the Synoptics; or all
four evangelists *felt themselves to be bound by a pre-
canonical tradition in which the broad lines of the story
were already fixed.* /13/
Clearly, it is the latter alternative for which Dodd
consistently opts.   But it is his method of attacking the
historical questions which I am emphasizing.

Out of this approach, Dodd forges a theory as to how the
pre-canonical traditions came together as *gospels*.   He lays
this out, for instance, when dealing with the various accounts
of the anointing of Jesus, /14/ and again in dealing with the
feeding of the multitude, /15/ and yet again as part of his
conclusion.   *In nuce,* he argues that whereas the form critics
are right to see the *pericopae* of the gospels being formulated
according to the varying needs and conditions of the early
church, 'yet there is no sufficient reason for assuming that
such formulation was a *creatio ex nihilo.*' /16/   Rather:

. . . the materials out of which they were formed were
already in existence, as an unarticulated wealth of
recollections and reminiscences of the words and deeds of

Jesus--mixed, it may be, with the reflections and
interpretations of his followers. It was out of this
unformed or fluid tradition that the units of narrative
and teaching crystallized into the forms we know. At the
early, unformed, stage we have to think, not of discreet
narratives, with their individual features sharply marked,
as we have them in the gospels, but of a host of
remembered traits and turns of expression, often disjoined
and without context, but abounding in characteristic
detail . . . . But the precise occasions with which
these features of [Jesus'] Ministry were associated were
perhaps not always remembered, or were remembered
differently by different witnesses; for the association of
ideas is a very individual thing, and it often affects our
recollection of events. /17/

This sweeping theorizing is supported by a glut of detail,
penned in Dodd's inimitable prose. The work is invaluable, not
only for its mind-stretching breadth, but also for its attention
to and presentation of the minutest consideration.

Because in this paper I am primarily concerned with
historical matters, it is worth drawing attention to two of
Dodd's asides, both of which touch on historical questions, in
order to gain a little more insight into his approach.

In the first, Dodd is dealing with John's account of the
arrest of Jesus. He notes, as part of his argument which does
not now concern us, that in the account of Peter's attack on
the High Priest's slave, the 'one original contribution which
John makes to the narrative is the naming of his assailant and
his victim.' /18/ Although Dodd recognizes that the insertion
of names into a traditional story is often taken to be prompted
by the forces of legendary accretion, and that 'story-tellers
do delight in individualizing their characters by supplying
them with names;' yet, he insists, 'it is not true that the line
of development is always in that direction, nor are the names
supplied always fictitious. In the Gospels, Mark's Jairus has
lost his name in Matthew, his Bartimaeus in Matthew and Luke,
and his Alexander and Rufus have vanished from both. On the
other hand, in introducing Caiaphas for Mark's vague ὁ ἀρχιερεύς
Matthew has certainly not invented a fictitious name.' /19/
From these observations Dodd goes on to a very even-handed
weighing of the matter, and ultimately decides that 'we have no
sufficient evidence for either accepting or rejecting the name

of Peter and Malchus as traditional.' /20/   (Note again, in passing, Dodd's use of 'traditional' to mean 'historical' in the sense 'historically correct.')

As a second example, we may note that when Dodd treats John 18:13, he concludes that it is 'hardly possible to acquit the evangelist of a misconception of the High Priest's tenure of office.' /21/   Dodd then briefly argues his case.   Whether or not we find it convincing is beside the point at the moment. The important thing to observe is that although Dodd is primarily engaged in a literary investigation, his focus is repeatedly turned to historical questions.   The title of the book is important: *Historical Tradition* (by which Dodd almost always means material passed on to the evangelist, material that is historically correct) *in the Fourth Gospel*.   Thus, although the vast majority of the book is given over to the minute defence of John's literary independence from the synoptic gospels, such literary concerns are essentially little more than Dodd's *method* for tackling historical questions.   This point cannot be emphasized too strongly;   for the reliability of Dodd's conclusions about the historical matters which most concern him turns not only on how well he utilizes his chosen methodological approach, but also on the validity of that approach to answer the historical questions Dodd wants answered.

III

It may be useful to give some brief account of how *HTFG* has been received, both in the period immediately after its publication and in the decade and a half that have elapsed since then.   This account is limited to a few of the initial reviews and a scattered selection of later developments.

Most of the reviews quite properly give primary attention to describing the content and argument of *HTFG*.   When it comes time for assessment, *HTFG* and its author receive generous, sometimes even euphoric praise.   Marcel Simon, writing of *HTFG*, says, 'Much is original and new.   Nothing is unimportant. There can be no doubt about the impact of this book on the further development of gospel criticism.   The author has made it perfectly evident that every attempt to resume "the quest of the historical Jesus" must of necessity take into account . . . the strain of tradition recovered from the fourth gospel. .'/21/ This laudatory verdict is endorsed to a greater or lesser extent by as wide a variety of scholars as H. K. McArthur, /22/ A. N. Wilder, /23/ F. W. Beare, /24/ A. J. B. Higgins, /25/ and G.

Johnston. /26/   Even E. Haenchen in the midst of an attack on
much of Dodd's thesis admits that Dodd 'Grosses geleistet hat',
/27/ and I. H. Marshall from the conservative side calls it 'the
kind of book which no scholar of the Gospel can possibly afford
to neglect', while pointing out that Dodd's approach 'does not
remove the element of historical risk in the study of the
Gospels'. /28/

Along with such generous praise, reviewers found plenty to
criticize.   The following is a representative sample of
criticisms that impinge on the historical questions which are
our focus in this paper:

1. Quite a number of reviewers, while praising Dodd's work in
HTFG, remain unconvinced that John is independent of all of the
synoptic gospels.   Mark, and perhaps Luke, are still thought by
some to constitute source material which the fourth evangelist
mined.   Bruce Vawter admits he 'is not entirely satisfied that
(Dodd) has completely disposed of the striking verbal
correspondences between Jn. and Mk.' /29/   Others, such as
Ernst Haenchen, appear more convinced.   Haenchen comments:
'Dabei verwendet er ausserordentlich viel Raum für den Nachweis,
dass Johannes nicht von den synoptischen Evangelien abhängig ist.
Man wird es als ein besonderes Verdienst des Buches betrachten
dürfen, dass dieser Nachweis wirklich gelungen ist.' /30/   A
more nuanced position is offered by Harvey K. McArthur:

> But is the argument which Dodd develops actually
> conclusive?   In the opinion of this reviewer Dodd has made
> clear the implausibility of any hypothesis which suggests
> that the Fourth Gospel was created by someone who took the
> three Synoptics and then wove them into a mosaic with
> liberal admixtures of his source materials and theology.
> Unfortunately the rejection of this hypothesis does not
> automatically establish the one which Dodd suggests as an
> alternative, namely, that the Johannine tradition was
> parallel to but not dependent on the one(s) found in the
> Synoptics.   There is at least one mediating possibility.
> Is it conceivable that the Fourth Gospel emerged in a
> community which had known the Synoptics but which had
> developed its own "oral tradition" from this base with
> additions from still other sources?   This possibility
> assumes indirect but not direct dependence on the Synoptics.
>
> Dodd does not really consider this alternative in the

course of his detailed investigations although he does
endeavor to eliminate it as a possibility in his
concluding summary (pp. 423-432).   Against such a
hypothesis he argues (a) that the time gap between the
Synoptics and John was scarcely such as to have allowed so
extensive a development, and (b) that it is unlikely that
any one Christian community used all three Synoptics at
this early date.   To the second of these considerations it
may be replied that it is at least equally unlikely that
the Fourth Gospel emerged in a community which knew *none* of
the Synoptic Gospels. /31/

2.   Reviewers of a more sceptical turn of mind criticize Dodd
for what they judge to be a too conservative assessment of the
historical trustworthiness of the traditions John uses.   'One
can agree that the fourth gospel has old independent reports on
John the Baptist,' comments Amos Wilder.   'But here as
elsewhere one must ask, how old and how primitive? . . .
Moreover, even "primitive" tradition, whether Johannine or
synoptic, can be misleading if we fail to recognize that its
retrospective interest in the *person* of Jesus represents a
changed perspective.   The whole reservoir of primitive
tradition, narrative and sayings, upon which the four gospels
are built had already been radically reshaped by the
translation of the earliest witness into various expressions
and forms of christological piety and faith.' /32/   Marcel
Simon agrees: 'To (Dodd), the process at work in the shaping
of the tradition was one of selection.   This might well be
true in a number of cases.   It is doubtful, however, that it
accounts for every single passage: the possibility of
fictitious additions is not to be excluded altogether.' /33/
Perhaps we should follow 'the sceptical mind' which is 'even
prepared to assert that John is an artist of great dramatic
power and much of his work reads like that of a superb
historical novelist.' /34/

3.   Reginal Fuller not only thinks that 'younger scholars in
particular will find it difficult' to place in the itineraries
the confidence which Dodd is able to place in them; but he is
also an able representative of those who reject Dodd's
treatment of eschatological statements in John:

More serious, to the reviewer's mind, is the judgment on
the tradition-history of the predictions of Jesus' going
away and seeing his disciples again.   These Dodd holds to

be a more primitive, and indeed substantially authentic, version of Jesus' future predictions, whereas the two synoptic types of prediction--those which speak of death and resurrection and those which speak of the parousia-- he holds to be later reinterpretations.   It is regrettable that more attention has not been paid to the Johannine 'Son of man' sayings.   Siegfried Schultz's study of these has resulted in a very different view of the Tradition-history behind the Fourth Gospel, viz., from an original Palestinian apocalyptic to a 'Jewish-heterodox' *Neuinterpretation*.   /35/

4.   Fuller praises *HTFG*'s lacᵏ of interaction with secondary literature.   'Most of us *Neutestamentler*,' he says, 'spend our time taking in each other's dirty washing and decking it out with extensive bibliographical footnotes.   Dr. Dodd's work is refreshingly independent, with an absolute minimum of that type of footnote.' /36/   But quite a number of others interpret the same evidence far more negatively.   William E. Hull objects in particular to Dodd's failure to interact with the source critics, with A. Guilding's thesis, /37/ and with Cullmann./38/ A. J. B. Higgins has similar complaints; /39/ and Ernst Haenchen is utterly blistering on Dodd's failure to interact with German scholarship. /40/

5.   The last point to be made in this list is not so much an overt criticism of Dodd by the reviewers, as notice of a perceptive observation made by two or three reviewers--an observation which accurately underscores the paucity of the material in John which Dodd judges to be genuinely authentic, *despite the appearance of a far more conservative stance*.   The appearance is maintained by the tone of the writing, the turn of phrase;   and, certainly, as compared with the work of Bultmann, *HTFG* is a very conservative book indeed. Nevertheless, George Johnston is correct when he says of Dodd: 'At the same time, he reminds us that John is a theologian of profound subtlety, who exploits in the interest of his own spirituality whatever traditional units he has preserved.   It will not do, therefore, to jump to hasty conclusions about the factual accuracy of the Gospel narratives *as they stand*.' /41/   F. W. Beare spells this out more pointedly;   and, for a final extensive quote, I shall cite him at length:

> Professor Dodd has greatly strengthened the case for taking the Fourth Gospel seriously as a quarry for historical facts concerning Jesus of Nazareth.   I am left

with the feeling that when its evidence has all been
sifted and weighed, it does not add greatly to the meagre
store of facts which are supplied by the Synoptics. Where
it differs from them, it is not to be automatically ruled
out of consideration; the 'pre-canonical' traditions which
it has employed have as much title to be looked upon as
reliable as those which the Synoptists had at their
disposal.   But I wonder if the total effect of this
investigation may not be misleading, in that it does not
take into account the unreality of the general picture of
Jesus in this Gospel.   These fragments of 'historical'
traditions are embedded in a complex theological structure
from which they can be recovered in any degree only by an
extraordinary exhibition of critical virtuosity on the part
of the searcher.   To set the matter in perspective let us
recall briefly that John the Baptist did not in fact hail
Jesus as the Lamb of God (the question here is rightly put
by Dodd: 'What measure of historical truth, then, if any,
can we assign to the statement of the Fourth Gospel that
John the Baptist bore witness to Christ?' - p. 301).   Jesus
did not talk to a ruler of the Jews about regeneration, did
not talk with a woman by a well in Samaria about his own
Messiahship and about the spirit-nature of God; did not
discourse to the multitudes about his descent from heaven
as the Bread of Life. . .   Above all, the Jesus of history
did not address his hearers in the structured dialogue and
monologue of the Fourth Gospel; and if there are bits of
teaching--parables, sayings, brief dialogue here and there
--which may be traced to a pre-canonical tradition (as Dodd
has succeeded in doing), it must be said that in the Gospel
these are submerged in the Evangelist's own constructions
and all but dissolved in his theological expositions. . .
And in general, the value and interest of this Gospel
surely lie in the developed theology of the Evangelist and
not in such occasional fragments of actual *verba Christi* as
may be uncovered by patient search.

   This is not to suggest that Professor Dodd himself
fails to give due weight to these considerations.   It is a
caution, rather, to his readers against an over-enthusiastic
reversion to the historical approach to this Gospel.
British scholarship has an unquenchable longing for brute
historical and biographical fact, and there is a perpetual
danger that the wish may give birth to the persuasion that
the facts are more readily ascertainable than is actually
the case.   After all has been said, and every last

particle of primitive gold-dust extracted, the Fourth
Gospel is in its total character a much less reliable
source of historical (especially biographical) information
than Mark, even though it may in some instances preserve a
more accurate recollection of what occurred.   The 'new
look' on the Fourth Gospel has already, in my opinion, set
a number of my colleagues dancing down a false path. . . .
/42/

In my view, Beare's analysis of *HTFG* is profoundly accurate,
irrespective of whether or not one wishes to follow him in his
degree of scepticism.

Since the publication of *HTFG*, research into the fourth
gospel has not abated in the slightest.   At the risk of
coverage that is much too shallow, it may nevertheless be worth
summarizing some of the major trends in johannine research
during the last fifteen years, as such trends impinge on the
concerns of *HTFG* and especially on the problems of historicity.

1.   Source criticism came into its own in the fourth gospel with
the massive commentary by the late Rudolf Bultmann /43/ (which
of course antedates *HTFG*), and reached its apex in R. T.
Fortna's *The Gospel of Signs*. /44/   There have been many other
attempts, and not fewer rebuttals; but as I have detailed this
debate elsewhere, and indicated my reservations about the
validity of the most popular conclusions, /45/ I shall refrain
from repeating old material.

Of course, source critics are not necessarily interested
in the historical trustworthiness of the sources they purport
to uncover; but there is almost invariably some interplay
between their concern to isolate a source or sources, and
questions of historicity. /46/   According to Fortna's
reconstruction, the signs source is supplemented by material
from within the johannine community; and on the face of it this
material, which often claims to be authentic, and the utterances
actually dominical, is not to be so highly rated.   Temple's
sources turn on idealogical factors, not the least of which
is the implausibility of genuine miracles. /47/   Schnackenburg
is much more cautious about delineating the signs source with
precision; but one of his tools for doing so is the
identification of seams separating tradition from redaction, and
his means for establishing such identification are historical as
well as linguistic, stylistic, and theological. /48/

In short, source criticism aims at a much more specific
recovery of the traditions behind the fourth gospel than what
Dodd attempts, and assumes that those traditions are written,
not oral.   But precisely because I remain unpersuaded by the
validity of the source critical methods currently being used on
the fourth gospel, I remain equally sceptical about source
critical methods as a viable approach to questions of
historicity.

2.   *HTFG* has probably enjoyed its biggest impact in influencing
others to hold that John is not dependent on any completed
synoptic gospel.   The major commentaries of Brown, Sanders/
Mastin, Schnackenburg, Morris and Lindars, not to mention the
substantial survey by Kysar, /49/ all opt for some variation of
the view that the synoptics and John enjoy common tradition,
written and/or oral, but no literary dependence.   As a result,
some such conclusion as the following is reached: 'If John did
not use the Synoptic Gospels, the way is opened for an
independent assessment of the historical value of his material.
It cannot be taken for granted that he is more reliable than the
Synoptists, or less so.   Each item has to be taken on its own
merits.' /50/

But it would be quite wrong to give the impression that the
thesis has gone unchallenged.   Indeed, one might even speculate
that it is on the verge of being overthrown.   J. A. Bailey
argues that in some instances John uses Luke directly, whereas
in other passages where there is close agreement the two
Evangelists independently follow similar traditions. /51/
Similarly G. Richter, at least as far as John 18:1-12 is
concerned: /52/ John, he contends, depends on Luke.   J.
Blinzler comes to a more nuanced conclusion when he argues that
the Fourth Evangelist had knowledge of Mark, and perhaps of
Luke, and reproduced some of it from memory, but without copies
in front of him while he worked. /53/   Günter Reim attempts to
cut the Gordian knot by appealing to a lost *fourth* Synoptic
Gospel, earlier than the three canonical synoptics, as the
prime source of the fourth gospel. /54/   Anton Dauer, in his
massive study of John 18:1-19:30, thinks the synoptic gospels
influenced the fourth gospel while the latter was still at the
stage of oral tradition; but even he is unwilling to rule out
the possibility of direct literary dependence. /55/

More recently, C. K. Barrett has revised his 1955
commentary /56/ and remained quite unrepentant about his belief
that John knew Mark, and probably Luke.   Barrett argues his

case at greater length in an important article; /57/ and he is
now joined by detailed contributions from F. Neirynck /58/ and
M. Sabbe. /59/   Boismard proposes a complex theory of three
editions of the fourth gospel; but in this view the second and
third editions reflect direct dependence on the synoptics. /60/

This is only a smattering of the recent literature on the
subject; but perhaps it is fair to say that there is no longer
any substantive consensus.   C. K. Barrett concedes perhaps a
little, but also demands an attractive accountability, when he
writes:

> It is certain that John did not 'use' Mark, as
> Matthew did.   The parallels cannot even *prove* that John
> had read the book we know as Mark.   Anyone who prefers
> to say, 'Not Mark, but the oral traditions on which Mark
> was based', or 'Not Mark, but a written source on which
> Mark drew', may claim that his hypothesis fits the
> evidence equally well.   All that can be said is that we
> do not have before us the oral tradition on which Mark
> was based; we do not have any of the written sources
> that Mark may have quoted; but we do have Mark, and in
> Mark are the stories that John repeats, sometimes at
> least with similar or even identical words, sometimes at
> least in substantially the same order--which is not in
> every case as inevitable as is sometimes suggested.
> Gardner-Smith's rather lame comment on the sequence of
> the feeding miracle and the walking on the lake remains
> as an implied criticism of his own position: 'they go
> well together, and they were no doubt associated in oral
> tradition' (p. 33).   The fact is that there crops up
> repeatedly in John evidence that suggests that the
> evangelist knew a body of traditional material that
> either was Mark, or was something much like Mark; and
> anyone who after an interval of nineteen centuries feels
> himself in a position to distinguish nicely between 'Mark'
> and 'something much like Mark', is at liberty to do so.
> The simpler hypothesis, which does not involve the
> postulation of otherwise unknown entities, is not
> without attractiveness. /61/

I confess I began a careful re-reading of *HTFG* already
prejudiced in favour of its position; but, having been alerted
by some of the articles and books cited above, I began to sense
special pleading here and there; /62/ and I now find myself a

cautious convert to Barrett's position.

In short, there is little clear-cut consensus on the problem of the literary relationship between John and the synoptics.   But I have already shown that Dodd's work in this regard was primarily his way of approaching questions of historicity in the fourth gospel.   So now we must ask ourselves how the problem of synoptic/fourth gospel literary relationship and the problem of the historical trustworthiness of the fourth gospel should properly be related.   How does current revisionism in the one area affect the other?   These questions will be probed a little farther on.

3.   Since the publication of *HTFG*, there has arisen a notable succession of commentators who have embraced some kind of 'developmental theory' /65/ of composition.   R. E. Brown postulates five separate stages leading up to what we call the Gospel of John. /64/   B. Lindars traces the fourth gospel's genesis to a series of homilies, put together in at least two major stages. /65/   Schnackenburg accepts the existence of a signs source, an early edition of the Gospel which incorporated that source and possibly other material of a kerygmatic or liturgical nature, and 'further drafts' (no specifications as to how many) plus a final redaction. /66/   W. Wilkens, though he has not written a commentary, has reconstructed what he believes to be the history of the fourth gospel's formation from a basic Passover framework. /67/   The only two exceptions to the adoption of some formulated developmental theory among recent major commentators are C. K. Barrett /68/ and L. Morris /69/--and that for entirely different reasons.

This is not to suggest that these developmental theories have sprung up because of the influence of *HTFG*.   But there is one obvious connection.   Insofar as the commentators have adopted the view that the material in the fourth gospel emerges from an oral tradition relatively independent of the synoptics, to that extent it is easier to postulate the existence of some definitive johannine 'circle' or johannine 'school' which produced the fourth gospel over an extended period of time. /70/ Such a perspective may well impinge on the question of historicity.

4.   There has been an increasing tendency, partly as a result of Dodd's influence, to recognize the accuracy of many topographical and historical details in the fourth gospel, while, ironically, simultaneously downplaying the historical

worth of most of its content.   Barrett thinks John is not
really interested in historical accuracy.   Those who adopt
developmental theories see the theology and teaching of the
johannine community almost everywhere, and the theology and
teaching of Jesus almost nowhere--except in tiny snippets
which may sometimes be retrieved by form criticism.   So
firmly entrenched is this approach (with the single notable
exception of L. Morris) that scholars who might be expected to
make somewhat more conservative estimations (because of their
practice elsewhere) prefer instead to use ambiguous language.
A fine example of such language is provided by Vanderlip, who
writes: 'We would probably not be far wrong if we were to hold
that the conversations between Jesus and the individuals
mentioned in the Gospel of John actually took place, but that
the recording of what was said and the manner in which the
dialogues are developed should be attributed for the most part
to the creative mind of the writer.   The conversations are the
framework for Johannine instruction.' /71/   Interpreted
sympathetically by all sides, this passage could be accepted by
all sides: there are surely few johannine scholars whose
position would necessarily contradict the statement.   But that
is to say nothing more than that the statement is marvelously
ambiguous; it certainly does not indicate any marked degree of
genuine and detailed consensus among the scholars themselves.
To this problem I shall return; but Dodd's influence,
directly or indirectly, is not too far away.

5. One other work deserves mention at this point.   In its
main thesis it leans but little on *HTFG*, even though it follows
Dodd in finding no literary dependence of the fourth gospel on
the synoptics.   I speak of J. L. Martyn's *History and Theology
in the Fourth Gospel*.   This little book was first published in
1968.   It exerted an influence out of all proportion to its
size; and then in 1979 it reappeared in a revised and
slightly enlarged form. /72/

     This book bears directly on the question of the historical
trustworthiness of the fourth gospel, and so I shall attempt to
challenge some parts of it.   .

     Martyn contends that much of the fourth gospel is a two
level drama, self-consciously presented in such a way as to
present bits of christian tradition about the historical Jesus,
and also to respond in a slightly disguised fashion to the
conflict going on between church and synagogue in the
Evangelist's own day.   At the first level, the Evangelist

presents the *einmalig* events, by which Martyn means the events
which happened 'back there' in Jesus' time.   At the second
level, the Evangelist addresses his own situation.   Martyn
believes that much of the *einmalig* material can also be applied
to the events of the Evangelist's own day, but that most of the
material which he discusses (especially John 3, 5, 6, 7 and 9)
is not really at the *einmalig* level at all, and does not
seriously pretend to teach us anything about the historical
Jesus, but is concerned solely with the *Sitz im Leben* of the
Evangelist.

Martyn finds this pattern particularly evident in John 9.
At the *einmalig* level, the narrative seems to tell us certain
things about Jesus, his disciples, a blind man and his parents,
and the Jewish authorities of Jesus' day.   But at the second
level, we are to discern a Jew of the Evangelist's day who is
healed and converted and living in the Jewish quarter of the
Evangelist's city.   Because the cure (whether of a physical
nature or not is immaterial, according to Martyn) is
attributed to Jesus, discussion sets in which leads to a
confrontation with the local Jewish council.   The council
interviews the man, and then his parents, who are frightened
out of plain speaking because they are aware of a resolution,
already passed by the council, to excommunicate from the
synagogue anyone who confesses that Jesus is the Messiah.
When the healed man leaves the courtroom, he is again
confronted by the christian preacher (under the literary guise of
Jesus), and led to faith in Jesus Christ.   The preacher
declares the significance of his mission and proceeds with a
sermon (John 10).

In Martyn's view, none of the material in this narrative
from 9:8 on has any reference to the *einmalig* level.   Even the
word *History* in the title of the book does not refer to the
history of Jesus and his times, but to the history of the
Evangelist--a point of clarification Martyn himself carefully
provides. /73/   From this base Martyn moves out to several
other passages in the fourth gospel, treating them in similar
fashion;   and then reaches out yet further to speculate on the
theological considerations which prompted the fourth evangelist
to write.

IV

Virtually everything I've said so far has been by way of
background and introduction to what follows.   The literature

on the problems of historicity connected with the fourth
gospel is so vast, and much of it so intricate, that many
volumes would be necessary to interact with it in any detail.
In what remains of this paper, I have opted instead to offer a
number of personal reflexions, almost all of them strictly
methodological and/or programmatic. I shall use these
reflexions as a springboard to interact with some of the
literature presented so far. I should perhaps add that what
follows is more by way of personal progress report by a student
seeking to deal fairly with the evidence and arrive at his own
conclusions, than of authoritative analysis by a distinguished
scholar after a lifetime of careful sifting and study.   Not
least in this particular, therefore, my work stands over
against *HTFG*!   At the same time I shall occasionally point to
areas which stand in urgent need of additional careful study.

1. *None of us approaches the problem of historicity in the
fourth gospel (or any other sensitive question, for that
matter) with an entirely 'open' mind, an entirely objective
approach; and therefore all of us need to recognize our own
'presuppositions' and not to dismiss others because of their
'presuppositions'.*

     The late Rudolf Bultmann is an outstanding example of a
man with strong and crucial presuppositions: (a) he held to
the existence of a full-blown pre-christian Gnosticism, a
perspective which massively influenced his interpretive
judgments; and (b) he held that it is impossible for
twentieth century man to believe in the world of angels,
devils, literal incarnation, physical resurrection, turning
water literally into wine, and so forth. /74/   He did not
prove, nor attempt to prove, (b): he affirmed it.   He did
attempt to prove (a), but because there is no conclusive
literary evidence for well-developed pre-christian Gnosticism,
he fell far short of convincing everyone. /75/

     Bultmann is not alone in having crucial presuppositions;
indeed every scholar has presuppositions, recognized or
unrecognized.   I myself approach the Bible with what most
would consider a 'high' view of Scripture: I expect it to
tell me the truth (which incidentally leaves me with a wide
range of hermeneutical possibilities).   My view of Scripture
is more like Bultmann's presupposition (a) than his (b), since
I have come to it from long study and a serious attempt to
weigh the evidence.   In my view the total 'fit' for a high
view of Scripture is far superior to any of the alternatives.

I freely confess I cannot 'prove' the correctness of this view
the way I can 'prove' the truth of the binomial theorem; but
then, neither could Bultmann 'prove' his pre-christian
Gnosticism.   Yet these two beliefs--one for him, one for me--
each function as a more-or-less non-negotiable point as we
approach any particular text: they are non-negotiable, that is
to say, short of a personal Kuhnian revolution; /76/ and such
revolutions do occur. We all know scholars who once adopted a
high view of Scripture but who came in time to abandon this
view, and we know of others, like R. V. G. Tasker and W.
Ramsey, who began without such a belief and came in time to
embrace it.

In describing Bultmann's non-negotiables, and my own, my
intention is both to illustrate the fact that everyone has such
patterns of thought, but also--an inevitable consequence of
this--to show that having non-negotiables does not exclude
anyone from debate.   Scholars concerned to disagree with
Bultmann have had to do more than point out Bultmann's
presuppositions: they have had to wrestle with him on his own
terms, and also seek to present another total 'fit' as
superior to the wholistic picture adopted by Bultmann.

These more-or-less non-negotiable (short of a Kuhnian
revolution) patterns in our belief structures occur at many
different levels.   For instance in a fascinating and scarcely
recognized article R. Kysar compares the results of C. H. Dodd
and R. Bultmann as each of these giants seeks to delineate the
closest literary affinities to the johannine prologue. /77/

Kysar tabulates their use of material from the O.T.,
classical literature, the Apocrypha, the Pseudepigrapha,
Rabbinic literature, the Hermetica, Philo, sub-apostolic
writings, the Odes of Solomon + miscellaneous.   He finds,
first, striking dissimilarity in what they cite: a total of
only 20 references in common out of 320 cited.   But further he
notes that the differences exhibited in the relationship
between the sheer amount of evidence, and their respective
conclusions, convey vastly different criteria for the use of
evidence.   Dodd piles up the examples, apparently believing
that the number of examples in support of his hypothesis at
least partly determines its validity; thus he has an
especially large number of references to Philonic and Hermetic
material.   Bultmann ignores such a consideration.   He quotes
the Old Testament prodigiously, but discounts virtually all of
this evidence.   His heavy use of the apocryphal and

pseudepigraphical literature is more understandable, since he
believes they betray the existence of pre-christian Gnosticism;
but even so, he thinks that the Odes of Solomon provide the
best examples of conceptual roots of the prologue--even though
the Odes claim a meagre 11% of his quotations.   Moreover, not
only are both Dodd and Bultmann sadly deficient in rabbinic
parallels, using only secondary literature, they both cite much
later literature as exemplars of the thought-forms which, they
contend, influenced the prologue: Dodd, the Hermetica, and
Bultmann, the Odes and Mandaic sources.

I am not at present quibbling with their results.   I am
interested solely in their methods, belief patterns, and, to a
lesser extent, training (it is not for nothing that the
rabbinic parallels offer such slim pickings: contrast A.
Schlatter /78/).   We might in a similar fashion point out that
it is not altogether surprising that Dodd finds the fourth
gospel's realized eschatology to be more primitive: the entire
pattern of his earlier work tends to downplay the apocalyptic
element.   I have already pointed out that *HTFG* has been
criticized in this area.   Clearly, there is a different
weighing of the evidence according to people's presuppositions.

When we approach the question of the historicity of the
fourth gospel, therefore, we must not only make our
definitions of 'history'clear, and what we think *can* be
demonstrated by the 'historian's method;' but we also need to
be as self-consciously aware as possible of our non-negotiables
(again, I repeat, non-negotiables not in an absolute sense, but
in a Kuhnian sense).   D. E. Nineham writes, 'It is of the
essence of the modern historian's method and criteria that they
are applicable only to purely human phenomena, and to human
phenomena of a normal, that is a non-miraculous, non-unique
character.' /79/   Such an approach eliminates *a priori* the
possibility that Jesus is literally the incarnation of the Son
of God, or that he turned water into wine.   It cannot
possibly envisage a God who acts in history except in an
entirely pantheistic sense--in which case, he must be painfully
difficult to detect, and in any event not by 'historical'
means.   If 'historical method' is permitted to include the
investigation of anything in the time-space continuum, then
much more is open to us as, at least, a possibility.

Similarly, when Dodd says (as I indicated earlier) that
he cannot see any way of identifying traditional materials
(i.e. historical materials, in the sense that the materials

describe what really happened) in the fourth gospel where
comparison with the synoptics fails us, short of giving undue
weight to subjective impressions, he has enunciated a terribly
limiting methodological non-negotiable.   Does he accept as
historical in extra-biblical ancient sources only that which is
attested independently elsewhere?   Where an author proves
reliable on incidental details that are to some degree
verifiable, is there not a presumption of his reliability in
areas where he is not at all verifiable?   Are there no
broader historical or theological reasons for thinking John to
be somewhat more credible than what Dodd's principle allows?
I would answer yes; but apparently Dodd's non-negotiable
requires that he answer no.

I may go farther.   Is it possible that the scholarly
consensus regarding a 'school' or 'circle' or 'community,' and
regarding a long series of editorial steps and of redactional
activity, has unwittingly provided a new generation of scholars
with several functional non-negotiables which are rarely tested?
If someone like Morris argues that John the son of Zebedee wrote
the fourth gospel, he is fairly easily dismissed, precisely
because, for most of us, the idea of John as author has already
been filtered out by our functional non-negotiables.   Indeed,
these non-negotiables are often absorbed unwittingly by our
reading, even though we ourselves have never examined the
primary data first-hand.   And even those few who have carefully
weighed the evidence and concluded, on balance, that it is
improbable that John is the fourth evangelist--among whom Dodd
must surely rank near the top in the care and fairness of his
approach--even these, once this tentative position is reached,
adopt the position as a functioning non-negotiable in the
future, short of a Kuhnian revolution.

It is extremely important that this first reflection not
be misunderstood by taking it to answer a question not within
its purview.   I am interested in pointing out that all of us
are finite, that none of us begins any inquiry with an entirely
blank mind, that we must be self-critical especially in those
areas where we adopt functional non-negotiables.   However,
such a cautious warning does not entail the conclusion of the
new historians, over-reacting against the crude objectivism of
von Ranke, that history is so non-objective that there is no
possible way of evaluating alternative reconstructions and
interpretations.   The task of the historian is not quite the
same as the task of the physicist; but it is remarkably

similar to the task of the geologist.   Certain recent critical
discussion which carefully defines the term 'objectivity' as
applied to history has shown conclusively that 'if we press the
criterion of objectivity too hard, it applies to no form of
inquiry; slacken it slightly and history edges its way in with
the rest.' /80/   I hope to deal with this question in two
subsequent articles.   For the moment I wish only to make it
clear that by this first reflection I do not mean to shut up
historical inquiry to unmitigated subjectivism.   Nevertheless,
even after such a fundamental *caveat* is registered, it is
important, methodologically speaking, that we make clear,
especially to ourselves and hopefully to others as well, just
what non-negotiables we are harbouring at the moment, and how
strong they are (their strength is, of course, entirely
relative).   In so doing, we will not only be able to learn
from each other, but also detect more accurately where and why
we disagree.   In time, we may even weaken the strength of some
of our non-negotiables, and change one of our fundamental
positions, and come a little closer to the truth.

2.   *The barrier commonly erected between history and theology*
is not only false, but is methodologically indefensible.

        This point has been discussed many times in articles and
books.   The only justification for raising it again is that
the distinction between history and theology is still being
used in many quarters as a methodological test for assessing
theologically motivated statements as non-historical.

        This is not in any way to deny that the Evangelists were
theologians with a set of doctrines and theological interests
they were earnestly attempting to propagate.   The straw man
raised by some critics--that either the Evangelists were
dispassionate observers giving us cold historical facts, replete
with endless specimens of *ipsissima verba Jesu,* or else they
were theologians concerned with conveying theological truth and
only incidentally (and even accidentally) including solid
history--forces upon us a needless choice.   The first alternative is so demonstrably untrue that the impression is given
we are shut up to the second; and that is methodologically
indefensible.   Of course the Evangelists were theologians.
Sometimes we are able to detect with fair probability some of
the theological motivations which prompted a particular
Evangelist to treat, say, the Passion Narrative, just as he
did.   In John's case, the conceptual collapsing of the death,

burial, resurrection and exaltation of Jesus into one
soteriological event is unique among the Evangelists, rather
dramatic; and certainly this bears detailed study. /81/

Yet this is a far cry from saying that, because John is
motivated by theological concerns, therefore he is untrustworthy
with respect to his historical witness wherever that witness has
been influenced by his theology. Some secular analogies may
help to clarify this point. In World War II, when the first
trickle of gruesome reports from Auschwitz, Dachau and other
death camps first started reaching the Allies, they were almost
universally dismissed. Everyone knew Hitler was leaning on the
Jews a little; and it was thought that the Jewish voices being
raised, and the handful of escapees who made it to the outside,
were grossly exaggerating the facts in order to manipulate the
Allies. After all, they were scarcely neutral witnesses.
Yet the fact remains that those few committed Jewish witnesses
were correct; and the fact that they passionately believed
what they were saying to be true did not in the final analysis
vitiate that truth. Similarly, a person telling of his true
love may not say anything untrue about her, even though his
account may be biased.

Another example from World War II is perhaps even more
revealing. Two recent books, William Manchester's *American
Caesar* /82/ and Herman Wouk's *War and Remembrance* /83/ both
describe the Battle of Leyte Gulf. Both are thorough and
careful historical works, and both authors draw largely on the
same sources (though I doubt if any of them would be
recoverable). Yet their accounts differ enormously, both
because of what they include and exclude and because of the
differing perspectives from which they are told, Wouk telling
the story through Navy eyes, Manchester focussing on General
MacArthur, politics and the army side. In one sense these
two accounts are distortions, at least from the point of view
of omniscience. But it does not follow that either is
inaccurate or untrue; I was not able to detect any *necessary
contradiction*. If we require that what they present to be
factual be in fact factual, even if not *exhaustively* true, then
we have required as much as is reasonable of a finite
intelligence.

Of course, I am not arguing that bias doesn't matter, nor
that a deep commitment or a conceptual framework *cannot* distort
the facts, wittingly or unwittingly. I am not surreptitiously
jumping from the preceding examples to the illegitimate

conclusion that John *must* therefore be historically accurate,
even though he is a committed witness.   Nor am I trying to
ignore or surreptitiously skirt the genuine differences between
the fourth gospel and the synoptics, concerning which I shall
say more a little further on.   My argument is purely
methodological and much more modest in its conclusion.   It is
simply that *no* historical account is *ever* purely 'objective' in
this strong sense; that it is the function of historians /84/
to make sense of the whole; that because a man is committed to
the truth of what he claims are facts does not *per se* jeopardize
the truthfulness of those alleged facts; and therefore any
method which attempts to retrieve the historical by rejecting
automatically those historical claims which the witness feels
strongly about is both naive and indefensible. /85/

At a theoretical level, Dodd is not, of course, unaware of
this falsely erected barrier.   'In seeking to interpret the
facts he records,' Dodd writes, 'the Fourth Evangelist is not
necessarily exceeding the limits proper to history.   For it is
the function of the historian, as distinct from the chronicler,
to expose the course of events as an intelligible process . . .'
/86/   He can even say that John 'is concerned to affirm with
all emphasis the historical actuality of the facts which (the
tradition) transmitted.' /87/   Yet a little further on Dodd
comments:

> It still remains, however, a part of the task of the
> student of history to seek to discover (in Ranke's oft-
> quoted phrase) 'wie es eigentlich geschehen ist'--how it
> actually happened.   To what extent and under what
> conditions may the Fourth Gospel be used as a document for
> the historian in that sense?

> The answer to that question depends upon the sources
> of information which were at the disposal of the
> evangelist, if we assume (as I think we may, in view of
> what has been said) that he intended to record that which
> happened, however free he may have felt to modify the
> factual record in order to bring out the meaning. /88/

There is no way to avoid the feeling that Dodd is trying to
have his cake and eat it too.   But the real problem comes up in
Dodd's methodological approach to many individual passages.   Of
the many examples, we may note two.   In discussing the foot-
washing episode in John 13:1-17, /89/ Dodd detects at the heart
of the account a simple episode, an 'exemplary story,' in which

Jesus washes his disciples' feet and tells them he has done this to leave them an example which they are to imitate.   This narrative Dodd is prepared to assess as something John drew out of the tradition (which, for Dodd, means it is historical), *once the theological commentary has been stripped away*.   This theological commentary must be attributed to the Evangelist (which, for Dodd, means it is non-historical).   This may or may not be a sound conclusion; but it is certainly not a sound method for arriving at a conclusion.

As a second example we may note Dodd's summary statement at the end of his chapter on 'The Reunion.' /90/ He writes: 'The extent to which the narrative has been *subjected to the influence of the specifically Johannine theology* is confined to a few (*readily separable*) passages . . . .' /91/

I contend, simply, that this is methodologically indefensible.   To appeal to johannine theology, or even to johannine drama, is not itself an adequate basis for separating out the historical from the later accretion.   I am reminded of the comment of David Halberstam, author of such best-selling non-fiction works as *The Best and the Brightest* and *The Powers that Be*:

> A real writer of non-fiction books is as much a dramatist as a journalist.   It does not lessen the responsibility for accuracy, but the writer owes the reader something additional.   It is the writer's fault, not the reader's, if the reader puts down the book. /92/

Perhaps John does not want us to put down his book.

3. *If scholarship is to advance in this area of the historical trustworthiness of the fourth gospel, arguments based on vague or imprecise or slippery language must be strenuously avoided.* It is quite legitimate, of course, to attempt to formulate a truly mediating position to which two or more polarized parties are invited to move; and one might even allow ambiguity in area X if there is some need to skate around X in order to get to Y--and Y is the topic of the paper at hand.   But what is unacceptable is ambiguity in talking about area X when it is precisely area X that is being studied.   Genuine uncertainty-- an agnostic position--is, of course, quite another matter; and there is no problem with a statement like 'I am unsure of the historical worth of this *pericope*'.   But a statement like 'We shall not be far wrong if we judge that this *pericope* springs

from some primitive tradition which has been creatively handled
by the Evangelist' may sound good, but is too imprecise to be
useful.

Probably a great deal of *unwitting* ambiguity has been
promoted by talk about the mutual influence of independent oral
traditions, and the like.   This could mean not much more than
that Christians in the first century sometimes talked to each
other.   Alternatively it could be taken to support theories
which postulate communities with their own independent
theologies, communities hermetically sealed off from one another
but capable of springing the odd leak.   We are talking about
that for which we have all too little direct evidence, and so we
use catch-all terminology.

I have illustrated what seems to be unacceptable ambiguity
from George Vanderlip.   Another example is found in some parts
of Stephen Smalley's recent treatment of history in the fourth
gospel, though this is in many ways a useful and competent work.
/93/   For example, when he comes to discuss his first concrete
example, John 2:1-21, he suggests (but does not really argue)
that the story has 'an authentically historical base'; but he
writes in such a way that it is unclear (1) whether he believes
that the historical base included a miracle or only something
'unexpected', (2) whether he believes Jesus' conversation with
his mother was originally part of the wedding story, or
something added later, (3) whether the master of the banquet had
any conversation with the bridegroom (verse 10 being a Johannine
link and reflecting Johannine theology).   In any case, Smalley
tells us that 'John finally worked over this material in his own
way with his own style . . .' /94/   If so, it amazes me how
well we are able to get back to an alleged source, various
accretions, and a final reworking.   But my main objection is
that at some points the language is too vague to be useful.

On this point, Dodd normally fares very well.   He is
usually extremely clear, with the result that whether one agrees
with him or disagrees, one usually enjoys a pretty good idea of
what the debate is about.

4.   *Extremely complex and detailed literary and critical
theories are usually much less plausible than is often thought;
yet somehow, unfortunately, they convey a general impression of
convincing coherence even after detail after detail has been
demonstrated to be implausible.*

The best argument for this reflection is the history of the
source criticism of the fourth gospel in the twentieth century.
/95/   But because this paper is interested in methodological
questions surrounding problems of historicity in John, I shall
turn attention to J. L. Martyn's book. /96/

Martyn begins his study of John 9 by noting in vv. 1-7
three elements very often found in the miracle story form: (a)
a description of the sickness;   (b) the sick person healed;   (c)
the miracle confirmed.   (a) is found in 9:1;   (b) in 9:6, 7;
and (c) appears to lie in 9:8, 9.   This latter identification,
however, Martyn rejects;   for vv. 8, 9 begin a new scene in
which Jesus is no longer present.   This proves, to Martyn, that
the original ending of the story has been changed in order to
incorporate *a dramatic expansion* of the story, which runs from
vv. 8-41.   The structure of this entire 'added part' is based
'on the ancient maxim that no more than two active characters
shall normally appear on stage at one time, and that scenes are
often divided by adherence to this rule.'   This generates the
following scenes: vv. 8-12, the blind man and his neighbours;
vv. 13-17, the blind man and the Pharisees;   vv. 18-23, the
Pharisees and the blind man's parents;   vv. 24-34, the Pharisees
and the blind man;   vv. 35-38, Jesus and the blind man;   vv. 39-
41, Jesus and the Pharisees.

Already a host of objections spring to mind.   I shall
venture a little further reflexion on form criticism below.
At the moment, we may profitably note: (1) Granted that the
miracle story form is not typical, one must at least ask the
question whether the difference is to be accounted for by
supposing that John changed it in order to create a 'dramatic
expansion,' or by supposing that the story is so primitive that
it has not yet even reached the smoothly rounded contours
idealized by the form critics.   Martyn has opted for the former
without even considering the latter.   (2) The very first
section, vv. 1-7, has *three* active characters: Jesus, his
disciples, and the blind man.   This is not uncommon in the
fourth gospel (e.g. 1:40-42;   2:1-11 *[unless one is going to
postulate several scenes!]*;   4:39-43;   several panels in 18-21).
(3) Moreover, Martyn's synthesis provides neither theological
nor form-critical explanation for vv. 2-5.   (4) It is not
obvious that vv. 39-41 should be considered a scene embracing
Jesus and the Pharisees *over against* vv. 35-38 (Jesus and the
blind man).   On the face of it, Jesus is still addressing the
blind man, and anyone else who wants to listen, in v. 39;   and
some Pharisees are listening in.

Martyn, however, on the above bases alone, concludes: 'He
who reads the chapter aloud with an eye to the shifting scenes
and the skillfully handled crescendos cannot fail to perceive
the artistic skill of the dramatist who created this piece out
of the little healing story of verses 1-7.' He feels close
comparative study 'will surely lead one to conclude that the
skilled dramatist is the Evangelist himself.' I am reminded of
Halberstam's comments. In any case, it now appears clear, and
Martyn makes it evident later on, that vv. 8-41 bear no relation
to the historical Jesus: they are a creation.

The purpose of this creation is to produce a two-level
story in which, at the *einmalig* level, the reference is to Jesus
(even though the story from v. 8 on never happened at that
level), and at the second level, the level of John's readers,
Jesus stands for an early christian preacher. Vv. 1-7 really
refer, not to Jerusalem near the Temple, but to some street in
the Jewish quarter of John's city. Some poor Jew, afflicted
with blindness (whether of a physical nature or not, Martyn
cannot decide), is restored in sight by the faithful witness of
the johannine church to the power of Jesus. No matter that the
disciples' contribution in vv. 1-7 scarcely sounds like faithful
witness. In the next scene (vv. 8-12), the cured man is found
conversing with neighbours and acquaintances near his home in
the Jewish quarter of John's city. Vv. 13-17 purport to be the
Sanhedrin of Jerusalem at the *einmalig* level (which never
happened from v. 8 on), but in fact refers to the Gerousia in
John's city. A voice from offstage must insert v. 14, as also
one or two later snippets which John does *not* record but which
Martyn finds essential to his 'drama.' Vv. 18-23, scene 4,
again picture the Gerousia, and presuppose the recent adoption
of the *Birkath ha-Minim,* a position Martyn defends in his second
chapter. Scene 5, 9:24-34, still in the courtroom, forces
choice between Moses and Jesus. In Scene 6, vv. 35-38, the
christian preacher (under the guise of Jesus) instrumental in
the man's healing leads him to solid faith. This leads to
scene 7, vv. 39-41, where the voice of Jesus Christ speaks
through the preacher-disciple. Martyn rather has to frame it
this way, since the text still has Jesus speaking in the first
person. A sermon follows in chapter 10.

I cannot enter into extended debate with Martyn without
writing a book as long as his. But every step of the way,
including most of his footnotes, Martyn overcomes difficulties
by affirming his theory at the expense of what the text says.
His reconstruction turns on many points, most of which I find

implausible.   To name but a few. (1) Would first century
readers understand that Martyn's reconstruction was what the
fourth gospel was really getting at?   I could believe that
some who were in the *Sitz im Leben* Martyn constructs might apply
certain elements of this chapter to their own situation;   and I
could even believe that John told the story at least in part so
that they would be encouraged by it.   But that is a far cry
from saying that most of it has no historical grounding in the
experiences of Jesus of Nazareth, and that John wrote it out of
pastoral concern, knowing full well that what he apparently
says happened in fact didn't, or alternatively that he wrote in
such a way his readers knew he was passing on pastoral advice in
the form of a Jesus-story with no basis in historical reality.
(2) Martyn bases the doubling between Jesus and the preacher--
disciple on such verses as 9:4; 14:12.   The resurrected Jesus
continues his ministry through his church.   I am unpersuaded
of his interpretation of these verses, but, that aside, Martyn
fails to reckon with the pronounced uniqueness of Jesus in the
fourth gospel.   Even if his *ministry* continues *in some respects*
by the Paraclete's working in his disciples, I doubt that John
would feel free to make the easy identification Martyn requires.
(3) Martyn requires a strong Christian-Jew antithesis; but this
interpretation of the fourth gospel and of its references to
'the Jews' has been strongly--and rightly--challenged. /97/
(4) Martyn bases a great deal on equating this instance of
expulsion from the synagogue with the *Birkath ha-Minim*; but of
this I shall say more later.

Quite literally a score of points of detail from Martyn's
first chapter are in fact as implausible as those I've
specified, perhaps more so.   But the point is that extremely
complex theories about questions of historicity tend to promote
such implausible details, even though that very wealth of detail
engenders a quiet confidence that the general picture must be
right, despite the fact that not all the details can be
substantiated.   As a result, Martyn's work has, by and large,
been warmly received.   I do not wish to sound too cynical; but
I suspect that when scholars have had time to assess his
arguments point by point in great detail, Martyn's book will
lose its prominence.   Of course, if he had written, instead of
this detailed book, some shorter essay merely suggesting, in
general terms, that John wrote the fourth gospel in such a way
as to encourage Christians in their witness to Jesus in their
own city, his work would not have had the impact that it has.
The irony is that something like the latter conclusion is being
drawn from it, even though the detailed arguments which he

adduces to support it are not themselves very plausible.

   Something similar occurs with a literary reconstruction of
the fourth gospel like that of R. E. Brown.   His five
successive stages are quite detailed; but they have not really
won the day.   In the case of his work, it is not so much that
any of his arguments is notoriously implausible, as that it is
extremely difficult to imagine how one could go about proving
his theory—even in the limited sense of attempting to have it
assessed as highly probable by a broad spectrum of scholars for
a sustained period of time.   R. Kysar says something similar:

> My point is that the theories advanced by Brown and Lindars
> are such that no amount of analysis of the gospel materials
> will ever produce convincing grounds for them.   If the
> gospel evolved in a manner comparable to that offered by
> Brown and Lindars, it is totally beyond the grasp of the
> johannine scholar and historian to produce even tentative
> proof that such was the case. /98/

Yet the fact remains that the scholarly world is, by and large,
convinced that John's Gospel did indeed evolve through periods
of substantial development.   And once again one must suppose
that if instead of detailed developmental theories whose details
are either implausible or highly speculative, we had been
presented only with general ideas about literary development,
those ideas would not have had the impact that the detailed
theories have enjoyed.

   We find ourselves in a Catch-22 situation.   In the last
reflection I complained about vague and ambiguous language; now
it almost appears that I'm complaining about precise language.
In fact, that is not quite the case.   Rather I'm complaining
about detailed theories whose details do not stand up to close
investigation, or whose details cannot in the nature of the case
be investigated.   There must surely be some cases where we are
forced to say, 'I don't know'—a point to which I shall return.
Moreover, methodologically speaking, I'm not sure these newer,
more complex and detailed theories deal any better with the hard
evidence than some of the older, simpler theories which have by
and large been rejected.

5. *Not a few form-critical arguments used in the service of
research into questions of historicity will not stand close
scrutiny.*

This reflection can be worked out in two or three ways.
In the first place, sober study is showing that form criticism
cannot possibly do all that was once expected of it.   Recent
essays by Schürmann, Hooker, Stanton, Travis, Longenecker,
Ellis /99/ and others are warning us against the abuse of the
tool.   These essays are of the greatest importance.   It is
obviously not possible to repeat all their arguments here; but
I cannot forbear to mention a few.   Schürmann has provided
sociological reasons for thinking the disciples took notes,
recording in written form, during the *pre-Passion period*,
various sayings and teaching of Jesus; and Ellis has extended
the list of reasons for thinking so.   This means that form-
critical arguments, which are normally formulated for *oral*
material, must be used with extreme caution.   Form critical
studies that serve as controls to gospel form criticism have,
as Stanton notes, most commonly been done on folklore and
Jewish traditions.   'The similarities are often striking,' he
says, 'but form critics have often paid insufficient attention
to the dissimilarities.' /100/   He goes on to point out that
the forms were not restricted to one *Sitz im Leben*: almost
every form of oral tradition was used in a wide variety of
ways.   Perhaps it is not surprising that there is wide
divergence of scholarly opinion about the most likely *Sitz* in
any particular case.   Hooker points out, among other things,
that just because the form of a pericope is established, and
even a plausible *Sitz im Leben* which may well provide the
setting in which an earlier story was preserved, shaped and
passed on, it does not follow that the *Sitz* in any sense
provided the setting for the *creation* of the story.

> The trap into which the form-critic so often falls is
> that he equates the *Sitz im Leben* with the *origin* of the
> material; the *Sitz im Leben* is not simply the 'setting'
> of the material but, according to Fuller, its 'creative
> milieu'.   Now this is all right so long as by 'creative'
> is meant 'that which licked the material into its present
> shape.'   But at this stage the form-critic makes the
> mistake of confusing form with content.   Because he has
> no knowledge of earlier forms, and because he can see the
> relevance of the material in its present form to the life
> of the early community, as he understands it, he thinks he
> has discovered the origin of the *material*.   Of course, he
> *may* be right: but he is making an assumption on the basis
> of insufficient evidence. /101/

Hooker goes on to give a probing critique of the principles of

'dissimilarity' and 'coherence' which are used to answer the
sort of objection she has just made.   She points out that in
reality the principles do not offer objective criteria: what is
really operative is the scholar's own understanding of the
situation.

Of course, Hooker is not trying to comfort conservatives.
She is merely pointing out that the tools we use in New
Testament study cannot in the nature of the case answer the
sorts of questions being put to them.   This surely means that
one must opt for agnosticism on these matters, or make decisions
at least partly prompted by larger considerations.

Dodd himself, in *HTFG*, occasionally offers a word of
warning about form criticism, even though form criticism is not
the least important of his tools in this book.   For instance,
he writes: 'It may fairly be objected to the work of some of
the form-critics in the field of the New Testament that they
have not always sufficiently allowed for the disparity in the
span of time to be taken into consideration.' /102/   Most of
the comparative studies deal in centuries;   in the New
Testament we are working with decades.   However, Dodd feels
that, when all allowance is made, form criticism has become an
invaluable tool for recognizing afresh the importance of oral
tradition in the New Testament period.   Put so generally, few
would disagree.   However, the cogency of *HTFG* turns on the
supposition that the tradition is *oral*.   Suppose Schürmann and
Ellis are right, as I think they are: how would Dodd modify
his argument?

There is a second way in which form-critical arguments are
proving to be tricky things, and need to be handled with more
caution.   It is this: really close parallels crop up in highly
diverse places, but the scholar arbitrarily (from a strictly
methodological point of view) fixates on one of them.   For
example, in an important chapter of *HTFG* called 'Discourse and
Dialogue in the Fourth Gospel,' /103/ Dodd argues that he has
isolated a particular form of dialogue characterized by the
following four elements: (1) an oracular utterance by Jesus:
(2) blank incomprehension or crude misunderstanding by an
interlocutor;   (3) a reproachful retort by Jesus;   and (4) an
explanation or extension of the enigmatic saying.   Dodd claims
that the closest parallels are found in the *Corpus Hermeticum,*
much later Gnostic literature.   But now E. E. Lemcio has
isolated precisely the same pattern in the Old Testament, and
arguably, in Mark as well. /104/   What effect does such

research have on Dodd's work?   In this particular instance, of
course, Lemcio has provided new evidence (although in one sense
the evidence was available from the start).   In not a few
instances, however, difference in scholarly opinion turns not on
the evidence, but on the weighing and interpretation of that
evidence.   Form criticism is not a 'tool' in the sense that a
bunsen burner or a mass spectrometer is a tool; but the
terminology has contributed to blinding us, making us unable to
see the crucial distinctions.

6. *The verifiable johannine accuracies ought to be given more
weight than is common at present.*   I am referring to details of
topography and the like. /105/   Of course one may say that John
used reliable sources or reliable tradition at these points, and
thus remove the credit for accuracy from the Evangelist himself.
But that simply pushes the argument one step farther back.   If
his sources and/or traditions are so good where they are
verifiable, why should they be judged largely suspect where they
are not verifiable? /106/   I suspect that the answer lies in
the opinion of many that the theological content ascribed to the
historical Jesus by John, and the actions and miracles ascribed
to him, *could not* be genuinely historical, owing to the fact
that some modern reconstructions of what *must* have been the case
have *a priori* ruled out of court much of the non-verifiable
evidence, and correspondingly minimized the significance of the
verifiable evidence.   This is methodologically unacceptable.
I am not saying that modern reconstructions have no place.   On
the contrary: they are the very stuff of the historian's task.
But if an ancient writer (or his sources!) is historically
reliable where he may be tested, and claims that certain statements and events are to be attributed to a certain historical
individual; and if the major barrier standing in the way of
accepting his claim is some modern reconstruction which denies
that such a claim could be true, is it not time to examine the
modern reconstruction again?

7. *There is a great deal of evidence for the view that the New
Testament documents are, by and large, 'accidental' or
'circumstantial' documents in some respects; and several
corollaries of this observation, all important to the historical
investigation of the New Testament, are being overlooked.*

It is still rather in vogue for New Testament scholars to
poke gentle fun at systematic theology, especially systematic
theology of the older sort which accepted the Bible as a given
and attempted to think through a 'system' that fairly embraced

all its teaching.   The New Testament documents, we are reminded,
do not present themselves as abstract reflections or as well-
organized dogmatics;   and the occasions which call forth these
documents are too occasional, circumstantial, or accidental to
allow fair handling of their material in such a fashion.

Ironically, New Testament scholars tend nevertheless to
systematize the individual documents of the New Testament--
indeed, to *hyper*systematize them.   As a result, there is a
rampant proclivity abroad to speak of Paul's Christology in
Romans as opposed to his Christology in, say, II Corinthians.
From this basis one may go on to speak of the development in
Pauline thought, or even the contradictions between his early
thought and his later thought on Christology.   In our
systematizing of the documents, we tend also to analyze the
possible backgrounds;   and where we cannot draw a reasonably
straight line from some document's peculiarity to something in
the alleged background, but can trace a straight line from that
peculiarity to later literature, we immediately suspect an
anachronism.   This seems to be an especially attractive
alternative if that peculiarity can in some way be fitted into
the biblical author's 'system,' as reconstructed by the critic.
Moreover, instead of systematizing theology using all the
material in the Bible as our chief source, we now systematize
history, and use our histmatics (if I may follow German
tradition and coin a word) to filter out unacceptable elements
in our texts, in much the same way that dogmatics (it is
alleged) filtered out unacceptable elements in the same texts.

Thus, it is very common to be told that the historical John
the Baptist could not possibly have pointed to the historical
Jesus and said, 'Look, the Lamb of God who takes away the sin of
the world!' (John 1:29);   or that the confession of Jesus'
messiahship and kingship (John 1:46,49) could not possibly have
taken place as early as John 1.   It is unthinkable;   and
besides, such early confessions seem to fly in the face of the
synoptics.

There are several methodological problems with histmatics,
and with the general failure to listen to the texts more
sympathetically.   *First,* in a crucial area like Christology, a
great deal of recent writing has resurrected something akin to
an older view: that 'high' Christology was not only very fast
in developing, but ultimately owes its main points to Jesus
himself.   Recent works by, *inter alios,* R. N. Longenecker,
C. F. D. Moule, I. H. Marshall, and M. Hengel, /107/ although

they disagree in many particulars, converge on this point.
Such research calls in question many widely held histmatic
structures.

Second, some modern studies have reminded us of the
'circumstantial' nature of the treatment of various themes in
New Testament books; /108/ and others, like J. D. G. Dunn's
Unity and Diversity in the New Testament, /109/ find that much
the same thing prevails with respect to the books themselves,
each one taken as a whole. I dissent profoundly from not a few
of Dunn's conclusions; but surely few would disagree with him
on the point in question: viz. that the New Testament books are
largely 'circumstantial' or 'accidental' documents in the
technical sense. They respond to circumstances, reflect
historical circumstances and perspectives, and are caught up in
the 'accidents' or history. Not one of them is meant to be
taken as a comprehensive, self-sufficient, and exclusive
portrayal of what Christianity ought to be.

It follows, then, that the modern student has to
reconstruct to the best of his ability just what happened.
There is in early Christianity obvious development of thought:
the least sceptical will admit to such, for instance, within
the Book of Acts. But when our information regarding the total
picture is so limited, and most of the primary sources so
'circumstantial' in nature, it is a major methodological error
to construct a large-scale histmatics based in part on a hyper-
systematizing (and hyperhistmatizing) of these 'circumstantial'
books, and in part on subjective assessments about what could or
could not have taken place.

Third, it is methodologically absurd to think that a
vibrant, thriving, not to say tumultous fledgling religion like
early Christianity, which took root simultaneously in several
different cultures and many different lands, and which embraced
people from a wide variety of ethnic, educational, social and
religious backgrounds, developed in a straight line, in such a
way that we can plot very much of the teaching as being early or
late. Probably in most conceptual areas, any given teaching
was both.

A modern analogy may be of help. Religious developments
within Western Christendom during the past one hundred years may
at a very general level be histmatized (or caricaturized!) something like this: Rationalism was on the ascendancy; an
increasing number of people adopted some modern variation of a

liberal Jesus or simply lost faith; popular piety and church
attendance decreased sharply; after the Great Depression and
World War II there was a short-lived resurgence of Christianity,
but it lacked a solid epistemological base and soon dissipated
its forces; a quasi-mystical, experience-oriented pop
Christianity developed in many places, along with a rising
invasion of Eastern cults.

How, then, would some future historian, twenty centuries
hence, who develops a histmatics of the twentieth century along
the above lines, handle the obvious anomalies?   It takes but
little imagination to speculate what theories our imaginary
fortieth century historians will propound to explain such
twentieth century phenomena as the large numbers of overseas
missionaries, the Bible sales, the growth and influence of the
(by and large) conservative charismatic movement, the re-birth
of Reformed theology, or the like.   The histmatic structure
would not be quick to allow the possibility that the same
writer could have written a technical essay on source criticism
/110/ and then a popular refutation of current attempts to
revive Dean Burgon. /111/   The latter work must surely have
been written eighty or ninety years ago.   But such a conclusion,
based as it is on the histmatic reconstruction, fails to allow
for the strange fact that in popular conservative circles Dean
Burgon again stalks through the land.

Simiarly, it would not be all that surprising to learn that
christian Jews and christian Gentiles in the first century
retained a wide variety of postures *vis-à-vis* one another.   It
would not be surprising to discover that a decision made at
Jerusalem was ignored, in different ways, both by some Jewish
Christians in Jerusalem and by some Gentile Christians elsewhere.   It should not be thought surprising that an historical
Stephen (Acts 7), at an early date, begins to see and expound
the implications for the Temple of a salvation made available
exclusively through Jesus of Nazareth--an exclusivistic framework already proclaimed by Peter (Acts 4:12), although the
cultic implications were not worked out by him (at least, not
that we know of!).   It is surely not a cause for surprise that
these legitimate implications of Christ's cross-work and
resurrection, though spelled out in Jewish circles, are actually
put into practice among less purely Jewish churches; for
tradition dies hard.

Fourth, Dodd is surely right when he argues, again and
again, that the fourth evangelist presents himself as one

concerned to give true historical data.   'For unquestionably
the tradition, in all its forms, *intends* (the emphasis is
Dodd's) to refer to an historical episode, closely dated *sub
Pontio Pilate,* apart from which (this is the uniform
implication) there would have been no church to shape or hand
down such a tradition.' /112/   Elsewhere, he comments, '. . .
it is important for the evangelist that what he narrates
happened.' /113/   Again, in discussing John 19:35, Dodd
remarks: 'In any case, whether the witness is the evangelist or
another, I can see no reasonable way of avoiding the conclusion
that the evangelist intends to assure his readers that his
account rests, whether directly or indirectly, on the testimony
of an eyewitness.   Not only so, he formally affirms that the
testimony is genuine (ἀληθινή) and that the witness must be
believed to be a veracious witness (ὅτι ἀληθῆ λέγει).' /114/
Dodd is surely entirely correct in what he believes the
Evangelist *intends* to provide. /115/

     If we apply these insights--that (1) even doctrines such as
a high Christology appeared remarkably early; that (2) the New
Testament books, being of a largely 'circumstantial' nature,
ought not be forced into a procrustean histmatics against their
own evidence; that (3) there was inevitably enormous diversity
among the first followers of Jesus, both before and after the
cross and resurrection; and that (4) the fourth evangelist
intends to be taken seriously as a historian, as well as a
theologian--then surely there are no insuperable historical
problems with John the Baptist's declaration.   *Must* such a
designation of Jesus have arisen solely in the post-Easter
church?   Is there not evidence, both synoptic (e.g. Mark 10:45)
and from the fourth gospel, which indicates that Jesus saw
himself as a suffering redeemer--evidence which can be removed
only by a methodologically questionable application of
histmatics?   And if, just if, Jesus saw himself in those terms,
and really was nothing less than that, would it be altogether
surprising if his forerunner pointed him out to be that?   And
if there is no clear precursor to such a statement in the ante-
cedent Jewish literature, is that fact any more difficult than
the broader fact that there is no unambiguous linking, in the
Jewish literature, of the messiah and the suffering servant at
any level?   And if God has actually done the unthinkable in the
incarnation, complete with angelic announcement (no less!),
should it be thought entirely strange if he instructs his Son's
forerunner to introduce a category which, though no doubt
somewhat strange at first, and still not entirely perspicuous
within the framework of John's gospel, nevertheless ultimately

claimed a significant role in the terminology of redemption?
Even using the criteria which we have already adjudged to be
rather too subjective, John 1:29 does not fare too badly.   The
saying, it is true, enjoys little 'coherence' with first century
Judaism (but then again, neither does the incarnation); but it
is sufficiently 'dissimilar' from johannine themes as to earn a
point or two there. /116/   And incidentally, might not a gospel
writer (or any other writer, for that matter) incorporate
material that he finds interesting, or contributing to a minor
point in his belief structure, or moving--even though that
material does not contribute directly to the writer's most
obvious themes?

Moreover, in the apocalyptic fervour of much of first
century Judaism, I can well imagine the sort of confessions we
find in 1:45,49.   This does not mean that those who uttered
them grasped their full christian significance, nor that they
never doubted again, still less that some straight line of
development would then exclude an authentic Caesarea Philippi
confession (which, we recall, was promptly followed up by an
insolent rebuke to the one just acknowledged to be the Messiah!).
The depth of grief and shock experienced by the disciples after
the cross, attested by Luke especially, surely presupposes an
assessment of Jesus before the cross that was, at least at
times, enormously high.   I suspect, moreover, that John deals
selectively with this material in such a way as to point out
that men often acknowledge Christ in some fashion, and fall away,
acknowledge him, and turn away, and so forth: such a repetition
becomes a theme for the fourth evangelist.   His approach by
this means focuses attention on Christ, his significance, his
steadfastness, his grace (is he not full of grace and truth,
1:14?), in contrast to the fickle disciples who at best are
constantly misunderstanding the significance of what they affirm
they believe.   By contrast, the synoptists centre attention
more broadly on the rising faith and growing understanding of
the disciples.   These disciples are not without setbacks; but
there is a genuine *crescendo* in their belief.   For the fourth
evangelist, the cross/exaltation is almost exclusively the
determining factor.   But my point in any case is *that there is
no methodological reason for denying that the real historical
basis is large enough to support both interpretations*.

There are obvious differences between the presentation of
Jesus by the synoptists and the presentation of Jesus by John;
and I do not wish to underestimate or minimize such differences.
My contention, however, both here and in the ninth reflection,

is that it is *methodologically* unsound to histmatize the fourth
gospel and the synoptics separately and then set the two
histmatic structures against each other.   It is
methodologically superior to suppose that what actually
happened is much bigger than any of the presentations, and
certainly big enough to support the presentations of both the
fourth gospel and of the synoptics (and for that matter any of
their sources).   I have tried to indicate the direction in
which I would pursue such an argument for a number of standard
problems;   but the work still needs to be done comprehensively
and rigorously across a very broad range of data.

8.   *In the light of these and similar methodological
reflections, many of the standard evidences of anachronism or of
historical error in the fourth gospel do not seem to rest so
much on a methodological base as on an ideological base.*

   It is often argued, or, worse, presupposed, that John
commonly takes some saying of Jesus which he found in the
tradition, and expounds it at length in such a way as to give
the impression that Jesus himself had given the entire
exposition.   Sometimes this alleged procedure is justified on
the grounds that christian prophets regularly spoke words of the
exalted Christ, through the power of the Spirit;   and the church
wittingly or unwittingly mingled the statements of the exalted
Christ, spoken through some christian prophet, with the words of
Jesus during his pre-Passion ministry.   It is further pointed
out that in at least one place, namely John 3, it is extremely
difficult to ascertain where the purported words of Jesus end
and the words of the Evangelist begin.

   There has recently been presented solid evidence that the
creative role of prophets was much smaller than many have
contended. /117/   Moreover, if in one passage John does not
make it clear where Jesus stops and he begins, in virtually
every other case there is no ambiguity at all about where John
expects his readers to see Jesus' words finishing.

   More important, there is quite substantial evidence not
only that Jesus spoke cryptically at times, and that his cryptic
utterances were not properly understood until after his
resurrection/exaltation and his sending of the Paraclete;   *but
also that John faithfully preserved the distinction between what
Jesus said that was not understood, and the understanding that
finally came to the disciples much later* (e.g. John 2:18-22;
7:37-39;   12:16;   16:12f., 25;   21:18-23;   compare Luke 24:6-8,

44-49).   It is not at all obvious that John is confused on this
matter.   One might even argue plausibly that anyone who
preserves this distinction so faithfully and explicitly is
trying to gain credence for what he is saying;   and if he errs
in this matter it will be because of an unconscious slip, not by
design.

I propose, then, to touch lightly on three areas which are
often thought to exemplify anachronisms, literary fiction, or
the like.   I shall not deal in a detailed way with any of them,
but merely indicate the line of thought I would be inclined to
explore.

(a)   *The Farewell Discourse*.   Very few believe that John 14-16
represents a summary of material that Jesus actually gave.
Most will acknowledge as dominical only the occasional isolated
logion.   In general, that is Dodd's approach in *HTFG*.

If for the sake of argument the previous reflexions may be
judged reasonably sound, I would be inclined to reflect further
along the following lines.   The old saw about the language
being typically johannine I acknowledge: whatever John
discusses, it comes out in his own idiom.   I shall venture more
on that topic in a moment.   But it should at least be pointed
out that the same language equally blankets sayings assessed as
dominical.   The criteria often used to separate out the
johannine reflection from the dominical aphorism (did Jesus
speak only in aphorisms?) I have already rejected as
methodologically indefensible.   I know no objective test that
will suffice.   However, although on the basis of John's
language, I do not take these words to be the *ipsissima verba*
of Jesus;   and although the language is that of johannine idiom;
and although there is nothing that requires or even suggests
that this is all that Jesus said on this occasion;   yet I cannot
help noting that *John presents these chapters to us as the
teaching of Jesus,* on a certain night, at a certain time in
history.   On the face of it, he gives the impression that he
expects us to believe that these chapters represent what Jesus
said.   If someone objects that historians in the ancient world
were prone to making up speeches and placing them on the lips
of their heroes, I protest that only *some* writers in the ancient
world exhibit this propensity.   The debate at this point is
well chronicled with respect to the speeches in Acts; /118/ and
I shall refrain from repeating it.

I might also be inclined to find my view reinforced by the

break at the end of John 14.   Far from indicating a seam,
14:31-15:1 evidences a momentous recollection of detail.   Jesus
and his disciples leave the room in response to his quiet
Ἐγείρεσθε, ἄγωμεν ἐντεῦθεν.   They leave the city, walking in
several clumps: twelve men can scarcely walk in one group in
the narrow streets of Old Jerusalem and along the narrow path
across the Kidron and up the Mount of Olives.   This
circumstance explains the description surrounding the dialogue
in 16:17-19.   Moreover, as they pass by vineyards, Jesus finds
in them another metaphor to use on this most awesome of nights;
and he begins, 'I am the true vine . . .' (15:1).   I cannot
prove that it was so; but I suggest this is a methodologically
superior way of approaching the hard literary evidence we
actually possess. /119/

(b)   *Excommunication in John 9:22*. Although almost all the
commentators see an anachronism here, it is J. L. Martyn, /120/
in his second chapter, who devotes most time and energy to
proving it.   He argues that there are four crucial points in
the text: (i) that there is a formal decision, (ii) made by the
Jewish authorities, (iii) to bring against christian Jews--i.e.
Jews who confess that Jesus is the Messiah; and (iv) that the
measure taken is drastic excommunication.   Martyn then tests
the options against these four findings, and concludes that the
punishment in question cannot be the light punishment called the
נזיפה, nor the temporary ban referred to either as the נדוי or
the שמתה, and still less the permanent excommunication known as
the חרם, if only because there is no unambiguous evidence for
the latter until the third century AD.   For various reasons,
Martyn also disallows the sort of exclusions from the synagogue
found in the Book of Acts.   This drives him to adopt the
conclusion that ἀποσυνάγωγος in John 9:22 presupposes
ברכת המנים the *Birkath ha-Minim*, or 'benediction against
heretics,' established as the twelfth of the Eighteen
Benedictions by the Council of Jamnia *at the end of the first
century AD*.

I see no way of proving that Martyn is wrong; but the
evidence that he is right is not particularly compelling either.
There are three principle points to observe.   *First*, his four
criteria are rather overwrought.   There was indeed some kind
of formal decision (9:22); but it may have been an *ad hoc*
decision.   It was approved by 'the Jews;' but scholars have
shown how tricky an expression that is. /121/   In this context
it may refer to no more than the Jews in question, the Jews who
went after the cured blind man, the Jews who reacted against

Jesus, the Jews who were the authorities in the local synagogue.
There is certainly no evidence that the voice of Jamnia was
involved.   If it be objected that any kind of excommunication
of Jesus' disciples is inconceivable at so early a date,
especially since Jewish Christians and Jewish non-Christians
quite clearly lived side by side for many decades, then I would
answer that what is in view is *ad hoc* opposition of the sort
that put Jesus on the cross, that stoned a Stephen or sent a
Saul to Damascus - even though these were merely sporadic
outbreaks of violence surrounded by sustained periods of
relative calm.   Moreover when Martyn contends that 'drastic
excommunication' is intended, and not some temporary ban which
implicitly suggests a disciplinary step designed to bring about
repentance, he bases his argument on the force of ἀπό in the
compound ἀποσυνάγωγος.   But surely he is leaning very heavily
on etymology, as any quick glance at ἀπο-compound entries in a
Greek lexicon quickly reveals.   No doubt ἀπό indicates
exclusion from the synagogue; but it does not necessarily
indicate permanent exclusion, nor preclude the possibility that
disciplinary exclusion is in view.

   Second, other options are possible, even if our sources of
knowledge are not very good.   Some kind of excommunication
stretches back to Ezra 10:8.   *Taan.* 3:8 contains a saying of
Simeon b. Shetah which threatens excommunication; and he is
normally dated *c.* 80 B.C.   The Dead Sea Scrolls betray
excommunication at Qumran (cf. 1QS 5:18; 6:24-7:25; 8:16f.,
22f.; CD 9:23).   So there is certainly evidence that
excommunication was an available option to synagogue
authorities in Jesus' day.   The adverb ἤδη (9:22) almost
suggests that it is rather surprising that the authorities took
this step so early; it is difficult to imagine what the
significance of the word might be if the excommunication
involved were post-Jamnian.   And incidentally, the *Birkath ha-
Minim* does not actually speak of excommunication, although it
is probably presupposed.   But the point is that some ambiguity
attaches to that identification as well.

   Third, if we grant that 'the Jews' were angry enough at
Jesus to plot his death (cf. 11:54), it does not seem
unreasonable that they might be angry enough to plot the
excommunication of his followers, even during his ministry.
/122/   These were not, after all, normal times: not every
itinerant preacher was capable of arousing the authorities to
wrath.

Some years ago D. R. A. Hare explored the connection between the *Birkath ha-Minim* and the excommunication found here, and concluded that the connection was entirely unproven. /123/ J. A. T. Robinson comments, 'Unless one *begins* with a later date for the gospel, there is no more reason for reading the events of 85-90 into 9.22 than for seeing a reference to Bar-Cochba in 5.43, which has long since become a curiosity of criticism.' /124/

(c)   *The Eucharistic Discourse in John 6.*   The literature on this chapter is immense.   I should say I do not find the various partition theories convincing, including the view that 6:51*c*-57 is a late addition. /125/   The studies by P. Borgen provide a wealth of illustrative material;   but his central thesis fails to convince. /126/

For the sake of economy I shall for the moment avoid close interaction with the secondary literature, and ask a rather simple (some might say naive) question: if we were to suppose that this is a fair statement of Jesus' teaching (however johannine the language, however selectively the Evangelist has presented his material, however many lacunae there may be), what implausible conceptions would we be required to ascribe to the historical Jesus?   I ask the question this way because, on the face of it, John expects his readers to believe that Jesus interacted with the crowds, as recorded, and that he gave the content ascribed to him.   There is no *formal* ambiguity surrounding where Jesus ends and John begins.   If then I take the record seriously, as it stands, does it compel me to adopt some ridiculous position(s) about the historical Jesus?   If so, what?   If not, what solid reason is there for rejecting the record as it stands?

To answer my own question, then, I would say there is nothing implausible about the record as it stands, provided that five things are true: (i) Jesus sometimes used metaphors of the sort, 'I am the door,' 'I am the vine,' 'I am the good shepherd,' 'I am the light,' and the like.   If he did, and if such metaphors sometimes became extended metaphors, or even mixed metaphors, in his hand, then there is no inherent implausibility in this one.   If it were not for the fact that we who live after the institution of the eucharist tend to read the eucharist back into these words, would we have any difficulty in accepting the bread of life metaphor as dominical, even when it is pushed to the extreme of being identified with Jesus' flesh (not body, as in the eucharistic institution) and

blood?   (ii) Jesus knew he was going to die, and knew too that
his death was for a redemptive purpose, a purpose which would
be applied to his followers by the Spirit he would himself
bestow once he had been exalted beyond the other side of death.
(iii) Jesus knew that he had come from his Father in a unique
way, and as a result saw himself as the exclusive means of
reconciling men to his Father so that they could receive
eternal life.   (iv) Jesus himself preached an 'already . . . not
yet' brand of eschatology which expected to gather a community
of disciples during the interim period, and expected a world-
wide mission.   (v) Jesus himself stands behind the institution
of the eucharist which, granted that John 6 is authentic, had
not yet been celebrated at this time.   It is not necessary to
insist, on the basis of this reconstruction, that Jesus gave
these words because he was planning to institute the eucharist.
However, when John by means of his gospel passed on this
teaching from Christ, the eucharist was already well established
in the church; and it would have been unlikely that Christians
could read these lines *without* making some kind of connection.
Sensitive to such connections, John is saying that this material
is what the historical Jesus taught, not less than the
institution of the eucharist.   If this reconstruction is
plausible, John may be warning against a view of the eucharist
which guarantees life by the simple ingestion of the physical
elements.   He restores the balance by pointing out some
parallel teaching from the historical Jesus, who insists
ultimately it is the Spirit who gives life; the flesh counts
for nothing.   The words that Jesus speaks are Spirit and life
(6:63).

      If these five things are true, then there is no
implausibility entailed by taking John 6 seriously, as it
stands, as a report of what the historical Jesus said.   But
are these five things true?   Each of them is attested
repeatedly in the gospels.   When any of them is doubted, that
doubt does not spring from the application of a neutral literary
tool capable in itself of screening out inauthentic statements,
but from the application of a histmatic framework.
Dispassionate historical analysis with as few axes to grind as
possible would not, I submit, entertain grave difficulty in
affirming any of the five points listed.   If so, why should the
content of John 6 provide any insuperable barrier to an
assessment which accepts it as authentic--as, on the face of it,
it claims to be?

9.   *The likely implications of the fact that John has stamped*

his entire gospel with his own style need to be reckoned with
more thoroughly than is usually the case.

John is, linguistically speaking, remarkably uniform.
This datum has implications for source criticism; but I need
not repeat them here.   From the point of view of questions of
historicity, the fact that the fourth gospel sounds more or less
the same, linguistically speaking, whether Jesus is talking or
John is talking, surely means, at the very least, that either we
have few *ipsissima verba* of Jesus preserved for us by this
Evangelist, or, if there are a few more than we might suspect,
it is impossible to isolate them with any confidence.   By and
large, we cannot appeal, as Jeremias does in the case of the
synoptic gospels, to Aramaisms.   Whatever historical material
John preserves is not amenable to being isolated by linguistic
means.

Yet this simple observation surely calls in question Dodd's
essential approach when he tries to determine what is historical.
To make this clear, a couple of modern analogies may be helpful.
In preparing this paper I read about a score of reviews of *HTFG*.
A few of these reviews provide no description of what *HTFG*
actually says, but cheerfully launch right into generalities of
praise and blame.   Most, however, devote a good deal of their
space to describing the contents of the book.   All reviewers, I
presume, read the book, or at least long sections of it; a few
of the later reviewers, I imagine, also read the early reviews.
Yet each reviewer summarizes the book in his own words,
selecting those parts which for any reason attracted him--and
the reasons are not all detectable.   Here and there the
reviewers quote phrases or sentences from *HTFG*; but if there
were no quotation marks, the situation that prevails in the
biblical manuscripts, I'm quite sure I would not be able to
isolate the *ipsissima verba* of Dodd with any degree of
confidence.   Yet the fact remains that those reviewers
accurately describe what Dodd's work is all about.   When they
say something like, 'Dodd says that . . . ,' they tell us in
truth what Dodd says.   Admittedly, they don't tell us *all* that
Dodd says; and they put it in their own idiom; yet only the
most rigid pedant would criticize any of these reviews on the
ground that Dodd really didn't *say* those things.   Now of
course it's possible for a reviewer to misunderstand an author,
and ascribe to him things he did not say.   But, short of
reading the book oneself, it is very difficult to detect such
passages.   Moreover, a careless reviewer may ascribe to the
author *an implication* of what the author said, even though the

author would not accept that implication as an entailment of his thought.   However, if the reviewer has built a good record of making distinctions between what the author actually says and what the reviewer thinks might be entailed by what he says, one's confidence in the reliability of the reviewer is increased.

Or again, consider a learned society meeting where an address is given by a brilliant lecturer.   One auditor gives a five minute summary of the two hour address to a close friend. This friend respects the auditor's reporting.   He is aware, of course, that the address was given in German, and the report in English--and reduced at that;   but he feels on balance that the report of the lecturer's content is accurate.   The friend then gives a one minute precis to his students, beginning his remarks with a preamble such as, 'The great German scholar Schmidt says that . . . . '   And by all common usage, his statement is correct--even though Schmidt said more, and perhaps with slightly different thrust, and in a different language.   And so we come to John.   Does he know the synoptics?   At very least we must admit John wrote in such a way that it is in the highest degree unlikely that such dependence could be demonstrated.   Brown insists, '(If) one posits dependency, one should be able to explain every difference in John as the deliberate change of Synoptic material or of a misunderstanding of that material.' /127/   Dodd in *HTFG* operates with the same rule. /128/   However, might not the dependency be there, in the sense that John had read, pondered, and even partly memorized the synoptics (or one or two of them)--and then decided to write his own book?   This does not threaten the historicity of the fourth gospel unless we insist that its writer was shut up exclusively to the synoptic gospels he had read as the sole source of any accurate knowledge of the historical Jesus.   But that, surely, is highly implausible.   Luke 1:1-4 reminds us that many accounts of Jesus' ministry were in circulation in the early period.   And quite apart from the question of the authorship of the fourth gospel, its writer was at most only decades removed from the events, not centuries.

Brown objects, 'However, any explanation of Johannine differences that must appeal as a principle to numerous capricious and inexplicable changes really removes the question from the area of scientific study.' /129/   I am not sure what 'scientific' means in such a context.   More troubling, I find that the words 'capricious' and 'inexplicable' are loaded. They suggest that the only alternative to an explanation of every change would be an appeal to the 'capricious.'   Why not the far simpler theory--that John wrote his own book, in his own style, with his own themes? It happens every day. . Ancient writers were free to copy the works of others as they saw fit, without being branded plagiarists; but they were also free not to copy them. If the fourth evangelist had access to all sorts of excellent information, in addition to the synoptics, what is implausible about the suggestion that he freely composed his own book? Add various editions and redactors if need be, although in my view they add more problems than they solve; but the result is the same.

If this reconstruction is at all plausible, it follows that Dodd's effort in *HTFG* to retrieve historical snippets, as magnificent as that effort is and as important as it may be when placed over against a more radical scepticism, is *methodologically* far, far too restrictive in what it allows to be judged historical. His method is not big enough even to check for the various kinds of possible dependency on the synoptic gospels; and his use of form criticism to isolate a pre-johannine tradition is methodologically equivocal. Even after this tradition has been isolated, it is extremely difficult to discern anything other than very subjective 'tools' being used to decide what parts of that tradition reach back to the historical Jesus. One simply cannot with confidence use his tools on the sort of book which the fourth gospel appears to be; or, rather, the application of his tools to this kind of book will indeed succeed in straining out some historical gnats; but the historical camels will get clean away.

In short, the uniformity of johannine language makes recovery of alleged snippets from the historical Jesus methodologically difficult, even dubious. However, far from serving as a counsel of despair, we must recognize that John, like many writers, has written up all of his material himself. If this renders retrieval of snippets by source or form criticism a methodologically doubtful task, then *mutatis mutandis* it avoids identifying great passages from the fourth gospel which are not among the snippets, as *not* being historical. This, of course, does not necessarily mean that they *are* historical; but at least it will enable us to recognize the limitations of literary tools in the historical enterprise, and leave open several options now illegitimately closed.

10. *We must, I fear, return again to the knotty question of authorship.*

One of the many splendid features of *HTFG* is the
eminently fair way in which this matter is discussed. /130/
Dodd ultimately decides that, on balance, the weight of
evidence goes against the tradition that the author of the
fourth gospel was John the son of Zebedee.   Yet he goes on to
argue:

> If the balance of probability should appear to be on the
> side of authorship by John son of Zebedee, much of what is
> written in the following pages would require some
> modification, but I do not think it would all fall to the
> ground.   The material ascribed here to tradition would
> turn out to be the apostle's own reminiscences; but even
> so, it would be obvious that they had been cast at one
> stage into the mould of the corporate tradition of the
> Church--as why should they not be, if the apostle was
> actively immersed in just that ministry of preaching,
> teaching and liturgy which *ex hypothesi* gave form to the
> substance of the Church's memories of its Founder? /131/

But there is more to it than that.   If on balance the author
was John the son of Zebedee, more than just a little of Dodd's
argument falls away.   Most of Dodd's argument is form critical.
He himself points out that comparative form critical studies
(e.g. of the Maori civilization) demand a *much* longer time span.
Yet there he treats what he admits to be a genuine possibility,
an eyewitness author, as if it would scarcely affect his
conclusions.   Whether or not his conclusions would be affected,
his method would certainly be: see, for instance, the form of
his argument on pp. 37, 43, 54, 59, 75, 96, 128ff., 166, etc.,
of *HTFG*.   If the fourth evangelist is a *bona fide* eyewitness,
and yet form criticism can be used anyway by simply replacing
the word 'tradition' with 'apostolic reminiscences,' then on
what is the entire discipline of form criticism based?   Where
are the parallel studies that allow this kind of eyewitness
phenomenon to be included?   This is still merely a
methodological question; but it will not go away. /132/

Before proceeding with further methodological questions, I
should perhaps confess my own conclusions.   By about the same
margin that Dodd weighs the evidence and opts for non-apostolic
authorship, I weigh the evidence and opt for apostolic authorship.   So far in this paper, however, wherever I have used the
words 'John' or 'johannine' as a reference to the author, it
has been without prejudice, in accordance with established

scholarly convention.   I do not think that any of my
arguments so far has demanded, explicitly or implicitly, that
the author be John son of Zebedee.

What makes the study of recent discussions of johannine
authorship most interesting is the kind of argument which each
scholar finds convincing.   We must face the embarrassing fact
that, apart from the discovery of the Dead Sea Scrolls and
some more biblical manuscripts (neither of which contribute
much to the debate, except for early papyri which impose a
terminus ad quem in the first third of the second century), we
possess no more hard, literary evidence on the subject than the
church has enjoyed for centuries.   Yet, of recent major writers
on the fourth gospel, none save Leon Morris (whose work is
certainly worth consulting) /133/ defends the apostolic authorship of the fourth gospel, even though that was almost the
universally held view until two centuries ago; and, in Britain,
the predominant view until a few decades ago.   Since the hard
evidence has changed but little, the *methods* for arriving at
such different answers must have changed.

Compare, for instance, the commentary by Westcott /134/
with the work of some recent writers.   Westcott championed
apostolic authorship, and did so in a classic statement that
has often been repeated.   He proceeded in concentric circles
from circumference to centre, seeking to show *by asking
questions of the text* that the Evangelist was (a) a Jew; (b) a
Jew of Palestine; (c) an eyewitness; (d) an apostle; and (e)
John son of Zebedee.

More recent treatments often accept the flow of this
argument, if not all the details (e.g. many think the evidence
for eyewitness is not all that good), but then say that on the
basis of other factors, to which I shall turn in a moment, we
must nevertheless conclude that John the son of Zebedee did not
write the book.   Some of his disciples wrote it following his
death, giving him the credit for the bulk of the material.
Not infrequently this is related to the famous evidence of
Papias about the 'elder John.'   Others think that the beloved
disciple is either a symbolic person or the idealization of an
unknown historical person: such modern reconstructions I shall
avoid in this discussion.

I do not propose to review all the evidence at the
moment, but to point out the kinds of arguments that those

scholars advance who justify their abandonment of the *prima
facie* evidence in favour of agnosticism or speculation, once
they have admitted the relative strength of that evidence.
Dodd himself, for instance, twice makes a fair amount out of
the fact that, although the convincing characterization helps
to confirm that the author was an eyewitness, two of the
pericopae richest in characterization 'are represented by the
evangelist himself as occasions when no eyewitness was
present--the conversation with the Samaritan woman, and the
examination before Pilate.' /135/ On this basis, Dodd
suggests that all of the characterization in the Gospel is
better accounted for by supposing the Evangelist was endowed
with consummate skill as a writer than by supposing he was an
eyewitness.   I am not sure the two possibilities should be
placed in antithesis; but, that aside, the Samaritan woman
herself seems a likely source of information, judging by the
open way she approached her fellow townspeople; and, as for
the *in camera* session with Pilate, if some personal secretary
or court scribe, later converted, did not share the information
(a possible but probably desperate expedient), I would suggest
that the information came from Jesus himself, after his
resurrection.   Is it possible to imagine extensive contacts
with his disciples over a forty day spread without one of them
asking what had happened at his trials?

What other arguments are used among recent writers to
deny that the author was the apostle John? Some note that
according to Acts 4:13 John was uneducated, and conclude that
an uneducated man could scarcely have composed the fourth
gospel.   On this basis we are going to run into trouble with
the traditions about R. Akiba--or, for that matter, with
people with whom I am personally acquainted who became
Christians as adults and only then embarked on serious study,
including post-graduate training.

The point is that methodologically speaking, the
deciding features in this shift of viewpoint are arguments
which pit possible but unnecessary inferences from an
assortment of texts, against explicit statements and their
entailed implications.   This is methodologically improper.
A great deal of the modern debate about the authorship of the
fourth gospel is being carried on at this methodological level.

One final area for methodological reflexion cannot be
avoided.   The vast majority of contemporary scholars are

convinced that the fourth gospel was not written by one person, but by a 'school' or 'circle' or 'community.' I remain unpersuaded that 'schools' write anything except symposia, or discrete books with a common *Weltanschauung*; yet the proposal seems to have received substantive support by the work of R. A. Culpepper. /136/ Culpepper examines such 'schools' as the Pythagorean school, the Academy, the Lyceum, the Stoa, the school at Qumran, and the like, developing a list of nine constants. Then he studies the fourth gospel and the johannine epistles in the light of these constants, and concludes that there is indeed such a thing as a johannine 'school.'

Despite the fact that this work has been well received, several major *methodological* objections must be raised. *First,* most of Culpepper's constants are not distinguishable from the characteristics of the church—indeed, of any vibrant religion. For instance, according to Culpepper a school in the ancient world was made up of disciples who traced the beginnings of their discipleship to a wise and good man. They treasured the founder, and cherished the traditions surrounding him. Members of the school were in the first instance students of the master, and used the ordinary means of learning and transmitting traditions. These schools adopted certain requirements for admission, and could expel members. Some distance from the host society was maintained in order to ensure perpetuity, a perpetuity also served by the beginnings of institutional structure. And so on. With the best will in the world, I cannot see how a community with constants such as these must be classed as a 'school' in any technical sense, unless Culpepper includes within the range of his definition 'church.' But then, of course, it might be wiser to speak of 'the christian school,' rather than 'the johannine school.'

My *second* methodological problem is that Culpepper seeks to avoid this obvious conclusion by some highly dubious exegetical steps. He establishes a *johannine* 'school,' as opposed to a *christian* 'school,' by requiring that the beloved disciple be understood to be the idealization of 'John,' the founder of the 'school,' and by insisting that he discharged to the community the role of the Paraclete. This stands at the heart of the book's evidence for the existence of a johannine 'school.' True, there are genuine parallels between the beloved disciple and the Paraclete—as between

the Paraclete and Jesus, Jesus and the disciples, Jesus and
his Father, and so on. But in each case there are *also*
fundamental distinctions to be drawn. It is methodologically
inadequate to note the parallels and to make the jump
advocated by Culpepper without weighing with equal rigour the
many *distinctions* between the beloved disciple and the
Paraclete. This weakness largely vitiates the book's central
thesis.

My *final* methodological objection is that when dealing
with John's gospel Culpepper has to assume large elements of
what is to be proved. For instance, that disciples of the
beloved disciple transmitted traditions is demonstrated, in
Culpepper's mind, by the existence of the fourth gospel and
the johannine epistles. But that will scarcely be convincing
evidence for a 'school' to those who have not already adopted
that viewpoint, but who still think, *mirabile dictu*, that John
the son of Zebedee wrote the documents in question. On the
face of it, the author of the fourth gospel stands with his
readers as a disciple of Jesus Christ.

V

This paper has been primarily methodological in nature;
yet even at that level, it has barely scratched the surface.
Many historical problems in the fourth gospel have not even
been touched (e.g. John 3:13; John's use of Christological
titles; the proper place of the cleansing of the temple);
and even some methodological questions of fundamental
importance have not been raised (e.g. questions surrounding
literary genre; proper and improper use of harmonization as
an historiographical tool). Such questions cry out for more
study.

But certain lessons, I hope, stand out. First, as great
a book as *HTFG* is, it is seriously deficient at a methodological
level. If we suppose we can establish as historical and
authentic only those things which Dodd's use of his tools
approves, we do the texts a serious injustice. Second, not a
little modern biblical research is in methodological disarray.
It is not that any of the literary tools we use is
intrinsically evil. On the contrary, all have their place.
But we err in treating them as if they guarantee objectivity,

or as if they can produce answers to questions they are
simply not able to handle.   But M. D. Hooker says it better
than I: 'My plea is that we should stop pretending to know
the answer when we do not.   My argument is that the tools
which are used in an attempt to uncover the authentic
teaching of Jesus cannot do what is required of them.' /137/

Finally, we must attempt to make reasonable sense of the
evidence as it stands; we must attempt to formulate historical
reconstructions which reasonably undergird the only evidence
that has come down to us.   This wholistic approach is
methodologically superior to those which on dubious grounds are
forced to discount a great deal of the evidence, or treat it
with a scepticism which is rooted much more in ideology than
in method. /138/

Notes

/1/ L. Morris, *The Gospel according to John* (NICNT; Grand
Rapids: Eerdmans, 1971).
/2/ R. Morgan, 'Biblical Classics II. F. C. Bauer: Paul,'
ExT 90 (1978-79) 4.
/3/ (London: Lutterworth, 1960).
/4/ The most significant examples include: W. F. Albright,
'Recent Discoveries in Palestine and the Gospel of John,' in
The Background of the New Testament and its Eschatology (edd.
W. D. Davies and D. Daube; Cambridge: University Press, 1956)
153-171; R. E. Brown, 'The Problem of Historicity in John,'
CBQ 24 (1962) 1-14; E. Stauffer, 'Historische Elemente im
Vierten Evangelium,' *Homiletica et Biblica* 22 (1963) 1-7.
/5/ 'Topography and Archaeology in the Fourth Gospel,' *SE* I
(edd. K. Aland *et al.*; 1959) 329-37.
/6/ Especially in his work, *New Testament Theology I: The
Proclamation of Jesus* (London: SCM, 1971).
/7/ C. H. Dodd, *The Interpretation of the Fourth Gospel*
(Cambridge: University Press, 1953).
/8/ *Ibid*. 444.
/9/ *Ibid*. 447.
/10/ (Cambridge: University Press, 1938).
/11/ *HTFG* 424: 'All through I have assumed that the tradition
we are trying to track down was oral.   That any authentic
information about Jesus must at first have been transmitted
orally does not admit of doubt, and all recent work has tended
to emphasize both the importance and the persistence of oral
tradition.   That some parts of it may have been written down

by way of *aide-mémoire* is always possible, and such written
sources may have intervened between the strictly oral
tradition and our Fourth Gospel.   If so, I am not concerned
with them . . . .'

/12/ *HTFG* 431;   italics mine.
/13/ *Ibid.* 30;   italics mine.
/14/ *Ibid.* 171-173.
/15/ *Ibid.* 216-222.
/16/ *Ibid.* 216.
/17/ *Ibid.* 171-172.
/18/ *Ibid.* 79.
/19/ *Ibid.*
/20/ *Ibid.* 80.
/21/ Review of *HTFG* in *JTS* 18 (1967) 189-92.
/22/ Review of *HTFG* in *The Muslim World* 55 (1965) 161-2.
/23/ Review of *HTFG* in *JBL* 83 (1964) 303-6.
/24/ Review of *HTFG* in *NTS* 10 (1964) 517-22.
/25/ Review of *HTFG* in *SJT* 17 (1964) 359-62.
/26/ Review of *HTFG* in *CJT* 11 (1965) 142-44.
/27/ Review of *HTFG* in *ThLZ* 93 (1968) 346-8.
/28/ Review of *HTFG* in *EQ* 37 (1965) 42-46.   For other reviews
from conservatives see F. C. Kuehner in *WTJ* 27 (1964) 39-41,
W. E. Hull in *RevExp* 66 (1969) 81-83, Andrew J. Bandstra in
Christianity Today 8 (Mar.13, 1964) 28.
/29/ Review of *HTFG* in *CBQ* 26 (1964) 267-70.
/30/ *Art. cit.* 347.
/31/ *Art. cit.* 162.   Cf. also A. Wikgren, review of *HTFG* in
Interpretation 20 (1966) 238.
/32/ *Art. cit.* 305-6.
/33/ *Art. cit.* 191.
/34/ G. Johnson, *art. cit.* 143.   More recently, R. Kysar (*The
Fourth Evangelist and His Gospel* [Minneapolis: Augsburg, 1975]
62) has come to much the same conclusion: 'What is
disappointing about (Dodd's) study is that this whole effort
carried with it a presupposition that "traditional" means
historically accurate.'
/35/ Review of *HTFG* in *JBR* 32 (1964) 270-71.
/36/ *Ibid.*
/37/ A. Guilding, *The Fourth Gospel and Jewish Worship* (Oxford:
Clarendon, 1960).
/38/ *Art. cit.* 82.
/39/ *Art. cit.* 361.
/40/ *Art. cit.*
/41/ *Art. cit.* 144.
/42/ *Art. cit.* 521-2.

/43/ The English translation is *The Gospel of John* (Oxford: Blackwell, 1971).

/44/ (Cambridge: University Press, 1970).

/45/ D. A. Carson, 'Current Source Criticism of the Fourth Gospel: Some Methodological Questions,' *JBL* 97 (1978) 411-29. Cf. also E. Ruckstuhl, 'Johannine Language and Style. The Question of Their Unity,' M. de Jonge, ed., *L'Evangile de Jean* (Leuven: University Press, 1977) 125-48.

/46/ The exception occurs, of course, when a critic seeks to establish his source on purely literary grounds.

/47/ S. Temple, *The Core of the Fourth Gospel* (London/Oxford: Mowbrays, 1975); discussed in D. A. Carson, *art. cit.*

/48/ E.g. he holds (as do many others) that the excommunication of 9:22 could not possibly have occurred in Jesus' day: cf. R. Schnackenburg, *Das Johannesevangelium*, 2. Teil (Freiburg: Herder, 1971) 316-17.

/49/ R. Kysar, *The Fourth Evangelist and His Gospel: An Examination of Contemporary Scholarship* (Minneapolis: Augsburg, 1975) esp. 54-66. Cf. also the influential work by B. Noack, *Zur johanneischen Tradition: Beiträge zur Kritik an der literarkritischen Analyse des vierten Evangeliums* (Copenhagen: Rosenkilde, 1954). It must not be thought, however, that this appeal to oral tradition is altogether new. True, the work of P. Gardner-Smith turned prevalent opinion around, and *HTFG* established the new consensus; but there have long been critics who appealed to oral tradition even when such an appeal was out of vogue. See, for example, J. Schniewind, *Die Parallelperikopen bei Lukas und Johannes* (Darmstadt: Wissenschaftliche Buchgesellschaft, repr. 1970 from a 1914 edition).

/50/ B. Lindars, *The Gospel of John* (London: Marshall, Morgan and Scott, 1972) 27.

/51/ J. A. Bailey, *The Traditions Common to the Gospels of Luke and John* (Leiden: E. J. Brill, 1963).

/52/ G. Richter, 'Die Gefangennahme Jesu nach dem Johannesevangelium (18:1-12),' *Bibel und Leben* 10 (1969) 26-39.

/53/ J. Blinzler, *Johannes und die Synoptiker* (Stuttgart: Katholisches Bibelwerk, 1965) 59.

/54/ G. Reim, *Studien zum alttestamentlichen Hintergrund des Johannesevangeliums* (Cambridge: University Press, 1974).

/55/ A. Dauer, *Die Passionsgeschichte im Johannesevangelium* (Münich: Kösel, 1972) esp. 335-336.

/56/ C. K. Barrett, *The Gospel According to St. John* (second edition; Philadelphia: Westminster, 1978).

/57/ C. K. Barrett, 'John and the Synoptic Gospels,' *ExT* 85

(1973-74) 228-233.
/58/ F. Neirynck, 'John and the Synoptics,' M. de Jonge, ed.,
L'Evangile de Jean (Leuven: University Press, 1977) 73-106.
/59/ M. Sabbe, 'The Arrest of Jesus in Jn. 18:1-11 and Its
Relation to the Synoptic Gospels,' M. de Jonge, ed.,
L'Evangile de Jean (Leuven: University Press, 1977) 203-234.
See also N. Perrin (*The New Testament: An Introduction* [New
York: Harcourt, Brace, Jovanovich, 1974] 229) who also affirms
that there is literary dependence.
/60/ M.-E. Boismard and A. Lamouille, edd., *L'Evangile de Jean*
(Paris: Editions de Cerf, 1977) esp. 16-70.
/61/ *The Gospel According to St. John* 45.
/62/ E.g., pp. 67-68, 103, 163, 165 and many others.
/63/ The expression is that of R. Kysar, *The Fourth
Evangelist* 38-54.
/64/ R. E. Brown, *The Gospel According to John* (London:
Geoffrey Chapman, 1966), 2 vols.
/65/ *The Gospel of John*.
/66/ The first of the three volumes of his commentary has been
translated into English: see *The Gospel according to John*
(London: Burns and Oates, 1968) I esp. 72-74.
/67/ W. Wilkens, *Die Entstehungsgeschichte des vierten
Evangeliums* (Zollikon: Evangelischer Verlag, 1958). Wilkens
has defended his proposal several times since its first
appearance (which antedates *HTFG*), and, most recently,
developed a redaction critical analysis based on his proposal:
cf. his *Zeichen und Werke* (Zürich: Zwingli Verlag, 1969).
/68/ *The Gospel According to St. John*.
/69/ *The Gospel According to John*.
/70/ The categories 'circle' and 'school' are, of course,
borrowed from O. Cullmann, *The Johannine Circle: Its Place in
Judaism, Among the Disciples of Jesus and in Early
Christianity* (London: SCM, 1976); and R. A. Culpepper, *The
Johannine School: An Evaluation of the Johannine-School
Hypothesis Based on an Investigation of the Nature of Ancient
Schools* (Missoula: Scholars Press, 1975), respectively.
/71/ D. G. Vanderlip, *Christianity According to John*
(Philadelphia: Westminster, 1975) 182.
/72/ (Nashville: Abingdon, 1979). All references to the
work are from the more recent edition.
/73/ *Ibid.* 12: 'The reader will quickly see that these points
of correspondence seem to me not only to illuminate important
aspects of the conceptual milieu in which the Fourth Evangelist
worked, but also--one might even say primarily--to point toward
certain historical developments transpiring in the city in

which he lived.   It is in the sense thus indicated that I
have employed the word history in the title.'
/74/ Bultmann's approach to Gnosticism appears everywhere in
his writings, but was first put into clear perspective in his
essay, 'Die Bedeutung der neuerschlossenen mandäischen und
manichäischen Quellen für das Verständnis des Johannesevangeliums,' *ZNW* 24 (1925) 100-146.   The most convenient place
to find Bultmann's famous 1941 essay on demythologization is in
Kerygma and Myth, ed. H.-W. Bartsch (London: SPCK, 1972) 1-44.
/75/ Of course, the debate antedates Bultmann, and after his
entry, embraces many people on both sides.   For a convenient
treatment of the position opposed to that of Bultmann, and
especially competent in the Mandean sources, see E. M. Yamauchi,
Pre-Christian Gnosticism (London: Tyndale, 1973).
/76/ I have coined the expression from the seminal study by
T. S. Kuhn, *The Structure of Scientific Revolutions* (Chicago:
University of Chicago Press, 1970).   It is not necessary to
follow Kuhn in detail in order to benefit from the rubric.
Part of the question in the paragraphs above turns on what we
mean by 'prove,' a notoriously slippery term: cf. the
important discussion by G. I. Mavrodes, *Belief in God: A Study
in the Epistemology of Religion* (New York: Random House, 1970)
esp. 17-48.   To prove anything in the historical realm is
rather unlike proving something in the realm of the physical
sciences, where experiments are in principle repeatable.
History, unfortunately, is not;   and therefore historical
investigation turns on witnesses of various kinds, and on the
cogency of competing reconstructions.   Of course, proof in the
physical sciences can be overthrown by more data or by a
Kuhnian revolution: at that point it shares the nature of
proof with historical investigation.   But the distinction
between the two disciplines needs to be borne in mind when one
comes across such expressions as 'the scientific study of the
Bible.'   The expression is painfully imprecise.   Does it mean
the study of the Bible based on solely naturalistic
presuppositions?   Or does it mean that the investigation of
the Bible is to be carried on as dispassionately and as
objectively as is possible for finite human beings?   It
cannot logically mean that the study of the Bible is to be
exactly like the study of, say, chemistry.
/77/ R. Kysar, 'The Background of the Prologue of the Fourth
Gospel: A Critique of Historical Methods,' *CJT* 16 (1970)
250-255.   Kysar bases his study on Dodd's treatment of the
prologue in *IFG* and in his essay 'The Background of the Fourth
Gospel,'   *BJRL* 19 (1935) 329-343;   and on Bultmann's

treatment of the prologue in his commentary and in his essay,
'Der religionsgeschichtliche Hintergrund des Prologs zum
Johannes Evangelium,' *Eucharisterion* (Fs. H. Gunkel; Göttingen:
Vandenhoeck & Ruprecht, 1923) II 3-26.
/78/ A. Schlatter, *Der Evangelist Johannes* (Stuttgart: Calwer,
1930).
/79/ D. E. Nineham, *Historicity and Chronology in the New
Testament* (London: SPCK, 1965) 3.
/80/ J. A. Passmore, 'The Objectivity of History,'
Philosophical Analysis and History (ed. W. H. Dray; New York/
London: Harper and Row, 1966) 75-94, esp. 91. This article
is of the utmost importance. See also W. L. Craig, 'The
Nature of History: An Exposition and Critique of the
Principal Arguments for Historical Relativism, as Propounded
by Carl Becker and Charles Beard' (M.A. Thesis, Trinity
Evangelical Divinity School, 1976), whose Appendix on the
historicity of the gospels is occasionally somewhat unsophisti-
cated but whose major analysis repays close study. I am indebted
to John D. Woodbridge for stimulating discussion on these
matters.
/81/ I have attempted to delineate some of John's
theological motivations in this regard in *Divine Sovereignity
and Human Responsibility: Some Aspects of Johannine Theology
Against Jewish Background* (London: Marshall, Morgan and Scott,
1980).
/82/ W. Manchester, *American Caesar: Douglas MacArthur* 1880-
1964 (Boston/Toronto: Little, Brown and Co., 1978).
/83/ H. Wouk, *War and Remembrance* (Boston/Toronto: Little,
Brown and Co., 1978). Wouk's work is a historical novel; yet
he has carefully explained where he meticulously follows the
events of history and where he departs from them.
/84/ In this paragraph (and generally elsewhere) I use the
terms 'historian,' 'historical,' 'history' and the like to
refer to what takes place in the space-time continuum, or, in
the case of 'historian,' to the person who studies what takes
place in the space-time continuum, without prejudice from
definitions which limit the possibility of what can take place
in the space-time continuum to the purely 'natural' (in the
technical sense). Such a definition does not require that
there be no reality outside the space-time continuum: e.g. no
events in God's heaven.
/85/ Cf. L. Morris, *Studies in the Fourth Gospel* (Grand
Rapids: Eerdmans, 1969) 70-74, 94-99, 112-118.
/86/ *IFG* 445.
/87/ *Ibid*.

/88/ *Ibid*. 447.

/89/ *HTFG* 60-63;   *IFG* 401-12.

/90/ *HTFG* 137-51.

/91/ *Ibid*. 151.   Dodd is here referring to most of the passion narrative, and draws attention to his treatment in *HTFG* at pp. 75-76, 97-98, 123-124, 135, 145-146;   and *IFG* 432-438.

/92/ Quoted by Jean Butler from a personal conversation with David Halberstam: cf. *Book-of-the-Month-Club News*, June, 1979, 5.

/93/ S. S. Smalley, *John: Evangelist and Interpreter* (Exeter: Paternoster, 1978) 162-190.

/94/ *Ibid*. 178.

/95/ Cf. D. A. Carson, art. *cit.*, n. 47, *supra*.

/96/ *Op. cit.*, n. 74, *supra*.

/97/ Of the many recent works which place this alleged antithesis in proper proportion, perhaps the best is that of R. Leistner, *Antijudaïsmus im Johannesevangelium? Darstellung des Problems in der neueren Auslegungsgeschichte und Untersuchung der Leidensgeschichte* (Bern: Herbert Lang, 1974). In discussing the Passion Narrative, Dodd came to the same sound conclusion: 'The statement, which is often made, that the Johannine account is influenced by the motive of incriminating the Jews cannot be substantiated, when it is compared with the other gospels' (*HTFG* 107).   The same general assessment can be extended to the entire fourth gospel.   Cf. also S. G. Wilson, 'Anti-Judaism in the Fourth Gospel? Some Considerations,' *Irish Biblical Studies* 1 (1979) 28-50.

/98/ *The Fourth Evangelist, op. cit.*, 53.

/99/ Respectively: H. Schürmann, 'Die vorösterlichen Anfänge der Logientradition,' in *Der historische Jesus und der kerygmatische Christus*, hrsg. H. Ristow and K. Matthiae (Berlin: Evangelische Verlagsanstalt, 1962), 342-70; M. D. Hooker, 'On Using the Wrong Tool,' *Theology* 75 (1972), 570-81; G. M. Stanton, 'Form Criticism Revisited,' *What About the New Testament?*, edd. M. D. Hooker and C. Hickling (London: SCM, 1975) 13-27; S. H. Travis, 'Form Criticism,' *New Testament Interpretation: Essays on Principles and Methods,* ed. I. H. Marshall (Exeter: Paternoster, 1977), 153-164; R. N. Longenecker, 'Literary Criteria in Life of Jesus Research: An Evaluation and Proposal,' *Current Issues in Biblical and Patristic Interpretation,* ed. G. F. Hawthorne (Grand Rapids: Eerdmans, 1975), 217-29; E. E. Ellis, 'New Directions in Form Criticism,' *Jesus Christus in Historie und Theologie,* hrsg. G.

Strecker (Tübingen: J. C. B. Mohr, 1975), 299-315.
/100/ *Art. cit.* 20.
/101/ *Art. cit.* 573.   Cf. also L. Morris, *Studies, op. cit.*
81-6.
/102/ *HTFG* 6.
/103/ *HTFG* 315-334.   Cf. also his earlier essay, 'The
Dialogue Form in the Gospels,' *BJRL* 37 (1954) 54-70.
/104/ E. E. Lemcio, 'External Evidence for the Structure and
Function of Mark iv. 1-20, vii. 14-23 and viii. 14-21,'
JTS 29 (1978) 323-338.
/105/ See references at nn. 5,6.
/106/ It must be admitted that some scholars (Bultmann being a
notable example) doubt that there is very much that is
historically reliable in the fourth gospel.   This division of
opinion is akin to that in modern *Actaforschung*:   the
Lightfoot-Ramsey-Bruce-Gasque line over against the Dibelius-
Haenchen axis.   As I read the evidence there are solid,
testable, and largely accidental bits of solid historical
information in both Acts and the fourth gospel;   and it is to
this sort of data that I refer.
/107/ Respectively: R. N. Longenecker, *The Christology of
Early Jewish Christianity* (London: SCM, 1970);   C. F. D. Moule
The Origin of Christology (Cambridge: University Press, 1977);
I. H. Marshall, *The Origins of New Testament Christology*
(Downers Grove: IVP, 1976);   M. Hengel, *The Son of God: The
Origin of Christology and the History of Jewish-Hellenistic
Religion* (London: SCM, 1976).
/108/ E.g., R. N. Longenecker, 'The "Faith of Abraham" Theme
in Paul, James and Hebrews: A Study in the Circumstantial
Nature of New Testament Teaching,' *JETS* 20 (1977) 203-212.
/109/ J. D. G. Dunn, *Unity and Diversity in the New Testament*
(London: SCM, 1977).
/110/ D. A. Carson, *Art. cit.* (cf. n. 47).
/111/ D. A. Carson, *The King James Version Debate: A Plea for
Realism* (Grand Rapids: Baker, 1979).
/112/ *HTFG* 7-8.
/113/ *IFG* 444.
/114/ *HTFG* 134; cf. L. Morris, *Studies* 119-123.
/115/ It must be admitted that some dispute this judgment.
C. K. Barrett (*Gospel* viii) says he does 'not believe that John
intended to supply us with historically verifiable information
regarding the life and teaching of Jesus, and that historical
traditions of great worth can be disentangled from his
interpretive comments.'   Formally, I agree;   unless (as I
suspect) Barrett means by 'verifiable' something like 'accurate.'
Cf. L. Morris, *Studies* 65-70;   and also p. 124 n. 110, where he

cites J. A. T. Robinson: 'It is astonishing how readily critics have assumed that our Evangelist attached the greatest importance to historicity in general and had but the slightest regard for it in particular.'

/116/ Cf. *HTFG* 269-271.

/117/ Cf. *inter alia* D. Hill, 'On the Evidence for the Creative Role of Christian Prophets,' *NTS* 20 (1973-74) 262-274; R. Bauckham, 'Synoptic Parousia Parables and the Apocalypse,' *NTS* 23 (1976-77) 162-176; J. D. G. Dunn, 'Prophetic 'I'-Sayings and the Jesus Tradition: The Importance of Testing Prophetic Utterances within Early Christianity,' *NTS* 24 (1977-78) 175-198.

/118/ Except for the most recent contributions, cf. W. W. Gasque, *A History of the Criticism of the Acts of the Apostles* (Grand Rapids: Eerdmans, 1975). In particular, cf. F. F. Bruce, 'The Speeches in Acts--Thirty Years After,' *Reconciliation and Hope,* ed. R. Banks (Exeter: Paternoster, 1974) 53-68; H. N. Ridderbos, *The Speeches of Peter in the Acts of the Apostles* (Madison: Theological Students Fellowship, repr. 1977); W. W. Gasque, 'The Speeches in Acts: Dibelius Reconsidered,' *New Dimensions in New Testament Study,* edd. R. N. Longenecker and M. C. Tenney (Grand Rapids: Zondervan, 1974) 232-250.

/119/ Cf. C. K. Barrett, 'The Bible in the New Testament Period,' *The Church's Use of the Bible Past and Present,* ed. D. E. Nineham (London: SPCK, 1963) 21: 'It is worthwhile to note that it is sometimes (the tradition's) sheer historical accuracy, its recounting things that Jesus said and did simply because he said and did them, that leads to a measure of diffuseness, of failure to concentrate upon the focal point.' Moreover, the ἐξῆλθεν in 18:1 does not prove that Jesus left the upstairs room at that point: compare the use of ἐξῆλθεν three verses later, in 18:4. The meaning of ἐξέρχομαι in the fourth gospel and johannine epistles is often theologically rather than spatially determined; and in a few instances it is closer in meaning to 'I go forward' than 'I go out'. Others suggest the exhortation at the end of John 14 marks the end of the meal and a time for cleaning up: there were no servants, after all, even for washing guests' feet. John 18:1 then refers to departure from the upstairs room, and ἐξῆλθεν in 18:4 to 'departure' from an *enclosed* garden. Such suggestions require historical imagination: let us admit it. But they have a certain verisimilitude, remain within the bounds of the text, and in any case require less imagination than certain complex source theories!

/120/ See n. 74.

/121/ Cf. n. 100.

/122/ For this observation I am indebted to R. A. Stewart, 'Judicial Procedure in New Testament Times,' *EQ* 47 (1975) 97-98.

/123/ D. R. A. Hare, *The Theme of Jewish Persecution of Christians in the Gospel of St. Matthew* (Cambridge: University Press, 1967) 48-56.   Cf. also C. F. D. Moule, *The Birth of the New Testament* (London: Adam and Charles Black, 1966) 107.

/124/ J. A. T. Robinson, *Redating the New Testament* (London: SCM, 1976) 273.

/125/ For a neat and fairly recent summary of current source analysis of John 6, cf. R. Kysar, 'The Source Analysis of the Fourth Gospel: A Growing Consensus?' *NovT* 15 (1973) 134-152. Apart from broader questions concerning the methodological legitimacy of source analysis in the fourth gospel, some useful counter-perspective may be gleaned from J. D. G. Dunn, 'John VI--A Eucharistic Discourse?' *NTS* 17 (1970-71) 328-338.

/126/ Viz., P. Borgen, 'Observations on the Midrashic Character of John 6,' *ZNW* 54 (1963) 232-240; idem, *Bread from Heaven: An Exegetical Study of the Concept of Manna in the Gospel of John and the Writings of Philo* (Leiden: E. J. Brill, 1965).   I acknowledge that the criteria he adduces in order to show that much of John 6 is midrashic require detailed discussion; but such discussion would take us beyond the limits of this paper.

/127/ R. E. Brown, *Gospel* I, xlv.

/128/ This crops up not only in those pages where he outlines his method, but also again and again in the course of the argument: e.g. *HTFG* 167: 'We ask, first, what motive John could have had for altering this at all.'

/129/ *Gospel*. xlv.

/130/ *HTFG*, 10-18.

/131/ *Ibid*. 17 n. 1.

/132/ J. A. T. Robinson (*Redating* 262-263) provides a trenchant catalogue of references in which Dodd clearly shows he thinks the Evangelist's relation to the tradition was external and second-hand.   The following comments by A. H. N. Green-Armytage (*John Who Saw* [London: Faber, 1951]) are slightly naive, but only slightly; and in any case they constitute a salutary warning: 'There is a world--I do not say a world in which all scholars live but one at any rate into which all of them sometimes stray, and which some of them seem permanently to inhabit--which is not the world in which I live.   In my world, if the *Times* and the *Telegraph* both tell one story in somewhat different terms, nobody concludes that one of them must have copied the other nor that the variations in the

story have some esoteric significance.   But in that world of
which I am speaking this would be taken for granted.   There,
no story is ever derived from facts, but always from somebody
else's version of the same story . . .   In my world, almost
every book, except some of those produced by Government
departments, is written by one author.   In that world almost
every book is produced by a committee, and some of them by a
whole series of committees.   In my world, if I read that Mr.
Churchill, in 1935, said that Europe was heading for a
disastrous war, I applaud his foresight.   In that world no
prophecy, however vaguely worded, is ever made except after the
event.   In my world we say, "The first world war took place in
1914-1918".   In that world they say, "The world-war narrative
took shape in the third decade of the twentieth century".   In
my world men and women live for a considerable time--seventy,
eighty, even a hundred years--and they are equipped with a
thing called memory.   In that world (it would appear), they
come into being, write a book, forthwith perish, all in a
flash, and it is noted of them with astonishment that they
"preserve traces of a primitive tradition" about things which
happened well within their own lifetime.'

/133/ L. Morris, *Studies* 139-292.
/134/ B. F. Westcott, *The Gospel according to St. John* (Grand
Rapids: Eerdmans, repr, 1971); orig. 1889).
/135/ *HTFG* 14; cf. *IFG* 450.
/136/ R. A. Culpepper, *The Johannine School*.
/137/ 'Wrong Tool' 570.
/138/ This paper was completed except for very minor revision
on October 1st, 1979.

Announcement in Nazara:
An Analysis of Luke 4:16-21*

Bruce Chilton,
Department of Biblical Studies,
University of Sheffield,
Sheffield, S10 2TN.

0)   *Introductory*

Luke 4:16-21 is unique to the third Gospel; the passage is of particular importance for understanding the Evangelist's theological intent and for arriving at a clear, historical appreciation of Jesus' message. It is a *Leitmotiv* of this discussion that a passage can have significance both theologically and historically, that history and theology are far from mutually exclusive, indeed that they are symbiotic in the process of gospel transmission. The theological relevance of the message of and about Jesus inspired a care for the details of that tradition, which in turn can open up previously unrealized theological meaning. The present passage offers us an insight into the relationship between traditional *given* and interpretative *application* in Luke's work.

In one sense, it seems almost too obvious to insist that gospel transmission is a process of both handing down data and explaining the relevance of those data, but often "Radicals" and "Conservatives" tend so to emphasize either the interpretative or the historical aspect of evangelical transmission that they fail to do justice to its dialectical nature. At the recent "Sixth International Congress on Biblical Studies" at Oxford, the unproductive nature of the confrontation between two opposite but equally one-sided viewpoints came home to me strongly in one evening session /1/. Prof. F.W. Beare, in the scheduled lecture, delivered himself of the opinion that the quest for the historical Jesus should be "bypassed" in that the Gospels are accounts of the Church's faith, not of Jesus' life. At the close of this lecture, Prof. J.D.M. Derrett offered an impromptu response in which he argued that Semitisms in the Gospels show that our Lord's voice is discernible in them. To the former position, one wants to object that the

Church's faith is faith in a historical datum; one cannot make
this dimension disappear with a wave of the form critical wand.
To the latter, one wants to point out, but might not out of
embarrassment at impugning the emperor's clothes, that more
than one person spoke Aramaic in the first century, and that
the Palestinian community showed no signs of being less vital
and creative than its sisters elsewhere. This is to say that
both views (and neither is unrepresentative) are inadequate
precisely because they attempt to do away with either the
historical or the interpretative element in the Gospels.
Remove either, and the Gospels as we have them, and the faith
to which they are a witness, are inexplicable.

While tradition and interpretation walk hand in hand in
our Gospels, they are not inseparable /2/. An appreciation of
the diction, syntax and theme of a passage, set against the
background of the work in which it appears, permits us to
determine what in it is the Evangelist's own contribution and
what he is simply handing down to us. At first meeting this
idea, for example as espoused by the great redaction critic
Heinz Schürmann, one might think that it is feasible (if
difficult), but irrelevant /3/. After all, the Gospels give us
their tradition and their interpretation *en bloc*; are we not
disturbing the unity of the literature by separating the two?
To a significant extent, this is a compelling criticism; there
is a tendency among Schürmann's followers to treat parts as if
they were not constituents of a whole, and this must be put
right /4/. But the entire point of Schürmann's method is to
understand documents as they are now by determining what was new
and what was old in them at the time they were produced. This
is not unnecessary hypercriticism: it is a crucial step in
attuning our ears to the books of the New Testament. We must
remember that our Gospels were not addressed to unbelievers;
their recipients had already responded to the message and
received instruction. To them, the Gospel according to Luke,
to take the work which is our concern as an instance, was not a
bolt from the blue. Rather, Luke offered a deliberately more
refined account of what was already known (cf. 1:1-4). His
audience knew the gospel story and would be ready to complain if
he did violence to it, but they also had need of a clearer
understanding of it, and this Luke sought to provide. Because
they were already familiar with much of the material which Luke
presented, they easily and naturally perceived his distinctive
contribution. This is to say that "tradition" and "redaction"
are not just modern *termini technici*: the terms represent

categories under which Luke's hearers - the people for whom he
intended the work - understood what was said to them. It
follows that we will never appreciate Luke's achievement fully
unless we learn to make the same sort of distinction between
what he is handing down and what he is embellishing.

Unfortunately, we cannot do this as unreflectively as Luke's
first hearers could, because they were directly familiar with
the gospel message before Luke, and we are not. It seems to me
that we are in the sort of situation that someone would be in
if, sometime in the future, he came across a modern sermon, but
he did not know of the Bible. Perhaps he would not at first
be able to see that the document was not like a speech in
Parliament or even a lecture in that a tradition (namely the
scripture) was influencing the argument at every turn. But in
any decent sermon, the Bible is not only referred to, but
alluded to, drawn upon for imagery, and pilfered for the
appropriate phrase. We, as the hearers of such a sermon, should
have no difficulty in distinguishing the scriptural data from
the preacher's interpretation. But our imaginary future
discoverer is not familiar with the Bible. Even so, if he had
any literary sensitivity he would soon see that the sermon was
not a free creation, but that it referred to a previous
tradition of some kind as authoritative. But he still would
not know what was traditional and what redactional unless he
could isolate either the tradition or the redaction. Now let
us give up this imaginary dilemma and return to the case at
hand. The modern reader of Luke is in a somewhat better
position. He can recover some of Luke's tradition directly -
namely the Old Testament. Indirectly, he has access (via
Matthew and Mark) to traditions at least very much like those
used by Luke /5/. Also, Luke is kind enough as to speak to
the reader occasionally (Luke 1:1-4; Acts 1:1-2) and this makes
it easier to recognize his voice elsewhere. After that,
however, the student is left to fend for himself. He does not
have direct access to Luke's tradition about Jesus except in
Luke's words, nor do Luke's words come to him except as
expressions of a tradition. This is why we must attend to the
language of a passage in order to distinguish between tradition
and redaction. By comparing the choice of words, the sort of
grammar and the motif thereby expressed with what appears
elsewhere in Luke's work, we can come to a reasonable judgement
as to whether a phrase is redactional or not. If not, we can
compare the diction of this tradition to other New Testament
diction, and to diction in literature of the New Testament

period, in order to determine whence it derived. This task is
not only a matter of attending to detail, although it certainly
involves that. Distinguishing tradition from redaction is
also a matter of using detailed information to acquire a sense
of how the Evangelist's mind worked, and of how the Church
before him thought, and of how Jesus fits into all this /6/.
Answers should not be pressed on these questions too quickly,
because our task is to respond to them from the evidence, not
to force the responses we should like to give onto the evidence.
Nonetheless, data is meaningless on its own, and synthesis is
a necessary part of the process of knowing; it is only when we
can perceive Luke's intent and the tradition's shape that we
can say our task is complete.

Luke 4:16-21 is part of a larger pericope (4:14-30) in
which Jesus' public ministry is introduced. There are several
indications that the present placement of the story, with
vv.18,19,21,24f. serving as a "keynote speech" /7/ for the
whole of Luke - Acts, is to be ascribed to our Evangelist. We
might first mention indications within the complex itself:
allusion is made to previous success in Capernaum (v.23).
This presupposes a situation later in the Galilean ministry,
which is where Matthew (13:54-58) and Mark (6:1-6) put their
rejection pericopae. Further, Luke at 4:43 shows that he
knows that Jesus' basic message concerned the kingdom of God,
and this betrays a familiarity with a programmatic kingdom
logion (similar to Mark 1:15 or Matthew 4:17) at the beginning
of the ministry. Perhaps vv.14,15 show Luke's awareness of
such material /8/. Luke therefore retains traces of the order
he altered, and consciously treats 4:16-21 (which Matthew and
Mark do not parallel) as Jesus' programmatic statement (to
which vv.14,15 serve as introduction and vv.22-30 as corollary).
For this reason, I wish in this paper to look at the language
of these verses in particular; here a very basic and innovative
assertion about Jesus' initial message is being made.

Before turning to the language of these few verses, let
us consider what 4:14-30 achieves in the context of Luke's
work. In a recent article, Waldemar Schmeichel explains the
function of the passage in terms of Luke's well-known emphasis
on the Spirit as leading Jesus:

> After the Isaiah statement 'The Spirit of God is upon me,'
> we never again hear that Jesus is being led by the Spirit
> or performs any function under its guidance! This is

particularly striking in contrast to the emphasis of
such leading immediately preceding the quote. Jesus'
movement throughout is controlled and motivated by
the Spirit, i.e., until 4:18. At that point Jesus
claims a Spirit anointment (not a Spirit experience!) /9/.

On the basis of this incisive observation, Schmeichel offers an
unfortunately tendentious interpretation. He suggests that the
motif of Spirit-leading is "aborted" at 4:18 in favour of the
prophetic rejection motif introduced in vv.22-30, a motif
which looks forward to the passion /10/. Schmeichel quite
correctly associates the citation of Isaiah 61 with the
references to Elijah and Elisha: Luke is indeed concerned to
show that Jesus, the one anointed with the Spirit by God, is
also rejected by his people (cf. Acts 10:38,39). But it is
thinking too schematically to say that the Spirit motif must
end where the rejection motif begins. It seems rather odd to
me that a theme should be thought of as "aborted" by reference
to it in a biblical citation, especially when that very citation
is the springboard for the dialog which leads to the expression
of the rejection motif! Rather, Luke has placed this passage
here to round off the preceding references to the Spirit (so
far I agree with Schmeichel) and (*pace* Schmeichel) to provide
a framework for understanding further references to the Spirit
both in association with Jesus (10:21; 12:10,12; 23:46) and in
association with the apostolic Church (Acts *passim*). Luke 4:18
establishes the unique identification between God's Spirit and
Jesus, and as such it completes the *praeparatio evangelica*
(Luke 1:5-4:13) and points ahead to the *missio evangelica* (with
euanggelizomai linking the two from 1:19 to Acts 17:18).

To see the passage as foundational for the *missio evangelica*
is hardly new; David Hill is to be numbered among those who have
argued that the rejection pericope points the way to Gentile
mission /11/. Schmeichel fulminates against this position:

But for this to be correct, would we not have to regard
Luke 4:16-30 (*sic,* but vv.14,15 really should be included
in this complex /12/) as a programmatic introduction not
only to the gospel but more centrally to the Book of
Acts as well? I do not know of any scholar who is
prepared to do that /13/.

As it happens, this position has at least been intimated in the
past /14/, and in any case I do not see his point, even granted

the premise; surely scholarly assent is not a *sina qua non* of
correct exegesis. Next, Schmeichel shows his flair for
schematic thinking in insisting that Elijah and Elishah are
not prototypes for Gentile mission:

> That they are paradigms of rejection I do not intend to
> question, but that they are more than that, that in fact
> they represent a resolution to rejection, i.e. a welcome
> elsewhere beyond the rejecting community, I find difficult
> to recognize in the text /15/.

Actually, of course, his difficulty does not arise from the
text, but - as his next paragraph shows - from a rationalistic
reading of the stories about the widow of Sarepta and Naaman
which has nothing to do with what Luke says. Schmeichel is
quite correct in saying that neither is "the first convert
in a new missionary field", but he fails even to argue that
this reservation ever occurred to Luke. As a matter of fact,
Schmeichel knows very well that Acts 13:42-52; 18:6; 28:28
explicitly connect Jewish rejection with Gentile mission, but
he insists that we should not "read this pericope from our
knowledge of" these passages /16/. On the previous page, he
asserts, "to recognize an anticipation of the experience of
the church in that of Jesus is a reading of the Nazareth
pericope from the perspective of Acts". Indeed it is, but
since Luke wrote both books with the same audience in mind, is
this procedure altogether unreasonable? I do not think it is.
We may not exclude the possibility that Luke saw Jesus'
ministry as paradigmatic for that of the Church as we analyze
the language of 4:16-21.

I) *Redaction critical*

The narrative portions of our passage (vv.16,17,20,21a) are
easily shown to be redactional, with three exceptions (*Nazara*
in v.16, *kai pantōn* and *en tē sunagōgē* in v.20) which will be
discussed in section two. On the whole, Luke can be seen to be
portraying Jesus' first public address as congruent with the
Christian missionary preaching which we know so well from
Acts: he understands the Church to be following the example of
her lord.

The construction "and he entered, according to his habit...
into the synagogue" (*kai ēlthen kata to eiōthos autō ... eis
tēn sunagōgēn*) is the first which suggests that Luke is presenting

us with a paradigm of mission preaching. The use of
eiserkhomai with *eis* is the usual way to speak of entering a
building in Koine, and no more weight should be attached to it
than is carried by the ordinary phrase (*kai ēlthen eis*) which
opens v.16. Similarly, the term "synagogue", even though it is
a normative one for the locus of mission activity both in the
third Gospel (4:15,44; 6:6; 13:10) and in Acts (9:20; 13;5,14;
14:1; 17:1,10,17; 18:4,19,26; 19:8), should not be pressed for
meaning since it is difficult to speak of events in a synagogue
without using it. *Kata to eiōthos autō*, however, is a different
matter, because nothing in the story demands a reference to
Jesus' habitual attendance at synagogues. From K.L. Schmidt to
Heinz Schürmann /17/, this has correctly been seen as a
redactional construction, and the latter cited Acts 17:2 as
the most pertinent parallel. It is striking that *eiserkhomai*
is also used in this passage and that Paul's entry into the
Thessalonian synagogue (v.1) is thereby described. In both
passages the dative of possession (*autō, tō Paulō*) is used to
stress that the habit of visiting synagogues belonged to Jesus
and Paul particularly. Incidentally, it is quite clear that
Jesus "custom" was not simply one of "habitually attending
sabbatical services" in Nazareth /18/; we already know from
v.15 that Jesus is an itinerant preacher, and that is how Luke
presents him here /19/. The statement that Jesus "came"
to Nazareth on this occasion (v.16) is not consistent with the
view that he was resident there at this time and entered the
synagogue as an ordinary participant. While these are the only
two uses of *to eiōthos* in Luke-Acts, *to ethos* appears ten times,
and all three occurrences in the Gospel are with *kata*. (In Luke
2:27 the form *kata to eithismenon tou nomou* appears). On the
evidence of a careful orchestration by which the closest
parallel in the Lukan corpus to Jesus' teaching in the
Palestinian synagogue is Paul's confuting in the Thessalonian
synagogue, the entire phrase *eisēlthen kata to eiōthos autō ...
eis tēn sunagōgēn* should be ascribed to Luke.

The phrase "on the sabbath day" (*en tē hēmera tōn sabbatōn*)
appears in the clause discussed in the previous paragraph, and
Schürmann has noted the parallels in Acts 13:14; 16:13 /20/.
It is perhaps significant that the first of these passages in
Acts also uses the *eiserkhomai ... eis* construction to describe
the entry of Paul and Barnabas into the synagogue at Pisidian
Antioch, and that the second refers to a sabbath prayer meeting.
This is of some interest because Luke usually avoids using the
plural of "sabbath" (as he does here) when he has a specific

occasion in mind. On the other hand, the plural is normally
used in Luke-Acts in connection with synagogue meetings (4:16,31;
13:10; Acts 13:14; 15:21; 16:13; 17:2). The single exception is
Luke 6:2, which is clearly an instance of traditional diction
(cf. Mark 2:24 and Luke 6:1). When Luke wanted to speak of a
single occasion which was part of the regular practice of
synagogue visiting (*kata to eiōthos*), it was natural for him to
use a word in the singular ("day") with a general qualification
("sabbath(s)").

    Two of the phrases so far discussed, *kata to eiōthos* and
tē hēmera tōn sabbatōn, also appear in the Septuagint /21/.
Luke knows very well what sort of vocabulary to use when
describing a scene in a synagogue. His style is peppered with
"Septuagintalisms", as H.F.D. Sparks dubbed them. He coined
this term in criticizing the notion that Semitisms are evident
in Luke's work /22/. The phrase *hou ēn tethrammenos* ("where he
was nurtured") also attracted his attention as the "one possible
indication of Aramaic influence" in this passage /23/. He is
quite right to doubt Aramaic provenience for two reasons: (1)
trephō is used three times by Luke (Luke 12:24; 23:29; Acts 12:20)
aside from in 4:16, and one of these usages (Acts 12:20) is in
an explanatory phrase, and (2) of the more than forty uses of
eimi imperfect in a periphrastic formation in the third Gospel,
nine are with the perfect passive participle of the other verb.
On the basis of such data, one cannot conclude with Matthew
Black that at Luke 4:16 "we have a true Semitic Pluperfect" /24/,
nor with Bruno Violet that *kai* frequency in the passage is "gut
semitisch" /25/. It appears rather that Luke knows how to tell a
story about a synagogue in Palestine. At the same time, he knows
how to present the material in such a way that it serves as a
paradigm for the mission of Paul and, derivatively, for that of
his own Church. The term "Septuagintalism" is felicitous because
it conveys Luke's mastery of literary colouring as he shows us
the significance of Jesus' visit to the Nazareth synagogue.

    Verses 16d,17,20a describe Jesus' behaviour in the
synagogue as part of the liturgical action: he stands to read,
a scroll is handed to him which he unrolls to the appropriate
place; after the reading he rolls it up again, hands it back
to the server, and sits down. By having Jesus stand to speak
and by emphasizing that what he says is found in the scroll,
Luke presents the action as a proper synagogue "reading" (*mqr'*),
not an "interpretation" (*trgwm*) or "homily" (*mdrš*). This by no
means requires us to conclude that the description is that of a
"sachkundiger Palästiner" /26/, as K.H. Rengstorf has suggested,

since we know from such passages as Acts 13:14f. that Luke was familiar with Diaspora synagogue practice. Linguistic analysis confirms that the description is of Lukan pedigree.

"To stand" (*anistēmi*) is used often in the third Gospel (twenty-nine times). It is most frequently found in participliar form (seventeen times), but it also appears in the indicative and subjunctive, as an imperative and an infinitive. Perhaps we should note that 4:16d is the only point at which the verb means more as an intransitive than to stand up on one's feet, since some sort of podium is probably in mind here. In Acts, however, the verb is four times used in the context of public address (1:15; 5:34; 13:16; 15:17, the third usage is also of synagogal address) and once in the context of prophecy (11:28), so Luke himself might well be expected to have used the term here. Similarly, "to read" (*anaginōskō*) also refers to public sabbath reading at Acts 13:27; 15:21.

If this analysis is correct, then another interpretative question can be addressed on the basis of the conclusions so far reached. Walter Grundmann, commenting on *anestē,* claimed that "Jesus handelt auch hier als Herr, der die Initiative ergreift", and Heinz Schürmann also speaks of an "Eigeninitiative" which is intimated here more than in Acts 13:15-42; 17:2; 18:4 /27/. It seems to me that the last two passages cited indicate more "initiative" - if not out and out audacity - than Jesus is pictured as showing by standing to read in Nazareth: no matter how *anestē* is read, *dialegomai* is simply the stronger verb. In any case, the continuity of *anestē* with Luke's liturgical vocabulary implies that we are not informed one way or another about the motivation for which Jesus stood to read; he simply got up to speak in the normal course of things.

"To give out" (*epididōmi*) is not a common word in the New Testament and it is used most often (Matthew 7:9,10/Luke 11:11, 12; Luke 24:30,42) in reference to giving someone something to eat. There is, however, common usage of the term in Hellenistic beaurocratic diction /28/ and Acts 15:30 (where the verb is also associated with *anaginōskō* in v.31) shows that Luke may have adopted this diction to his own purposes. Unfortunately, this is the only other use of the verb with such a meaning in Luke-Acts, so that great probability cannot be claimed for this argument. However, the fact that Luke alone among New Testament writers uses the term in this manner, and its demonstrable association with Hellenistic diction, makes the redactional

provenience of the term likely. The author of the third Gospel
is here describing Jesus' behaviour in a way which picks up
diction familiar to his hearers.

The fact that "book" or "scroll" (*biblion*) stands without
the definite article here has attracted the attention of those
who claim that Luke is to some extent reproducing a Semitic
source in his narrative. Bruno Violet suggested that *spr* in
the construct state lies behind the usage, and Heinz Schürmann
observes that Luke usually uses the plural *bibloi* for the books
of the Bible /29/. Neither of these arguments is convincing.
The absence of the article here is not only acceptable - it is
a convention among good Greek writers to omit the article
"when a person or object is first introduced", as J.H. Moulton
and N. Turner put it /30/. In fact, of course, Luke does use
the article with *biblion* later in v.17 and in v.20 - after the
book has been specified - and this indicates that the omission
in v.17 is literary and self-conscious. As to Schürmann's
point, it ought to be evident that a writer would not likely
use a plural noun in order to refer to a scroll (as distinct
from the writings contained therein), and in any case Luke was
not unfamiliar with the singular usage of the related term
biblos (3:4; 20:42; Acts 1:20; 7:42).

The singular usage without the article in 3:4 (as in all
of the singular usages cited) is striking because Isaiah is also
cited there, in relation to John. The actual phrase *tou
prophētou Ēsaiou* need not detain us. Luke refers to this prophet
five times (3:4; 4:17; Acts 8:28,30; 28:25) as either "Isaiah the
prophet" or "the prophet Isaiah". That the phrases are
interchangeable to him and alternated in the interests of variety
is shown by Acts 8:28,30. The reference to Isaiah in 4:17
therefore echoes the reference in 3:4, so that a contrapuntal
arrangement between John and Jesus material is developed (as
it is in chapters one and two). We therefore find reflected in
the use of the citation words the same sort of connection
between the two passages as their structural relation in the
narrative suggests /31/. The most straightforward conclusion
to be drawn from this is that both aspects of this arrangement
are the work of a single mind - Luke's.

"Having unrolled" (*anaptuxas*) is a key term in Luke's
arrangement of a symmetrical but variated description of
events in the synagogue. Words related to normal practice in
the synagogue in v.17 - *epidothē*, *biblion*, *anaptuxas* - are

modified and repeated in v.20 - *ptuxas, to biblion, apodous* -
in a manner which is evocative of ritual action. The use of
participles in this way is characteristic of what J.H. Moulton
has called Luke's "flowing style" /32/, so that once again
we can perceive the hand of this masterful, literate redactor.

"To find" (*heuriskō*) is often found in Luke-Acts (seventy-
nine times), but only at Acts 17:23 does it appear in a (albeit
distantly) similar context. While the similarity of the
construction *bōmon en hō epegegrapto* to *ton topon hou ēn
gegrammenon* is perhaps significant, the Acts passage is
hardly a true parallel to the present usage. "The place"
(*ho topos*) poses a similar problem. It also is frequently used
by Luke (thirty-four times), but never in reference to a
citation, and yet it is so common and flexible in Greek that
it seems ludicrous to posit a rabbinic *mqwm* as its immediate
source, especially since Walter Bauer reports its use for
"passage in a book" in Xenophon, Philo and Josephus /33/.
Taking account of the possibility that this sort of diction
influenced Luke, of the similar usage at Acts 17:23, and of
the Lukan pedigree of the surrounding material, it seems
probable that *heuren ton topon* is a product of redaction.

Once this phrase is seen as redactional, one has some
parameters within which to interpret the term *heuriskō,* i.e.
its uses elsewhere in the third Gospel. This is valuable
inasmuch as this word has been used to forward some remarkable
exegeses. Four commentators - Klostermann, Temple, Lohse and
Grundmann - read a providential overtone into the present
usage, in Temple's words:

> We are told that he unrolled the sacred scroll from
> its roller and found, without looking for them, the
> passages of Isaias that were appropriate to his
> purpose /34/.

But *heuriskō* regularly implies an element of searching, so
that M.-J. Lagrange says far more accurately that the use of
the verb "indique que Jésus trouva l'endroit qu'il avait en
vue" /35/. This reading is appropriate so long as one bears
in mind that Luke presents Jesus as having "found the place"
as a regular component in the course of the ritual events
described.

While "was written" (*ēn gegrammenon*) occurs nowhere else

in Luke's work, we do find *gegrammenon* with "is" (Luke 20:17)
and the participle also occurs in reference to scripture in
John's Gospel and at 2 Corinthians 4:13. *Antiquities* 9.214
presents us with the use of the same participle with an *ana*-
prefix, so that its place in Diaspora diction is again indicated.
Luke, it seems, picked up this diction at 20:17 and put it into
the past at 4:17. The use of "was" (*ēn*) should not be considered
odd; it simply serves to narrate a citation as distinct from
actually making one (cf. 3:4).

As we have seen, v.20 fills out the description of the
synagogue ritual in a way which is symmetrical to v.17. The
term "servant" or "attendant" (*huperetēs*) is applied by Luke
both to Christian preachers (1:2; Acts 26:16) and to lower
echelon officials; of more specific interest for our present
purpose, it refers in Acts 13:5, as here, to a function in
the context of the synagogue. Again, Jesus' action is set in
an environment with which a Church missionary would have been
familiar. This is also true in respect of the verb "to sit"
(*kathizō*), which is used by all the Synoptic Evangelists when
Jesus speaks *ex cathedra*, as we might say (Matthew 5:1; Mark
9:35; Luke 5:3), but by Luke in particular as the attitude of
preaching in the synagogue (Acts 13:14 cf. v.16; 16:13). By
his every action in the synagogue, Jesus is the
heilsgeschichtliche cornerstone of a mission theology.

In v.20b the key redactional phrase is "were staring at
him" (*ēsan atenizontes autō*). Since the imperfect of third
person *eimi* is used some forty times in a periphrastic tense
formation in the third Gospel, its usage here can hardly be
called unusual. *Atenizō* appears only at 2 Corinthians 3:7,13 in
the works of New Testament writers other than Luke, who uses the
verb twelve times. Consistently, he employs it to heighten the
dramatic impact of the scene in which it occurs. So, for
example, the servant girl is not merely *emblepsa* (Mark 14:67)
when she accuses Peter, she is *atenisasa* (Luke 22:56). The
same sense accompanies the use of the term all through Acts, and
it is worth pointing out that this overtone is not associated
with the term in Pauline diction.

Since Luke's use of this verb is deliberate, it seems
reasonable to conclude that it has some particular import here.
Eric Klostermann suggested that the tension implied is in
anticipation "auf den kommenden Vortrag" /36/. This exegesis
requires us to read *atenizō* in a manner which conflicts with

its meaning elsewhere in Luke-Acts. Regularly, the verb is
used with the understanding that the person who stares is
already in the grip of some powerful experience or emotion,
whether the subject is the servant girl, those who see the
risen or exalted Jesus (Acts 1:10; 7:55) or a vision (10:4;
11:6), those who speak with the power of the Spirit as a
present force (3:4; 13:19; 23:1) or those who look on in awe
at the efficacy of this power (3:12; 6:15). By analogy to this
usage, it is necessary to understand that in v.20b the
congregation is already upset; they are not merely waiting in
anticipation, something has occurred which disturbs them. We
are not told precisely what so affects them at this point,
and since Luke is not usually so ambiguous, it would seem that
a traditional reference to commotion in the synagogue has been
re-expressed in Lukan terminology. The reason for the
traditional reference will be discussed in the next section.

        This is the only place in Luke-Acts where "eyes"
(*ophthalmoi*) is the subject of the verb *atenizō*.   Heinz
Schürmann has suggested that "die seelische Funktion dem Glied"
is an indication of the Palestinian origin of the phrase /37/.
We have already seen that Luke has put a tradition notice into
his own words and, as we will see below, *pantōn* and *en tē
synagōgē* in v.20 are non-Lukan, so his suggestion cannot be
lightly put aside. Let us consider the other uses of "eyes"
in the third Gospel. In three cases, "eyes" are put in the
accusative with the verb "to raise" (6:20; 16:23; 18:13). This
itself may be considered a Semitic idiom (cf. Psalm 122:1 LXX),
but Luke has the phrase at one point (6:20) where the Matthean
parallel does not; the other two Lukan uses are in special
material. The uses of "eyes" in the nominative in the third
Gospel (2:30; 10:23/Matthew 13:16; 24:16,31, other than the
present instance) appear to be traditional. But the somewhat
unusual use of the nominative at 4:20 may simply be consequent
on Luke's decision to use *atenizō*, and Hans Conzelmann points
out that at 10:23f. (cf. Matthew 13:16) /38/, Luke arranges to
make the witness of eyes inclusive of that of ears in a manner
which parallels the presentation in 4:20f. (see also 17:22f.;
Acts 2:33). This thematic evidence suggests that Luke has
inserted *hoi ophthalmoi* here with syntax which is for him
unusual, but not aberrant, in order to indicate that Jesus has
arrested attention in the synagogue.

        The first part of v.21 is clearly Lukan. An article by
J.H. Hunkin provides the most detailed investigation of New

Testament "begin" (*arkhomai*) diction available. Hunkin lists thirteen instances in Luke in which *arkhomai* "distinctly" means "begin" and fourteen in which this meaning is doubtful. Of these pleonastic uses, ten appear with the infinitive of a verb of speaking, and in eight cases this verb is *legein* (3:8; 4:21; 7:24; 11:29; 12:1; 13:26; 20:9; 23:30) /39/. Only two of this group (7:24; 20:9) are paralleled (Matthew 11:7; Mark 12:1), so that we are left with six instances in which a specifically Lukan pattern may be detectable. In three of the last-mentioned six passages, the construction is used in logia of the Baptist (3:8) and of Jesus (13:26; 23:30). At 13:26; 23:30 the adverb "then" (*tote*) appears, and this seems to bring out the reason for which *arkhomai* occurs in these instances: in each case, the speaker is concerned with what will be said at a particular time or in a particular context. This is also how the verb is used in narration, in which three of our six passages are found (4:21; 11:29; 12:1). Here the verbs are used to indicate what Jesus says at a specific juncture. This diction appears to be Lukan: not only is it consistent and frequent, but Luke sometimes uses it when Matthew and Mark do not.

This consistency is not of a nature which would seem to support Schürmann's theory that Luke has a theology of "the beginning" (*arkhē*) which identifies 4:18,19 as "the word" of Acts 10:37 /40/. On two occasions, Jesus is reported to have started speaking while a crowd assembled (11:29; 12:1); *heilsgeschichtliche* overtones are absent here. On three other occasions, this purely narrative use may have historical significance. We are told at 7:24 that Jesus began to speak about John after the latter had sent a delegation to determine his identity, and at 20:9 that Jesus began to tell the parable of the vineyard after his authority had been questioned. It may be that Luke, by the use of *arkhomai* in selected instances, is holding to his promise to tell his tale in order (1:3). Even so, this can hardly be called the governing meaning of the term, because it is sometimes difficult to determine if the sequence in Luke's mind is really historical or only narrative. For example, the question of those sitting at table at 7:49 may indicate a turning point in the ministry (but sins have been forgiven before, see 5:20), or simply that the crowd at that point in the story was responding to Jesus' absolution of the woman. The wide use of *arkhomai* in Luke in a variety of contexts makes the narrative signification the preferred reading of the verb, although the use of the verb in this inaugural scene may reasonably be held to convey a programmatic meaning.

In his "Appendix on Semitisms" in the second volume of
Moulton's grammar, W.F. Howard points out that *ērxato* with the
infinitive "cannot be called a Hebraism, for though it is found
fairly often in the LXX ... it has no fixed Hebrew original" /41/.
In concluding his discussion, Howard says, "I venture to add
that its comparative frequency in the LXX may have inclined
Luke to use it". In view of the findings that the construction
is characteristic of Luke, and that the LXX is for him an
important resource as he describes the paradigmatic activity of
Jesus, Howard's venture amounts to a probability.

The use of "to" (*pros*) after a verb of speaking is
ubiquitously Lukan, with 103 occurrences as opposed to one
in Matthew and eight in Mark. The use of *de* and *hoti* in 4:21
can also be assigned to Luke insofar as they are consequent
upon the decision to employ the major components of the clause
and do not conflict with Lukan diction elsewhere in his corpus.

Overall, then, Luke makes evident to us the paradigmatic
significance of the Nazareth pericopé as he uses evocative
phrases, sometimes reminiscent of the language of the
Septuagint, to portray the activity of Jesus in the synagogue.
It is perhaps not too much to say that Luke's Jesus is a proto-
missionary of the apostolic Church. When this concern for the
mission of the Church is recognized, Luke's preference for this
passage over Mark 1:14,15 as the first statement in the public
ministry of Jesus becomes explicable, although he has taken
care to preserve a sense of Jesus' relation to John. The
Jesus of Luke's special tradition (vv.18,19, see below)
preaches, not the proximity of the kingdom, but precisely
what the Church preaches (cf. Acts 3:20; 4:27; 10:38): his
own anointing.

II) *Tradition critical*

Tradition criticism seeks to determine the provenience and
meaning of the material which our writers hand down to us. It
is obviously very important not to confuse traditional with
redactional elements; if, for example, we treated Luke's
language as an indicator of the provenience of 4:16-21 in the
tradition, we would conclude that it was a Diaspora formulation,
and we would read Luke's theology into the passage. Analysis
will show that this is far from appropriate, and that this
passage in Luke's work is based upon Aramaic tradition with a
theme of its own. In this instance, as in many others,

accurate tradition criticism is only practicable on a redaction
critical basis: one must first demonstrate that an element is
not redactional before treating it as traditional.

Before turning to the traditional citation and logion
incorporated at 4:16-21 (vv.18,19,21b), let us consider the
three traditional elements in the wording of vv.16,20: *Nazara,*
pantōn and *en tē sunagōgē*. *Nazara* appears only here and at
Matthew 4:13 in the New Testament, and it is scarcely feasible
that Luke invented what is evidently the Aramaic form of the
name /42/. Because "of all" (*pantōn*) in v.20 refers to a
definite group in its totality, its use without the article is
called "scarcely permissible" by C.F.D. Moule; he points out that
v.28 also has *pas* plural without the article and that both are
"striking instances of the oddity" /43/. They are striking
indeed, since both occur in the context of the Nazareth
pericope and both are contained in descriptions of the
congregation's reaction to Jesus' citation of Old Testament
passages. The coherent use of the construction in a single
story, coupled with Luke's refusal to use it elsewhere in
similar contexts (e.g. 4:36; 5:26, where the use without the
article is general and therefore not irregular), leads to the
conclusion that the usage here is traditional. The repetition
of the location of the action (*en tē sunagōgē,* as in v.28) is
curious. The synagogue was mentioned in v.16, and the events
of vv.17-20a can hardly have occurred anywhere else. This is
the sort of redundancy which Luke ordinarily avoids /44/.
Further, this phrase is what makes *pantōn* refer to a totality -
which is the reason for which it ought to have the article.
Since the phrase does not make sense in terms of Lukan style,
it is better assigned to the tradition before Luke.

What is the provenience of this traditional diction?
Obviously, "in the synagogue" does not tell us anything, but
Nazara suggests that we might be dealing with a Palestinian
tradition. Is *pantōn* a Semitism? To answer this question, it
is wise to use the Old Syriac New Testament manuscripts as a
guide /45/: Syriac is a sister language to Aramaic, and can show
us how the Gospel message was actually rendered in a Semitic
idiom at an early stage. *Pantōn* is what *klhwn* (*kl* = "all";
hwn = "them") renders at Mark 2:12; 4:31, to take some random
examples, but the Syriac term also corresponds to "all" in the
plural nominative (3:28) and accusative (2:12b; Luke 5:9; 7:16).
It seems, then, that a fixed Semitic construction could be
construed variously in Greek /46/. This means that a Greek

translator would not know whether a given *klhwn* should be
rendered "of them all" or "all those", since there is no
case distinction in the Semitic languages with which we are
concerned. *Pantōn* in v.20b can be explained by a decision to
render *klhwn* as a genitive, but to keep the word at the
beginning of the sentence in order to retain the emphasis on
the total focus upon Jesus at the outset. For this purpose,
pantōn after the noun would miss the vigourous assertion of
totality which "all" at the beginning of a sentence achieves.
This can be illustrated with reference to two English
translations of Luke 4:20b. The A.V. reads, "the eyes of all
them". This is the equivalent of Greek *hoi ophthalmoi tōn
pantōn,* and it does not have the impact of the less accurate
"all the eyes" of the N.E.B. If one wanted to keep the
emphasis of the N.E.B. rendering but also retain the case
indication, as in the A.V., one might say, "of all, the eyes".
In English this is clumsy; in Greek it is frightful. This
strained use of Greek (of which the English examples are a
pale reflection) is easily explained as an attempt to render
a word commonly used in Hebrew, Aramaic and Syriac without the
case indication endemic to Greek. *Pantōn* joins *Nazara* as a
sign of Semitic tradition.

The Old Syriac reading at v.20 might excite our interest
for more than linguistic reasons: the manuscripts have no word
for "eyes" here, and it was suggested in the previous section
that Luke introduced this term at this point. The possibility
must be entertained that the Old Syriac version offers us some
insight into the pre-Lukan form of the pericope. This may seem
surprising at first, but let us bear in mind that the oral
tradition about Jesus was not immediately silenced when it
achieved written form /47/, and that Syriac speakers would
have been in a good position to transmit this tradition
literally /48/.

The citation in vv.18,19 is striking for its fidelity to
the diction of the Septuagint and for its departure from the
text of Isaiah 61.1,2 in LXX. Precise verbal identity is
evidenced at every turn, but the LXX "to heal the broken in
heart" is omitted, a phrase from Isaiah 58:6, "set the bruised
free", is inserted, and the "proclaim" of Isaiah 61:2 LXX
appears as "preach". It has been suggested that Luke's memory
slipped /49/, but this is all but incredible for several
reasons: (1) as Adolf Schlatter has pointed out, the *en* of the
inserted phrase is unusual in Luke /50/, (2) Luke shows in

v.17 that he has a particular passage in mind, and (3) Luke
himself would never have missed out the healing phrase when
vv.23f. deal precisely with this topic /51/. All three
observations militate against the idea that Luke deliberately
changed the citation, and it is especially difficult to see
why an author who introduces Septuagintal diction into a
narrative would then depart from the text of the LXX when he
comes to the words which are at the heart of the story. One
can say not only probably but with a degree of certainty that
this passage is a product neither of Luke's memory nor of his
theology, but the voice of his tradition.

More precisely it is an echo of the tradition's voice,
because Luke, in citing the scripture, would have done so in
Septuagintal form, since that was the version which was
normative for him. Can we recover anything of the pre-Lukan
form of this citation? We again turn to the Old Syriac New
Testament, and again we encounter important new evidence.
While other Syriac versions - namely the Peshitta and the
so-called Palestinian Syriac Lectionary - move even closer to
the LXX by including "to heal the broken in heart", the older
translation gives us a startlingly new rendering of the
citation:

> The Spirit of the Lord is upon *thee*, because of which
> > he has anointed *thee*
> > to preach the gospel to the poor,
> and he has despatched me to preach
> > to the captives forgiveness, and to the blind sight
> > - and *I* will strengthen the broken with forgiveness -
> > and to preach the acceptable year of the Lord.

In the light of the tendency of Luke and of the subsequent
textual tradition to conform the citation to that of the
Septuagint, the Old Syriac reading is very striking indeed.
This tendency is evidence of the Church's struggle (both in
Palestine and the Diaspora) to be accorded legitimacy as the
true Israel, and such tampering with the biblical text as we
have seen above was hardly part of its programme. The
authorship of Jesus would explain how, despite its divergence
from the LXX, this tradition is still available in the Old
Syriac Gospels, and to a lesser extent in the Greek text of Luke
Unless Jesus had expressed himself in this way, it is difficult
to see why any version of the New Testament would have altered
the citation from the Old Testament. Further, the unusual claim

which is implicit in this odd form of the citation (see the
next section) explains why there was a traditional notice of
commotion among everyone in the synagogue.

In a recent review of *God in Strength*, Graham Stanton argues
that the Old Syriac readings do not represent dominical tradition:
"the surprising variants in the Old Syriac...seem to represent
either a corruption or error, or an attempt to make explicit the
Christology implied in the Greek textual tradition"/52/. The first
alternative is simply implausible; the variants are not isolated
mistakes, but form a coherent rendering of the Isaian text which
accounts for the traditional notice of commotion. The second assumes that the Old Syriac--unlike any other versions--tamper with
Old Testament citations in the New Testament in the interest of
Christology. No evidence has been adduced that they do so, and
we have already observed that the tendency in the manuscripts
considered is to bring such citations into line with known and
respected translations of the Old Testament. That is, the alternative suggestions fail to offer a tenable account of the history
of the texts' development, which is essential in textual study.

The diction in the logion following the citation (v.21b)
is clearly traditional. Luke never uses "today" (*sēmeron*)
when he himself is speaking; it is always attributed to someone
else in the third Gospel. The present usage is like several
other sayings attributed to Jesus in that *sēmeron* stands at
the beginning of the statement. The unvarying repetition of
this asseverative introduction, which is reminiscent of "amen"
usage /53/, is not characteristic of Luke: it is far more
suggestive of a tradition which transmitted the sayings of
Jesus in this fashion. Similarly, there are two uses of "fulfil"
(*plēroō*) in reference to scripture in the third Gospel (4:21;
24:44). In both cases, the verb is used in the passive, the
speaker is Jesus, and the saying is unparalleled. The use of
"scripture" (*hē graphē*) with "this" is surprisingly rare in the
New Testament, occurring elsewhere only at Mark 12:20 and Acts
8:35. Three passages in the third Gospel (1:44; 9:44; 12:3)
parallel the use of "ears" in 4:21. All of these are in logia,
but all use either *eis* (as at Acts 11:22) or *pros* with "ears"
in the accusative. What Bruno Violet called the "semitisch"
use of *en* with the dative here departs from regular Lukan
usage /54/, and the insertion of "eyes" shows that Luke was not
content with v.21 in its traditional form; he felt a further
phrase was needed for clarification.

The use of *en* with "ears" is not, I think, enough evidence
to suggest that the traditional diction was Semitic. On the
other hand, the logion is clearly traditional, it has the
characteristically dominical *sēmeron*, and we have already seen
that other traditional elements in this passage are Palestinian.
Further, it is a regular feature of synagogue worship to praise
God for "speaking and establishing" (*hmdbr wmqym*) what was said
in the prophetic lection /55/. It therefore seems that v.21 is
of a piece with the tradition which surfaces in vv.16,18,19,20.

III) *Historical*

One may not assume that everything redactional is specious
as history, nor that everything traditional is trustworthy.
Luke remained remarkably faithful to his tradition even as he
developed his own concerns, and it is possible that, by the
placement here of v.21, the tradition was already seeking to
domesticate Jesus' assertion by making it serve a function in
the synagogue liturgy (a function which dominical *sēmeron*
sayings do not elsewhere perform, cf. 19:5,9; 23:43). Having
said this, however, the citation (vv.18,19) in the Old Syriac
Gospels claims a high degree of reliability as a historical
datum because it serves neither the tradition's interest nor
Luke's. By coming to an appreciation of these words, we are
granted an insight into Jesus' approach to this scripture.

The citation has been altered to the extent that it becomes
a kind of conversation between someone who addresses "thee",
and the latter's response as "I". It is interesting that there
is in Isaiah 58:6 a similar play between "I" and "ye" (in the
Masoretic Text and the Targum) or between "I" and "thou" (in
the LXX, the Vulgate, the Peshitta and the Old Latin) /56/.
The roles are not the same, however, in that the "I" of Isaiah
58:6 is God, while that of Luke 4:18 is the person sent. The
"I" - "thee" formation is also paralleled - again with reversal
of roles - at Isaiah 42:6,7 (in the Masoretic Text, the Targum,
the LXX and the Peshitta), and it is noteworthy that the
servant of Isaiah 42 - upon whom the Spirit of God is said to
rest (v.1 cf. 61:1) - is sent to bring release to the
prisoners and new sight to the blind (v.7). The use of "I" in
the second half of Luke 4:18 is explicable as the influence of
diction preserved in the Peshitta, Vulgate and Arabic of
Isaiah 61:1. In sum, we see that Jesus availed himself of
various phrases then associated with Isaiah 61 to bring out the
meaning of the passage in a manner generally reminiscent of
Targumic practice.

So much, then, can we reconstruct of the method by which this "citation" was formed. We may now ask why it was formed, which is to ask: just what did Jesus achieve by this metamorphosis of Isaiah 61:1,2 - 58:6 - 42:6,7? This may be ascertained simply by describing the impact the changes would have on a hearer who expected Isaiah 61·1 in its usual form. Instead of upon "me", upon "thee"; and anointed "thee" instead of "me". Then a return to the usual text, indeed more than a return, for the "me" of Isaiah 61:1 becomes an emphatic "I". This must have generated general befuddlement, followed by the question: who is the "I" or "thou" of this declaration? Even when we take into account the possibility that Jesus was picking up phrases which would be somewhat familiar to his hearers, the fact remains that the changes he introduced radically alter the structure of the passage. The speaker of the citation ("I") is addressed with and identified by "thee"; the announcement as a whole asserts, "I (of whom it is said, 'The Spirit of the Lord is upon thee, etc.') have been sent to preach, and I will fulfill my charge". This design only emerges when the entire passage is considered, with "I" understood as the key of the statement. Unless this is done, "thee" only causes confusion. There is a deliberative focus by the use of "thee" on the function which "I" performs. This person is designated as the one anointed to preach good news: this is the constitutive element of his purpose (expressed by "thee" in a charge from God) from which all the other activities listed (with "me" and "I") derive. It can be said that the Spirit is upon "thee" for the sake of preaching good news, and that other verbs in the passage are "my" response to that controlling reality. Jesus assents to the divine charge which he himself posits in the strange use of "thee".

The Targum to Isaiah preserves diction which explains how the "thee" - "I" language of Jesus could have referred to an identifiable speaker to the hearers of this strange "citation". In the Masoretic Text, Isaiah 61 presents us with an "I" who is intimately involved in what the LORD does (see vv.8,10 especially), but he is not named. The Targum prefaces the chapter with the introduction, "the prophet says", and this is not surprising since this Targum, which is careful in its "prophet" diction, applies the verb "to prophesy" specifically to those sent by the LORD (see Targum Isaiah 50:5). The reference to "covenant" in Isaiah 61:8 is another possible association with the prophetic servant of 42:6 and the "I" - "thee" formation therein employed. The basic point, however, is that Jesus, by using the "I" - "thee" language, identifies

himself with the prophetic figure which is most prominently
featured in the Targum to Isaiah.

In a word, Jesus announced his own divine commission in the
synagogue. It seems to me that this is a matter of simple
historical fact, and it calls into question the commonly held
view that christological statements in the mouth of Jesus are
secondary. Jesus made this claim in a manner which provoked
a disturbed response, as the tradition reported. This
pre-Lukan tradition also seems self-consciously to have
portrayed Jesus as conforming to synagogue practice. This was
the point which fired Luke's literary expertise, and he turned
the Nazareth pericope into a paradigm for mission by making it
the inaugural scene in Jesus' public ministry and by describing
the scene in language redolent of the situation of Acts. Quite
clearly, the gospel message was interpreted as it passed through
the mouths of preachers until it reached Luke, and so achieved
written form; just as clearly, this interpretative procedure
was conservative of apparently irrelevant details (e.g., the
odd form of the biblical "citation") which make it possible
for us to distinguish redaction from various layers of
tradition, and to arrive at a reasonably assured historical
finding. There is no short cut to the historical Jesus. We
must follow the chain of interpretation and tradition which
began with him and his followers and (provisionally) ended
with the written witness, and, since the written witness is the
only hard evidence available to us, we must follow this chain
in reverse. Having done that, of course, we become another
link in the chain which leads *from* the New Testament, and we
are in a position to articulate the gospel message in our own
terms ...

Notes

* The research on the basis of which this article is written was
first presented in *God in Strength* (cf. n. 6). The present treatment differs from the earlier work in the following respects: (1)
Waldemar Schmeichel's important article (cf. n. 9) has been considered; (2) Graham Stanton's review of *God in Strength* (cf. n. 52
has been treated of; (3) and a somewhat less technical, more dis-
cursive approach has been developed for the readers of *Gospel
Perspectives*.

/1/   On 5 April 1978.

/2/   I would disagree with the statement of Frederick H. Borsch
that "since all we can hope to share with the disciples through
historical investigation is something of the character of their

response, the precise form of the transcendental cause to which
they felt themselves responding is, not only unrecoverable, but
not of primary significance to us" (*God's Parable,* (London: SCM,
1975) 22, where he is discussing the resurrection).
/3/   A little book entitled *Das Geheimnis Jesu* (Leipzig: St.
Benno, 1972) serves as a very valuable introduction to
Schürmann's thought. Schürmann's most notable contributions to
Lukan studies are his three part analysis of Luke 22:7-38
(Münster: Aschendorff, 1953-1957) and his commentary on Luke
in the Herder series.
/4/   The tendency might be said to dog purely statistical
efforts to reconstruct "Q": see, e.g., R.E. Edwards, *A
Concordance to Q* (Missoula: Scholars Press, 1975) and Wolfgang
Schenk, "The Relationship of Q and Mark" (paper delivered at
the Oxford Congress on 6 April). Schürmann himself might even
be faulted on this score (cf. "Sprachliche Reminiszenzen an
angeänderte oder ausgelassene Bestandteile der Spruchsammlung
im Lukas - und Matthäusevangelium" *N.T.S.* 6 (1959-1960) 193-210.
/5/   Since W.R. Farmer, *The Synoptic Problem* (New York:
Macmillan, 1964), we can say no more than that: Markan priority
can no longer be assumed, although I am inclined to think that
Mark generally preserves a form of tradition prior to Matthew
and Luke and upon which Matthew and Luke built.
/6/   Cf. "An evangelical and critical approach to the sayings
of Jesus" *Themelios* 3 (1978) 78-85 and *God in Strength - Jesus'
announcement of the kingdom:* Studien zum Neuen Testament und
seiner Umwelt (Monographien) 1 (Freistadt: Plöchl, 1979) 123-77.
/7/   So H.J. Cadbury, *The Making of Luke-Acts* (London: S.P.C.K.,
1968) 189.
/8/   Schürmann, "Der 'Bericht vom Anfang'. Ein
Rekonstruktionsversuch auf Grund von Lk 4,14-16" in:
*Traditionsgeschichtliche Untersuchungen zu den synoptischen
Evangelien* (Düsseldorf: Patmos, 1968) 67-80; cf. J. Delobel,
"La rédaction de Lc., IV, 14-16a et le Bericht vom Anfang" in
F. Neiryuck (ed.), *L'évangile de Luc:*B.E.T.L. 32 (1973) 203-223.
/9/   Schmeichel, "Christian Prophecy in Lukan Thought: Luke
4:16-30 as a Point of Departure" in G. MacRae (ed.), *Society of
Biblical Literature 1976 Seminar Papers* (Missoula: Scholars
Press, 1976) 299.
/10/   Schmeichel, 301.
/11/   David Hill, "The Rejection of Jesus at Nazareth (Lk.4:
16-30)" *Novum Testamentum* 13 (1971) 178.
/12/   This is shown conclusively by Schürmann, *art. cit.*
/13/   Schmeichel, 296.
/14/   So, for example, Walter Grundmann, *Das Evangelium nach
Lukas* (Berlin: Evangelische Verlagsanstalt, n.d.) 120 and

Heinz Schürmann, *Das Lukasevangelium* (Freiburg: Herder, 1969)
227 read *anestē* in a heilsgeschichtliche manner (see below).
/15/ Schmeichel, 295.
/16/ Schmeichel, 296.
/17/ Schmidt, *Der Rahmen der Geschichte Jesu* (Berlin:
Trowitzsch, 1919) 39; Schürmann, *Das Lukasevangelium* 227 n.45.
/18/ So P.J. Temple, "The Rejection of Jesus at Nazareth" *C.B.Q.*
17 (1955) 237.
/19/ Schmidt, 39.
/20/ *Das Lukasevangelium* 227 n.45.
/21/ As noted (respectively) by A. Plummer, *A Critical and
Exegetical Commentary on the Gospel According to S. Luke: I.C.C.*
(Edinburgh: Clark, 1905) 119 and A. Schlatter, *Das Evangelium
des Lukas aus seinen Quellen Erklärt* (Stuttgart: Calwer, 1931)
226.
/22/ H.F.D. Sparks, "The Semitisms of St. Luke's Gospel"
J.T.S. 24 (1943) 129-138. In a letter dated 24 July 1979, Earle
Ellis understandably objected that a theory of Lukan
"Septuagintalisms" would not account for the sporadic appearance
of such turns of phrase, nor for non-Septuagintal Lukan
Semitisms. I do not wish to suggest that Luke's only Semitic
source was the LXX, and I would agree that Luke does not employ
Septuagintal vocabulary and phrasing in a univocal manner.
/23/ Sparks, 136.
/24/ M. Black, *An Aramaic Approach to the Gospels and Acts*
(Oxford: Clarendon, 1967) 132.
/25/ Bruno Violet, "Zum rechten Verständnis der
Nazarethperikope" *Z.N.W.* 37 (1938) 259.
/26/ K.H. Rengstorf, *Das Evangelium nach Lukas* (Göttingen:
Vandenhoeck and Ruprecht, 1958) 67.
/27/ Grundmann, *Das Evangelium nach Lukas* 120; Schürmann, *Das
Lukasevangelium* 227.
/28/ W. Bauer (tr. W.F. Arndt, F.W. Gingrich), *A Greek-English
Lexicon of the New Testament and Other Early Christian
Literature* (Chicago: University Press, 1957) 292.
/29/ Violet, 260; Schürmann, 233.
/30/ J.H. Moulton and N. Turner, *A Grammar of New Testament
Greek* (III) *Syntax* (Edinburgh: Clark, 1963) 173.
/31/ It is also worth noting that, while Luke nowhere
incorporates Mark 1:14a into his work, a similar relationship
between John and Jesus obtains in the contrapuntal Isaiah
citations. Also, of course, Luke 3:20 establishes that the
events of 4:14f. are in fact *meta to paradothēnai ton Ioannēn*,
even if this is not said in so many words. To a significant
extent the traditions available to Luke caused him to present
the material in this way.

/32/ Moulton, *Grammar* III 158.

/33/ Bauer, 830.

/34/ Temple, "The Rejection" 230. Cf. E. Klostermann, *Das Lukasevangelium* (Tübingen: Mohr, 1929) 63; E. Lohse, "Lukas als Theologe der Heilsgeschichte" *Evangelische Theologie* 14 (1954) 267 n.39; Grundmann, *Das Evangelium nach Lukas* 120.

/35/ M.-J. Lagrange, *Évangile selon Saint Luc* (Paris: Gabalda, 1948) 138.

/36/ Klostermann, *Das Lukasevangelium* 63. In a letter dated 4 July 1978, Peter Davids expressed this more accurately, "it seems to me that the word indicates that something in the behaviour of the person arrested attention and the explanation usually lies in the words which follow".

/37/ Schürmann, *Das Lukasevangelium* 234.

/38/ H. Conzelmann (tr. G. Buswell), *The Theology of St. Luke* (London: Faber, 1961) 105 n.3.

/39/ Hunkin, "'Pleonastic' *arkhomai* in the New Testament" *J.T.S.* 25 (1924) 394.

/40/ Schürmann, *Das Lukasevangelium* 231 n.89.

/41/ J.H. Moulton and W.F. Howard, *A Grammar of New Testament Greek* (II) *Accidence and Word-Formation with an Appendix on Semitisms in the New Testament* (Edinburgh: Clark, 1929) 455.

/42/ Schürmann, *Das Lukasevangelium* 227.

/43/ C.F.D. Moule, *An Idiom Book of New Testament Greek* (Cambridge: University Press, 1953) 109.

/44/ In the inaugural exorcism story, he omits Mark's reference to the synagogue (Luke 4:31 = Mark 1:21) so that the reference in the body of the story stands alone (4:33 = 1:23). In Acts 13:14f., Luke only repeats "synagogue" (v.43) after thirty verses, and then the point is not locative, but temporal.

/45/ A.S. Lewis, *The Old Syriac Gospels* (London: Williams and Norgate, 1910); F.C. Burkitt, *Evangelion Da-Mepharreshe* (Cambridge: University Press, 1904). Here supplemented with readings from the Peshitta edition of the British and Foreign Bible Society (1966). For a defense of the method here employed, cf. Matthew Black, *An Aramaic Approach to the Gospels and Acts* (Oxford: Clarendon, 1967) 197-204,247.

/46/ This impression is strengthened by the reading of the so-called Palestinian Syriac Lectionary (A.S. Lewis and M.D. Gibson (London: Kegan Paul, Trench, Trübner, 1899)), which is a more slavish translation of the Greek New Testament. Here a relative *d* is added in order to follow the particular meaning of the Greek (w^c*ynyhwn dkwl ḥyn*).

/47/ Cf. Thorleif Boman, *Die Jesus-Überlieferung im Lichte der neueren Volkskunde* (Göttingen: Vandenhoeck and Ruprecht, 1967).

/48/ Cf. Helmust Koester, "*GNŌMAI DIAPHOROI*: The Origins and

Nature of Diversification in Early Christianity" *H.T.R.* 58
(1965) 279-318 and "One Jesus and Four primitive Gospels"
H.T.R. 61 (1968) 203-247.

/49/ Plummer, 121.

/50/ Schlatter, 226, 227.

/51/ For points 2 and 3, cf. T. Holtz, *Untersuchungen über die
alttestamentlichen Zitate bei Lukas* (Berlin: Akademie, 1968)
40, 41. In my above-mentioned book, I compare this citation
to others of comparable length in Luke-Acts, and argue that it
is quite unusual in this context.

/52/ *J.S.N.T.* 8 (1980) 75. On p. 73, Prof. Stanton intimates
that I am unaware of the distinction between redaction criticism
and tradition criticism. P. 67 of *God in Strength* proves
otherwise.

/53/ Cf. K. Berger, "Zur Geschichte der Einleitungsformel
'Amen, ich sage euch'" *Z.N.W.* 63 (1972) 55. Its use as an oath
formula here is attested by Beza's Latin text, which reads *certe
(Jesu Christi Domini Nostri Novum Testament* (Vignon: 1598)).

/54/ Violet, 261 n.20.

/55/ J.H. Hertz, *The Pentateuch and Haftorahs. Genesis* (London:
Oxford University Press, 1929) 430.

/56/ In comparing ancient Old Testament versions, whose
readings sometimes inform us of the first century understanding
of the scripture, the indispensable tool is still Brian
Walton's *Biblia Sacra Polyglotta* (London: 1655-1657).

The Empty Tomb of Jesus /1/

William Lane Craig
2065 Half Day Road
Deerfield, IL 60015

Until recently the empty tomb has been widely regarded as
both an offense to modern intelligence and an embarrassment
for Christian faith; an offense because it implies a nature
miracle akin to the resuscitation of a corpse and an
embarrassment because it is nevertheless almost inextricably
bound up with Jesus's resurrection, which lies at the very
heart of the Christian faith. But in the last several years,
a remarkable change seems to have taken place, and the
scepticism that so characterized earlier treatments of this
problem appears to be fast receding. In this essay I wish to
assess the evidence for the historicity of Jesus's empty tomb.

I Cor 15.3b-5

In order to do this, we need to look first at one of
the oldest traditions contained in the New Testament concerning
the resurrection. In Paul's first letter to the Corinthians
(AD 56-57) he cites what is apparently an old Christian formula
(I Cor 15.3b-5), as is evident from the non-Pauline and Semitic
characteristics it contains. It reads:

. . . ὅτι Χριστὸς ἀπέθανεν ὑπὲρ τῶν ἁμαρτιῶν ἡμῶν
         κατὰ τὰς γραφάς,
    καὶ ὅτι ἐτάφη,
    καὶ ὅτι ἐγήγερται τῇ ἡμέρᾳ τῇ τρίτῃ κατὰ τὰς γραφάς,
    καὶ ὅτι ὤφθη Κηφᾷ, εἶτα τοῖς δώδεκα·

Does this formula bear witness to the fact of Jesus's empty
tomb?

'He Was Buried'

Some exegetes have maintained that the statement of the
formula 'he was buried' implies, standing as it does between
the death and the resurrection, that the tomb was empty. But
many critics deny this, holding that the burial does not stand

in relation to the resurrection, but to the death, and as such
serves to underline and confirm the reality of the death.   The
close *Zusammenhang* of the death and burial is said to be evident
in Rom 6, where to be baptized into Christ's death is to be
baptized into his burial.   Hans Grass maintains that for the
burial to imply a physical resurrection the sentence would have
to read ἀπέθανεν. . . καὶ ὅτι ἐγήγερται ἐκ τοῦ τάφου.   As it is,
the burial does not imply that the grave was empty.   Grass also
points out that Paul fails to mention the empty tomb in the
second half of I Cor 15, an instructive omission since the empty
tomb would have been a knock-down argument against those who
denied the bodily resurrection. /2/   It is also often urged that
the empty tomb was no part of the early *kerygma* and is therefore
not implied in the burial.

Now while I should not want to assert that the 'he was
buried' was included in the formula in order to prove the empty
tomb, it seems to me that the empty tomb is implied in the
sequence of events related in the formula.   For in saying that
Jesus died--was buried--was raised--appeared, one automatically
implies that the empty grave has been left behind.   The four-
fold ὅτι and the chronological series of events weighs against
subordinating the burial to the death. /3/   In baptism the
burial looks *forward* with confidence to the rising again: 'We
were buried therefore with him by baptism into death, so that
as Christ was raised from the dead by the glory of the Father,
we too might walk in newness of life' (Rom 6.4).   Even clearer
is Col 2.13:   '. . . and you were buried with him in baptism,
in which you were also raised with him through faith in the
working of God, who raised him from the dead.'   And even if one
denied the evidence of the four-fold ὅτι and the chronological
sequence, the very fact that a dead-and-buried man was raised
itself implies an empty grave.   Grass's assertion that the
formula should read ἐγήγερται ἐκ τοῦ τάφου is not so obvious
when we reflect that in I Cor 15.12 Paul does write ἐκ νεκρῶν
ἐγήγερται (cf. I Thess 1.10; Rom 10.9; Gal 1.1; Mt 27.64; 28.7).
/4/   In being raised from the dead, Christ is raised from the
grave.

Grass's argument that had Paul believed in the empty tomb,
then he would have mentioned it in the second half of I Cor 15
turns back upon Grass.   For if Paul did not believe in the empty
tomb, as Grass contends, then why did he not mention the purely
spiritual appearance of Christ to him as a knock-down
argument for the immateriality of Christ's resurrection body?

Grass can only reply that Paul did not appeal to his vision
of Jesus to prove that the resurrection body would be heavenly
and glorious because the meeting 'eluded all description.' /5/
But could Paul not have said he saw a heavenly light and heard
a voice (Acts 22.6-7; 26.13-14)? In fact the very ineffability
of the experience would be a positive argument for immateriality,
since a physical body is not beyond all description. Actually
Grass seems to misunderstand Paul's intention in discussing the
resurrection body in I Cor 15.35-56. Paul does not want to
prove that it is physical, for that was presupposed by everyone
and was perhaps what the Corinthians recoiled at. He wants to
prove that the body is in *some* sense spiritual, and thus the
Corinthians ought not to stick at it. /6/ Hence, the mention
of the empty tomb would be wholly beside the point. There would
be thus no reason to mention the empty tomb, but good reason to
appeal to Paul's vision, which he does not do. This suggests
that Grass's analysis is mistaken.

         Finally as to the absence of the empty tomb in the *kerygma*,
the statement 'he was buried' followed by the proclamation of
the resurrection indicates that the empty tomb was implied in
the *kerygma*. The formula is a summary statement, and it could
very well be that Paul was familiar with the historical context
of the simple statement in the formula, which would imply that
he not only presupposed the empty tomb, but actually knew of it
as well. The tomb is alluded to in the preaching in Acts 2.24-
32. The pointed contrast between David's death and burial and
Jesus's not being held by death is the fact that whereas David's
tomb is with us to this day, God raised (ἀνέστησεν) Jesus up.
The empty tomb seems clearly in view here. The empty tomb is
also implicit in Paul's speech in Antioch of Pisidia, which
follows point for point the outline of the formula in I Cor 15.
3-5: '. . . they took him down from the tree, and laid him in
a tomb. But God raised him from the dead; and for many days he
appeared to those who came up with him from Galilee to Jerusalem.'
(Acts 13.29-31). No first century Jew or pagan would be so
cerebral as to wonder if the tomb were empty or not. That the
empty tomb is not more explicitly mentioned may be simply
because it was regarded as *selbstverständlich*, given the
resurrection and appearances of Jesus. Or again, it may be that
the evidence of the appearances so overwhelmed the testimony of
legally unqualified women to the empty grave that the latter
was not used as evidence. But the gospel of Mark shows that
the empty tomb was important to the early church, even if it
was not appealed to as evidence in evangelistic preaching. So

I think it quite likely that the formula and Paul at least
accept the empty tomb, even if it is not explicitly *mentioned*.

'On the Third Day'
        A second possible reference to the empty tomb is the
phrase 'on the third day.' Since no one actually saw the
resurrection of Jesus, how could it be dated on the third day?
Some critics argue that it was on this day that the women found
the tomb empty, so the resurrection came to be dated on that
day. Thus, the phrase 'on the third day' not only presupposes
that a resurrection leaves an empty grave behind, but is a
definite reference to the historical fact of Jesus's empty
tomb. But of course there are many other ways to interpret
this phrase: (1) The third day dates the first appearance of
Jesus. (2) Because Christians assembled for worship on the
first day of the week, the resurrection was assigned to this
day. (3) Parallels in the history of religions influenced the
dating of the resurrection on the third day. (4) The dating
of the third day is lifted from Old Testament scriptures.
(5) The third day is a theological interpretation indicating
God's salvation, deliverance, and manifestation. Inasmuch as
the first four theories have been subjected to searching
criticism by both Lehmann and Bode, it seems best to me in the
interests of economy to simply refer the reader to their
discussions /7/ and to proceed immediately to the fifth
hypothesis.

        The theory that the third day is a theological
interpretation indicating God's salvation, deliverance, and
manifestation is, I think, the only serious alternative to
regarding the third day motif as based on the historical events
of the resurrection, and this theory has been eloquently
expounded by Lehmann and supported by Bode as well. /8/ To
begin with there are nearly 30 passages in the LXX that use the
phrase τῇ ἡμέρᾳ τῇ τρίτῃ to describe events that happened on
the third day. /9/ On the third day Abraham offered Isaac
(Gen 22.4; cf. Gen 34.25; 40.20). On the third day Joseph
released his brothers from prison (Gen 42.18). After three
days God made a covenant with his people and gave the law
(Ex 19.11, 16; cf. Lev 8.18; Num 7.24; 19.12, 19; Judg 19.8;
20.30). On the third day David came to Ziklag to fight the
Amalekites (I Sam 30.1) and on the third day thereafter heard
the news of Saul and Jonathan's death (II Sam 1.2). On the
third day the kingdom was divided (I Kings 12.24; cf. II Chron
10.12). On the third day King Hezekiah went to the House of

the Lord after which he was miraculously healed (II Kings 20.5, 8). On the third day Esther began her plan to save her people (Esther 5.1; cf. II Macc 11.18). The only passage in the prophets mentioning the third day is Hos 6.2. These LXX passages taken together show us that the third day is a theologically determined time at which God acts to bring about the new and the better, a time of life, salvation, and victory; on the third day comes the resolution of a difficulty through God's mighty act.

A second step is to consider the interpretation given to such passages in Jewish Midrash (Midrash Rabbah, Genesis [Mikketz] 91.7; Midrash Rabbah, Esther 9.2; Midrash Rabbah, Deuteronomy [Ki Thabo] 7.6; Midrash on Psalms 22.5). /10/ From Jewish Midrash it is evident that the third day was the day when God delivered the righteous from distress or when events reached their climax. It is also evident that Hos 6.2 was interpreted in terms of resurrection, albeit at the end of history. The mention of the offering of Isaac on the third day is thought to have had a special influence on Christian thought, as we shall see.

A third step in the argument is comparison of other Rabbinical literature concerning the third day with regard to the resurrection (Targum Hosea 6.2; B. Sanhedrin 97a; B. Rosh Hashanah 31a; P. Berakoth 5.2; P. Sanhedrin 11.6; Pirkê de Rabbi Eliezer 51.73b-74a; Tanna de-be Eliyyahu, p. 29). /11/ These passages make it evident that the rabbis were interpreting Hos 6.2 in the sense of an eschatological resurrection.

Now, according to Lehmann, when one brings together the testimonies of the Midrash Rabbah, the rabbinic writings, and the passages from the LXX, then it becomes highly probable that I Cor 15.4 can be illuminated by these texts and their theology. Of particular importance here is the sacrifice of Isaac, which came to have a profound meaning for Jewish theology. In pre-Christian Judaism the sacrifice of Isaac was already brought into connection with the Passover. He became a symbol of submission and self-sacrifice to God. The offering of Isaac was conceived to have salvific worth. In the blood of the sacrifices, God saw and remembered the sacrifice of Isaac and so continued His blessing of Israel. According to Lehmann, this exegesis of Gen 22 leaves traces in Rom 4.17, 25; 8.32 and Heb 11.17-19. This last text particularly relates the resurrection of Jesus to the sacrifice of Isaac. When we consider the formula in I Cor 15, with its Semitic background, then it is probable that

the expression 'on the third day' reflects the influence of
Jewish traditions that later came to be written in Talmud and
Midrash. Thus, 'on the third day' does not mark the discovery
of the empty tomb or the first appearance, nor is it indeed any
time indicator at all, but rather it is the day of God's
deliverance and victory. It tells us that God did not leave the
Righteous One in distress, but raised him up and so ushered in
a new eon.

Lehmann's case is well-documented and very persuasive;
but doubt begins to arise when we inquire concerning the *dates* of
the citations from Talmud and Midrash. /12/ For all of them are
hundreds of years later than the New Testament period. Midrash
Rabbah, which forms the backbone of Lehmann's case, is a
collection from the fourth to the sixth centuries. Pirḳê de
Rabbi Eliezer is a collection from the outgoing eighth century.
The Midrash on Psalm 22 contains the opinions of the Amoraim,
rabbinical teachers of the third to the fifth centuries. The
Babylonian Talmud and the so-called Jerusalem Talmud are the
fruit of the discussions and elaborations of these Amoraim on
the Mishnah, which was redacted, arranged, and revised by Rabbi
Judah ha-Nasi about the beginning of the third century. The
Mishnah itself, despite its length, never once quotes Hos 6.2;
Gen 22.4, 42.17; Jonah 2.1; or any other of the passages in
question which mention the third day. The Targum on Hosea, says
McArthur, is associated with Jonathan b. Uzziel of the first
century; but this ascription is quite uncertain and in any case
tells us nothing concerning Hos 6.2 in particular, since the
Targum as a whole involves a confluence of early and late
material. Thus all the citations concerning the significance of
the third day and interpreting Hos 6.2 in terms of an
eschatological resurrection may well stem from literature
centuries removed from the New Testament period.

Lehmann believes that these citations embody traditions
that go back orally prior to the Christian era. But if that is
the case then should not we expect to confront these motifs in
Jewish literature contemporaneous with the New Testament times,
namely, the Apocrypha and Pseudepigrapha? One would especially
expect to confront the third day motif in the apocalyptic works.
In fact, it is conspicuously absent. The book of I Enoch, which
is quoted in Jude, had more influence on the New Testament
writers than any other apocryphal or pseudepigraphic work and is
a valuable source of information concerning Judaism from 200 BC
to AD 100. In this work the eschatological resurrection is

associated with the number seven, not three (91.15-16; 93).
Similarly in IV Ezra, a first century compilation, the
eschatological resurrection takes place after seven days
(7.26-44). A related work from the second half of the first
century and a good representative of Jewish thought
contemporaneous with the New Testament, II Baruch gives no
indication of the day of the resurrection at history's end
(50-51). Neither does II Macc 7.9-42; 12.43-45 or the Testament
of the Twelve Patriarchs (Judah) 25.1, 4; (Zebulun) 10.2;
(Benjamin) 10.6-18. All these works, which stem from
intertestamental or New Testament times, have a doctrine of
eschatological resurrection, but not one of them knows of the
third day motif. Evidently the number seven was thought to
have greater divine import than the number three (cf. Rev 1.20;
6.1; 8.2; 15.1, 7). In II Macc 5.14; 11.18 we find 'three days'
and 'third day' mentioned in another context, but their meaning
is wholly non-theological, indicating only 'a short time' or
'the day after tomorrow.' Lehmann's case would be much stronger
were he able to find passages in Jewish literature contemporary
with the New Testament which employ the third day motif or
associate the resurrection with the third day. It appears that
this interpretation is a peculiarity of later rabbinical
exegesis of the Talmudic period.

    Moreover, there seems to be no indication that the New
Testament writers were aware of such exegesis. Lehmann states
that the conception of the offering of Isaac as a salvific event
is characteristic of the New Testament. But this is not the
question; the issue is whether the interpretation of the
offering of Isaac *on the third day* plays a role in the New
Testament. Here the evidence is precisely to the contrary:
Rom 4.17, 25 not only have nothing to do with the offering of
Isaac (it is to Gen 15, not 22 that Paul turns for his doctrine
of justification by faith), but refer to Jesus's resurrection
without mentioning the third day; Rom 8.32 makes no explicit
mention of Isaac and no mention, implicit or explicit, of the
resurrection, not to speak of the third day; Heb 11.17-19 does
not in fact explicitly use Isaac as a type of Christ, but more
importantly does not in any way mention the third day. This
latter passage seems to be crucial, for in this passage, of all
places, one would expect the mention of the third day theme in
connection with the resurrection. But it does not appear. This
suggests that the connection of the sacrifice of Isaac with a
third day motif was not yet known. In the other passage in which
the offering of Isaac is employed (James 2.21-23), there is also
no mention of the third day motif. (And James even goes on to

use the illustration of Rahab the harlot and the spies, again
without mentioning the three day theme, as did later Rabbinic
exegesis.) Hence, the appeal to the offering of Isaac as
evidence that the New Testament knows of the rabbinic exegesis
concerning the theological significance of the third day is
counter-productive.

Finally, Lehmann's interpretation labors under the same
difficulty as the fourth hypothesis, namely, it *requires* that
the gospel traditions concerning the discovery of the empty tomb
and the first appearances be false. For if these traditions
are accurate, then the events of Easter morning could not but
have had an effect on when the early believers thought that the
resurrection had occurred. Thus, insofar as the gospel
traditions are thought to be credible, Lehmann's theory is
undermined.

Suppose it is objected that these traditions are in fact
false. It seems to me that the question which then needs to be
asked is whether the disciples would have adopted the language
of the third day. For suppose the first appearance of Christ
was to Peter a week later as he was fishing in Galilee. Would
the believers then have said that Jesus was raised on the third
day rather than, say, the seventh? Lehmann says yes; for the
'third day' is not meant in any sense as a time indicator, but
is a purely theological concept. But were the disciples so
speculative? Certainly Luke understands the third day as a time
indicator, for he writes 'But on the first day of the week. . . .
That very day. . . . it is now the third day. . . . the Christ
should suffer and on the third day rise from the dead' (Lk 24.1,
13, 21, 46). Lehmann and Bode's response is that Luke as a
Gentile did not understand the theological significance of the
third day, which would have been clear to his Jewish
contemporaries, and so mistook it as a time indicator. /13/ This
cannot but make one feel rather uneasy about Lehmann's hypothesis
for it involves isolating Luke from all his Jewish contemporaries
And I suspect that this dichotomy between historical understandin
and theological significance is an import from the twentieth
century. The Rabbis cited in the Talmud and Midrash no doubt
believed both that the events in question really happened on the
third day and that they were theologically significant, for they
include in their lists of events that occurred on the third day
not only events in which the third day was important
theologically (as in the giving of the law) but also events in
which the third day was not charged with theological significance

(as in Rahab and the spies). There is no reason to think that
the New Testament writers did not think Jesus actually rose on
the third day; John, for example, certainly seems to take the
three day figure as a time indicator by contrasting it with the
46 years it took to build the temple (John 2.20). But in this
case, it is doubtful that they would have adopted the language
of the third day unless the Easter events really did take place
on the third day. This suggests that while the LXX may have
provided the *language* for the dating of the resurrection, the
historical events of Easter provided the *basis* for dating the
resurrection. The events of Easter happened 'on the first day
of the week,' but the language of the 'third day' was adopted
because (1) the first day of the week was in fact the third day
subsequent to the crucifixion, and (2) the third day in the LXX
was a day of climax and of God's deliverance.

I think this is the most likely account of the matter.
This means that the phrase 'on the third day' in the formula of
I Cor 15 is a time indicator for the events of Easter, including
the empty tomb, employing the language of the Old Testament
concerning God's acts of deliverance and victory on the third
day, perhaps with texts like Jonah 2.11 and Hos 6.2 especially
in mind. The phrase is a fusion of historical facts plus
theological tradition.

Paul's Knowledge of the Empty Tomb
On the basis of our study of the phrases 'he was buried'
and 'on the third day,' therefore, we may conclude that Paul
accepted an empty tomb as a matter of course. Paul certainly
believed that the grave was empty. But did he *know* the empty
tomb of Jesus? Here we must go outside the confines of I Cor 15
and take a larger view of the historical context in which Paul
moved. We know from Paul's own letters that Paul was in
Jerusalem three years after his conversion, and that he stayed
with Peter two weeks and also spoke with James (Gal 1.18-19).
Therefore Peter, with whom Paul spoke during those two weeks in
Jerusalem, must have also believed the tomb was empty. A Jew
could not think otherwise. Therefore, the Christian community
also, of which Peter was the leader, must have believed in the
empty tomb. But that can only mean that the tomb was empty.
For not only would the disciples not believe in a resurrection
if the corpse were still in the grave, but they could never have
proclaimed the resurrection either under such circumstances.
But if the tomb was empty, then it is unthinkable that Paul,
being in the city for two weeks six years later and after that
often in contact with the Christian community there, should

never hear a thing about the empty tomb. Indeed, is it too
much to imagine that during his two week stay Paul would want
to visit the place where the Lord lay? Ordinary human feelings
would suggest such a thing. In fact, it could be argued that
if Paul was in Jerusalem prior to his trip to Damascus, as Acts
reports, then he probably would have heard of the empty tomb
then, not, indeed, from the Christians, but from the Jewish
authorities in whose employ he was. For even if the Christians
in their enthusiasm had not checked to see if the tomb of Jesus
were empty, the Jewish authorities could be guilty of no such
oversight. So ironically, Paul may have known of the empty tomb
even before his conversion. So I think that it is highly
probable that Paul not only accepted the empty tomb, but that
he also knew that the actual grave of Jesus was empty.

The Evidence of the Gospels

With this conclusion in hand, we may now proceed to the
gospel accounts of the discovery of the empty tomb to see if
they supply us with any additional reliable information. Found
in all four gospels, the empty tomb narrative shows sure
evidence of traditional material in the agreements between the
Synoptics and John. It is certain that traditions included that
on the first day of the week women, at least Mary Magdalene,
came to the tomb early and found the stone taken away; that they
saw an angelic appearance; that they informed the disciples, at
least Peter, who went, found the tomb empty with the grave
clothes lying still in the grave, and returned home puzzled;
that the women saw a physical appearance of Jesus shortly
thereafter; and that Jesus gave them certain instructions for
the disciples. Not all the Synoptics record all these
traditions; but John does, and at least one Synoptic confirms
each incident; thus, given John's probable independence from
the Synoptics, these incidents are traditional. That is not to
say they are historical.

A Pre-Markan Empty Tomb Tradition
The story of the discovery of the empty tomb was in all
likelihood the conclusion or at least part of the pre-Markan
passion story. About the only argument against this is the
juxtaposition of the lists in Mark 15.47 and 16.1, which really
affords no grounds for such a conclusion at all. /14/ At the
very most, this could only force one to explain one or the other
as an editorial addition; it would not serve to break off the
empty tomb story from the passion narrative. Pesch argues
convincingly, I think, that the empty tomb story is no

independent pericope, but is bound up with the passion story
and the immediate context and is tied to the burial story by
verbal and syntactical similarities. /15/

But perhaps the most telling argument in favor of 16.1-8's
belonging to the passion story is that it is unthinkable that
the passion story could end in defeat and death with no mention
of the empty tomb or resurrection. The passion story is
incomplete without victory at the end. Confirmation of the
inclusion of 16.1-8 in the pre-Markan passion story is the
remarkable correspondence to the course of events described in
I Cor 15: died--was buried--rose--appeared; all these elements
appear in the pre-Markan passion story, including Christ's
appearance (v 7). Thus, there are very strong reasons for
taking the empty tomb account as part of the pre-Markan passion
story.

Like the burial story, the account of the discovery of
the empty tomb is remarkably restrained. Bultmann states,
'. . . Mark's presentation is extremely reserved, in so far as
the resurrection and the appearance of the risen Lord are not
recounted.' /16/ Nauck observes that many theological motifs
that might be expected are lacking in the story; (1) the
proof from prophecy, (2) the in-breaking of the new eon, (3) the
ascension of Jesus's spirit or his descent into hell, (4) the
nature of the risen body, and (5) the use of Christological
titles. /17/ Although kerygmatic speech appears in the mouth
of the angel, the fact of the discovery of the empty tomb is
not kerygmatically colored. All these factors point to a very
old tradition concerning the discovery of the empty tomb.

The Anointing of the Body

Mark begins the story by relating that when the sabbath
was past (=Saturday night), the women bought spices to anoint
the body. The next morning they went to the tomb. The women's
intention to anoint the body has caused no end of controversy.
It is often assumed that the women were coming to finish the
rushed job done by Joseph on Friday evening; John, who has a
thorough burial, mentions no intention of anointing. It is
often said that the 'Eastern climate' would make it impossible
to anoint a corpse after three days. And it would not have
violated sabbath law to anoint a body on the sabbath, instead
of waiting until Sunday (Mishnah Shabbat 23.5). Besides, the
body had been already anointed in advance (Mark 14.8). And
why do the women think of the stone over the entrance only
after they are underway? They should have realized the venture

was futile.

But what in fact were the women about? There is no
indication that they were going to complete a task poorly
done. Mark gives no hint of hurry or incompleteness at the
burial. That Luke says the women saw 'how' the body was laid
(Luke 29.55) does not imply that the women saw a lack which they
wished to remedy; it could mean merely they saw that it was
laid in a tomb, not buried, as was customary for criminals, thus
making possible a visit to anoint the body. The fact that John
does not mention the intention of anointing proves little,
since Matthew does not mention it either. So there seems to be
no indication that the women were going to complete Jesus's
burial. In fact what the women were probably doing is precisely
that described in the Mishnah, namely the use of aromatic oils
and perfumes that could be rubbed on or simply poured over the
body. Even if the corpse had begun to decay, that would not
prevent this simple act of devotion by these women. This same
devotion could have induced them to go to try together to open
the tomb, despite the stone. (That Mark only mentions the stone
here does not mean they had not thought of it before; it serves
a literary purpose here to prepare for v 4.) The opening of tombs
to allow late visitors to view the body or to check against
apparent death was Jewish practice, /18/ so the women's
intention was not extraordinary. It is true that anointing
could be done on the sabbath, but this was only for a person
lying on the death bed in his home, not for a body already
wrapped and entombed in a sealed grave outside the city.
Blinzler points out that, odd as it may seem, it would have been
against the Jewish law even to carry the *aromata* to the grave
site, for this was 'work' (Jer 17.21-22; Shabbath 8.1)! /19/
Thus, Luke's comment that the women rested on the sabbath would
probably be a correct description.

Sometimes it is asserted that Matthew leaves out the
anointing motif because he realized one could not anoint a corpse
after three days in that climate. But Mark himself, who lived
in the Mediterranean climate, would surely also realize this
fact, if it be true. In point of fact, Jerusalem, being 700
meters above sea level, can be quite cool in April; interesting
is the entirely incidental detail mentioned by John that at
night in Jerusalem at that time it was cold, so much so that the
servants and officers of the Jews had made a fire and were
standing around it warming themselves (John 18.18). Add to this
the facts that the body, interred Friday evening, had actually
been in the tomb only a night, a day, and a night when the women

came to anoint it early Sunday morning, that a rock-hewn tomb
in a cliff side would stay naturally cool, and that the body
may have already been packed around with aromatic spices, and
one can see that the intention to anoint the body cannot in any
way be ruled out. The argument that it had been anointed in
advance would, if anything, actually favor the historicity
of this intention, for after 14.8 Mark would have little
reason to invent a second and superfluous anointing by the
women.

The Women at the Tomb
The gospels all agree that around dawn the women visited
the tomb. Which women?--Mark says the two Maries and Salome;
Matthew mentions only the two Maries; Luke says the two Maries,
Joanna, and other women; John mentions only Mary Magdalene.
There seems to be no difficulty in imagining a handful of women
going to the tomb. Even John records Mary's words as 'we do
not know where they have laid him' (John 20.2). It is true that
Semitic usage could permit the first person plural to mean
simply 'I' (cf. John 3.11, 32), but not only does this seem
rather artificial in this context, but then we would expect
the plural as well in v 13. In any case, this ignores the
Synoptic tradition and only makes an isolated grammatical point.
When we have independent traditions that women visited the tomb,
then the weight of probability falls decisively in favor of
Mary's 'we' being the remnant of a tradition of more than one
woman. John has perhaps focused on her for dramatic effect.

Arriving at the tomb the women find the stone rolled away.
According to the Synoptics the women actually enter the tomb
and see an angelic vision. John, however, says Mary Magdalene
runs to find Peter and the Beloved Disciple, and only after
they come and go from the tomb does she see the angels. Mark's
'young man' is intended to be an angel, as is evident from his
white robe and the women's reaction. /20/ Although some critics
want to regard the angel as a Markan redaction, the exclusion
of the angelophany from the pre-Markan passion story is
arbitrary, since the earliest Christians certainly believed in
the reality of angels and demons and would not hesitate to
relate such an account as embodied in vv 5-8. It is quite
unlikely that the pre-Markan tradition lacked the angel, for
the climax of the story comes with his words in vv 5-6, and
without him the tomb is ambiguous in its meaning. John confirms
that there was a tradition of the women's seeing angels at the
tomb, especially in light of the fact that he keeps the angels
in his account even though their role is oddly superfluous.

Many scholars wish to see v 7 as a Markan interpolation
into the pre-Markan tradition. But the evidence for this
seems weak, in my opinion. The fundamental reason for taking
16.7 as an insertion is the belief that 14.28 is an insertion,
to which 16.7 refers. But what is the evidence that 14.28 is
an interpolation? The basic argument is that vv 27 and 29 read
smoothly without it. /21/ This, however, is the weakest of
reasons for suspecting an insertion (especially since the
verses read just as smoothly when v 28 is left in), for the
fact that a sentence can be dropped out of a context without
destroying its flow may be entirely coincidental and no
indication that the sentence was not originally part of that
context. In fact there are positive reasons for believing
14.28 is not an insertion. Jeremias points out that it
continues the image of the shepherd in v 27; προάγειν is a
technical term of shepherding (cf. John 10.4, 27). The
emphasis of Jesus's words lies not on v 27, but on v 28: the
sheep will not only be scattered but reassembled. /22/ Pesch
explains that through the use of the *passivum divinum*, the
death and resurrection through God are counter-balanced: God
strikes the shepherd, but raises him up. In contrast to the
scattering of the disciples is Jesus's reassembling them in
Galilee. /23/ Furthermore, it is not just 14.28 and 16.7 that
presuppose each other; it is death *and* resurrection of Christ
that is predicted, so that 14.27 and 16.6 belong together as
well. It is futile to object that in 14.29 Peter only takes
offense at v 27, not v 28, for of course he only objects to
Jesus's telling him they will all fall away, and not to Jesus's
promise to go before them (cf. the same pattern in 8.31-32).
On this logic one would have to leave out not only the
prediction of the resurrection, but also the striking of the
shepherd, since Peter jumps over that as well. There seem to
be thus no good reasons to regard 14.28 as a redactional
insertion and good reasons to see it as firmly welded in place.
If there is an insertion, it is all of vv 27-31; cf. Luke 22.31-
34; John 13.36-38. This means that 16.7 is also in place in
the pre-Markan tradition of the passion story. The content of
the verse reveals the knowledge of a resurrection appearance of
Christ to the disciples in Galilee.

Mark 16.8 has caused a great deal of consternation, not
only because it seems to be a very odd note on which to end a
book, but also because all the other gospels agree that the
women did report to the disciples. But the reaction of fear
and awe in the presence of the divine is a typical Markan
characteristic. /24/ The silence of the women was surely meant

to be just temporary, /25/ otherwise the account itself could not be part of the pre-Markan passion story.

The Disciples' Visit to the Tomb

According to Luke the disciples do not believe the women's report (Luke 24.11). But Luke and John agree that Peter and at least one other disciple rise and run to the tomb to check it out (Luke 24.12, 24; John 20.2-10). Although Luke 24.12 was regarded by Westcott and Hort as a Western non-interpolation, its presence in the later discovered p^{75} has convinced an increasing number of scholars of its authenticity. There are no good reasons for denying that it was originally part of the Gospel of Luke. This is of exceeding significance, for it proves that there was tradition not only that the disciples were in Jerusalem (*contra* the flight to Galilee hypothesis), but also that they knew of the empty tomb. That Luke and John share generically the same tradition is evident not only from the close similarity of Luke 24.12 to John's account, but also from the fact that John 20.1 most nearly resembles Luke in the number, selection, and order of the elements narrated than any other gospel. /26/ Most recent works agree that the visit of the disciples to the tomb is traditional.

Luke 24.24 makes it clear that Peter did not go to the tomb alone; John names his companion as the Beloved Disciple. This would suggest that John intends this disciple to be a historical person, and his identification could be correct. /27/ The authority of the Beloved Disciple stands behind the gospel as the witness to the accuracy of what is written therein (John 21.24), and the identification of his role in the disciples' visit to the empty tomb could be the reminiscence of an eyewitness. So although only Peter was named in the tradition, accompanied by an anonymous disciple(s), the author of the fourth gospel claimed to know who this unnamed disciple was and identifies him. Whether this identification is correct or not, what seems to be clear is that the Beloved Disciple was thought to be a real historical person who went with Peter to the empty tomb and whose memories stand behind the fourth gospel as their authentication.

If the Beloved Disciple in chap. 20 is then conceived as a historical person, is his presence an unhistorical, redactional addition inserted by some later editor? The fact that v 8 is in style and content from the evangelist suggests that this is not so. That ὃν ἐφύλει instead of ὃν ἠγάπα is used

in v 2 also indicates that the evangelist himself wrote these
words and not a later redactor. In fact the unity and
continuity of vv 2-10 preclude that the evangelist wrote only
of Peter and Mary's visit and that the Beloved Disciple was
artfully inserted by a later editor. Luke 24.24 reveals that
Peter did not go to the tomb alone, so one cannot exclude that
the Beloved Disciple went with him. Thus, the evangelist, who
knew the Beloved Disciple and wrote on the basis of his
memories, includes his part in these events.

If it be said that the evangelist simply invented the
figure of the Beloved Disciple, then 21.24 becomes a deliberate
falsehood, the close affinities between chaps. 1-20 and 21 are
ignored, it becomes difficult to explain how the person of the
Beloved Disciple should come to exist and why he is inserted
in the narratives, and the widespread concern over his death is
rendered unintelligible. The evangelist and the gospel
certainly stem out of the same circle that appended chap. 21
and adds its signature in 21.24c. Therefore, it seems to me
that the role of the Beloved Disciple in 20.2-10 can only be
that of a historical participant whose memories fill out the
tradition received. There seems to be no plausible way of
denying the historicity of the Beloved Disciple's role in the
visit to the empty tomb. /28/

It might be urged against the historicity of the disciples'
visit to the tomb that the disciples had fled Friday night to
Galilee and so were not present in Jerusalem. But not only does
Mark 14.50 not contemplate this, but it seems unreasonable to
think that the disciples, fleeing from the garden, would return
to where they were staying, grab their things, and keep on
going all the way back to Galilee. And scholars who support
such a flight must prove that the denial of Peter is
unhistorical, since it presupposes the presence of the disciples
in Jerusalem. But there seems to be no good reason to regard
this tradition, attested in all four gospels, as unhistorical.
In its favor is the fact that it is improbable that the early
Christians should invent a tale concerning the apostasy of the
man who was their leader.

Sometimes it is said that the disciples could not have
been in Jerusalem, since they are not mentioned in the trial,
execution, or burial stories. But could it not be that the
disciples were hiding for fear of the Jews, just as the gospels
indicate? There is no reason why the passion story would want
to portray the church's leaders as cowering in seclusion while

only the women dared to venture about openly, were this not
historical; the disciples could have been made to flee to
Galilee while the women stayed behind. This would even have
had the advantage of making the appearances unexpected by
keeping the empty tomb unknown to the disciples. But, no, the
pre-Markan passion story says, 'But go, tell his disciples and
Peter that he is going before you to Galilee; there you will
see him. . .' (Mark 16.7). So the disciples were probably in
Jerusalem, but lying low.

Besides this, it is not true that the disciples are
missing entirely from the scene. All the gospels record the
denial of Peter while the trial of Jesus was proceeding; John
adds that there was another disciple with him, perhaps the
Beloved Disciple (John 18.15). According to Luke, at the
execution of Jesus, 'all his acquaintances. . . stood at a
distance and saw these things' (Luke 23.49). John says that
the Beloved Disciple was at the cross with Jesus's mother and
bore witness to what happened there (John 19.26-27, 35). So
it is not true that the disciples are completely absent during
the low point in the course of events prior to the resurrection.
There are therefore a number of traditions that the disciples
were in Jerusalem during the weekend; that at least two of
them visited the tomb cannot therefore be excluded.

It is often asserted that the story of the disciples'
visit to the tomb is an apologetic development designed to
shore up the weak witness of the women. Not only does there
seem to be no proof for this, but against it stand the
traditions that the disciples were in Jerusalem. For if the
women did find the tomb empty on Sunday morning, and reported
this to the disciples, then it seems to me implausible that the
disciples would sit idly by not caring to check out the women's
news. That one or two of them should run back to the tomb with
the women, even if only to satisfy their doubts that the women
were mistaken, seems very likely. Hence, I see no good reason
to deny the story's historical credibility.

Assessment and Conclusion

Having examined the testimony of Paul and the gospels
concerning the empty tomb of Jesus, what is the evidence in
favor of its historicity?

1. *Paul's testimony implies the historicity of the empty
tomb*. Paul accepted the empty tomb of Jesus, as is evident

from the sequence 'died--was buried--was raised' and from the
expression 'on the third day' in the formula in I Cor 15. Few
facts could be more certain than that Paul at least *believed*
in the empty tomb. But the question now presses, how is it
historically possible for the apostle Paul to have accepted the
empty tomb of Jesus if in fact the tomb was not empty? Paul
was in Jerusalem six years after the events themselves. The
tomb must have been empty by then. But more than that, Peter,
James, and the other Christians in Jerusalem with whom Paul
spoke must have also accepted that the tomb was found empty at
the resurrection. It would have been impossible for the
resurrection faith to survive in face of a tomb containing the
corpse of Jesus. The disciples could not have adhered to the
resurrection; even if they had, scarcely any one would have
believed them; and their Jewish opponents could have exposed
the whole affair as a poor joke by displaying the body of
Jesus.

Moreover, all this aside, had the tomb not been empty, then
Christian theology would have taken an entirely different
route than it did, trying to explain how resurrection could
still be possible, though the body remained in the grave. But
neither Christian theology nor apologetics ever had to face
such a problem. To my mind, it seems inconceivable that Pauline
theology concerning the bodily resurrection could have taken
the direction that it did had the tomb not been empty from the
start. Thus Paul's acceptance of the empty tomb is strong
evidence in favor of its historicity.

2. *The presence of the empty tomb pericope in the
pre-Markan passion story supports its historicity*. The empty
tomb story was part of, perhaps the close of, the pre-Markan
passion story. According to Pesch, /29/ geographical
references, personal names, and the use of Galilee as a horizon
all point to Jerusalem as the fount of the pre-Markan passion
story. As to its age, Paul's Last Supper tradition (I Cor 11.
23-25) presupposes the pre-Markan passion account; therefore,
the latter must have originated in the first years of existence
of the Jerusalem *Urgemeinde*. Confirmation of this is found in
the fact that the pre-Markan passion story speaks of the 'high
priest' without using his name (14.53, 54, 60, 61, 63). This
implies (nearly necessitates, according to Pesch) that Caiaphas
was still the high priest when the pre-Markan passion story
was being told, since then there would have been no need to
mention his name. Since Caiaphas was high priest from A.D. 18-
37, the *terminus ante quem* for the origin of the tradition is

A.D. 37.   Such an early date is also suggested by the
correspondence between the events listed in the pre-Pauline
formula in I Cor 15 and the closing events of the pre-Markan
passion story. The third line of the formula corresponds to
the story of the discovery of the empty tomb, the ἐγήγερται
mirroring the ἠγέρθη. Since the formula probably antedates
Paul's visit to Jerusalem in A.D. 36-38, /30/ the traditions
encapsulated therein must be equally as old, which would go to
support Pesch's dating.

Now if this is the case, then any attempt to construe the
empty tomb account as an unhistorical legend seems doomed to
failure. It is astounding that Pesch himself can try to
convince us that the pre-Markan empty tomb story is a fusion
of three *Gattungen* from the history of religions: door-opening
miracles, epiphany stories, and stories of seeking but not
finding persons who have been raised from the dead! /31/ On
the contrary: given the temporal (even if not as old as Pesch
argues) and geographical proximity of the origin of the
pre-Markan passion story to the events themselves, it would
seem most plausible to regard the empty tomb story as
substantially accurate historically.

3. *The use of 'the first day of the week' instead of 'on
the third day' points to the primitiveness of the tradition.*
The tradition of the discovery of the empty tomb is probably
very old and very primitive because it lacks altogether the
third day motif, which is itself extremely old, as evident by
its appearance in I Cor 15.4. According to Bode, if the empty
tomb narrative were a late and legendary account, then it could
hardly have avoided being cast in the prominent, ancient, and
accepted third day motif./32/ This can only mean that the
empty tomb tradition ante-dates the coming to prominence of the
third day motif in the church. This conclusion is strengthened
by the fact that τῇ μιᾷ τῶν σαββάτων, while being quite awkward
Greek, would be smooth and natural in Aramaic; this Semitism
lends weight to the hypothesis of a primitive tradition embodied
here. And once more, I would argue that the proximity of the
tradition to the events themselves makes it idle to regard the
empty tomb as a legend. It makes it probable that on the first
day of the week the tomb was indeed found empty.

4. *The nature of the narrative itself is theologically
unadorned and non-apologetic.* The resurrection is not
described, and we have noted the lack of later theological
motifs that a late legend might be expected to contain. This

suggests the account is primitive and factual, even if
dramatization occurs in the role of the angel. Very often
contemporary theologians urge that the empty tomb is not a
historical proof for the resurrection because for the disciples
it was in itself ambiguous and not a proof. However, that fact
seems to lend weight to the historical credibility of the
empty tomb story precisely because it was not an apologetic
device of early Christians. Rather it was, as Wilckens nicely
puts it, 'a trophy of God's victory.' /33/ The very fact that
they saw in it no proof insures that the narrative is
substantially uncolored by apologetic motifs and in its
primitive form.

5. *The discovery of the tomb by women is highly probable*.
Given the low status of women in Jewish society and their lack
of qualification to serve as legal witnesses, /34/ the most
plausible explanation, in light of the gospels' conviction that
the disciples were in Jerusalem over the weekend, why women and
not the male disciples were made discoverers of the empty tomb
is that the women were in fact the ones who made this discovery.
This conclusion is confirmed by the fact that there is no reason
why the later Christian church would wish to humiliate its
leaders by having them hiding in cowardice in Jerusalem, while
the women boldly carry out their last devotions to Jesus's
body, unless this were in fact the truth. Their motive of
anointing the body by pouring oils over it is entirely
plausible and was probably the reason why the women went to the
tomb. Furthermore, the listing of the women's names again seems
to preclude unhistorical legend at the story's core, for these
persons were known in the *Urgemeinde* and so could not be easily
associated with a false account.

6. *The investigation of the empty tomb by the disciples
is historically probable*. Behind the fourth gospel stands the
Beloved Disciple, whose reminiscences fill out the traditions
employed. The visit of the disciples to the empty tomb is
therefore attested not only in tradition but by this disciple.
His testimony has therefore the same first hand character as
Paul's and ought to be accepted as equally reliable. We thus
possess testimony for the empty tomb that cannot be disregarded.
The historicity of the disciples' visit is also made likely by
the plausibility of the denial of Peter tradition, for if he
was in Jerusalem, then having heard the women's report he would
quite likely haved checked it out. The inherent implausibility
of and absence of any evidence for the disciples' flight to
Galilee render it highly likely that they were in Jerusalem,

which fact makes the visit to the tomb also likely.

7. *It would have been impossible for the disciples to*
proclaim the resurrection in Jerusalem had the tomb not been
empty. The empty tomb is a *sine qua non* of the resurrection.
The notion that Jesus rose from the dead with a new body while
his old body lay in the grave is a purely modern conception.
Jewish mentality would never have accepted a division of two
bodies, one in the tomb and one in the risen life. When
therefore the disciples began to preach the resurrection in
Jerusalem, and people responded, and the religious authorities
stood helplessly by, the tomb must have been empty. The fact
that the Christian fellowship, founded on belief in Jesus's
resurrection, could come into existence and flourish in the
very city where he was executed and buried seems to be powerful
evidence for the historicity of the empty tomb.

8. *The Jewish polemic presupposes the empty tomb.* From
Matthew's story of the guard at the tomb (Matt 27.62-66;
28.11-15), which was aimed at refuting the widespread Jewish
allegation that the disciples had stolen Jesus's body, we
learn that the Christians' Jewish opponents did not deny that
Jesus's tomb was empty. When the disciples began to preach
that Jesus was risen, the Jews responded with the charge that
the disciples had taken away his body, to which the Christians
retorted that the guard would have prevented any such theft.
The Jews then asserted that the guard had fallen asleep and
that the disciples stole the body while the guard slept. The
Christian answer was that the Jews had bribed the guard to say
this, and so the controversy stood at the time of Matthew's
writing. The point of interest for us is not the historicity
of the guard or the bribe, which nearly all New Testament
scholars reject. Rather the point is that the whole heated
polemic presupposes the empty tomb. Mahoney's objection, that
the Matthaean narrative presupposes only the preaching of the
resurrection, and that the Jews argued as they did only because
it would have been 'colorless' to say the tomb was unknown or
lost, fails to perceive the true force of the argument. /35/
The point is that the Jews did not respond to the preaching of
the resurrection by pointing to the tomb of Jesus or exhibiting
his corpse, but entangled themselves in a hopeless series of
absurdities trying to explain away his empty tomb. The fact
that the enemies of Christianity felt obliged to explain away
the empty tomb by the theft hypothesis shows not only that the
tomb was known (confirmation of the burial story), but that it
was *empty*. (Oddly enough, Mahoney contradicts himself when he

later asserts that it was more promising for the Jews to make
fools of the disciples through the gardener-misplaced-the-body
theory than to make them clever hoaxers through the theft
hypothesis. /36/ So it was not apparently the fear of being
'colorless' that induced the Jewish authorities to resort to
the desperate expedient of the theft hypothesis.) The
proclamation 'He is risen from the dead' (Matt 27.64) prompted
the Jews to respond, 'His disciples. . . stole him away'
(Matt 28.13). Why? The most probable answer is that they
could not deny that his tomb was empty and had to come up with
an alternative explanation. So they said the disciples stole
the body, and from there the polemic began. Even the gardener-
hypothesis is an attempt to explain away the empty tomb. The
fact that the Jewish polemic never denied that Jesus's tomb
was empty, but only tried to explain it away, seems to be
compelling evidence that the tomb was in fact empty.

Taken together these eight considerations furnish good
evidence that the tomb of Jesus was actually found empty on
Sunday morning by a small group of his women followers. As a
simple historical fact, there seems to be no good reason to
deny this. As Van Daalen has remarked, it is extremely
difficult to object to the fact of the empty tomb on historical
grounds; most objectors do so on the basis of theological or
philosophical considerations. /37/ But these, of course,
cannot change objective, empirical fact. And, interestingly,
more and more New Testament scholars seem to be realizing this.
According to Jacob Kremer, who has specialized in the study of
the resurrection, 'By far, most exegetes hold firmly. . . to
the reliability of the biblical statements concerning the empty
tomb. . .', /38/ and he lists 28 prominent scholars in support:
Blank, Blinzler, Bode, von Campenhausen, Delorme, Dhanis,
Grundmann, Hengel, Lehmann, Léon-Dufour, Lichtenstein, Mánek,
Martini, Mussner, Nauck, Rengstorff, Ruckstuhl, Schenke,
Schmidt, K. Schubert, Schwank, Schweizer, Seidensticker,
Strobel, Stuhlmacher, Trilling, Vögtle, Wilckens. I can think
of at least 17 more that he neglected to mention: Benoit,
Brown, Clark, Dunn, Ellis, Gundry, Hooke, Jeremias, Klappert,
Ladd, Lane, Marshall, Moule, Perry, J. A. T. Robinson,
Schnackenburg, and Vermes. Schnackenburg concurs with Kremer's
judgment: '. . . most exegetes accept the historicity of the
empty tomb, so that this question is not the decisive point in
discussion about the resurrection.' /39/ Thus, in the opinion
of most contemporary scholars, the empty tomb has moved from
the realm of offense and embarrassment to that of
straightforward fact.

Notes

/1/ This research was funded through a grant from the Alexander von Humboldt Foundation and conducted at the Universität München and Cambridge University. The full results of this research will appear in two forthcoming volumes: *The Historical Argument for the Resurrection of Jesus* and *The Historicity of the Resurrection of Jesus*.

/2/ Hans Grass, *Ostergeschehen und Osterberichte* (4th ed.; Göttingen: Vandenhoeck & Ruprecht, 1970), 146-7.

/3/ See Werner Kramer, *Christos, Kyrios, Gottessohn* (ATANT 44; Stuttgart and Zürich: Zwingli Verlag, 1963), 15; Franz Mussner, *Die Auferstehung Jesu* (BH 7; München: Kösel Verlag, 1969), 60-1; Ulrich Wilckens, *Auferstehung* (Stuttgart and Berlin: Kreuz Verlag, 1970), 20; Joseph Schmitt, 'Le "milieu" littéraire dans la "tradition" citée dans I Cor., XV, 3b-5,' in *Resurrexit* (ed. Edouard Dhanis; Rome: Editrice Libreria Vaticana, 1974), 178. The four-fold ὅτι serves to emphasize equally each of the chronologically successive events, thus prohibiting the subordination of one event to another.

/4/ This phrase implies a bodily resurrection, according to Archibald Robertson and Alfred Plummer, *First Epistle of Saint Paul to the Corinthians* (2d ed; ICC; Edinburgh: T & T Clark, 1967), 351; Jacob Kremer, 'Zur Diskussion über "das leere Grab",' in *Resurrexit*, 144; Robert H. Gundry, *Soma in Biblical Theology* (Cambridge: Cambridge University Press, 1976), 177; cf. Paul Hoffmann, *Die Toten in Christus* (3d rev. ed.; NTA 2; Münster: Aschendorff, 1978), 180-5.

/5/ Grass, *Ostergeschehen*, 172.

/6/ See discussion in William Lane Craig, 'The Bodily Resurrection of Jesus,' in *Gospel Perspectives I: Studies of History and Tradition in the Four Gospels* (ed. R. T. France and David Wenham; Sheffield, England: JSOT Press, 1980), 50-65.

/7/ See Karl Lehmann, *Auferweckt am dritten Tag nach der Schrift* (QD 38; Freiburg: Herder, 1968), 176-261; Edward Lynn Bode, *The First Easter Morning* (AB 45; Rome: Biblical Institute Press, 1970), 110-17; cf. Harvey K. McArthur, '"On the Third Day",' *NTS* 18 (1971): 81-6.

/8/ Lehmann, *Auferweckt*, 262-90; Bode, *Easter*, 119-26.

/9/ Wengst observes that Lehmann actually produces only 25 passages, not 'nearly 30' and of these only nine can be truly said to have the theological significance that Lehmann sees in the third day (Gen 22.4; Ex 19.11, 16; Judg 20.30; I Sam 30.1, 2; II Kings 20.5, 8; Esther 5.1; Hosea 6.2). (Klaus Wengst, *Christologische Formeln und Lieder des Urchristentums* [SNT 7; Gütersloh: Gerd Mohn, 1972], 96.)

/10/ Full citations may be found in Lehmann and MacArthur.

/11/ Full citations may be found in Lehmann and MacArthur.

/12/ Conzelmann dismisses Lehmann's case out of hand on this consideration alone. (Hans Conzelmann, *Der erste Brief an die Korinther* [KEKNT 5; Göttingen: Vandenhoeck & Ruprecht, 1969] 302.) See also Wengst, *Formeln*, 96.

/13/ Lehmann, *Auferweckt*, 174; Bode, *Easter*, 125-6.

/14/ Mark 15.40-41, which first names the women, cannot be an independent piece of tradition, since it makes sense only in its context. But neither can these verses be editorially constructed out of 15.47 and 16.1 because then the appellation 'the younger' is inexplicable, as is the fusion of what would normally designate the wife of James and the wife of Joses into one woman, the mother of James and Joses. But if 15.40-41 are part of the pre-Markan tradition, then so are probably 15.47 and 16.1. For rather than repeat the long identification of Mary in 15.40, the tradition names her by one son in 15.47 and the other in 16.1; thus 15.47 and 16.1 actually presuppose each other's existence. And their juxtaposition is by no means a useless duplication: the omission and re-introduction of Salome's name suggests that the witnesses to the crucifixion, burial, and empty tomb are being here recalled.

/15/ Rudolf Pesch, *Das Markusevangelium* (2 vols.; HTKNT 2; Freiburg: Herder, 1977), 2:519-20.

/16/ Rudolf Bultmann, *Die Geschichte der synoptischen Tradition* (8th ed.; FRLANT 12; Göttingen: Vandenhoeck & Ruprech 1970), 309.

/17/ Wolfgang Nauck, 'Die Bedeutung des leeren Grabes für den Glauben an den Auferstandenen,' *ZNW* 47 (1956): 243-67; also Kremer, '"Grab",' 153.

/18/ Semachoth 8; Ebel Rabbathi 4.11. See further Ernst Lohmeyer, *Das Evangelium des Markus* (KEKNT 2; Göttingen: Vandenhoeck & Ruprecht, 1937), 351.

/19/ Joseph Blinzler, 'Die Grablegung Jesu in historischer Sicht,' in *Resurrexit*, 83.

/20/ On νεανίσκος as angel, cf. II Macc 3.26, 33; Luke 24.4; Gospel of Peter 9; Josephus *Antiquities of the Jews* 5.277. The white robe is traditional for angels (cf. Rev 9.13; 10.1). In Mark fear and awe are the typical response to the divine. The other gospels understood Mark's figure as an angel.

/21/ It is sometimes urged that the Fayum Gospel Fragment, a third century compilation from the gospels which omits v 28, testifies to a tradition lacking this verse. But as a compilation the fragment by its very nature omits material and is no evidence for the absence of v 28 in the passion tradition. See M.-J. Lagrange, *Evangile selon saint Marc* (Paris: Librairie Lecoffre, 1966), 383; William L. Lane, *The Gospel according to Mark* (NLCNT; London: Marshall, Morgan & Scott, 1974), 510; Pesch, *Markusevangelium*, 2:381.

/22/ Joachim Jeremias, *Neutestamentliche Theologie* (2d ed.; Gütersloh: Gerd Mohn, 1973), 282.

/23/ Pesch, *Markusevangelium*, 2:381-2.

/24/ See helpful chart and discussion in Bode, *Easter*, 37-9.

/25/ See the helpful discussion of the women's silence in Bode, *Easter*, pp. 39-44. He distinguishes five possible interpretations: (1) The silence explains why the legend of the empty tomb remained so long unknown. (2) The silence is an instance of Mark's Messianic secret motif. (3) The silence was temporary. (4) The silence served the apologetic purpose of separating the apostles from the empty tomb. (5) The silence is the paradoxical human reaction to divine commands as understood by Mark. But (1) is now widely rejected as implausible, since the empty tomb story is a pre-Markan tradition. (2) is inappropriate in the post-resurrection period

when Jesus may be proclaimed as the Messiah. As for (4), there
is no evidence that the silence was designed to separate the
apostles from the tomb. Mark does not hold that the disciples
had fled back to Galilee independently of the women. So there
is no implication that the disciples saw Jesus without having
heard of the empty tomb. It is pointless to speak of
'apologetics' when Mark does not even imply that the disciples
went to Galilee and saw Jesus without hearing the women's
message, much less draw some apologetic conclusion as a result
of this. In fact there were also traditions that the disciples
did visit the tomb, after the women told them of their discovery,
but Mark breaks off his story before that point. As for (5)
this solution is entirely too subtle, drawing the conclusion
that because people talked when Jesus told them not to,
therefore, the women, having been told to talk, did not.
Therefore (3) is most probable. The fear and silence are Markan
motifs of divine encounter and were not meant to imply an
enduring silence.

/26/ Robert Mahoney, *Two Disciples at the Tomb* (TW 6;
Bern: Herbert Lang, 1974), 209.

/27/ See Raymond E. Brown, *The Gospel according to
John* (AB 29; Garden City, N.Y.: Doubleday & Co., 1970),1119-20.

/28/ I find it implausible either that the Beloved
Disciple should have lied to his students that he was there when
he was not or that the entire Johannine community should lie
in asserting that their master had taken part in certain
historical events when they knew he had not. See excellent
comments by Brown, *John*, 1127-9. Nor do I find plausible
attempts to construe the Beloved Disciple as a mere symbol. For
no agreement can be reached as to what he is intended to
symbolize. (For a survey of the broad field of alternatives,
see Alv Kragerud, *Der Lieblingsjünger im Johannesevangelium*
[Oslo: Osloer Universitätsverlag, 1959], 46-51; Thorwald
Lorenzen, *Der Lieblingsjünger im Johannesevangelium* [SBS 55;
Stuttgart: Katholisches Bibelwerk, 1971], 74-82.) Had the
author intended him to symbolize something else, then he would
surely have made the meaning of the symbol clearer; otherwise it
is pointless. In any case, the fact that a person may be used
as a symbol does not imply that the individual so used is
therefore unhistorical. Peter is certainly a historical person,
the same Peter that we find in the synoptics, and it would be
strange to have him accompanied by a purely symbolic figure who
was not also a historical individual. Finally, in John 21.20-4

the Beloved Disciple is clearly a historical person widely known
in the Christian church as an original disciple who would live
to see the Parousia and whose witness underlies the gospel. He
was either still alive or had just recently died. (That he had
been long dead is excluded by the urgency of v 23.) If he was
still alive, then his being an unhistorical symbol in chap. 20
is impossible, since his witness underlay the gospel, and he
could not have allowed himself to be mistaken for the symbolic
figure invented by the evangelist. By the same token, had he
recently died, then, even if his disciples had written chap. 21,
they could not have mistakenly identified the symbol of chaps.
1-20 with their historical master, since they knew who he was
and whether he had in fact done the things ascribed to the
Beloved Disciple in the gospel. The hypothesis that these
disciples retrojected their master back into the gospel as the
Beloved Disciple is dealt with in the text and would still imply
that the Beloved Disciple is at least meant to be a historical
person, not a mere symbol. Thus, it is difficult to deny the
historicity of the Beloved Disciple's role apart from the
hypothesis of deliberate misrepresentation.

/29/ Pesch, *Markusevangelium*, 2:21; cf. 2:364-77.

/30/ See Grass, *Ostergeschehen*, 95.

/31/ Pesch, *Markusevangelium*, 2:522-36. Pesch thinks
the stone's being rolled away is the product of door-opening
miracle stories. When it is pointed out that no such
door-opening is narrated in Mark, Pesch gives away his case by
asserting that it is a 'latent' door-opening miracle! The
angelic appearance he attributes to epiphany stories, though
without showing the parallels. Most astounding of all he
appeals to a *Gattung* for seeking, but not finding someone for
the search for Jesus's body, adducing several dubious texts
(e.g., II Kings 2.16-18; Ps 37.36; Ez 26.21) plus a spate of
post-Christian or Christian-influenced sources (Gospel of
Nicodemus 16.6; Testament of Job 39-40) and even question-begging
texts from the New Testament itself. He uncritically accepts
Lehmann and MacArthur's analysis of the third day motif, which
he erroneously equates with Mark's phrase 'on the first day'.
His assertion that the fact that the women were known in the
Urgemeinde cannot prevent legend since many legends are attested
about the disciples is a *petitio principii*. He fails to come
to grips with his own early dating and never shows how legend
could develop in so short a span in the presence of those who
knew better. For a critique of Pesch's position as well as a

timely warning against New Testament exegesis's falling into
the fallacies of the old *Religionsgeschichtliche* school, see
Peter Stuhlmacher, ' "Kritischer müssten mir die Historisch-
Kritischen sein!",' *TQ* 153 (1973):   244-51.

/32/ Bode, *Easter*, p. 161; Brown agrees: '. . . the
basic time indication of the finding of the tomb was fixed in
Christian memory before the possible symbolism in the three-day
reckoning had yet been perceived.' (Brown, *John*, p. 980.) The
fact that τῇ μιᾷ τῶν σαββάτων is probably a Semitism also points
to the early origin of the phrase.

/33/ Wilckens, *Auferstehung*, 64.

/34/ On the low rung of the social ladder occupied by
women in Jewish society, see J Sot 19a; B Kidd 82b. On their
lack of qualification to serve as legal witnesses, see M Rosh
Ha-Shanah 1.8.

/35/ Mahoney, *Disciples*, 159.

/36/ Ibid., 243.

/37/ D. H. van Daalen, *The Real Resurrection* (London:
Collins, 1972), 41.

/38/ Jacob Kremer, *Die Osterevangelien--Geschichten um
Geschichte* (Stuttgart: Katholisches Bibelwerk, 1977), 49-50.

/39/ Rudolf Schnackenburg, personal letter.

On Discerning Semitic Sources in Luke 1-2

Stephen C. Farris,
Westminster College,
Cambridge, England.

'An Orgy of Hebraic Greek'/1/. So W. L. Knox described the first two chapters of Luke's Gospel. Almost all scholars would agree that the Greek of Luke 1-2 differs considerably from the language of the rest of Luke-Acts but there is no such agreement as to the explanation of this phenomenon, this Hebraic 'orgy'. Some scholars argue forcefully that the Semitic Greek of these chapters results from the translation of a Hebrew or Aramaic source or sources. Others argue, equally forcefully, that Luke is here writing 'Biblical Greek', imitating the LXX just as we might emulate the literary style of King James' men. The difficulty of the problem can more clearly be appreciated when one remembers that the LXX itself is 'translation Greek'. Those who hold that the linguistic character of the first two chapters of Luke is the result of deliberate imitation of the LXX are saying, therefore, that these chapters are 'imitation translation Greek'. Translation Greek or imitation translation Greek? This is the difficult choice that faces those who investigate the literary origins of Luke 1-2/2/.

It is not surprising, therefore, that Raymond Brown could write as recently as 1977, 'The linguistic opponents have fought one another to a draw at the present moment of our historical research'/3/. One cannot, he argued, decide the question of Semitic sources behind Luke 1-2 on linguistic grounds. Brown, however, seems not to have considered the works of Raymond A. Martin. In two articles/4/ and a book/5/ Martin developed a method which purports to enable the user to determine whether or not Semitic sources lie behind a Greek document. If Martin's method actually works, the linguistic draw may have been broken. Scholars no longer need play Mr. Micawber, 'waiting for something to turn up'. Something has now turned up. But will it work?

Raymond Martin informs us in the preface to his book, *Syntactical Evidence*,/6/ that he first took an interest in the question of translation Greek when a student at Princeton

Seminary. He maintained that interest while a missionary in
India, publishing at that time the two articles mentioned
earlier. One might imagine that Dr. Martin absorbed some of the
legendary patience of the Orient, for the development of his
method must have involved the most tedious and painstaking of
studies. The method was then fully described in *Syntactical
Evidence*. There, Martin declares that he has isolated seventeen
criteria which enable one to discover the presence of Semitic
sources behind Greek documents. A description of those criteria
will display not only the nature of the method but also Martin's
industry and thoroughness./7/

Martin had, as do all investigators, a considerable sample
of translation Greek, the LXX. The observation of the relative
frequency or infrequency there of certain syntactical features,
when compared with works originally composed in Greek, lies at
the basis of his method. The results of this sort of approach
can easily be shown in graphical form and it may assist the
reader to consult Martin's graphs of the 17 criteria which are
appended to this article as the various criteria are discussed.
/8/ On those graphs the first section on the left shows the
incidence of the phenomenon in question in translated Greek: the
second shows the same with respect to writings originally
composed in that language.

The first eight criteria have to do with the relative
infrequency of the appearance of certain prepositions compared
to the frequency of the appearance of ἐν. The preposition ב
appears very frequently in Hebrew or Aramaic and is usually
represented in translation by ἐν. Certain other prepositions
which are relatively common in original Greek do not have
common Semitic equivalents. The following table shows the
eight prepositions which Martin uses as criteria and a numeral
with each: the numeral is the number of occurrences of the
relevant prepositions per occurrence of ἐν which Martin
considers the dividing line between original and translation
Greek; thus, for example, if διά with genitive occurs more than
.06 times for each occurrence of ἐν, then we are on the original
Greek side of the line; if it occurs less than .06 times per ἐν,
then we are on the translation Greek side. Since ἐν is usually
more frequent than the other prepositions, the numeral each time
has a decimal point. The same number is shown by a horizontal
line on the graphs.

1. διά with the genitive case   .06
2. διά in all occurrences   .18
3. εἰς   .49
4. κατά with the accusative case   .18
5. κατά in all occurrences   .19
6. περί   .27
7. πρός with the dative case   .024
8. ὑπό with the genitive case   .07

A glance at the graphs shows that the dividing line is a somewhat artificial one./9/ For example, the frequency of κατά in Numbers and of πρός with the dative case in Joshua is well 'above the line'. However, one can see that the bulk of the translated Greek appears below the dividing line and almost all the original Greek above it. The graphs also show the writings from which Martin derived these criteria. On the translated Greek side he was able to use the LXX version of the entire Hebrew Old Testament. For original Greek he used writings of considerable variety, both highly literary texts and the papyri, as well as Josephus and 2-3-4 Maccabees.

For the next nine criteria Martin was not able to take such a wide sample since the process of counting was more difficult than merely looking up the appropriate entry in a concordance. With respect to these nine criteria he studied the following texts:

Translated Greek	*Lines of Greek Text /10/*
Genesis 1-4, 6, 39	382
1 Samuel 3, 4, 22	194
1 Kings 17	58
2 Kings 13	71
Daniel - Hebrew Sections - LXX	482
Daniel - Hebrew Sections - Theodotion	460
Daniel - Aramaic Section - LXX	595
Daniel - Aramaic Section - Theodotion	634
Ezra - Hebrew Sections	328
Ezra - Aramaic Sections	211
Total Lines of Translated Greek	3418

Original Greek

Plutarch's Lives   325
    Demosthenes I, II, III, XXI
    Cicero I, II, XXX, XLIX
    Alexander L, LI, LII

Original Greek	*Lines of Greek Text*
Polybius - The Histories	192
Book I. 1-4	
Book II, 7	
Epictetus - The Discourses	138
Book III, Chapter II	
Book IV, Chapters II and III	
Josephus	215
Contra Apionem, Book I. 1-4	
Antiquities, Book XIV. i	
Papyri (Numbers 1, 2, 3, 16, 18-115, 117	630
121, 127)	
Total Lines of Original Greek	1500

Criterion 9. The Frequency of καί Coordinating Independent
Clauses in Relation to the Frequency of δέ.

The criterion involves the relative frequency of the use
of καί copulative./11/. Semitic conjunctions are never
postpositive and are, of course, very common indeed. There is
a considerable difference in the handling of this feature in
translation Greek between the literalness of Theodotion on the
one hand and the relative freedom of the LXX version of Genesis
on the other. However, original Greek, according to Martin's
figures, always has less than two occurrences of καί copulative
for every occurrence of δέ.

Criterion 10. Separation of the Greek Article from its
Substantive.

Nothing can be inserted between a Hebrew article or its
equivalent in Aramaic, the emphatic state, and its substantive.
This is not the case in Greek. As one might, therefore, expect,
Martin found that a relatively small percentage of articles are
separated from their substantives in translation Greek, 5% or
less./12/

Criterion 11. The Infrequency in Translation Greek of
Dependent Genitives Preceding the Word on which They Depend.

The genitive is expressed in Hebrew and Aramaic by
constructions which follow rather than precede the substantive
on which they depend. This is not necessarily the case in
original Greek. In Martin's sample of translation Greek
there are always 22 or more dependent genitives following their
substantives for every such genitive preceding its substantive.

Criterion 12. The Greater Frequency of Dependent Genitive
Personal Pronouns in Greek which is a Translation of a Semitic
Language.
    Prononimal suffixes are extremely common in Hebrew and
Aramaic and are usually translated by dependent genitive
personal pronouns. As one can see from the graph such pronouns
are therefore more common in translated Greek. This is one of
several criteria expressed as a number of lines of text for
each occurrence of the phenomenon in question. In this case
the point of division is nine lines per occurrence.

Criterion 13. The Greater Frequency of Genitive Personal
Pronouns Dependent upon Anarthrous Substantives in Translation
Greek.
    This criterion is closely related to the last and is based
on the fact that nouns with pronominal suffixes are normally
anarthrous in the Semitic languages. It appears that in
translation Greek genitive personal pronouns dependent on
anarthrous substantives occur every 77 lines or less.

Criterion 14. The Infrequency in Translation Greek of
Attributive Adjectives Preceding the Word They Qualify.
    Criterion 14 also rests on an observation of word order.
Attributive adjectives normally follow the word they qualify in
the Semitic languages but may frequently precede it in Greek.
Here the dividing line is at .35 attributive adjectives
preceding for every one following the word it qualifies./13/

Criterion 15. The Relative Infrequency of Attributive
Adjectives in Translation Greek.
    Attributive adjectives are used relatively infrequently in
Hebrew and Aramaic and one might therefore expect that Greek
translated from these languages would share that characteristic.
Martin's calculations show that this is, in fact, the case.
One may well be puzzled by Martin's positioning of the line of
demarcation, however. As one can see on the graph a
considerable part of his sample of translation Greek has
attributive adjectives appearing more frequently than once
every 10.1 lines, the dividing line here.

Criterion 16. Frequency of Adverbial Participles.
    While Greek frequently expresses subordination by the use
of an adverbial or circumstantial participle the Semitic
languages do not do so. Infrequent use of such participles
may therefore be a sign of translation Greek. Martin found

that translated Greek possessed such participles no more
frequently than one every 6 lines.

Criterion 17.   The Frequency of the Dative Case.
     This criterion is closely related to the first eight in
that it measures the relative frequency of ἐν. Dative,
locative and instrumental ideas are often expressed with the
preposition ב in Hebrew and Aramaic but need not be expressed
with ἐν in Greek. According to Martin's figures one might
suspect the presence of translation Greek when there are less
than 2 instances of the dative without the use of ἐν for every
instance with it/14/.

     After all these criteria have been applied to the texts in
question, the counting done, and the appropriate calculations
made in each case, Martin finds the total number of criteria
which indicate the presence of original Greek and subtracts
from it the number of criteria indicating translation Greek.
The result can be either a positive or a negative number
depending on whether the criteria showing original Greek
(positive result), or translation Greek (negative result),
predominate. For example, when one applies the criteria to
Genesis 39 one finds 4 original Greek frequencies, 10
translation Greek frequencies and 3 for which there is
insufficient evidence to make a determination. One subtracts
10 (translation Greek frequencies) from 4 (original Greek
frequencies) and comes up with a net score of -6.

     A table showing the results of Martin's study may be
useful here./15/

Text	Net result
Genesis 1-4, 6, 39	-4
1 Samuel 3, 4, 22	-11
1 Kings 17	-6
2 Kings 13	-12
Daniel Hebrew LXX	-10
Hebrew Theodotion	-12
Aramaic LXX	-12
Aramaic Theodotion	-13
Ezra Hebrew	-14
Ezra Aramaic	-12

Plutarch - Selections   +16
Polybius - Books I, II   +15
Epictetus Books III, IV   +17
Josephus - Selections   +16
Papyri - Selections   +17

Clearly there is a considerable difference with respect to
these criteria between original and translation Greek in *the
sample which Martin studied.*

Martin also considered the possibility that Semitic sources
might be embedded in documents that, as a whole, had been
originally composed in Greek. This sort of Semitic source
might very likely be quite short and, as a result, more
difficult to identify. He therefore divided his material into
smaller units of text and subjected these units to the analysis
described earlier in this article. Predictably he found that
'as the unit of text which is being analysed becomes smaller,
syntactical variations due to content and style become more
pronounced'./16/ To this point all the text units with which
Martin had worked were 58 lines or longer. He divided these
texts into smaller units of 50-31 lines or 30-16 lines or 15-4
lines in length. Once more a table may be useful in
summarizing the results of such a study./17/ The table shows
the range of net results when the criteria are applied to the
shorter units of original and translation Greek.

Unit Length	Original Greek	Translation Greek
31-50 lines	+13 to +7	+1 to -8
16-30 lines	+12 to +3	+4 to -9
4-15 lines	+12 to 0	+7 to -6

With units of 31-50 lines there is no overlap between the
results for original and translation Greek. With units of 16-
30 lines there is some overlap although the bulk of the
material is still separated. There is a rather considerable
overlap when one considers units of 4-15 lines in length.
This overlap is caused primarily, however, not by the more
frequent appearance of translation Greek frequencies in original
Greek texts but by less frequent appearances of such frequencies
in translation Greek. Never, even in the shortest units, did
translation Greek frequencies predominate in an original Greek
text. Martin concluded: 'the differences between the original
Greek and the translated Greek is (sic) sufficient in all units
of 31-50 lines in length, in most units of 16-30 lines in

length, and in many units of 4-15 lines to indicate that they
are indeed translation rather than original Greek'./17/
Nevertheless, he must admit that, in this last case, at least a
third of the translation Greek appeared on the 'wrong' side of
the dividing line and thus could not certainly be detected by
means of this method./19/

The most adequate summary of the results of this study is
Martin's own:
For units of 31 to 50 lines in length, 'these criteria
clearly indicate translation Greek if *in such a section one or
fewer net original Greek frequencies or one or more translation
Greek frequencies occur*'.
For units of 16 to 30 lines of length: '*if one or fewer
net original Greek frequencies or one or more translation Greek
frequencies occur this indicates translation of a Hebrew or
Aramaic document*. If 2 to 4 net original Greek frequencies
occur this *probably* indicates translation of a Semitic
document'./20/
For units of 4 to 15 lines in length: '*only if one or more
net translation Greek frequencies appear is translation from
Hebrew or Aramaic definitely indicated*'./21/

Martin then applied his method to the Acts of the
Apostles. This, he argued, is an ideal test case since the
book has two halves of more or less equal length but of quite
different character. The second half of the book, 15:35-28:31,
can hardly be drawn from Semitic sources but 'it is quite
generally conceded that at least in some parts of the first
half of Acts the writer does use Aramaic sources'./22/ (One
might quarrel with the adverb generally.) Martin found that the
second half of the book displayed 16 net original Greek
frequencies, the same, in fact, as Plutarch. Even the smallest
units studied were safely above the lowest limit for original
Greek frequencies. The first half of Acts, on the other hand,
displayed only 8 net original Greek frequencies, a figure which
falls in the gap between the frequencies displayed by the
original and translation Greek frequencies analyzed earlier in
the book./23/ Furthermore, the figures for every indicator
except one, διά + genitive, are closer to translation Greek
frequencies than the comparable second half figures. When one
turns to the smaller units of text one finds that a number of
these units display translation Greek frequencies. No smaller
units in any of the original Greek which Martin had studied
previously had displayed such frequencies. Similarly, none of

the smaller units of translation Greek had displayed the
original Greek frequencies one finds in many of the other units
and in Acts 1-15:35 as a whole. 'The explanation for this non-
conformity to either original or translation Greek is clear.
Acts 1-15:35 contains some material which was originally
composed in Greek and also some which has been translated from
Semitic sources.'./24/

It is not my intention to dwell longer on the Acts of the
Apostles than is absolutely necessary. The reader who wishes
to know more of the question of Semitic sources in Acts must
himself consult Martin's study. Let it only be said that the
results of the study of the second half of Acts where there can
hardly be a question of Semitic sources may be useful for
purposes of comparison with the Infancy Narratives where there
may be such sources./25/

The reader who has consulted Martin's graphs which
illustrate the results of his study can hardly have failed to
notice that I have applied the method to Luke 1-2. The method
has one great advantage for this purpose; it is almost
inconceivable that an author would consciously imitate the
syntactical features analyzed by it. It has been argued that
Luke here has adopted a 'Septuagintalizing' style, imitating the
vocabulary, the concerns and rhythms of the LXX. It would, I
suggest, take an extremely hardy proponent of this theory to
argue that Luke discovered and reproduced the correct
frequencies of the various syntactical features discussed
earlier in this paper. It is one thing to imitate the
vocabulary of the Old Testament and give a writing some of its
atmosphere by inserting characteristic expressions like καὶ
ἐγένετο; any moderately literate modern could imitate the
Authorised Version in a similar fashion. It is quite another
consistently to reproduce some of its more obscure
characteristics which do not depend on subject matter or
vocabulary. Conscious imitation of these phenomena appears
unthinkable. One cannot totally discount the possibility that
a writer extremely sensitive to literary nuances, 'a first-
century James Joyce'/26/ might, in the course of his imitation
of the LXX, unconsciously reproduce as a by-product of that
imitation some of these characteristics, some of the time. One
could hardly expect him to do so consistently. These criteria
do not concern themselves with idiom, with vocabulary, or
theology, which are the natural subjects of imitation; they
consist of the obscure unconsidered building blocks of language.

Furthermore, we know that Luke, where certainly
uninfluenced by Semitic sources, as in Acts 15:36ff., wrote
Greek that displays frequencies characteristic of original
Greek. Martin's study shows that Acts 15:36ff. exhibits the
same net number of original Greek frequencies as Plutarch and
that not one of the smaller units displays translation Greek
frequencies. It is not the case, therefore, that Luke's own
style was necessarily Semitic.

When we turn to the infancy narratives and apply Martin's
criteria we find that Luke 1-2 as a whole and also in its
various parts, consistently displays translation Greek
frequencies as the following chart makes clear./27/

Section	Lines	Net
Chapter 1 without hymns	107	-12
Hymns of Chapter 1	30	-4
Chapter 2:1-40 without hymns	57	-5
Hymns of Chapter 2	5	-2
2:41ff.	23	-2
Chapter 1 total	137	-14
Chapter 2 total	80	-5
Hymns total	35	-4
Grand total	217	-16

Every one of these units, even Luke 2:41ff.,/28/ is safely
within the translation Greek frequency range.

A standard test of statistical significance was applied to
the results gained by the application of each of the 16
criteria to Luke 1-2 as a whole. (It is a weakness in Martin's
study that he nowhere mentions the application of such tests to
his results.) To do this one forms a 'null hypothesis' to be
falsified, in this case, that the data for Luke 1-2 belongs to
the normal distribution of values for original Greek. In all
16 cases the results were 'significant at the 1% level' or
better. This means that the results for Luke 1-2 were more
extreme than 99% of the values one might expect for original
Greek. Such a level of significance is considered 'fairly
conclusive' evidence that the null hypothesis is untrue./29/
In fact most of the 16 results were significant at well beyond
this level even when the values of the writer nearest to
translation Greek were taken as the mean value for original
Greek rather than the actual mean. The Greek of Luke 1-2
differs significantly from the original Greek *in the sample*

which Martin studied.

Several points ought to be made before proceeding. The
score for Luke 1-2 as a whole, -16, shows a higher number of
translation Greek frequencies than even the samples of the LXX
which Martin examined. This makes a striking contrast with the
+16 of the second half of Acts. Of the two chapters it is
clear that the first is more Semitic in style than the second
both in total score and with respect to the data for each
individual criterion./30/ However, it would be inaccurate to
suggest in a similar fashion that the hymns, on the basis of
this data, must be considered less Semitic than the narrative.
The lower score, -4, for the hymns as a whole, is a reflection
of the lesser number of lines. In a shorter unit a single
expression such as διά στόματος τῶν ἀγίων ἀπ' αἰῶνος προφητῶν,
Lk 1:70, can have a much greater statistical effect than in a
larger unit of text. Furthermore, there is always bound to be
a greater number of criteria for which there is not enough data
to come to a conclusion. In fact, with respect to many of the
criteria, the hymns appear more Semitic than does the narrative.

Considering the results one can hardly escape the
conclusion that Luke 1-2 is translated from a Semitic source or
sources. But is the method reliable? This is the question
which must be considered in the rest of this article.

Martin's method certainly appears to be impressive; the
graphs create a strong visual impression in its favour and
there is a persuasive explanation of the significance of each
of the criteria. Furthermore, the method gives the impression
of being 'scientific' and 'objective'. The method is, however,
by no means easy to apply. The eye skips a line; the finger
presses the wrong button on the calculator; the same word is
counted twice. More importantly, the user could wish at times
for slightly more specific directions concerning what 'counts'
and what does not under some of the criteria.

There are, however, certain problems and difficulties
which are of a more serious nature and which may point to flaws
in the method itself. One difficulty has to do with the number
of criteria. Criteria 1-8 purport to be eight separate
indicators showing the relative infrequency of various
prepositions. One might well suppose, however, that there is
but one criterion here, the relative frequency of ἐν.
Furthermore, criterion 17 which compares the number of

occurrences of the dative without the use of ἐν to the number of
such occurrences with it is, at least in part, a measure of the
frequency of ἐν. Are there nine separate criteria here - or
just one?

It seems best, however, to retain Martin's method intact
in this respect. That the texts in question agree or disagree
with translation Greek not only with respect to the frequency
of ἐν but also with respect to the relative infrequency of
seven other prepositions, each according to its proper
proportion, is worthy of note. Furthermore, in order
conveniently to compare the results of this study with the
results of Martin's own study the retention of his system is
advisable.

Another problem lies in the fact that one can find the
same phrase being counted several times under different
criteria thus having a strong, perhaps too strong, influence on
the overall result. Consider, for example, the unusual
expression mentioned earlier, διά στόματος τῶν ἁγιών ἀπ'
αἰῶνος προφητῶν αὐτοῦ, Lk. 1:70, which for various reasons has
sometimes been considered an insertion by Luke into the hymn.
Here we have one expression which counts in six different
criteria and by its singular presence makes several of them come
down on the original Greek side with respect to the hymns.

There are also several more minor flaws in the system
which have to do with the counting. The only one worth
mentioning here is that for a particular criterion among the
first eight to be counted, at least one of the relevant
prepositions must be present. For example, if in a particular
passage there are 10 instances of ἐν and 4 of εἰς the criterion
can be considered to indicate translation Greek. If, on the
other hand, there are 10 instances of ἐν but none of εἰς the
criterion may not be counted at all, even though the point of
the criterion is that εἰς is relatively infrequent in
translation Greek compared to ἐν.

A more serious problem involves the question of the
relative importance of the criteria. In Martin's system all
seventeen of the criteria are of equal value numerically. One
criterion, one vote. My own impression is that the last nine
criteria ought to be of more significance than the relative
frequency of the individual prepositions. The latter seem
'lightweight' by comparison in that one is using some of the

same data, the number of occurrences of ἐν, repeatedly. Once
it is admitted that the various criteria are not equal value,
however, the certainty of the mathematical rules disappears.
One net score of -3 might be more significant than the next -3
depending on which criteria made up the score. In fact, if
the criteria are of unequal significance it is hard to imagine
reducing the data to a numerical score at all. After
considering all the data one might merely be left with an
impression of translation Greek or original Greek, hardly a
completely objective process.

There remains a still more serious problem. In a review
of *Syntactical Evidence* John J. Collin wrote, 'M's criteria
make no allowance for the possibility of a poor quality Greek
influenced by Semitic idiom'./31/ If Martin's method cannot
distinguish between Greek translated from a Semitic language
and Greek written by one influenced by Semitic idiom its
usefulness for application to the New Testament, mainly written
as it is by Semites, will be limited. I have chosen several
texts for analysis in an effort to determine whether or not
this is the case.

The first text chosen is Luke 5:12-6:11 and the second is
its parallel in Mark, Mk 1:40-3:6. The third text is Luke 12:
13-13:9 of which the central portion appears to be drawn from Q.
/32/ The other two sections of the text, Lk. 12:13-21 and 13:
1-9, contain material peculiar to Luke. There are some who
claim that the Synoptic Gospels are translated from Aramaic.
/33/ Furthermore, if there is any historical root in the life
of Jesus, or even in the situation of the early Aramaic-
speaking church, to the sayings and stories recounted in these
texts, there must certainly have been a Semitic substratum in
their tradition history. One cannot, therefore, predict with
confidence the result of an analysis of these texts. It will
be useful, however, to have data from the Lukan texts for
purposes of comparison with Luke 1-2 and with Acts. The
passage from Mark was chosen in order to discover whether the
characteristics studied in Martin's method could be passed from
one Greek document to another dependent on it.

I know of no scholar who suggests that Romans and
Galatians were composed in Hebrew or Aramaic. From these books
I have chosen a passage of doctrinal exposition, Romans 5, and
a passage which contains biographical narrative, Galatians 1-
2:5./34/ Finally, there are two texts of somewhat different

character, Revelation 3 and 4-5:10. The former is the
concluding section of the letter to the seven churches while
the latter forms the beginning of the apocalyptic vision
itself. This latter section contains narrative, direct
discourse, and hymnic materials, as do the infancy narratives
of Luke. Of the author of Revelation R. H. Charles wrote,
'while he writes in Greek, he thinks in Hebrew'./35/
Revelation, it appears, may serve as our example of 'poor
quality Greek influenced by Semitic idiom'.

The results of the analysis are as follows:

Text	Lines	Net Result
Luke 5:12-6:11	91	0
Mark 1:40-3:6	89	+2
Luke 12:13-13:9	109	-2
Lukan passages (total)	200	0
Romans 5	50.5	+2
Galatians 1-2:5	56	+3
Paul (total)	106.5	+3
Revelation 3	59	-2
Revelation 4-5:10	61	-5
Revelation (total)	120	-5

The bulk of this material displays frequencies which fall
into the gap between the results for translation Greek and
those of original Greek in Martin's study./36/ Revelation with
a net score of -5 is the only exception, having a score similar
to that of the Genesis selections, -4, and 1 Kings 17, -6. The
passages from Paul, which display the most original Greek
frequencies in this sample, do not approach the scores of the
original Greek examined by Martin. The exact significance of
this data may not immediately be clear but it does appear that
the method may not always be able to differentiate between
translation Greek and Greek composed by one who thinks in a
Semitic language.

With respect to the relative frequency of prepositions the
concordances enable one to accumulate data for the entire New
Testament. In more than half the cases for which a
determination is possible, 98 out of 184, the frequencies are
typical of 'translation Greek'. In fact, it appears that Acts
is one of the few books in the New Testament in which original
Greek frequencies predominate. However, these figures do not
prove that the frequencies Martin has isolated are not

characteristic of translation Greek but only suggest that such frequencies may also be characteristic of Greek written by one influenced by Semitic idiom.

All these considerations must throw doubt on the ability of this method reliably to distinguish between translation Greek and much of the rather Semitized Greek of the New Testament. /37/ I suggest, however, that the use of Martin's method might well help us come to a conclusion about Semitic sources in Luke 1-2. It is important to remember that none of the passages from the rest of the New Testament show the consistent translation Greek frequencies of Luke 1-2. Not even Rev. 4-5: 10 comes close to doing so. In the case of every available criterion the former chapters exhibit frequencies characteristic of translation Greek. (It may be worth mentioning in passing that if all the criteria point in the same direction the objection that these criteria are of differing significance loses its force.)

Secondly, the results of the wider application of the method throw doubt primarily on the ability of the method to distinguish between Greek translated from a Semitic language and Greek written by a person heavily influenced by Semitic idiom. But Luke was not necessarily the latter as the testimony of Acts 15:35ff. shows. He was quite capable of writing Greek free from the sort of Semitic characteristics we have been studying, when not influenced by Semitic sources, or by sources written in the kind of Semitic-like Greek of much of the New Testament.

Consider yet another table.

Acts 15:35ff.	+16
Luke, selections from the Gospel	0
Luke 1-2	-16

Luke had no Semitic sources for the latter half of Acts and he wrote a text which consistently shows the characteristics of original Greek. In other words, it appears that Luke's normal Greek, that is, the Greek which he wrote when certainly not influenced by Semitic sources, is similar to the sample of original Greek which Martin studied. In the selections from the Gospel, on the other hand, he appears to have been dependent on Semitic-like sources. In these chapters Luke displayed translation and original Greek frequencies about equally. It appears that Luke's Greek may be rather similar to that of his source with respect to

Martin's criteria.

    With respect to Luke 5:12-6:11 and its source in Mark, it
appears that in every case except criterion 9, the ratio of καί
to δέ, there is a marked similarity between the figures for the
two gospels. The ratio is 6.75 to 1 in Mark but only 1.77 to 1
for Luke. Luke is considerably less Semitic here than is Mark
and it rather looks as if Luke has improved on the language of
his source at this point. Even in the case of the two criteria
in which Mark falls on the original Greek side of the divide
and Luke on the other, the figures are remarkably similar. In
criterion 11 the figures for dependent genitives are:

	Post-	Pre-
Luke	29	0
Mark	27	2

In criterion 17 the numbers of datives without ἐν are almost
identical, 17 for Mark, 16 for Luke. The difference in the
result of the calculations derives from the fact that Luke uses
ἐν slightly more frequently than does Mark, for example in the
characteristic construction ἐν τῷ + infinitive. In some cases
Mark appears the more Semitic, in other cases, Luke, but the
similarity between the two is obvious. In fact, Luke 5:12-6:11
is usually closer to Mark in its frequencies than it is to Luke
12. The most plausible explanation for all this is that Luke's
style with respect to these seventeen criteria absorbs some of
the characteristics of his source. The fact that Luke altered
the language of his source with respect to the καί/δέ ratio,
which is probably the most immediately noticeable of the
Semitisms discerned by Martin's method, but did not alter
Mark's language with respect to the other criteria may well
indicate that the use of the syntactical features discerned by
them is below the level of conscious control. The absorption
of these Semitic characteristics may not be related to any
desire to imitate Semitic style but rather to the level of
Semitism of his source. That is to say, Luke's language is
not conditioned here by his own literary strategy but by the
character of his source.

    What then of Luke 1-2 with its 'score' of -16? This is
radically different even from that of the Greek of Luke 5:12-
6:11. What can be the explanation of this? With respect to
Martin's criteria it appears that:
1. *Luke 1-2 is dissimilar to original Greek.*
2. *Luke 1-2 is similar to translation Greek.*
3. *Luke could absorb characteristics discovered by Martin's*

method from a source.

Given these three observations, the most plausible explanation for the Hebraic colouring of Luke 1-2 must surely be that Luke has once again absorbed some of the style of a source. Furthermore, if even Revelation, written in Greek by an author thinking in Hebrew, does not display the consistently Semitic frequencies of Luke 1-2, it seems reasonable to suppose that the source was not simply Semitic Greek but rather had actually been composed in one of the Semitic languages. The 'draw' of which Raymond Brown wrote was the effect of the arguments of proponents of a Septuagintal imitation theory on the one hand, and proponents of a Hebrew source theory on the other. (That the language of the Semitic source was Aramaic rather than Hebrew is no longer a widely held position.) The application of Raymond Martin's method produces evidence which appears to break the draw in favour of the advocates of a Hebrew source theory.

It was said of a certain man that he used statistics the way a drunk uses a lamp-post - to lean on rather than for illumination. I trust that the statistics so liberally scattered through this paper have not produced the confusion of a drunkard but rather that illumination which is the purpose not only of lamp-posts but of statistics and indeed, of New Testament studies.

Notes

/1/ W. L. Knox, *The Sources of the Synoptic Gospels*, H. Chadwick, vol. II, Cambridge: The University Press, 1957, p. 40.

/2/ See R. Laurentin, 'Traces d'Allusions Etymologiques I', *Biblica*, 37, (1956), pp. 435-456. Laurentin presents in the concluding seven pages of that article an excellent summary of scholarly opinion with respect to this question. As Laurentin notes, the present consensus is that Hebrew rather than Aramaic was the language of the hypothetical Semitic source. Scholars have believed that they have discovered various sorts of evidence that these chapters were translated from Hebrew, the presence of mistranslation, nonLXX Hebraisms, and metre and word-play, especially etymological allusions, in a restored Hebrew text. There is obviously no space here for a discussion of these arguments or of the counter arguments of

those who deny the use of Semitic sources. It remains only to
repeat that these arguments concern the possible existence of
a Hebrew rather than an Aramaic source.

/3/ R. E. Brown, *The Birth of the Messiah*, Garden City, NY:
Doubleday, 1977, p. 246.

/4/ R. A. Martin, 'Some Syntactical Criteria of Translation
Greek', *VT* X, 1960, pp. 295-310, and 'Syntactical Evidence of
Aramaic Sources in Acts I-XV', *NTS* 11, 1964, pp. 38-59. In
the latter article Martin applied those criteria which he had
developed at that point in time to Luke 1-2.

/5/ R. A. Martin, *Syntactical Evidence of Semitic Sources in
Greek Documents, Septuagint and Cognate Studies 3*, Missoula,
Mt.: Scholars' Press, 1974, hereafter *Syntactical Evidence*. I
am grateful to the SBL and to Dr. Martin for permission to
quote from the book and to reproduce its graphs. I must also
thank Dr. Martin for correcting several errors in the rough
draft of this article (any remaining errors are mine, not his)
and for informing me of three articles in which he has
published the results of the application of his method to
other texts. These are: R. A. Martin, "Syntactical Evidence
of a Semitic Vorlage of the Testament of Joseph" in *Studies on
the Testament of Joseph*, ed. G. W. Nickelsburg, *Septuagint and
Cognate Studies* 5, Missoula Mt.: Scholars' Press, 1975, pp.
105-23, and in the same series, Martin, "Syntax Criticism of
the Testament of Abraham" in *Studies on the Testament of
Abraham*, ed. G. W. Nickelsburg, *Septuagint and Cognate Studies*
6, Missoula Mt.: Scholars' Press, 1976, pp. 95-120, and
"Syntax Criticism of the LXX Additions to the Book of Esther",
JBL 94 (1976), pp. 65-72.

/6/ R. A. Martin, *Syntactical Evidence*, p. v.

/7/ See pages 5-38 of *Syntactical Evidence*.

/8/ The originals of these graphs may be found in *Syntactical
Evidence* as the individual criteria are discussed in pp. 5-38.

/9/ Martin is aware of this problem. See *Syntactical Evidence*,
p. 6.

/10/ Martin took as standard line length that of the United
Bible Society New Testament, i.e. approximately 51 letter
spaces. See *Syntactical Evidence*, p. 17, n. 1 and Appendix 1
"Line Adjustments", pp. 109-110.

/11/ It appears that the idea of using this phenomenon as a
criterion came from N. Turner's article 'The Relation of Luke
1 and 2 to Hebraic Sources and to the rest of Luke-Acts' *NTS*
2, 1955-56, pp. 100-115. See *Syntactical Evidence* p. 16.

/12/ Martin has erred here in expressing percentage as a
decimal figure. For example, with respect to Genesis the

number should be either 3% or .03 separated articles for every
unseparated one. It is not .03%!

/13/ Martin excludes the following adjectives from his count:
numerals, πᾶς, πολύς, ἕτερος, ποιός, αὐτός.

/14/ Martin excluded from his data the use of the dative with
forms of λέγω, εἶπον, δίδωμι.

/15/ Martin, *Syntactical Evidence*, p. 39.

/16/ Martin, *Syntactical Evidence*, p. 45.

/17/ A more detailed presentation of these results may be
found in the tables in *Syntactical Evidence*, pp. 49, 51, 53.

/18/ Martin, *Syntactical Evidence*, p. 45.

/19/ Martin, *Syntactical Evidence*, p. 52.

/20/ Martin, *Syntactical Evidence*, p. 50.

/21/ Martin, *Syntactical Evidence*, p. 52.

/22/ Martin, *Syntactical Evidence*, p. 87.

/23/ See the table on pp. 206-7 of this article.

/24/ Martin, *Syntactical Evidence*, p. 97.

/25/ It is generally conceded (and here the adverb is, I think,
appropriate) that the same author composed Luke and Acts.

/26/ L. Gaston, 'The Lucan Birth Narratives in Tradition and
Redaction', *1976 SBL Papers*, p. 212.

/27/ Tables containing pertinent data gleaned from the
application of Martin's method and the other NT passages
discussed later in this article will be included in my
dissertation on the hymns of Luke 1-2 which will, I
anticipate, be submitted to Cambridge University shortly.
(Note: Luke 1:1-4 has been excluded from my calculations.)

/28/ The dividing line for units of this length, 23 lines, in
Martin's system, is +1.

/29/ C. Chatfield, *Statistics for Technology: A Course in
Applied Statistics*, 2nd edition, London: Chapman & Hall, 1978,
p. 138. I wish to thank Mr. G. Walsham of Fitzwilliam College,
Cambridge for assisting me with this question. It need hardly
be said, however, that any statistical errors are mine rather
than his.

/30/ I tentatively suggest that Luke slightly expanded his
source in the account of Jesus' birth and presentation thus
introducing more original Greek characteristics.

/31/ The review may be found in *CBQ* 37, 1975, pp. 592-3.

/32/ I shall assume the correctness of the two-source theory
in this paper.

/33/ See, for example, C. C. Torrey, *Our Translated Gospels*,
London: no date, Hodder & Stoughton, and other works, and more
recently, J. C. O'Neill, 'The Synoptic Problem' *NTS* 21, 1975,
pp. 273-85.

/34/ The sample was extended beyond the end of the first
chapter in order to obtain a text of more than 50 lines in
length.
/35/ R. H. Charles, *The Revelation of St. John*, vol. I, *I.C.C.*
Edinburgh: 1920, p. cxliii. This conclusion seems to have
found wide agreement among commentators although Torrey in
The Apocalypse of John, New Haven: 1958, argues for translation
from Aramaic. But see John Sweet, *Revelation*, London: 1979,
p. 16, where Charles' position is essentially reaffirmed.
/36/ See the chart on pp. 206-7 of this article.
/37/ The New Testament is obviously full of this sort of Greek
and one might well expect it to be the middle term between
translation and original Greek. It is not entirely surprising,
therefore, that the results for the passages studied here fall
into the gap between the two types of Greek. Moreover, those
texts which were certainly composed in Greek, albeit by a
'Hebrew of the Hebrews', do show a predominance of original
Greek frequencies. The texts from the Gospels, which may rest
on an Aramaic substratum, show fewer such frequencies. In
Revelation, the Greek written by an author thinking in Hebrew,
the translation Greek frequencies predominate, although not so
strongly as in most of the translated Greek studied by Martin.

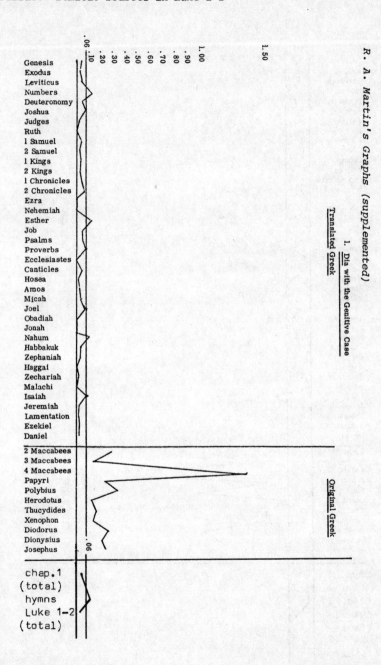

R. A. Martin's Graphs (supplemented)

1. Dia with the Genitive Case

Translated Greek

Original Greek

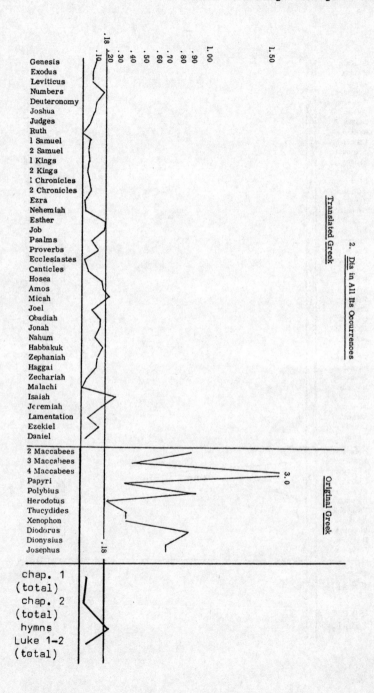

2. Dia in All Its Occurrences

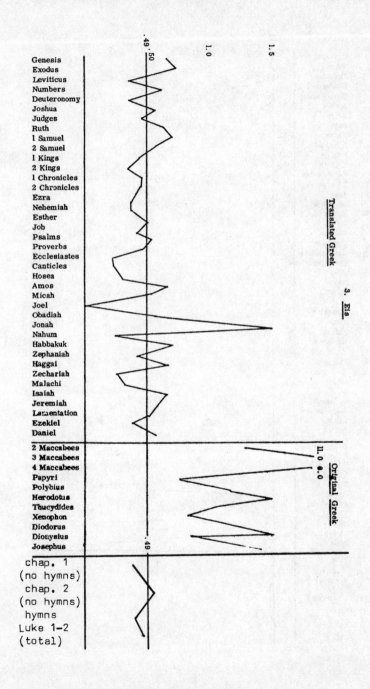

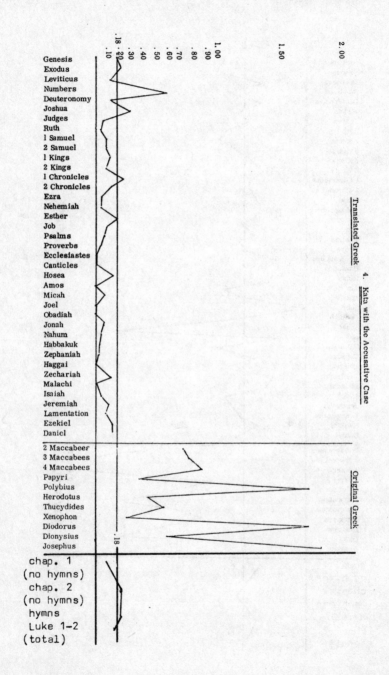

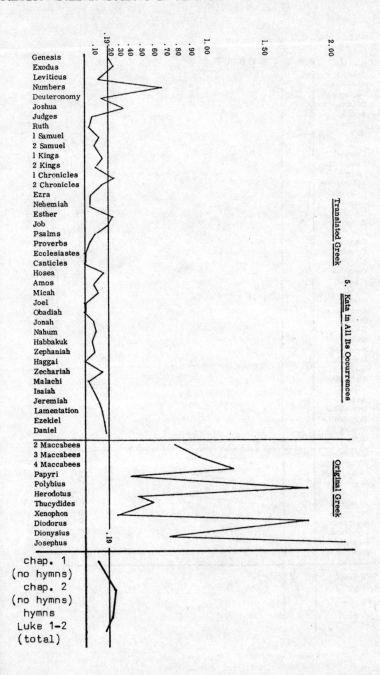

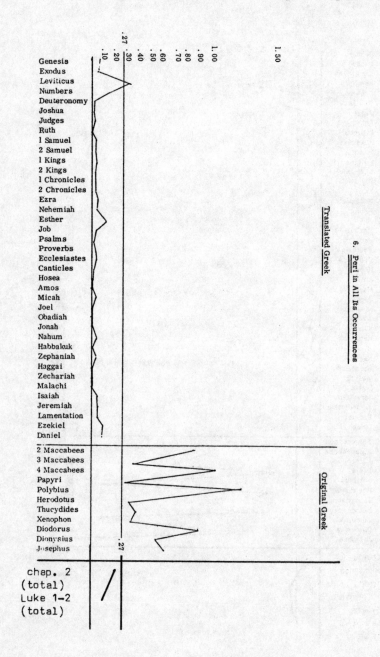

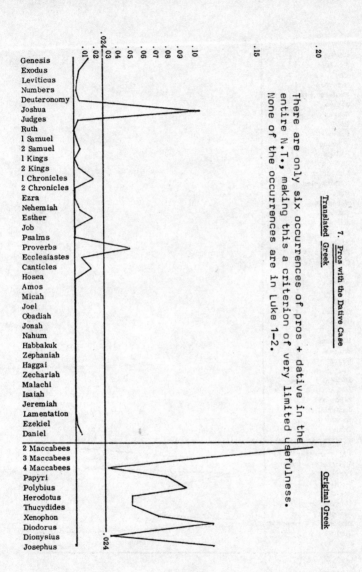

7. <u>Pros with the Dative Case</u>

<u>Translated Greek</u>

<u>Original Greek</u>

There are only six occurrences of pros + dative in the entire N.T., making this a criterion of very limited usefulness. None of the occurrences are in Luke 1-2.

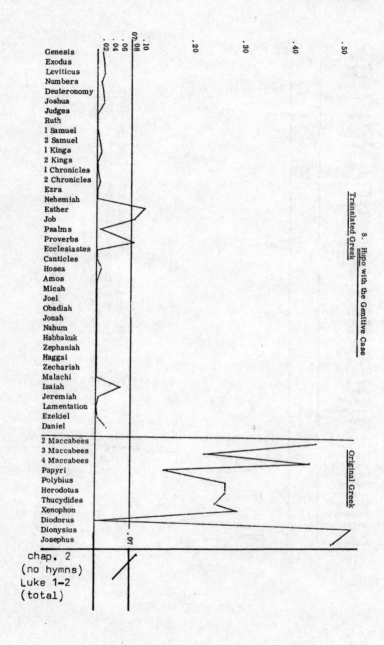

8. **Hupo with the Genitive Case**

Translated Greek

Original Greek

chap. 2
(no hymns)
Luke 1-2
(total)

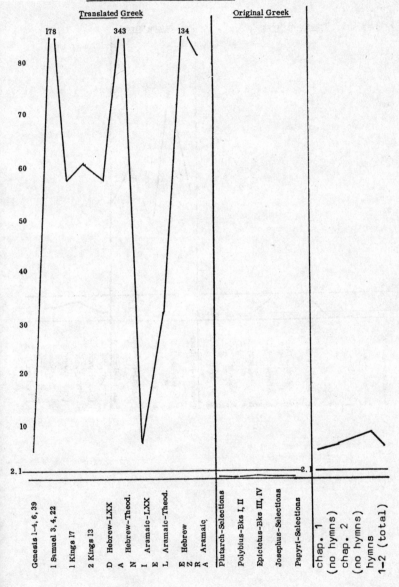

9. Number of <u>Kai</u>'s Copulative for Each <u>De</u>

10. Separation of the Greek Article

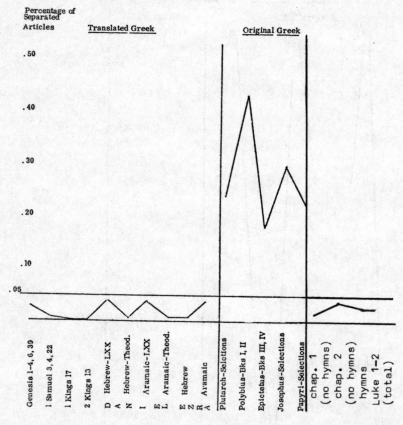

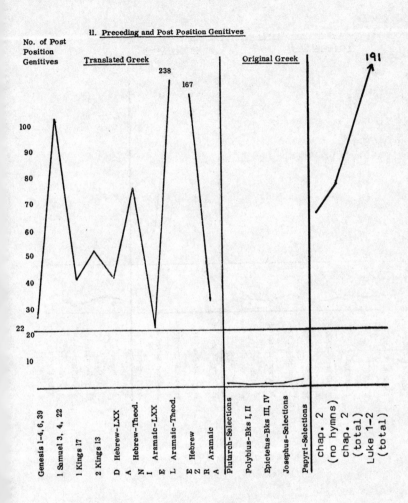

ii. **Preceding and Post Position Genitives**

No. of Post Position Genitives

Translated Greek

Original Greek

191

238

167

100
90
80
70
60
50
40
30
22
20

10

Genesis 1-4, 6, 39
1 Samuel 3, 4, 22
1 Kings 17
2 Kings 13
D Hebrew-LXX
A Hebrew-Theod.
N
I Aramaic-LXX
E
L Aramaic-Theod.
E Hebrew
Z
R Aramaic
A
Plutarch-Selections
Polybius-Bks I, II
Epictetus-Bks III, IV
Josephus-Selections
Papyri-Selections
chap. 2 (no hymns)
chap. 2 (total)
Luke 1-2 (total)

232   Gospel Perspectives II

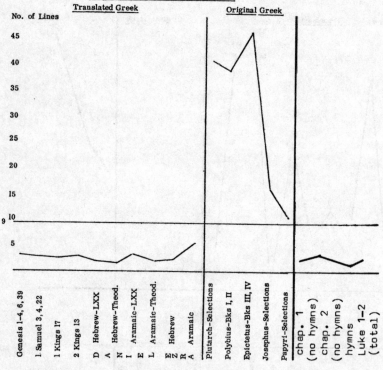

12. Dependent Genitive Personal Pronouns

13. <u>Genitive Personal Pronouns Dependent on Anarthrous Substantives</u>

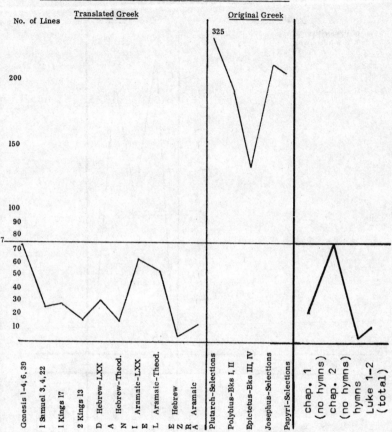

14. <u>Attributive Adjectives Preceding the Word They Qualify</u>

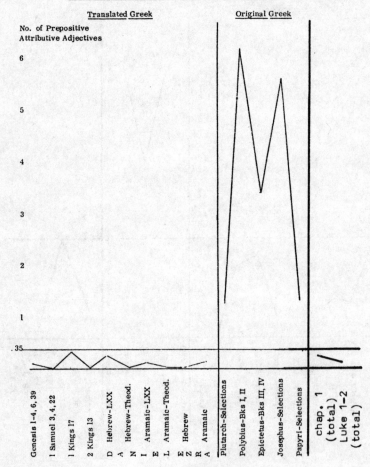

15. Frequency of Attributive Adjectives

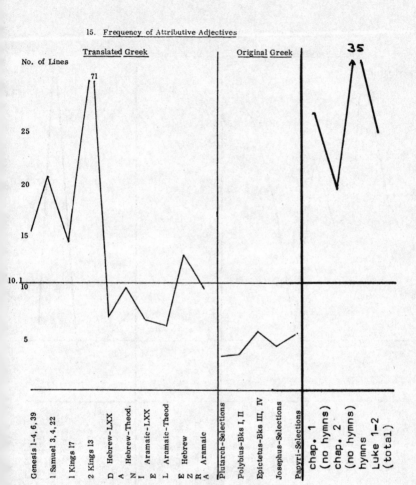

16. Frequency of Adverbial Participles

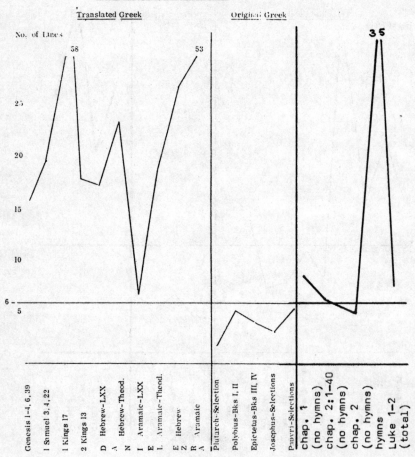

17. <u>Frequency of the Dative Case</u>

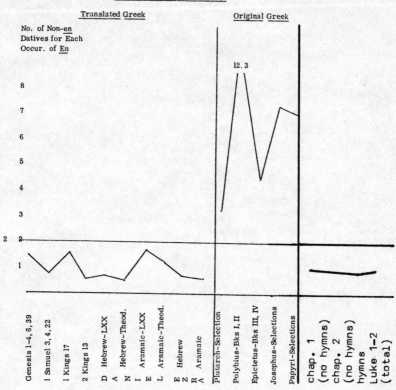

<u>Translated</u> Greek

<u>Original</u> Greek

No. of Non-<u>en</u>
Datives for Each
Occur. of <u>En</u>

8

7

6

5

4

3

2   2

1

12.3

Genesis 1-4, 6, 39
1 Samuel 3, 4, 22
1 Kings 17
2 Kings 13
D Hebrew-LXX
A Hebrew-Theod.
N Aramaic-LXX
I
E Aramaic-Theod.
L
E Hebrew
Z
R Aramaic
A

Plutarch-Selection
Polybius-Bks I, II
Epictetus-Bks III, IV
Josephus-Selections
Papyri-Selections

chap. 1
(no hymns)
chap. 2
(no hymns)
hymns
Luke 1-2
(total)

Scripture, Tradition and History in the Infancy Narratives of Matthew

R. T. France,
Tyndale House,
36 Selwyn Gardens,
Cambridge, CB3 9BA.

I Matthew 1-2 as history

Until recently doubts as to whether the New Testament infancy narratives /1/ are accounts of actual events have generally centred on three main approaches.

(a) *External evidence*.

Luke's introduction of the census into his infancy narrative immediately lays him open to verification from our (admittedly scanty) knowledge of the contemporary history of the Roman Empire, and the difficulty of squaring the two has been a fertile source of attack on Luke's historical reliability. But Matthew offers no such hostage to fortune. Apart from the existence of Herod as King in Jerusalem and his son Archelaus' succession as ruler of Judaea, his narrative simply does not intersect with contemporary events as they have come down to us; there is no scope for conflict, and therefore for falsification, here.   There is, of course, the question of verisimilitude, of how far Matthew's stories 'ring true' in the historical setting of the time, and to this question we shall return, but direct external evidence bearing on the events he records simply does not exist /2/.

This in itself may be seen as a problem. *Why* does secular history include no mention of a visit of foreign dignitaries which 'troubled all Jerusalem' (Mt. 2:3), or of a massacre in Bethlehem (2:16)?   And why do Christian sources supply no independent witness to these events so closely linked to the birth of the Messiah, or to his living in Egypt as a child?

To take the latter point first, the more remarkable fact is surely that these stories appear even in Matthew.   For New Testament Christianity, as opposed to the later atmosphere which produced the apocryphal gospels, was remarkably

uninterested in the story of Jesus outside the period of his
public ministry, as is witnessed by the gospels of Mark and
John, and by the silence of the rest of the NT.   Whether such
events were known or not in the first-century church, there is
little in the focus of interest of the NT writings to encourage
us to believe that they would have been much spoken of.
Matthew, as we shall see, records these events for reasons
other than biographical curiosity.   As mere events, they were
of no more pressing interest than all the other forgotten
events of Jesus' life before his baptism.

As for the silence of non-Christian sources, two factors
must be borne in mind.   First is the scantiness of our
knowledge.   A great deal happened in Palestine in the first
century of which we have no record.   Silence is only
significant in the case of events such as one of our extant
sources might have been expected to know about and to think
worth recording.   And secondly, it is doubtful whether the
events in Mt. 1-2 are of such a character.   If the
crucifixion of Jesus achieved no non-Christian record at the
time, and only began to be noticed in the light of the
movement which arose from it /3/, can we assume that the visit
of the magi and the killing of a few children in Bethlehem/4/,
if they actually happened, would have been known to, say,
Josephus nearly a century later, or, if he had known of them,
that he would have thought them worth including in his record?

(b) *Matthew compared with Luke.*
Scholarly exegesis is very conscious of the need to read
the Matthaean and Lucan infancy narratives as independent
accounts, and not to interpret one in terms of the other,
mixing the magi with the shepherds in the manner of popular
tradition.   But both passages purport to deal with the birth
and childhood of the same historical person, and therefore if
the claim is made that both are historical accounts their
compatibility becomes an important factor.   Independent
accounts of the same event must at least avoid contradiction
if both are to be taken seriously as historical sources.   Do
Matthew and Luke contradict one another?

There is, of course, a lot of common ground: the
betrothed couple called Mary and Joseph, the latter of
Davidic descent, the conception without human intercourse by
the Holy Spirit, the angelic revelation of the name Jesus,
the birth in Bethlehem in the reign of Herod, and the

upbringing in Nazareth /5/; all these are found in both
Matthew and Luke, and they add up to a basic 'story-line'
presumably agreed in earlier Christian tradition.

But, quite apart from the wide area of independent
material where the two accounts do not overlap at all, there
is one problem about the consistency of the basic 'story-line'
itself /6/. This concerns the parental home, which according
to Luke was at Nazareth until just before Jesus' birth (Lk.
1:26, 39, 56; 2:4f), after which the family apparently
returned to Nazareth from Jerusalem when Jesus was forty days
old (Lk. 2:22, 39). In Matthew no mention is made of the
parental home before Jesus' birth at Bethlehem, but the move
to Nazareth does not come until after the visit of the magi
(when Jesus was a 'child' in a 'house', aged 'two years old or
under') and an unspecified period in Egypt concluding after
Herod's death, and then it looks more like an unexpected new
domicile rather than a return home (2:22f).

This difference, by which 'even the most determined
harmonizer should be foiled'/7/, does not of course affect the
agreed sequence of birth at Bethlehem and upbringing at
Nazareth, nor does Matthew contradict Luke's statement that
Mary and Joseph came from Nazareth; he clearly did not know
that this was the case, to judge by the wording of 2:22f, but
he does not offer any alternative domicile before the birth.
The discrepancy lies rather in the chronology, where Lk.
2:22, 39 apparently does not leave room for the Bethlehem and
Egypt events of Mt. 2. But chronological compression is not
uncommon in the gospels; if Luke, not having any further
incident to record between those when Jesus was 40 days and 12
years old, fails to insert a pedantic note to the effect that
the Jerusalem visit was followed by a return to Bethlehem and
a period of even a few years before the ultimate return to
Nazareth, and therefore gives the impression of a direct
return there from Jerusalem, what does this imply? Probably
that he did not know of the occurence of these events; or
that he knew of them, but preferred a flowing narrative to a
pedantic footnote. Whichever is the case, this hardly seems
a firm basis on which to impugn the historicity of what he, or
Matthew, *does* record.

What emerges most clearly from the comparison of
Matthew's infancy narratives with Luke's is that they are
independent /8/. Each clearly knows of events of which the

other is ignorant, and each writes in very different style and
for different purposes.   But neither falsifies the explicit
statements of the other, for apart from the shared 'story-line'
outlined above, Matthew and Luke, like Matthew and secular
history, simply do not intersect.

(c) *Supernatural phenomena.*
     Undoubtedly the main reason for doubt over the
historical character of the NT infancy narratives is not that
they conflict either with one another or with other
historical sources, but that they record events which fall
outside our normal experience.   In these two chapters
Matthew records no less than five dreams by which God
communicated with men, three of them featuring 'an angel of
the Lord'; a star which not only conveyed a factual message
but which also moved in such a way as to indicate a specific
location; and above all the conception of a child by the
Holy Spirit without human intercourse.   Such experiences do
not belong to the world most of us know; that sort of thing
just does not happen to us, and so, it is frequently
concluded, it did not happen then.

     The virgin conception has been endlessly discussed, and
involves much wider data than the section of Matthew we are
considering here.   No one would defend it as a biologically
normal event, nor would most of us thank anyone who produced a
scientifically authenticated example of an allegedly parallel
conception today.   It is precisely as a unique divine
provision for a unique occasion that it is recorded by the NT
writers and has been accepted in Christian theology.   If for
some this puts it outside the pale of historical possibility,
there are others who do not find it impossible to believe
that God is not bound by the normal operation of his creation,
indeed who would think it strange if the climactic event of
God's long-awaited coming did not break through the limits of
everyday experience.

     But many Christians who are prepared to accept the
historicity of so important an occurrence as the virgin
conception are less comfortable with the angels and the star.
Are these not rather peripheral, unnecessary extravagances
which detract from the sober reality of the Saviour's birth?
But modern Western tastes as to what is appropriate do not
settle the question of historicity.   For Matthew they were
clearly appropriate, and he gives no clue that he considered

them other than factual.   In fact Matthew is not given to
introducing angels gratuitously into his story.   The only
angel who appears 'publicly' in Matthew is the one who moved
the stone (Mt. 28:2ff), where he is an agent in the supremely
supernatural event of the resurrection.   Otherwise, angels
appear only in Jesus' private experience in the wilderness
(Mt. 4:11) and here in Mt. 1-2 where in each case they are
seen in dreams, not in waking experience.   Dreams are, of
course, not susceptible to historical verification; it might,
however, be salutary for Western Christians who dismiss
guidance through dreams as a flight of the imagination, to
spend some time among African Christians in order to realise
how accepted a part of Christian experience this can be, as it
was of course an accepted feature of the world to which
Matthew (and Joseph and the magi) belonged.

Dreams, of course, are all in the mind.   But a moving
star is a public spectacle.   Attempts to identify the star of
Mt. 2 with a natural phenomenon have included mainly a
comet /9/, the special conjunction of Saturn and Jupiter in
the constellation of Pisces in 7 BC /10/, and a nova,
probably that mentioned by Chinese astronomers in 5/4 BC /11/.
But no known phenomenon clearly accounts for the movement of
the star and its 'coming and standing over' Bethlehem as
recorded in verse 9 /12/, so that even if one (or more!) of
the above suggestions might account for the initial interest
of the magi, it seems that Matthew is speaking of guidance by
abnormal means, appropriate indeed to the magi, but outside
their, and our, scientific experience.   If such an event is
deemed impossible, then, for all the labours of astronomers,
Matthew's star cannot be historical.   Like the virgin
conception, it confronts us with a choice which involves
fundamental philosophical questions as to the limits of what
is possible.   To this question we shall return.

II   Matthew 1-2 as midrash

Most scholarly objections to Mt. 1-2 as factual history
do not focus nowadays on the traditional lines just described,
but on the belief that to ask such questions of this passage
at all is a category mistake.   These stories are not meant to
be history; they belong to a different literary genre.   In
this connection the dominant word of the last decade has been
'midrash' /13/.

It is questionable how much light the word 'midrash'
itself throws on the discussion, as it is used in widely
varying ways.   Everyone agrees that its etymological meaning
is something like 'interpretation' or 'study' (of Scripture),
and that it is the name for a literary genre within
post-Jamnian Judaism which is essentially a commentary on a
passage of Scripture, but which typically ranges far beyond
what we would regard as exegesis of the text in its search for
the true meaning of the inspired words.   The main area of
uncertainty is whether the word should be applied only to the
literary genre so described, or also to the hermeneutical
techniques which are characteristic of this genre, or further
to the attitude to Scripture which gave rise to these
techniques, or to some or all of these at once.

There is scope here for some slipperiness of language
which can make mutual understanding difficult.   This paper,
therefore, while it will be concerned with the debate
represented by the term 'midrash' as applied to Mt. 1-2, will
be cautious in its use of that term, preferring to specify
whether I am speaking of Matthew as commenting on a
consecutive portion of Scripture or on some 'sacred'
tradition, or as delighting in tracing the application of
assorted scriptural passages to the events he describes, or as
using to this end hermeneutical techniques which we might find
questionable or unconvincing.   Above all, I shall try not to
assume that one of these activities necessarily implies the
others; the term 'midrash' easily becomes an illegitimate
bridge from what Matthew can be shown to be doing to what he
is assumed to have done because other 'midrashists' did it.
To agree that Matthew shares some characteristics of Jewish
midrash is not to make him in all ways typical of the
genre /14/.

In particular we must not lose sight of the important
point that, however much Matthew may or may not have shared
the outlook and techniques of the compilers of midrashim, his
infancy narratives (and of course still more the rest of his
gospel) do not take the form of a commentary on any given
section of the OT.   The OT occupies a very prominent place in
them, but the structural framework of Mt. 1-2 is a series of
traditions about the birth and childhood of Jesus, into which
scriptural themes and quotations are woven as the narrative
suggests them.   The 'given' was the story of Jesus; various
OT passages and themes find their coherence in this tradition,

but could not by themselves form the basis for these chapters.
Mt. 1-2 is not, then, commentary on any part of the OT; in
that sense it is not, in literary form, a midrash /15/.

From this point the defender of the historical
character of the narrative might be tempted to go on to rule
midrash out of court as an inappropriate category, and so to
play down the significance of scriptural themes in these
chapters.   But this will not do.   Mt. 1-2, even if it is not
a commentary on a given passage of Scripture, is saturated
with scriptural themes, and one of the author's principal
aims and delights is to trace the connections between these
themes, and to weave them together into an exposition of the
significance of the events recorded.   In the process we are
confronted with several examples of the use of Scripture
which C. F. D. Moule characterises as 'to our critical eyes,
manifestly forced and artificial and unconvincing' /16/ and
which resemble both in conception and in execution what we
find in Jewish midrashim.

In other words, even if Mt. 1-2 is not, formally
speaking, midrash, it shares a mentality and techniques
which can fairly be called 'midrashic'.   The deeper one digs
into the language and conception of these chapters, the
richer becomes the variety of scriptural material uncovered.
Matthew did not just quote a few proof-texts; he delighted
to weave scriptural themes into his narrative with an
enthusiasm unmatched even at Qumran.

In an article restricted only to the four formula-
quotations of Mt. 2 /17/, I have tried to demonstrate that
much more was involved than the obvious application of each
quoted text to that point in the narrative where it is
introduced.   Beneath this 'surface meaning' are further
'bonus' ideas for those who are prepared to dig deeper,
those with a specially close knowledge of the context or
original form of the text quoted, or those who shared
certain common traditions of interpretation with the author.
And in the narrative of chapters 1-2, apart from the formula-
quotations, the range of scriptural material becomes far
wider, involving typological connections, some more some less
explicit, with numerous themes of Israel's past.   Thus M. M.
Bourke /18/ finds in Mt. 1-2 numerous echoes of the stories
(in Scripture and later tradition) of Moses, Abraham, Jacob
the man, and Israel the nation (particularly the Exodus

experience), while W. D. Davies /19/ finds here the themes of
a new creation, a new David, a new Moses, a new Israel, a new
Exodus, among 'a complexity of emphases...which interpenetrate
so closely that to dissect them is to distort' (p. 73).   The
story of the Magi in particular is generally agreed to include
deliberate echoes of many scriptural themes beyond the one
formal quotation it includes: the star (cf. Num. 24:17) is
only the most obvious of a number of possible allusions to
Balaam /20/; the homage of the magi and their gifts have been
traced especially to Ps. 72:10ff and Is. 60:1ff; and the
echoes of the Queen of Sheba's visit to Solomon have also led
to the whole story being seen as a midrash on 1 Kings 10 /21/.
The figure of Joseph in chapter 1 has been seen as modelled on
that of the OT Joseph /22/, while the clearly artificial
structuring of the genealogy gives rise to many fascinating
speculations as to the scriptural connections it was meant to
evoke in the erudite reader /23/.

So one major purpose of his infancy narratives was to
explore the theme of Jesus' fulfilment of Scripture, and to
this end his wording has been ingeniously chosen to bring out
a wide range of parallels from the OT and Jewish tradition.
If that is a distinguishing mark of midrash, then Mt. 1-2 is
boldly midrashic in character, whatever its literary genre.

III   Midrash and history

But what has all this to do with the historical value of
the infancy narratives?   Put simply, it leads some to this
equation: Jewish midrashim were given to imaginative
expansion of the material which Scripture and tradition
provided, and Matthew is midrashic, therefore Matthew may be
assumed to be relying as much on his and other Christians'
imagination as on historical tradition.   If an incident
helped to draw out the scriptural significance of Jesus, its
historicity was not an issue.   Christian tradition, like
Jewish, was subject to pious elaboration, and a writer such as
Matthew would be the last to resist such a development.

Now it is undeniable that such pious elaboration was a
feature of later Christianity.   The story of the magi, for
instance, gradually developed from its basic Matthaean form
to include their description as kings, their being three in
number, their differing geographical origins and subsequent
histories, and a number of different sets of names for them/24/.

But the fact that later Christians felt free to
elaborate earlier tradition does not *per se* prove that
Matthew or his predecessors also did so.   It is here that the
word 'midrash' must be used with caution.   R. E. Brown
describes this later Christian elaboration as 'Christian
midrash' /25/, 'midrashim in the strictest sense' /26/.
This is valid in so far as these Christian traditions are
doing what was often done in Jewish midrash.   But this is not
the characteristic of midrash which we have seen above to be
typical also of Mt. 1-2.   The description of Matthew as
'midrashic' is valid only in relation to those aspects of his
work which are demonstrably parallel to Jewish midrashim; it
does not entitle us to import into our understanding of
Matthew a whole package labelled 'midrash' which includes the
imaginative creation of ostensibly historical details.
Matthew may or may not have included such fictional
elaborations, but this must be shown from the evidence of
Matthew, not from the later practice of 'midrashic'
Christianity /27/.

A clear example of this questionable inference from
Matthew's midrashic interests to the fictional character of
the events he describes may be seen in M. D. Goulder's
treatment of the story of the magi /28/.   Beginning with Gen.
25:19 - 28:8, which he sees as the lectionary reading
underlying this section of the gospel, Goulder draws together
a complex collection of scriptural themes which he finds
reflected in Matthew's narrative (Is. 60; Ps. 72; Song of
Solomon; Joseph's dreams; the migration to Egypt; Num.
24:17; the pillar of cloud and fire; Nebuchadnezzar and
Daniel; and more).   He then continues: 'Midrashic
reference is to be intuited rather than proven.   Schniewind
maintains that we have to do here with remembered history,
and who can prove him wrong?'   Yet Goulder has said nothing
so far against the historicity of the narrative; he has
merely explored ('intuited') its scriptural background.
But he now assumes that this midrashic reference is in
opposition to 'remembered history' as the foundation of the
narrative, that what is recorded as reflecting OT themes was
therefore invented for this purpose.   Matthew, having been
labelled a 'midrashist', is credited with 'making stories up',
since this is one of the 'general traits of midrash' /29/.
The possibility is not considered that Matthew received a
historical tradition, perceived in it certain links with the
OT, and so wrote it up in such a way as to draw out these

connections.   While I do not find all Goulder's 'midrashic
references' convincing, I agree with him that Mt. 2:1-12 is
full, deliberately full, of scriptural echoes.   But I cannot
see why this fact puts it outside the category of
'remembered history'.

This example, which seems typical of Goulder's
approach /30/, is mentioned here as one of the more egregious
instances of the assumption without supporting evidence that
'midrashic' material is necessarily unhistorical /31/.
There may be arguments for and against the historicity of the
magi, but in the absence of such arguments the passage from
'midrashic' to 'unhistorical' does not seem compelling.

So the introduction of the word 'midrash' is not by
itself sufficient to remove Mt. 1-2 from the realm of factual
history.   What is needed is some plausible account of the
origin of the traditions these chapters record.

IV   Did Matthew make it all up?

Goulder's thesis is that Matthew's gospel is
essentially a midrash on Mark with the aid of OT passages
derived from a lectionary (and therefore that the infancy
narratives, having no Marcan basis, derive almost entirely
from the evangelist's free creativity on the basis of the OT
and other Jewish traditional material).   In addition to the
assumption that Matthew's 'midrashic' character indicates
that he made stories up, two connected arguments are used to
support this thesis.   First, following Kilpatrick's lead,
his discussion of each pericope includes a list of
'characteristic Matthaean diction' found in it, and an
appendix is devoted to isolating 'a vocabulary of
characteristic words' /32/.   The argument is that
'Matthaean diction' indicates Matthaean origin.   It does, of
course, indicate Matthaean *composition*, and each section of
the infancy narratives provides evidence of this (though the
magi pericope in particular includes sufficient
'non-Matthaean' vocabulary to require some qualifications) /33/
This shows, then, that Matthew did not here incorporate
earlier traditions unchanged into his gospel.   But this is
hardly surprising; no one today expects to find Matthew
merely recording tradition in traditional words, without
placing on it the stamp of his own theological interests and
linguistic preferences.   But Matthaean wording proves

nothing about the *origin* of the traditions he records.

Similarly, a note at the end of Goulder's book /34/ offers 'what seems to be statistical proof' that Matthew had no sources other than Mark: whereas in Marcan passages only 18% of the words are characteristically Matthaean, in the infancy narratives the figure is 28% (and similar figures apply to the Q and M passages). But, assuming the statistics are correct and the 'characteristic vocabulary' is properly selected (and I have no reason to doubt either), what does this prove?   It certainly makes it unlikely that Matthew used other written sources comparable to Mark in the same way that he used Mark, and might therefore cause some discomfort to those who see Q as a unitary written source. But I for one would never have envisaged the infancy narratives coming to Matthew in a fixed literary form like Mark.   And an argument against Matthew's use of *written sources* is not an argument against his dependence on earlier *traditions*, retold in his own characteristic way, but not therefore necessarily the product of his own imagination. Unless Matthaean criticism is to be put back into the era of scissors-and-paste redaction, vocabulary statistics are not going to help us much in determining whether Matthew made up the stories he narrates, or whether he received them as factual tradition /35/.

It is, in fact, widely agreed that at least Mt. 1:18 - 2:23 rests largely on previous narrative traditions, whether these were independent stories or already collected in one or more groups of infancy traditions /36/.   The five formula-quotations in these chapters reinforce this view, as it is generally agreed that these, together with the other formula-quotations of the gospel, were added at a late stage (i.e. by the evangelist himself) as comments on already existing narratives /37/.   To remove each of these quotations with its introductory formula from the surrounding narrative would leave a coherent, indeed in most cases a more flowing, story.   But we shall return to this in the next section.

But to dismiss arguments for Matthew's invention of the stories he relates, and to affirm that they came to him as tradition, is not yet to solve the problem of the origin of those stories.   Matthew may have recorded them believing them to be factual, but did they arise through pious

imagination at an earlier stage?   After all Matthew was not,
we may assume, the only person in the first-century church to
be fascinated by the theme of Jesus as the fulfiller of
Scripture.   Is it not possible that the scriptural themes
which so clearly pervade the stories as Matthew tells them
were in fact the clay out of which the stories themselves were
originally moulded before they came to him as historical
narrative?   This question requires some examination of the
relation between Scripture and tradition in these chapters.

V Scripture and tradition

No other section of the gospels is so obviously linked to
the OT as Mt. 1-2.   This is true not only with regard to the
frequency and complexity of quotation and allusion, but also
in the very structure of the chapters.   The genealogy is a
clearly artificial structure whose numerical form is probably
based on a scriptural pattern /38/.   1:18 - 2:23 then falls
into five sections each centred on a formula-quotation.   And
these quotations come in not as additional comments on a story
told for its own sake, but as themselves the focal point of
the stories in which they are set.   Thus when Matthew's
infancy narratives are compared with Luke's, the difference is
immediately apparent.   Luke is a story-teller;   his
narratives are about real people, in whose individual
characters he is clearly interested, and about real situations
which are sketched out so that the reader can enjoy them and
enter into them.   But Matthew's five pericopes are almost
skeletal, the bare facts set down only as far as is necessary
to provide the setting for the claim to fulfilment.   Even the
birth of Jesus itself is only hinted at, not narrated.
Where Matthew does indulge in a little story-telling,
particularly in the story of the magi, it is quickly apparent
that the details are built around further OT allusions,
adding more scriptural weight to the explicit claim of the
formula-quotations.

Structurally speaking, then, these chapters are built
around OT quotations and allusions.   A consecutive story of
Jesus' birth and infancy told for its own sake would not look
like Mt. 1-2.

Does this mean, then, that here Scripture gave rise to
tradition, that the 'stories' are imaginative creations out
of the text?   That does not follow.   To include a number of

stories because they are seen as clear fulfilments of OT
texts, and to tell them in such a way as to highlight that
fulfilment, is not at all the same exercise as starting with
a given text, and concocting an imaginary story as its
supposed fulfilment, for at least three reasons.

1. *Why these texts?*
The midrashist had a text in front of him on which he set
out to comment and elaborate.   He might draw in many other
texts, to us quite obscurely related, in the process, but he
had a given text as his starting point.   But Matthew had not.
The five formula-quotations which form the framework of the
narrative had no known previous connection with each other,
nor were they individually at all obvious as a selection on
which to construct an exposition of the significance of Jesus.
Some (especially Jer. 31:15) seem to us quite inappropriate;
one is not recognisable as a straight quotation from the OT
at all (Mt. 2:23).   The connection of these five passages
with one another, and their presence in Matthew's narrative,
is not because they were a given starting-point for him, but
because each in its own way was, for Matthew, relevant to an
incident in Jesus' infancy and *therefore* played a part in the
aim of these chapters to draw out the significance of Jesus'
origins.   Thus it was the incidents which brought the texts
into Matthew's scheme, not vice versa.   The only framework
Matthew had for his account was not, as for the midrashist, a
scriptural text, but a collection of traditions about Jesus.
Without such traditions already in existence, there is no
reason for these particular texts to appear at all /39/.

Once they have come in, it is natural that Matthew tells
his story in such a way as to emphasize their relevance, and
so the account becomes structured around the texts, as noted
above.   But the process must have begun with the traditions
which suggested the texts in the first place /40/.

2. *The form of the quotations.*
While it is true that the narrative has been constructed
in such a way as to highlight the relevance of the
quotations, it is equally true that in some cases the wording
of the quotation has been adapted to fit the narrative
context /41/.   The alterations to the text of Micah 5:1, and
the insertion into it of words from 2 Sam. 5:2, serve to draw
out more unambiguously the status of the Messiah born in
Bethlehem, an expedient which was only required if Jesus'

birth in Bethlehem was a fixed datum of tradition.   More
remarkably, the enigmatic 'quotation' 'He shall be called a
Nazarene' is clearly the result of some fairly drastic
adaptation of OT words or ideas, so drastic that no one can be
sure from what OT texts it began.   Such free handling of the
wording of the OT would be incomprehensible if the fact of
Jesus' Nazarene origin were not already a fixed datum which
required scriptural authentication.   To invent Jesus'
upbringing in such an improbable place as Nazareth out of
whatever OT text lies behind Mt. 2:23 would be a prodigious
tour de force.   In any case, no one doubts that Jesus was
always known to have come from Nazareth.   The point here is
that it is that fact which accounts for Matthew's ingenious
'quotation' in 2:23, so that here at least it is
inconceivable that the text produced the tradition.

3.   *The idea of 'fulfilment'*.
The explicit object of the formula-quotations is to claim
that in the events of Jesus' infancy the OT was 'fulfilled'.
This is, of course, a major theme of Matthew's gospel as a
whole, and one which distinguishes him from current Jewish use
of the OT /42/.   Is it too simplistic to ask what meaning
'fulfilment' could have if the supposed event is in fact
known to be a fiction derived from the OT text itself?
What would be the point of proclaiming 'then was fulfilled..',
if nothing in fact happened 'then', nor at all outside the
author's own mind?   The notion of fulfilment when applied to
alleged events surely requires some *point d'appui* subsequent
to the prophecy itself, not just a meditation on the
significance of the prophet's words, clothed in the form of a
fictional narrative.   At least for the person who makes the
claim, the 'fulfilling' events must be factual, otherwise the
argument is meaningless.   In other words, if Matthew
introduced the formula-quotations, he did so because he
believed the stories to which he applied them to be
historical.   He may, of course, have been mistaken, but at
least Matthew's formula-quotations themselves cannot be the
source of the traditions.

As far as the formula-quotations themselves are
concerned, then, it seems clear that they were added by
Matthew to existing traditions, and were not themselves the
source of those traditions /43/.

But the formula-quotations, prominent as they are, are only one part of the OT material which is employed in Mt. 1-2, and from the compositional point of view they are apparently the latest.   More subtly woven into the stories are a variety of allusions to scriptural themes, some of which have been mentioned above /44/.   Even if it be granted, then, that the traditions preceded the formula-quotations, is it not possible that it was meditation on these other scriptural themes which gave rise to the infancy traditions before they came to Matthew and his church as factual accounts?   The most plausible such theme is that of the childhood of Moses.   Mt. 2 contains several possible echoes of the story as found in the early chapters of Exodus, including a near-quotation of Ex. 4:19 in Mt. 2:20 (though admittedly the period of Moses' life there in question is not his infancy).   But much more impressive are the echoes of later Jewish elaboration of the Moses story, as found particularly in Josephus and in the Palestinian Targum /45/. There is no doubt that Matthew's story is told in the light of these traditions, and that therefore the portrayal of Jesus in his infancy as a new Moses is part of the aim of these chapters.

From this observation some scholars move to the suggestion that the Mosaic colouring is not a typological theme embroidered onto an existing tradition about Jesus, but is the evidence of where that tradition began.   Thus P. Winter writes, 'The legend $\lceil$ of the killing of the children $\rceil$ owed its origin to the intention of portraying Jesus in the role of "the second Moses".   Its authors were led by a conscious urge to fill in the picture of Jesus with traits well known to a Jewish public from their traditional concepts of Moses.' /46/.   He goes on to develop the idea of an 'anonymous popular poetry' whereby 'these stories had developed artlessly in the secrecy of legend and folk tale', which provided the material for Matthew's infancy narratives /47/.   I have discussed this suggestion elsewhere /48/, and have pointed out first that there is not sufficient evidence in the pre-Matthaean material of the rest of the gospel for an interest in Jesus as a 'new Moses' to support the case, and secondly that within Mt. 1-2 the Mosaic typology is only one of a number of typological themes /49/ which run side by side in a rich diversity, brought together only by their common relevance to the stories of Jesus in which they are embedded.   I argued

therefore that the Mosaic typology should not be seen as the
original warp onto which the stories were woven, but as one
of several strands woven into the warp of the stories of Jesus.

Such an argument is not open to conclusive demonstration.
What to one scholar seems the most probable explanation of the
mentality and literary technique of a first-century author may
seem anachronistic to another. But I would return to my
question about the 'fulfilment' theme. Assuming that the
presence of all these scriptural themes in Mt. 1-2 is evidence
of a desire (not necessarily Matthew's, but at some earlier
stage of tradition) to point out how Jesus has fulfilled the
scriptural pattern (and that is how typology is normally
understood), would not this argument be rendered ineffective
(or at least reduced to the level of a confidence trick) if
the supposed points of correspondence were in fact purely
imaginary? It could be that it *was* all a confidence trick,
but that seems to me an interpretation to be avoided where a
more rational procedure can be suggested. But if the
traditions about Jesus were received as factual, then it
would be both a more convincing and a devotionally
satisfying approach to tell them in such a way as to bring
out their typological significance. It is hard to enter
into the mind of a Christian in the first few decades after
Jesus' death who would invent a fictional incident in order
to establish a typological significance for Jesus and then
pass it on as a factual tradition; and yet, if these
traditions are not historically based, *someone* at some time
must have done that.

This argument seems to be strengthened by the
recognition of an apologetic aim in these chapters.
Stendahl's valuable article 'Quis et Unde?'/50/ has shown
how these chapters establish the scriptural grounds for the
identity and the geographical origins of Jesus as the
Messiah. There is, of course, great christological
value in such a study for the Christian believer, but
Stendahl rightly stresses its apologetic importance for the
outsider, particularly with reference to the geographical
theme of the second chapter. Such an apologetic is evoked
by the existence of facts which need to be explained /51/.
One does not invent inconvenient facts in order to defend
them!

From a literary point of view, therefore, it seems more
probable that tradition came before scripture, that the
scriptural texts and allusions were woven into existing
narratives at various stages of the tradition before
Matthew as well as in his redaction because they seemed to
the early Christians to be relevant to the stories as
prediction and type to fulfilment.   The scriptural themes of
these chapters are rich and prominent, and given such
narrative tradition to relate to, they very naturally come to
expression in the telling of the stories, first by more
subtle typological colouring, then at Matthew's hand by
explicit quotations which dominate and give shape to the
narratives.   But if there was no narrative there in the
first place, the whole development lacks a plausible
starting-point.

VI   Verisimilitude and historicity

The results of this study have so far been largely
destructive, in that they have indicated the inadequacy of
various approaches to the question of the historical basis of
Matthew's infancy narratives.   In the nature of the case,
such an argument proves nothing constructively, but I hope it
does at least caution against a too hasty dismissal of these
infancy narratives as imaginative fiction.   I believe that
it leaves the question of historicity still open, where many
would have thought it already closed.   Indeed I would go
further and affirm that in the absence of any other probable
starting-point for these traditions, it is *prima facie* likely
that they are what they purport to be, records of actual
events.   In principle, the most probable starting-point for
any narrative tradition is the occurrence of the event it
relates, and nothing has so far caused us to abandon that
explanation of Mt. 1-2.

But are these events credible in the real world of
first-century Palestine?   Do they ring true?   It is true,
of course, that verisimilitude does not in itself prove
historicity, for a historical novel aims for verisimilitude
in its depiction of fictional events.   But it may be
questioned how much Matthew's literary method has in common
with that of the writer of historical novels, or indeed how
far verisimilitude was the concern of the writers of
exemplary fiction in the world to which he belonged.   At

least some comment on the historical verisimilitude of the
setting and events of Mt. 1-2 is relevant to our theme, as it
is a great deal easier to accept the historical origin of
credible traditions than of incredible ones!

Here, of course, the supernatural elements in the
stories mentioned above, particularly the moving star and the
virginal conception, necessarily come to the fore. We shall
return to them, but first I would like to comment on the
historical setting of the narratives apart from these
elements.

One striking feature of the Matthaean infancy
narratives is that, apart from the story of the magi, they
focus almost exclusively on Joseph and are told from his
standpoint. Some explanation of this is surely needed, for
while his legal paternity of Jesus is necessary, following
the genealogy, to establish Jesus' Davidic status, this does
not account for the almost 'biographical' interest in his
reactions in chapter 1 or his prominence in the itinerary of
chapter 2. This can hardly be attributed to Matthew's
special interest in view of the fact that there is not a
single reference to Joseph in Matthew's gospel outside these
chapters. Do these stories, then, derive from some other
source with a special interest in Joseph? But Joseph was
not a figure of importance in any Christian circles
represented elsewhere in the NT, for he is barely
mentioned, and then as little more than background scenery.
It is not easy to think of a more likely explanation for
this unusual interest in Joseph than the very traditional
view that the stories derive ultimately from Joseph himself.
How they found their way from him to Matthew's gospel must
remain a mystery, but nothing that we know of first-century
Christianity suggests any other plausible source. And if
that is the case, the implications for the factual origin of
the traditions are obvious.

Be that as it may, the setting of most of the narrative
of Mt. 1-2 is the experience of an obscure descendant of
David, who is not himself a major actor in the events, but
rather the bewildered victim of extraordinary circumstances.
His main function is as the recipient of divine
instructions by means of dreams (no less than four dreams in
the 19 verses in which he figures). The expectation of

divine revelation through dreams was commonplace in the
ancient world, however foreign it may be to some (but not all)
modern cultures, and Joseph's prompt obedience to such
revelation, even when it countermanded the dictates of his
very conventional conscience (1:19-20), is just what we would
expect in an ordinarily pious man of his period. His choice
of Egypt as a place of exile, even if we are not prepared to
accept that it was specified in his dream, was in line with
the practice of other Palestinians who feared reprisals from
the government /52/; as a neighbouring country with a
sizeable Jewish population it was an obvious refuge.   And
his subsequent avoidance of Judaea under Archelaus, and
expectation of safety instead in Galilee, accords with the
political circumstances as we know them.   In short, Joseph
and his experiences ring true in the south-east
Mediterranean world of the turn of the era, and the
distinctive focus of these stories accords well with an
origin in Joseph's own reminiscences.

But if Joseph can be believed, surely the magi
following the star are too extraordinary to be true.   The
behaviour of the star is generally agreed to be
inexplicable by normal astronomical means.   But apart from
this feature, to which we shall return, commentators have
pointed out the intrinsic verisimilitude of the visit of the
magi /53/.   Astrological interest in Babylon and other
parts of 'the East' is well attested, and the willingness of
such sages to draw political conclusions from their
researches and to travel west on the basis of their results
is attested by the famous visit to Italy of Tiridates and
other eastern magi in AD 66 /54/.   The belief that the
birth of great men was heralded by special stars is also
widely attested.   The gifts brought by the magi are
regularly mentioned as precious products of Arabia and other
'eastern' lands, and would have caused no surprise as
valuable exotic produce.   Thus the basic story-line of the
visit of the magi is not in itself historically improbable,
whatever may be thought of the description of the
astronomical phenomenon which caused it.

Moreover, it may be suggested that astrologers are not
the most likely group to be introduced into Christian
fiction by a church which soon found itself obliged to
combat astrological beliefs.   It was *kings* who became the
focus of Christian legend-building at this point, on the

basis presumably of OT passages such as Ps. 72:10f and Is.
60:1-3; had the story been fictional and inspired by
reflection on the OT, they might have been expected to be kings
from the beginning, certainly not magi.

But the other actor in the story of the magi and the
subsequent events looks too much like a stock character for
some interpreters to take his role as factual. Would the real
Herod have acted so perfectly the part of the fairy-tale
villain? But at least there can be no doubt that there was a
real Herod, and we have in Josephus' writings a very full
account of his reign. There is room for doubt over many of
the details of Josephus' accounts, but the main outline of
Herod's character and behaviour is not seriously contested,
despite Josephus' evident prejudice against him. Josephus
depicts a ruthless, cruel man, unpopular with his Jewish
subjects not only because of his mixed race but because of the
tyrannical nature of his rule. More relevant to our present
purpose, he depicts a man whose obsession with conspiracy, real
and imagined, led him to drastic measures in defence of his
throne, including the execution of his three eldest sons and of
his favourite wife, as well as several other potential rivals
among his relatives and several large groups of actual or
suspected conspirators /55/. The fact that the majority of
these incidents happened during the last four years of Herod's
reign, the period of Jesus' birth, is surely relevant to our
question. It is thus quite in character that Herod, in that
period, should be deeply alarmed by a report of the birth of a
rival, and should take drastic steps to eliminate that rival,
even at the cost of the indiscriminate killing of a few
children in a small village /56/.

More suspect as historical fact is Herod's incompetence
in failing to identify the potential rival either by having the
magi followed or by local enquiry as to which house they had
visited. But he had no reason to doubt the willingness of the
magi to co-operate, and it cannot be assumed that the local
population would be eager to supply information to their
Idumaean tyrant. Besides, the Herod of the last few years
was, according to Josephus, not entirely responsible for his
actions, and more given to violent reaction than to careful
planning /57/.

A further objection that the bad relations between Herod
and the Sanhedrin would have made the consultation of

Mt. 2:4-6 impossible assumes that Matthew's grandiloquent language is intended to describe a formal convening of the Sanhedrin;   a less formal consultation of those religious leaders prepared to co-operate would have been quite feasible.

In short, the basic story-line of chapters 1-2, focussed on the characters of Joseph, Herod and the magi, falls well within the bounds of historical probability.   These were the sort of things which, as far as our historical knowledge allows us to judge, could well have happened in that time and place.   They are not typical of life in the western world of the twentieth century, but those who live in the less sophisticated parts of the world even today will have less difficulty in identifying both with the raw tyranny and with the openness to supernatural guidance which characterise Matthew's stories.

But verisimilitude is not by itself proof of historicity, and when the events which occur in such a historically plausible setting are themselves incredible, verisimilitude may be attributed to careful fiction rather than to factual recording.

We discussed previously /58/ three aspects of the stories which may be thought to come in this category, the dreams with their angels, the moving star, and the conception without human intercourse.   Of these the first is less of a difficulty: dreams are not public events, and the evidence is impressive that, unfamiliar as this experience of revelation may be to most modern biblical scholars, it has been, and still is for many, a regular feature of life in a less materialistic environment.   But the star and the virginal conception remain firmly empirical, and starkly out of tune with scientific man's experience of reality.   Three courses seem possible.   One is to conclude from these impossible' elements that the stories as a whole, however plausible in other respects, are fictional;   a second is to accept the essential story-line, but to eliminate these supernatural elements as legendary accretion;   the third is to affirm that 'miraculous' happenings are not theoretically impossible, however uncommon they may be in our experience, and that in the setting of God's unique presence in the baby born in Bethlehem such happenings should not be ruled out of court.

No doubt readers of Matthew will continue to be divided
between these options, depending on their presuppositions
both as to Matthew's beliefs and literary methods and as to
the omnicompetence of scientific explanation. The latter
question in particular clearly falls outside the scope of
this paper. All I am concerned to point out here is that if
these supernatural elements are pronounced unhistorical, it is
on the basis of an overall philosophy which has no room for
such events, not because the narratives in which they find
their place are in themselves implausible. Or, to put it the
other way, the interpreter who holds to the historicity of
Matthew's stories may be criticised for holding to a world
view which goes beyond the limits of scientific materialism,
and would presumably happily accept that criticism and not
regard it as a matter for reproach, but this criticism will
be a philosophical one rather than historical. Given the
acceptability of miracle, historical verisimilitude is on his
side.

VII Conclusion

This paper has moved from the criticism of alternative
explanations of the traditions of Mt. 1-2, particularly in
terms of imaginative creation on the basis of scriptural
motifs, to the assertion that in fact the most plausible
origin from a literary point of view is in the historical
occurrence of the events narrated, and a consideration of
those events has suggested that, unless supernatural
occurrences are ruled out *a priori*, they could well have
happened. All this adds up to a *prima facie* case for the
historicity of the story-line of Matthew's infancy
narratives, even when full recognition has been accorded to
the rich variety of scriptural elements which have been drawn
into their formulation.

But has it all been worth doing? Does it matter
whether the events are historical or not? Can we not learn
as much from Matthew's scriptural meditations and
theological emphases whether the events around which he
weaves them happened or not?

We have noted above two reasons why Matthew himself is
likely to have regarded the question of historicity as
important. One is the apologetic aim of these chapters.
To engage in apologetics at all implies that the traditions

which are being explained are believed to be factual, or there would be no point in defending or explaining them. And it would hardly be wise to construct that apologetic by inventing fictional events to account for factual traditions. Such an apologetic could not hope to succeed in the face of the awareness of the church at large that no such incidents had happened, even if the inventor could succeed in squaring such deliberate deception with his Christian conscience.

The other factor is Matthew's evident concern with the idea of fulfilment, a concept which in his gospel relates almost invariably to the occurrence of events which are regarded as predicted or foreshadowed in the OT.   It is hard to see how Matthew could make this claim, or indeed what meaning it could have, if he did not believe the events to be factual.

If then we are to do justice to Matthew's own concerns, we cannot dismiss the question of historicity, and this paper has shown, I hope, that there is good reason to affirm the historical origin of his infancy narratives, both on literary grounds and in the relation of their contents to the history of the time.   To recognise this fact is not to impoverish Christian theology by diverting attention from the rich interpretative material of these chapters, nor to suggest that these chapters were written primarily to record events for their own sake, but rather to enable us to enter further into Matthew's fertile mind by seeing how he has found in the real events of which he speaks the fulfilment of many themes of OT scripture.   Historicity for its own sake might prove a barren study, but without it our theological understanding of the significance of Jesus will lack its essential foundation.

Notes

/1/ The term 'infancy narratives' is only partially correct as a description of the contents of Mt. 1-2 and Lk. 1-2, but its familiarity makes it a convenient label for these chapters in general.

/2/ See my article in *NovT* 21 (1979) 116-118 for some suggested external evidence on the killing of the children at Bethlehem; it is not impressive.

/3/ This is true of the earliest non-Christian references,
viz. Tacitus, *Annals* xv 44; *Sanhedrin* 43a; Josephus, *Ant.*
xviii 64 (if this Christianised passage rests on an original
mention by Josephus).

/4/ See my discussion in *NovT* 21 (1979) 114 of the scale of
the incident, and its exaggeration in later Christian
tradition.

/5/ See R. E. Brown, *The Birth of the Messiah* (London:
Geoffrey Chapman, 1977) 34-5 for fuller details.

/6/ Space forbids any discussion of the differing
genealogies, which lie outside the narrative proper, though
they agree on Jesus' Davidic lineage, however this was
arrived at!

/7/ *Ibid.* 189.

/8/ The attempt of J. Drury, *Tradition and Design in Luke's
Gospel* (London: Darton, Longman & Todd, 1976) 122-5, to show
that Luke's infancy narratives are dependent on Matthew's, is
based on points at which they share the same motif (name of
Joseph, conception by the Holy Spirit, angelic announcement,
etc.) or confront the same problem (the Bethlehem/Nazareth
discrepancy).   All such 'agreements' are more simply
explained by a common tradition on which each worked
independently, especially when it is observed that at almost
every point Luke's method of introducing the motif or solving
the problem is strikingly different from Matthew's.   If it
were not for an overall theory of literary dependence to be
proved, Drury could hardly have come to this conclusion on
the basis of the infancy narratives themselves.

/9/ Halley's comet was seen in 12 BC, but the date is too
early to be taken seriously by many in this connection.   See
however J. E. Bruns, *CBQ* 23 (1961) 54.

/10/ E.g. E. Stauffer, *Jesus and his Story* (ET, London: SCM
Press, 1960) 36-38; R. A. Rosenberg, *Biblica* 53 (1972) 105-109.

/11/ E.g. *Quarterly Journal of the Royal Astronomical Society*
18 (1977) 443-449; cf. J. Finegan, *Handbook of Biblical
Chronology* (Princeton UP, 1964) 246-248.

/12/ See however E. L. Martin, *The Birth of Christ
Recalculated!* (Pasadena: Foundation for Biblical Research,
1978) 11-21 for a theory which attempts to explain these
features by means of the 'movements' of Jupiter in 3/2 BC.

/13/ 'Haggadah' is also much used in this connection.   The
words are not interchangeable, but in writings on the NT they
tend to be used to a similar purpose, and since 'midrash' is
the more commonly used I shall concentrate on that,

while recognising that it is more specifically 'haggadic midrash' which is the intended point of comparison with the infancy narratives.

/14/ On the definition of 'midrash', and its applicability to Mt. 1-2, see my brief comments in *NovT* 21 (1979) 100-101 and literature there cited.

/15/ Cf. e.g. R. E. Brown, *Birth* 37: 'The purpose of midrash was to make the OT account intelligible, and that is not the purpose of the infancy narratives.   They were written to make Jesus' origins intelligible against the background of the fulfillment of OT expectations.'   This point refers only to the literary genre of the passage, without prejudice to the attitude to and handling of those OT passages which are woven in with the narrative.   Douglas J. Moo, in a useful introduction to his unpublished Ph.D. dissertation (St. Andrews) 'The use of the OT in the gospel passion texts', points out that the term 'commentary' is more appropriately applied to the Qumran *pesharim*, which deal with the OT text in every detail and consecutively, than to the midrashim, which are luxuriant discourses hung on the text as a peg (pp. 12-13).   But this proper distinction does not affect the point that the OT text is the structural principle for the midrashim, however far they may stray from it, and however little real grounding some of the resultant material may have in the text to which it is attached.

/16/ *The Origin of Christology* (Cambridge UP, 1977) 129.

/17/ 'The Formula-Quotations of Matthew 2 and the Problem of Communication', *NTS* 27 (1980/1) 233-252.

/18/ *CBQ* 22 (1960) 161-173.

/19/ *The Setting of the Sermon on the Mount* (Cambridge UP, 1963) 67-83.

/20/ See R. E. Brown, *Birth* 117.

/21/ J. E. Bruns, *CBQ* 23 (1961) 51-54.   For a very detailed search for underlying themes in this pericope, including pagan as well as Jewish allusions, see M. Hengel and H. Merkel, 'Die Magier aus dem Osten und die Flucht nach Ägypten' in *Orientierung an Jesus: zur Theologie der Synoptiker* (J. Schmid *Festschrift*), ed. P. Hoffman (Freiburg: Herder, 1973) 139-169.

/22/ E.g. H. C. Waetjen *JBL* 95 (1976) 225-6.

/23/ Besides the famous proposal of Gfrörer that the 3 sets of 14 generations are derived from the numerical value of 14 attaching to the 3 consonants of the name David, see e.g. M. J. Moreton, *Studia Evangelica* II (1964) 224 for the proposal that the 3 x 14 reflects the 42 months of apocalyptic; and H. C. Waetjen, *art. cit.* 210-212 for its derivation from the 14-stage eschatology of 2 Baruch 53-74, and apocalyptic scheme of 4

264 Gospel Perspectives II

ages of history (the fourth being introduced by Jesus). See
further M. D. Johnson, *The Purpose of the Biblical Genealogies*
(Cambridge UP, 1969) 189-208; M. D. Goulder, *Midrash and
Lection in Matthew* (London: SPCK, 1974) 228-233, for several
other suggestions on this point.

/24/ See R. E. Brown, *Birth* 197-200, for details; and for
other such expansion of the infancy narratives, *ibid.* 559.

/25/ *Ibid.* 198.

/26/ *Ibid.* 559.

/27/ See further M. M. Bourke, *CBQ* 22 (1960) 160-161.

/28/ *Midrash* 236-239.

/29/ *Ibid.* 33.

/30/ Cf. especially the discussion of the historicity of the
virginal conception, *ibid.* 234-5. It is, for Goulder, a clear
case of how 'an evangelist has found history in scripture'.

/31/ Cf. J. Drury, *Tradition* 123, for the implication that the
name of Mary's husband was invented by Matthew, on the grounds
of the name's 'midrashic aptness which casts some doubts on its
historicity'. It is amusing, and perhaps instructive, to note
that Joseph's name is one of the few features in Matthew's
account which Goulder does regard as historical, *Midrash* 230,
235 n.28.

/32/ *Midrash* 476-485.

/33/ *Ibid.* 238-9.

/34/ *Ibid.* 474-5.

/35/ Vocabulary may, of course, work the other way: the
presence of significantly non-Matthaean vocabulary does count
as *prima facie* evidence that at that point earlier tradition
has affected not only the content but the wording of Matthew's
account. See e.g. the comments on Mt. 2:16 in my article in
NovT 21 (1979) 113. It is the reverse argument, that Matthaean
vocabulary indicates Matthaean origin, which does not work.

/36/ For some recent statements, see e.g. E. Nellesen, *Das
Kind und seine Mutter* (Stuttgarter Bibelstudien 39. Stuttgart:
KBW, 1969) especially 77-80; A. Vögtle in M. Didier (ed.)
L'Evangile selon Matthieu: Rédaction et Théologie (BETL 29.
Gembloux: Duculot, 1972) 156-161; G. M. Soares Prabhu, *The
Formula-Quotations in the Infancy Narrative of Matthew* (An.
Bib. 63. Rome: Biblical Institute Press, 1976) 294-300
(summarising the whole dissertation); R. E. Brown, *Birth*
96-119.

/37/ See the references in the last note, especially Soares
Prabhu, *op. cit.*, chapter II for the redactional origin of the
quotations, and chapter IV for the literary priority of the
narrative.

/38/ See above note 23.

/39/ An alternative proposal for the origin of the scriptural material in Mt. 1-2 is Goulder's thesis of a lectionary background. This would, if proved, offer a series of given texts for Matthew to work from. But even if we accept that Matthew and his church used the lectionary reconstructed by Goulder (and this is not yet generally conceded), could Matthew have invented the genealogy and birth story out of Gen. 23:1 - 25:18, and the narratives of chapter 2 out of Gen. 25:19 - 32:3 (*Midrash* 227-242)? There are certainly a few interesting points of correspondence in Mt. 1-2 with these supposed readings from Genesis: Abraham's genealogy features prominently in Gen. 25, and Rachel's childlessness is a theme of Gen. 30. Other supposed correspondences are less plausible: Herod the *Edomite* (a point Matthew does not draw out) in the role of Esau, ancestor of Edom, or the homage of the magi as fulfilment of Isaac's blessing on Jacob (Gen. 27:29). Other of Goulder's themes from Genesis unfortunately occur outside the required 'lections': the miraculous birth of Isaac; Joseph the dreamer; Israel's descent to Egypt. Any or all of these themes may have occurred to Matthew and may have influenced his wording in these chapters, but the ingenuity required to create the narratives *de novo* out of a section of Genesis which in itself bears such remote resemblance to any of them would be very wonderful. Nor should it be forgotten that none of the explicit quotations comes out of the supposed lections, nor do any parts of Gen. 23-31 feature among the generally recognised scriptural allusions in Mt. 1-2. The one exception might be Daube's derivation of Herod's coup from that planned by Laban against Jacob according to the Passover haggadah on Dt. 26:5, which of course was based on, though it did not agree with, Genesis 31. This, if accepted, would be one of the most promising links with Goulder's lections in Mt. 1-2, yet he does not mention it; presumably he, with the majority of commentators, is not convinced by Daube. (For Daube's theory see his *The NT and Rabbinic Judaism* (London: Athlone Press, 1956) 189-192, and *NTS* 5 (1958/9) 184-6. For discussion, and citation of some contrary opinions, see my article in *NovT* 21 (1979) 106-7.)

/40/ I have developed this argument more fully with reference specifically to Mt. 2:16-18 in *NovT* 21 (1979) 103-104, and for chapter 2 as a whole cf. section I of my article 'The Formula-Quotations of Matthew 2 and the Problem of Communication', *NTS* 27 (1980/1) 234-237.

/41/ For a parallel case of OT wording drastically adapted to

fit the narrative details see 27:9f, and the comments of K.
Stendahl, *The School of St. Matthew* (Uppsala, 1954) 196-8.
/42/ For the lack of similar 'fulfilment' formulae in Jewish
writings see B. M. Metzger, *JBL* 70 (1951) 306-7 re the Mishnah,
and J. A. Fitzmyer *NTS* 7 (1960/61) 303-4 for Qumran.   Cf.
C. F. D. Moule *NTS* 14 (1967/8), especially 308-311.
/43/ Cf. R. E. Brown, *Birth* 100 for similar arguments.
/44/ See above pp. 245-6.
/45/ I have discussed these echoes, with reference to fuller
treatments, in *NovT* 21 (1979) 105-6.
/46/ *Hibbert Journal* 53 (1954-5), 38.
/47/ *Ibid.* 40-41.
/48/ *NovT* 21 (1979) 108-111.
/49/ See above pp. 245-6.
/50/ In W. Eltester (ed.) *Judentum, Urchristentum, Kirche.
Festschrift für J. Jeremias* (BZNW 26. Berlin: Töpelmann, 1960)
94-105.
/51/ Cf. Stendahl's insistence, *ibid.* 103, that 'in Mt. the
Virgin Birth story is theologically mute', i.e. that it was not
an idea introduced by Matthew to make a theological point, but
a known tradition for which explanation was now required.
/52/ 1 Kings 11:17; 11:40; 2 Kings 25:26; Jer. 26:21;
42:13ff; Josephus *Ant.* XII 387-8.
/53/ E.g. W. C. Allen (*ICC*) 14-15; W. F. Albright and C. S.
Mann (*Anchor Bible*) 13-16.
/54/ Dio Cassius 63:7; Suetonius, *Nero* 13.   For other
instances see R. E. Brown, *Birth* 174.
/55/ For details see my article in *NovT* 21 (1979) 114-5.
/56/ What can be inferred of population figures for Bethlehem
under Herod suggests a total of less than twenty involved in
the 'massacre' (see *ibid.* 114), hardly a remarkable figure by
the standard of Herod's purges recorded by Josephus.
/57/ See e.g. E. M. Smallwood, *The Jews under Roman Rule*
(Leiden: E. J. Brill, 1976) 103f; A. Schalit, *König Herodes*
(Berlin: de Gruyter, 1969) 648f.
/58/ See above pp. 242-3.

Johannes und Matthäus –
Zwiespalt oder Viergestalt des Evangeliums?

Gerhard Maier
Albrecht-Bengel-Haus
Ludwig-Krapf-Str. 5
7400 Tübingen

I. Zum Problem

Keinem Leser, der von den Synoptikern zu Johannes weiterschreitet, bleibt die Eigenart des Joh Ev verborgen. Gegenüber den Synoptikern mutet letzteres wie eine fremde Welt an/1/. Dieser Tatbestand wurde schon lange, bevor es eine sog. 'moderne Theologie' gab, diskutiert. So beschäftigt sich der Kanon Muratori (ca 200 n.Chr.) mit den verschiedenen Evangelienanfängen. Im Endergebnis hält er an der Verfasserschaft des Zwölferapostels Johannes und an der Dignität des vierten Evangeliums für den Gottesdienst und den Kreis der heiligen Schriften fest. Luther sieht im Joh Ev sogar das 'zarte, rechte Hauptevangelium', 'den andern dreien weit, weit vorzuziehen', weil es die Predigt Christi stärker betone./2/ Für Coccejus sind die Unterschiede zwischen den Synoptikern und dem Joh Ev ein Erweis der Echtheit aller Evangelien. Zeigen sie doch, daß zwischen den Evangelisten keine Absprache getroffen wurde. Hier wird gerade die Unterschiedlichkeit zu einem Argument für die Inspiration./3/ Bengel findet bei Johannes und Matthäus mehr 'Präzision und Pünktlichkeit' als bei Markus und Lukas. Für ihn bedeutet die Inspiration als geschichtlicher Vorgang, daß die persönliche Eigenart und die persönlichen Gaben jedes Evangelisten von Gott benutzt werden und vom Ausleger beachtet werden müssen./4/ Es ist ohne weiteres deutlich, daß mit dem Einsetzen der historischkritischen Forschung mehr und mehr die Unterschiede zwischen Johannes und den Synoptikern hervortraten. Bekanntlich hatte dieser Fortschritt der Forschung für das Joh Ev einschneidende Folgen, soweit es seine geschichtliche und theologische Würdigung betrifft. Das gilt vor allem für die deutsche Theologie. Hatten Schleiermacher u.a. noch an der geschichtlichen Zuverlässigkeit des vierten Evangeliums festgehalten, so stellte schon Karl Gottlieb Bretschneider 1820 die Alternative auf: 'Es kann... nicht sein, daß sowohl der Jesus der drei Evangelien wie der des vierten zu gleicher Zeit

geschichtlich wahr ist.'/5/ Der Tübinger Stiftsrepetent David
Friedrich Strauß erklärte in seinem 'Leben Jesu' (1835/6) das
Joh Ev als ungeschichtliche, mythische Übertünchung des wahren
Lebens Jesu./6/ Ferdinand Christian Baur, das einflußreiche
Haupt der kritischen Tübinger Schule, faßte das Joh Ev als
geschichtliche Einkleidung einer Idee auf und gab es damit
ebenfalls historisch preis./7/ Am Ende des 19. Jhds
konstatierte Karl von Hase: 'In der deutschen Theologie ist
eine Zeit gekommen, daß, wer es wagt im 4. Evangelium einen
werthvollen Quell für die Geschichte Jesu zu erkennen, fast
seine wissenschaftliche Ehre dransetzt'./8/

Allerdings lassen sich im 20. Jhd. einige wesentliche
Korrekturen an diesem Bild beobachten. Dazu gehören A.
Schlatters Untersuchung über Sprache und Eigenart des vierten
Evangelisten (1902), K. Kundsins Nachweis der guten
palästinischen Ortskenntnisse im vierten Evangelium (1925), E.
Stauffers Bemerkungen über 'Historische Elemente im 4.
Evangelium'/9/ (1960), und O. Cullmanns Arbeiten (zuletzt:
'Der johanneische Kreis', 1975). Auch R. Schnackenburg
versuchte, 'das strukturell Gemeinsame' der vier kanonischen
Evangelien hervorzuheben (1972). Insgesamt darf jedoch nicht
übersehen werden, daß nach wie vor zwei wesentliche Schranken
für ein angemessenes Verständnis des Johannesevangeliums
gegeben sind. Die eine Schranke besteht in der Neigung, die
geschichtliche Zuverlässigkeit des vierten Evangeliums
zugunsten der Synoptiker stark herabzusetzen. Die zweite
Schranke liegt in einer Überbetonung der Unterschiede zwischen
den Synoptikern und Johannes, die Gefahr läuft, die
Gemeinsamkeiten aus dem Auge zu verlieren./10/

Anders verlief die Entwicklung in England. Seit dem
Konferenzpapier, das J. A. T. Robinson 1957 unter dem Titel
'The New Look on the Fourth Gospel' vorlegte, spricht man
öfters von einem 'new look' bez. der johanneischen Forschung.
/11/ Doch schon zuvor unterschied sich die englische Forschung
an wichtigen Punkten und in charakteristischer Weise von der
deutschsprachigen. So betont C. K. Barrett in seinem
Johanneskommentar: 'the differences between John and the
Synoptic Gospels must not be exaggerated'./12/ Auch A. M.
Hunter hält die geltend gemachten Differenzen zwischen den
Evangelien für 'overdrawn'./13/ Johannes enthalte 'an
excellent historical tradition about Jesus' und sei bisweilen
zuverlässiger als die Synoptiker./14/   C. H. Dodd beschließt
seine grundlegende Untersuchung über 'Historical Tradition in

the Fourth Gospel' (Cambridge, 1963) mit der These: 'behind
the Fourth Gospel lies an ancient tradition independent of the
other Gospels, and meriting serious consideration as a
contribution to our knowledge of the historical facts
concerning Jesus Christ' (S. 423). Noch einen Schritt weiter
geht S. S. Smalley in einer jüngst erschienenen Untersuchung.
Er setzt voraus, daß das vierte Evangelium auf einer von den
Synoptikern unabhängigen Tradition basiert, und zieht daraus
den Schluß: 'If the Johannine tradition is independent, its
claim to be historically valuable is high. This means that the
Fourth Gospel can no longer be disregarded in any study of the
Gospels, but must be taken into one purview with the Synoptics'.
/15/ Allerdings ist dieser 'new look on John' weitgehend von
der Annahme abhängig, daß Johannes die Synoptiker nicht kannte
bzw. auf einer anderen Tradition fußt als die Synoptiker./16/
Wesentlich ist ferner die Voraussetzung der Zwei-Quellen-
Theorie, die dazu drängt, vor allem das Verhältnis des Johannes
zu Markus ins Auge zu fassen./17/

Der Zweck unserer Studie ist es, erneut Gemeinsamkeiten
zwischen Johannes und der synoptischen Tradition
herauszuarbeiten, die den Graben zwischen Johannes und den
übrigen Evangelien überbrücken helfen bzw. in seinem
wirklichen Ausmaß sehen lernen. Natürlich kann es nicht darum
gehen, Unterschiede und notwendige Differenzierungen zu
verwischen. Diese betreffen ja nicht nur den Stil und die
Umwelt der einzelnen Evangelien, nicht nur die Stoffauswahl und
die chronologischen Daten, sondern vor allem auch die
Darstellung Jesu, seine Worte und sein Auftreten als das des
endzeitlichen Erlösers: Kurzum die Christologie./18/ Nachdem
aber die Vergangenheit weit mehr mit den wirklichen oder nur
angeblichen Differenzen befaßt war, müssen wir uns heute wieder
stärker auf das alle Evangelien Verbindende konzentrieren, um
ein angemessenes Bild zu erhalten.

Dabei wählen wir auf Seiten der Synoptiker Matthäus aus,
um unseren Vergleich durchzuführen. Diese Auswahl empfiehlt
sich schon aufgrund der Tatsache, daß das Verhältnis Johannes/
Matthäus seltener untersucht wurde als das Verhältnis Johannes/
Markus oder Johannes/Lukas./19/ Ferner empfindet man den
Graben zwischen Johannes und Matthäus als besonders breit. Das
gilt sowohl in zeitlicher - Joh ist das jüngste der
kanonischen Evangelien/20/, Mt evtl doch das älteste von ihnen
/21/ - als auch in sachlicher Hinsicht. Exemplarisch sei hier
B. H. Streeter zitiert. Er glaubt zwar, daß Johannes das Mt
Ev gekannt hat, meint dann jedoch: 'John made little use of

Matthew because he did not like its apocalyptic and Judaistic
tendencies'./22/   Umso notwendiger ist es, sich dem Verhältnis
Johannes/Matthäus zuzuwenden. Sollte sich im Verlauf der
Untersuchung herausstellen, daß Johannes und Matthäus spezielle
Gemeinsamkeiten aufweisen, die im Verhältnis Johannes/Markus
oder Johannes/Lukas nicht gegeben sind, ist dies nur eine
Anregung für neue Untersuchungen. Im Rahmen unserer Studie ist
es freilich nicht möglich, der Ursache solcher spezieller
Gemeinsamkeiten nachzugehen oder gar die Frage zu erörtern, ob
und inwieweit Johannes das Mt Ev 'benutzt' hat.

Eine methodische Vorbemerkung sei noch gestattet. Aus
Gründen, die hier nicht weiter dargelegt werden können, kann
ich mich nicht entschließen, die Zwei-Quellen-Theorie
anzuwenden./23/ Dennoch meine ich, daß die meisten der
folgenden Beobachtungen und Ergebnisse auch dann ihren Wert
behalten, wenn die Zwei-Quellen-Theorie im Recht sein sollte.

II.   Duktus und Struktur bei Matthäus und Johannes

Stellt man das Joh Ev z.B. neben das koptische Thomas-
Evangelium, dann springt sofort ein gravierender Unterschied in
die Augen: Johannes bietet nicht nur Jesus-Worte, sondern auch
Jesus-Geschichte. Sein Evangelium folgt einem Aufriß und einer
Zielsetzung, die es durchaus mit dem Matthäus-Evangelium
vergleichbar erscheinen lassen./24/

Es ist hier weder Platz noch Ort, näher auf die
Bestimmung dessen einzugehen, was 'Geschichte' bei Johannes,
bei Matthäus und schließlich in der Moderne bedeutet. Wir
halten hier nur fest, was C. H. Dodd im Blick auf alle
kanonischen Evangelien sagte: 'The Gospels profess to tell us
what happened' - auch Johannes!/25/ In der Tat gehört es 'to
the specific character of Christianity that it is an historical
religion... It remains, therefore, a question of acute interest
to the Christian theologian, whether their (i.e. of the
Gospels) testimony is in fact true'./26/

Wir beobachten nun einen weithin gemeinsamen Aufriß der
Jesusgeschichte bei Matthäus und Johannes. Beide weisen auf
den göttlichen Ursprung Jesu hin, Matthäus, indem er
gewissermaßen die Toledoth Jesu erzählt, die doch in der
wunderbaren Geburtsgeschichte alle menschliche Erfahrung
aufsprengt (1,1-25); Johannes, indem er eben dieses Ineinander
der 'normalen' Menschengeschichte mit dem Wundergeschehen -

'Das Wort ward Fleisch' - in einen Prolog faßt, der die
Täufergestalt mit der zugleich protologischen und
eschatologischen Gestalt Jesu verwebt (1,1-18). Beide datieren
den Beginn des öffentlichen Wirkens Jesu in die Zeit des
Täufers (Mt 3,1ff; Joh 1,19ff). Beide verknüpfen den Anfang
ihrer Erzählung in auffallender Weise mit dem AT (vgl. Mt 1,1
mit Gen 5,1; 22,18 und Joh 1,1 mit Gen 1,1). Das deutet darauf
hin, daß Jesus in einem bestimmten Sinn die Geschichte des AT
fortsetzt. Schon diese Konzeption enthält offensichtlich
heilsgeschichtliche Elemente, was wiederum die beiden
Evangelien miteinander verknüpft. Aber auch der Anfang des
Wirkens Jesu weist verbindende Züge auf. Zwar kann man bei
Johannes von einem 'galiläischen Frühling' nicht sprechen.
Aber bis zur Scheidung unter den Jüngern in Joh 6,60ff
überwiegt bei Jesus der 'Erfolg', die Auseinandersetzung tritt
trotz 2,14ff; 5,10ff; 6,41ff zurück. Ähnliches beobachten wir
in Mt 4 - 10. Erst im Mittelteil beider Evangelien gewinnen
Kampf und Auseinandersetzung mit den Gegnern Raum (ab Mt 11,
2ff; Joh 7). Auf den ersten Blick scheint die Stellung des
Messiasbekenntnisses zu verschiedenartig: Matthäus stellt es an
den Schluß des Mittelteils (16,13ff), Johannes an dessen Anfang
(6,66ff) Doch hebt sich dieser Anstoß durch die Beobachtung,
daß Johannes im Mittelteil die Auseinandersetzungen in
Jerusalem berichtet, die Matthäus ausläßt, und infolgedessen
das Messiasbekenntnis auch bei Johannes die galiläische Epoche
abschließt. Sodann führen beide Evangelisten den Weg Jesu
zielstrebig auf die Passion zu. Hier ist es - gerade im
wichtigsten Abschnitt Jesu während seines irdischen Lebens! -
wo sie sich überraschend oft berühren, ja gelegentlich
ergänzen. Wir erinnern uns an das Urteil Dodds über die
johanneische Passionserzählung: 'As a whole it is singularly
plain and objective'./27/ Jedoch sind Leiden und Kreuz für
keinen von beiden der endgültige Zielpunkt. Dieser liegt
vielmehr eindeutig in der Auferstehung Jesu (Mt 28; Joh 20 -
21). Beide schildern diese Auferstehung leibhaft und
realistisch, als ein Ereignis, das sich gegen die Zweifel der
Jünger durchsetzt (Mt 28,17; Joh 20,24ff). Es geht ihnen - um
noch einmal einen Begriff Dodds/28/ aufzunehmen - um 'facts'.

Für die Struktur beider Evangelien sind ferner die
Zusammenfassungen von Jesusworten charakteristisch. Sicher:
auch Mk 4 und 13 enthalten ähnliche Redekomplexe, ebenso Luk 6;
15 und 21. Was jedoch Matthäus und Johannes von den anderen
Evangelisten abhebt, ist zunächst die *Häufigkeit* solcher
längeren 'Reden' (Mt 5 - 7; 10,5ff; 13; 18; 23; 24 - 25; Joh 3,

10ff; 5,19ff; 6,35ff; 10,1ff; 13,31 - 17). Zweitens ist ihr
Umfang gewachsen. Drittens *gliedern* Matthäus und Johannes ihre
Evangelien stärker und bewußter mit Hilfe dieser Reden. So
schließt Mt 5 - 7 die Lehrtätigkeit Jesu in dessen Frühzeit ab;
10,5ff das Missionsunternehmen in Israel; 18 die galiläische
Tätigkeit und 24/25 den Unterricht an den Jüngern vor der
Passion (vgl. die ähnlichen Redewendungen in 7,28; 11,1; 19,1;
26,1). Bei Johannes schließt die 'Brotrede' (6,35ff) die
galiläische Wirksamkeit Jesu ab und leitet gleichzeitig zum
Messiasbekenntnis hinüber; die 'Hirtenrede' (10,1ff) enthält
Jesu abschliessende Einladung an die Öffentlichkeit Israels
und leitet zugleich hinüber zum Passionsgeschehen; Joh 14 - 17
bilden als 'Abschiedsreden' eine Art Vermächtnis des von der
Erde scheidenden Messias an seine Jünger. Viertens aber
verbinden sowohl Matthäus als auch Johannes mit den 'Reden'
eine *theologische bzw. katechetische Ordnung* in übergreifenden
Zusammenhängen, der erstere mehr thematisch, der letztere eher
assoziativ./29/ Hier spiegelt sich offenbar ein besonderes
Interesse an Jesus als dem Lehrer oder Offenbarer - dem
Enthüller des wahren Gotteswillens -, das Matthäus und
Johannes noch mehr miteinander verbindet als andere
Evangelistenpaare.

Man kann sich dies vor allem an den sog. 'Abschiedsreden'
klar machen. Wiederum gilt: Das Phänomen der 'Abschiedsreden'
ist nicht auf Matthäus und Johannes beschränkt (vgl. Mk 13;
Luk 21). Jedoch ist ihr Umfang bei Matthäus und Johannes
beträchtlich größer als bei Markus und Lukas (Mt 18; 24; 25;
Joh 13,31 - 17). Außerdem sprengen sie bei Matthäus und
Johannes die *eschatologische* Thematik, die bei Markus und
Lukas so gänzlich dominiert. Mehr noch: Es ist die
ekklesiologische Sicht, die sowohl bei Matthäus (18) als auch
bei Johannes (13,34f; 14,8ff.15ff; 15,1ff; 16,5ff) neben die
eschatologische tritt - bei Johannes noch stärker und
vollständiger als bei Matthäus. Die gemeinsame Betonung der
Jesusworte, die der Gemeinde gelten, verbindet das erste und
das vierte Evangelium noch einmal aufs engste. Von daher ist
es alles andere als ein 'Zufall', daß diese beiden die
kirchlichen 'Hauptevangelien' geworden sind./30/

Die beiderseitige spezifische Gewichtung des lehrenden
bzw. offenbarenden Jesus führt uns zu einer weiteren
strukturellen Eigenart. Es handelt sich um die Unterscheidung
und um die Bewertung von Volksevangelisation und
Jüngerbelehrung. Auch hier ist zunächst sachlich

festzustellen: Alle Evangelien kennen diese Unterscheidung
(vgl. z.B. Mk 1,21f; 2,2 mit 4,10ff; Luk 4,15; 8,4 mit 8,9ff).
Theorien wie die vom 'Messiasgeheimnis' in den Evangelien/31/
können leicht den Tatbestand verschleiern, daß Jesus nach
Ausweis aller Evangelien den Jüngern mehr Mitteilungen machte
als dem Volk oder den Gegnern. Selbst wenn die Evangelien
expressis verbis nichts darüber berichteten, müßten wir
logischerweise einen solchen Unterschied annehmen. Er ergibt
sich ganz natürlich aus dem Lehrer-Schüler-Verhältnis. Was
jedoch Matthäus und Johannes vor den andern Evangelien
auszeichnet, ist der Umfang der Jüngerbelehrung. So faßt
Matthäus die 'Bergpredigt' im Unterschied zu Lukas eindeutig
als Lehre für die Jünger zusammen (vgl. Mt 5,1f mit Luk 6,20
und 27). Dasselbe gilt für Mt 10,5ff und Mt 18, oder auch 15,
12ff, die weit mehr Stoff bieten als die markinischen oder
lukanischen Parallelen. Bei Johannes ist vor allem auf die
Kapitel 13,31 - 17 hinzuweisen, die ja ebenfalls eindeutig an
den Jüngerkreis gerichtet sind. Vielleicht darf man noch einen
Schritt weitergehen. Stärker als Markus und Lukas lassen
nämlich Matthäus und Johannes das Bestreben erkennen, die
Jüngerbelehrung am Ende des irdischen Wirkens Jesu zu
konzentrieren. Bei Joh 13,31 - 17 ist dies ohne weiteres
klar. Bei Matthäus ist auf Kapitel 18; 19,23 - 20,18; 24 und
25 hinzuweisen. Der Zusammenhang mit der ekklesiologischen
Sicht (s. oben) liegt auf der Hand. Darüberhinaus kann man
fragen, ob sich darin nicht die tatsächliche historische
Situation wiederspiegelt, in der Jesus unter der Erfahrung der
Ablehnung durch Israel und im Blick auf das nahende Kreuz sich
am Ende mehr und mehr seinen Jüngern zuwandte. Halten wir
jedenfalls fest: Matthäus und Johannes zeigen darin eine
eigenartige Verwandtschaft, daß sie der Jüngerbelehrung
besonderen Raum geben und zugleich das Wirken Jesu im
Jüngerkreis in der Schlußphase vor der Kreuzigung betonen.

Wir fragen noch nach der theologischen Intention der
beiden Evangelien. Zweifellos geht es ihnen - wie ja doch
allen kanonischen Evangelien - um die 'proclamation of the
gospel of Jesus Christ'./32/ Mit Hunter kann man dies noch
näher fassen als die Verkündigung der einzigartigen Sohnschaft
Jesu Christi, die den Synoptikern und Johannes gemeinsam ist.
/33/ Kürzlich hat P. Stuhlmacher die 'Versöhnungschristologie'
als das allen Evangelien Gemeinsame zu beschreiben versucht
und kam dabei zu der These: 'Das Evangelium von der
Versöhnung Gottes mit seiner Schöpfung durch die Sendung des

Messias Jesus Christus ist das Herzstück des Neuen Testaments'.
/34/ In der Tat wollen sowohl Matthäus als auch Johannes Jesus
als den auf Erden erschienenen Erlöser darstellen, um den
heilbringenden Glauben an Jesus zu wecken (Mt 1,21; 28,18 - 20;
Joh 20,31). Beide akzentuieren deshalb den Missionsbefehl (vgl.
Mt 28,18ff; Joh 20,21ff) - wie übrigens auch Lukas. Beide
sehen im Sühnetod die Vollendung des Auftrages Jesu, ja das
Ereignis, das eine neue Zeit einleitet, die zugleich die letzte
Zeit vor der Errichtung des Reiches Gottes sein wird (Mt 1,21;
20,28; 27,51ff; 28,18ff; Joh 19,30; 20,21ff; 21,23)/35/.
Zugegeben: Das alles sind sehr allgemeine Beobachtungen.
Deshalb darf man aber so grundlegende Intentionen keineswegs
für selbstverständlich erachten oder ausklammern.

     Was aber Matthäus und Johannes noch einmal in einzigartiger
Weise verbindet, ist ihr Verhältnis zum Alten Testament. Wir
bemerkten schon, daß beide Evangelien mit bekannten
alttestamentlichen Wendungen beginnen (vgl. Mt 1,1 mit Gen 5,
1; 22,18 und Joh 1,1 mit Gen 1,1). In beiden spielt der
Schriftbeweis eine größere Rolle als bei Markus und Lukas (zu
Johannes vgl. 1,23.45.49; 5,39.46f; 6,14; 7,38; 10,35; 12,14f.
38ff; 13,18; 15,25; 19,24.36f). Das ist angesichts der
zeitlichen und räumlichen Entfernung beider Evangelien/36/ eine
erstaunliche Tatsache. Noch erstaunlicher ist, daß beide mit
dem Reflexionszitat arbeiten. Nepper - Christensen hat
beobachtet, daß sogar die Form der johanneischen 'recht stark
derjenigen der Reflexionszitate im Mt ähnelt'/37/ (vgl. dazu
Joh 12,38; 13,18; 19,24; 19,36). Sowohl Matthäus als auch
Johannes legen also besonderen Wert auf die Erfüllung des Alten
Testaments, die in der Geschichte Jesu geschehen ist. Für
beide gilt in einem heilsgeschichtlichen und
geschichtstheologischen Sinne, was Johannes so formuliert hat:
'das Heil (σωτηρία!) kommt von den Juden' (Joh 4,22; vgl. Jes
2,3)./38/ Man kann diese Verbindung wohl kaum auf das Konto
irgendwelcher Traditionen setzen, die z.B. Johannes aufgenommen
haben soll. Hier handelt es sich vielmehr um bewußte
Darstellung seitens der verantwortlichen Endredaktoren - mit
andern Worten: der 'Evangelisten' selbst.

     Duktus und Struktur enthüllen also ein breites Feld von
Gemeinsamkeiten bei Matthäus und Johannes./39/ Ja, es hat sich
gezeigt, daß Matthäus und Johannes teilweise enger miteinander
verbunden sind als jeder von ihnen mit anderen Evangelien.
Letzteres gilt z.B. für die Form der beiderseitigen
Evangelienanfänge, die Zusammenfassungen von Jesusworten,

Umfang und Thematik der sog. Abschiedsreden, das verwandte
Interesse an dem lehrenden und offenbarenden Jesus, das Gewicht
und die Stellung der Jüngerbelehrung in der Gesamtstruktur des
Evangeliums, das ekklesiologische Interesse, die Akzentuierung
des Missionsbefehls, den Schriftbeweis, das Reflexionszitat und
die Verknüpfung mit dem Alten Testament.

Im Folgenden soll die Gemeinsamkeit an einzelnen Punkten
kondretisiert werden.

III. Einzelvergleiche

1. *Die ἐγώ-εἰμι -Aussagen*
Bekanntlich sind die ἐγώ-εἰμι -Aussagen des Joh Ev seit
langem umstritten. Beliebt war die Herleitung von der 'Gnosis'.
/40/ Auch wo man ein messianisches Selbstbewußtsein Jesu
verneinte, gerieten sie in den Verdacht, unhistorisch zu sein.
/41/

Es ist hier nicht möglich, die religionsgeschichtliche
Herleitung umfassend aufzurollen. Jedoch sollen Matthäus und
Johannes auf diesem umstrittenen Feld miteinander verglichen
werden.

Die erste Feststellung ist, daß eine Identifikationsformel, wie z.B.: 'Ich bin das Brot des Lebens,... das Licht
der Welt' usw., die für das Joh Ev typisch ist, im Mt Ev fehlt.
Mit dieser Feststellung ist allerdings das Problem noch
keineswegs erledigt. Man muß vielmehr mit E. Stauffer/42/ die
ἐγώ-εἰμι -Aussagen in den größeren Rahmen des 'christologischen
ἐγώ' einordnen. Stauffer findet ein solches christologisches
ἐγώ bei den Synoptikern 'an drei Stellen: in der Bergpredigt,
im Jubelruf und im Heilandsruf'./43/ Alle drei sind auch
matthäisch. Das ἐγὼ δὲ λέγω ὑμῖν, das fünfmal in Mt 5,22ff
erscheint, hebt Jesus von allen Lehrern Israels ab und macht
ihn zum einzigartigen Künder des Gotteswillens, der
eschatologischen Tora. Entsprechend der Deutung des
vorausgehenden Passivs: 'daß zu den Alten gesagt ist' spricht
Jesus entweder auf der Stufe des zweiten Mose (vgl. Dt 18,15)
oder - von Gott selbst. An dieser Stelle ist daran zu erinnern,
daß in Israel mindestens seit den Proverbia eine Gleichsetzung
von Tora und Weisheit möglich war und daß die personifizierte
Weisheit die Heilsgüter vermittelt: Leben (Prov 7,2), Wahrheit
(Prov 8,7), Erkenntnis (Prov 8,10), Rat und Tat, Macht und
Verstand (Prov 8,14), Liebe (Prov 8,17), Reichtum, Ehre,

Unvergängliches, Gerechtigkeit (Prov 8,18). Sie ist Gottes
'Liebling' und von 'Anfang' bei Gott (Prov 8,22.30). Der
Abschnitt Prov 8,22ff endet mit beinahe 'johanneischen' Sätzen:
'Wer mich findet, der findet das Leben; alle, die mich hassen,
lieben den Tod' (V. 35f). Ist Jesus die Quelle der
eschatologischen Tora, wie er es in Mt 5,21ff beansprucht,
dann ist er in Person auch der Geber aller jener Heilsgüter:
Leben, Wahrheit, Gerechtigkeit usw. Daß die Übertragung auf
einen konkreten Lehrer dem Judentum nicht unmöglich war,
beweist das Sirachbuch (verfaßt ca. 175 v.Chr). Hier
beschreibt Ben Sira seine Tätigkeit in einem Hymnus, der
prophetisches Selbstbewußtsein wiederspiegelt: 'So will ich
noch weiter gleich dem Frühlicht... Lehre leuchten und sie bis
in die Ferne leuchten lassen. Noch weiter will ich Belehrung
gleich Prophetenworten ausgießen...' (24,30ff). Ben Sira
vergleicht sich also mit dem Licht der Sonne, das aufgrund
seiner Lehre erstrahlt./44/ Wie gesagt enthält das ἐγώ der
Bergpredigt keine Identifikation. Es läßt letztere vielleicht
sogar bewußt offen. Aber es führt *sachlich* hinüber zu den
Identifikationsformeln mit ἐγώ εἰμι, die das Joh Ev wiedergibt.
Deshalb kommt E. Stauffer auch zu dem Schluß: 'Das
Johannesevangelium führt diese Gedanken (sc. der Synoptiker)
auf der ganzen Linie weiter'./45/

Einen Schritt näher am Joh Ev steht der Heilandsruf in Mt
11,28ff. Die Einladung: 'Kommt her zu mir alle' bezieht sich
evtl. direkt auf die entsprechende Einladung der personifizier-
ten Weisheit in Prov 1,20ff; 8,1ff und 9,1ff. Nichts steht der
Möglichkeit im Wege, daß Jesus sich selbst als die
personifizierte Weisheit betrachtete, als die ihn später die
Apostel verkündigten (vgl. Kol 2,9). Allerdings - und hierin
liegt ein bedeutender Unterschied zur alttestamentlichen
Weisheit - sah er sich in Mt 11,28ff vorwiegend als den
Erlöser, der die Beladenen auf geheimnisvolle Weise befreit.
Sein 'Ich' umfaßt nach dem Kontext die Sohnschaft, die
messianische Aufgabe, die Lehrautorität und die eschatologische
Erlösungskompetenz. Oder, wie Stauffer formuliert: 'In
seinem ἐγώ schneiden sich alle geschichtlichen und kosmischen
Linien'./46/ Die Identifikationsformeln des Joh Ev bleiben
auch demgegenüber noch etwas Besonderes. Aber sachlich ließe
sich Mt 11,28ff durchaus umformulieren zu einem: 'Ich bin die
Erquickung, ... die Ruhe, ... die Erlösung'. Die Entfernung
von Mt 11,28ff zu den Identifikationsformeln des Joh Ev ist
nicht größer als die zwischen innerjohanneischen Aussagen, von
- sagen wir etwa - Joh 7, 37f zu Joh 6,35.

Im Kontext des Mt Ev betrifft deshalb die Frage Jesu an
die Jünger: 'Wer sagt ihr, daß ich sei?' weit mehr als eine
Identifikation auf der rein menschlichen Ebene. Sie hat das
Messiasbekenntnis zum Ziel und entspricht sachlich durchaus
dem ἐγώ εἰμι Jesu vor dem Hohen Rat nach Mk 14,62 (vgl. Joh 20,
31)./47/

Es ist nun interessant, daß wir *sachlich* zu den
johanneischen Identifikationsformeln eine weitere Parallele bei
Matthäus finden können, wenn wir Mt 4,14ff in unsere Untersuchung
einbeziehen. In Joh 8,12 sagt Jesus von sich: 'Ich bin das
Licht der Welt'. In Mt 5,14 sagt Jesus von den Jüngern: 'Ihr
seid das Licht der Welt'. Nach Mt.4,14ff jedoch ist wieder
Jesus selber das 'Licht', das den Verlorenen aufgeht. Freilich
macht Matthäus diese Aussage im Rahmen eines Reflexionszitates
nach Jes 8,23f. Historisch ist es durchaus denkbar, daß Jesus
sich auf Jes 8,23f berief, und daß Matthäus die Erinnerung
daran in Gestalt von Mt 4,14ff festhielt, während sie Johannes
als Selbstaussage Jesu in Form einer Identifikationsformel
überlieferte. Die polaren Begriffe φῶς und σκοτία sind
jedenfalls beiden Evangelien gemeinsam und deuten doch wohl
auch bei Johannes auf Jes 8,23f zurück (vgl. Joh 8,18).

Ein absolutes ἐγώ εἰμι taucht bei Matthäus nur einmal auf,
und zwar in 14,27. Gegen Morgen erscheint Jesus, auf den
Wassern gehend, den Jüngern in der Not des Seesturms und
tröstet sie mit den Worten: 'Ich bins; fürchtet euch nicht!'
(ἐγώ εἰμι· μὴ φοβεῖσθε). Später deuten die Jünger das ἐγώ
als den θεοῦ υἱός (Mt 14,33). Damit sind wir erneut im Umkreis
des christologischen ἐγώ. . Auch dieses ἐγώ εἰμι des
Gottessohnes, der als solcher erst noch erkannt werden will,
ist offen im Blick auf konkretisierende Prädikationen. Es
bahnt also an, was Johannes expliziert - in Kontinuität mit dem
ἐγώ εἰμι der Synoptiker!

Schon E. Stauffer hat darauf aufmerksam gemacht, daß
dieses ἐγώ εἰμι in Mt 14,27 zurückweist auf das 'Ich bin' des
Alten Testaments und später der Apokalyptik, mit dem Gott sich
als Gott offenbart./48/ Vor allem ist hier an die grundlegende
Gottesaussage in Ex 3,14: 'Ich bin, der ich bin' zu denken.
Hat Jesus in Mt 14,27 und vergleichbaren Stellen seine
göttliche Herkunft und Vollmacht angedeutet? Eine solche
Vermutung wird bestärkt durch Mt 18,20, wo die Schechina Jesu
wie die Schechina Gottes behandelt wird, und durch Mt 28,20, wo
der Auferweckte in göttlicher Vollmacht das tröstende und

majestätische 'Ich bin bei euch alle Tage' spricht. Ist das
ἐγώ .. εἰμι an der letztgenannten Stelle wirklich nur im
alltäglichen Sinne gebraucht, sodaß das ἐγώ nicht betont werden
dürfte? Oder steht doch derselbe Herr im Hintergrund, der
Josua verheißend zurief: 'ich will mit dir sein' (Jo 1,5); und
der Israel tröstete: 'fürchte dich nicht, ich bin mit dir' (Jes
41,10)? Das vorgesetzte ἰδού legt jedenfalls einen starken
christologischen Akzent auf das ἐγώ. So darf man wohl auch Mt
28,20 als eine bewußte Anspielung auf Ex 3,14 sehen. Könnte
man sich entschließen, Mt 14,27 und Mt 28,20 für echte
Jesuslogien bzw. Worte des Auferstandenen zu halten, dann wäre
die Entwicklung der ἐγώ εἰμι -Aussage bei Johannes viel
verständlicher. Dann wäre auch ein Zugang zu Joh 10,30: 'Ich
und der Vater sind eins' gefunden. Halten wir fest: Ohne die
Besonderheit der johanneischen 'Ich bin'-Worte aufzuheben, sind
sie doch in den größeren Rahmen des 'christologischen ἐγώ'
einzuordnen, dem wir auch bei Matthäus und den Synoptikern
überhaupt begegnen. Sachlich finden sie bei den letzteren z.T.
echte Parallelen, z.T. werden sie dort angebahnt. Die ἐγώ
εἰμι -Aussagen des Johannes sind zwar für den Leser, der von
Matthäus herkommt, anders, aber nicht schlechthin fremd.

Eine Erklärung des beiderseitigen Verhältnisses wäre in
doppelter Weise denkbar. Entweder hat Johannes Aussagen Jesu,
die ihm mündlich oder schriftlich an die Hand gegeben waren,
weiterentwickelt zu den spezifisch johanneischen Ich-bin-Worten,
allerdings in Kontinuität zu den Aussagen bei den Synoptikern.
/49/ Oder aber er berichtet ergänzend zu den Synoptikern Jesus-
Worte in Gestalt von Identifikationsformeln./50/ Dabei muß man
immer die Möglichkeit offenlassen, daß Johannes umformuliert
(z.B. Menschensohn-Worte in Ich-bin-Worte) oder auch Matthäus
umformuliert (z.B. Ich-bin-Worte in Menschensohn-Worte)! Der
Vergleich von Matthäus und Johnnes ergibt immerhin eine gewisse
Wahrscheinlichkeit, daß Jesus schon vor dem Kreuzestod das 'Ich
bin' in christologischem Selbstbewußtsein gebraucht hat, ein
'Ich bin' freilich, dessen wahre Bedeutung sich erst den
Glaubenden erschließt./51/

2. *Die 'Sohnes'-Aussagen*
Fur die Christologie nicht weniger interessant ist der
Begriff des 'Sohnes'.

Die Bedeutung des 'Sohnes'-begriffes für das Joh Ev ist
bekannt. In einem ausführlichen Artikel im ThWNT kommt E.
Schweizer zu der Auffassung, 'daß Sohn Gottes für Johannes die

vom jüdischen Glauben scheidende Zusammenfassung des
Bekenntnisses geworden ist'./52/ Wie sieht es diesbezüglich
bei Matthäus aus?

Die Stammtafel Jesu weist in Mt 1,16 den berühmten Bruch
auf. Nicht 'Joseph zeugte Jesus', sondern Maria beschließt die
Stammtafel, 'von der Jesus, der Messias genannt wird, geboren
wurde'. V. 18ff stellen noch einmal klar, daß Jesus 'aus dem
heiligen Geist' im Leib der Maria gezeugt ist. An dem
supranatural-realistischen Charakter der Sohnschaft Jesu läßt
Matthäus also von Anfang an keinen Zweifel. Er entspricht
damit sachlich den Präexistenz-Aussagen des Joh Ev (vgl. Joh 1,
12.18; 3,13 usf.). Von da her bekommt auch das Reflexionszitat
in 2,15 seinen Sinn./53/ Die Bat Kol bei der Taufe und auf dem
Berg der Verklärung unterstreicht die Wichtigkeit des
Sohnestitels Jesu (3,17; 17,5). Gehen hier und bei der
Benutzung des Sohnestitels durch den Teufel und die Dämonen
(vgl. Mt 4,3.6; 8,29) die anderen Synoptiker parallel, so ist
Matthäus unter allen Evangelisten der einzige, der nicht nur
das Messiasbekenntnis als Sohnesbekenntnis beim Seewandel
vorbereitet (14,33), sondern auch das Messiasbekenntnis selber
ausdrücklich als Bekenntnis zum 'Sohne Gottes' faßt (Mt 16,16).
Der o.e. Satz Schweizers ließe sich also auch auf Matthäus
anwenden. Johannes erstreckt die Zweierbeziehung von Vater und
Sohn unter dem Gedanken der Sendung weiter auf die Jünger.
Dieselbe Dreierkette unter dem Sendungsgedanken bildet auch
Matthäus, vgl. Mt 10,40 (das reicher ist als die Lukasparallele
in Luk 10,16!) - mit Joh 13,20; 20,21. Ist das Bekenntnis des
Centurio zum gekreuzigten 'Sohne Gottes' auch bei Markus
überliefert (vgl. Mt 27,54 mit Mk 15,39), so gewinnt Matthäus
'Eine letzte Stufe' in 'dem Nebeneinanderstellen der Namen des
Vaters, des Sohnes und des heiligen Geistes' in Mt 28,20 /54/.
Mt 28,20 verwirklicht in seiner trinitarischen Fassung das in
Joh 10,30 ausgesprochene: 'ich und der Vater sind eins'. Mt
11,25ff war für W. Bousset die einzige Stelle mit einer 'den
Reden des vierten Ev. etwas verwandte(n) Tonart'./55/ Hier
wird Jesus in einzigartiger, wirklich 'johanneischer' Weise als
der mit dem Vater immer wieder einige Sohn, als der eine, der
den Vater kennt, der alles vom Vater empfängt und als der
einzige göttliche Offenbarer dargestellt (vgl. Joh 1,18; 3,35;
10,15; 17,25f; auch in Luk 10,21f überliefert).

Man kann sogar sagen, daß Betonung und Inhalt des
Sohnestitels unter allen synoptischen Evangelien bei Matthäus
dem Joh Ev am nächsten kommen. Hunter bemerkt mit Recht: Mt

11,27 'warns us against the unwisdom of magnifying the
theological differences between John and the Synoptics'./56/
Man wird wieder fragen dürfen, ob nicht diese Verwandtschaft
zwischen Matthäus und Johannes ihre natürlichste Erklärung
darin findet, daß der historische Jesus sich schon im
Jüngerkreis vor Ostern als der einzigartige Sohn des Vaters
zu erkennen gab./57/

3. Die messianischen Debatten

Die Anfrage des Täufers, ob Jesus der 'Kommende' sei (Mt
11,2; vgl. Ps 118,26) spiegelt mit Wahrscheinlichkeit auch die
Unruhe in seiner Jüngerschaft wieder. Joh scheint in 1,8.19ff
zu betonen, daß eben nicht der Täufer der Messias ist. Hat
Johannes hier den Täuferjüngern sagen wollen: Jesus und nicht
der Täufer ist der wahre Messias Israels? Offenbar blicken wir
hier in eine messianische Debatte zwischen Jesus und dem Täufer
bzw. zwischen ihren Jüngern hinein, die sich sowohl bei
Matthäus als auch bei Johannes niederschlug.

Nach Mt 12,23 bestand im Volk die Neigung, an die
Messianität bzw. die Davidssohnschaft Jesu zu glauben (vgl. 9,
27; 15,22; 20,30). Dasselbe berichtet Johannes in 7,26.31.40ff.
Zugleich lassen beide Evangelisten erkennen, daß darüber im
Volk, im Am-ha-arez, heftig diskutiert wurde. Noch beim Einzug
in Jerusalem sprach man Jesus als Davidssohn an (Mt 21,9; Joh
12,13). Freilich war man im Volk nicht an diesen Titel
gebunden. Man faßte Jesus auch als den wiedererstandenen
Täufer, als Elia, Jeremia, einen Propheten oder 'den' Propheten
aus Dt 18,15 auf (Mt 14,2; 16,14; 21,11; Joh 3,25ff; 4,19.29.
42; 6,14; 7,40ff; 9,17ff; 10,24ff). Schließlich hieß Jesus
auch der 'Nazarener', der 'Galiläer', der 'Kommende' oder
einfach der 'Messias' (Mt 21,9.11; 26,69; 27,17.22; Joh 6,14;
7,52; 19,19).

Nicht minder heftig diskutierten die Pharisäer über eine
mögliche Messianität Jesu. Von allen Religionsparteien der
Judenschaft waren sie für die Messianität Jesu am meisten
offen. Matthäus läßt erkennen, daß einige pharisäische Führer
bereit waren, Jesus als Messias zu betrachten (vgl. Mt 9,18ff
mit Mk 5,21ff). Dann entbrennt jedoch der Streit, ob Jesu
Vollmacht dämonisch bzw. satanisch oder ob sie göttlich ist (Mt
9,34; 12,22ff). In diese Diskussion schalten sich später die
sadduzäischen Führer ein (Mt 21,23ff). Schließlich kommt die
Mehrheit im Hohen Rat zu der Überzeugung, daß Jesu
Messiasanspruch Gotteslästerung sei (Mt 26,65ff). Am Ende wird

Jesus als der 'Verführer' gebrandmarkt, als der er im Talmud
fortlebt (Mt 27,63). Nur leise deutet sich bei der Diskussion
Jesu mit den Pharisäern nach dem Einzug in Jerusalem an, daß das
Problem 'Jesus Messias' noch keineswegs für alle Pharisäer
entschieden war (Mt 22,41ff).

      Johannes bestätigt oder ergänzt diese Angaben. Eine
historisch präzisere, weil eher differenzierende
Berichterstattung liegt z.B. dort vor, wo er uns in Nikodemus
die Minderheit der pharisäischen Partei darstellt, die an Jesus
glaubte (Joh 3,1ff; 7,50ff; 12,42; 19,39f). Ein Satz wie der
von Joh 12,42 hat zwar keine Parallele bei den Synoptikern,
aber die historische Wahrscheinlichkeit für sich. Joh 12,42
enthält nicht nur einen Tadel, sondern auch eine Entschuldigung
der jüdischen 'Obersten'. Von dort führt die Linie weiter zu
den Angaben der Apostelgeschichte (5,34ff; 6,7; 15,5; 21,20;
23,6ff). Joh 7 und 8 durchzieht der Kampf Jesu mit den
Pharisäern über die Frage, ob er der Messias sei. Dabei wird
wie bei Matthäus der Vorwurf erhoben, Jesus 'habe einen Dämon'
(7,20; 8,48.52; 10,20). Daß bei Johannes das Volk in diesen
Vorwurf einstimmt, darf nicht verwundern und läßt sich mit Mt
11,18 vergleichen. Die Vollmachtsfrage wird auch in Joh 9,16ff
analog zu Mt 21,23ff diskutiert (vgl. wieder Joh 3,2). Die
Ablehnung Jesu durch die Mehrheit wird in Joh 1,11 auf eine
Weise formuliert, die an Mt 21,37ff erinnert. Schließlich
bleibt es auch im Joh Ev bei der Brandmarkung Jesu als eines
'Verführers' (7,12.47; 19,7).

      Wieder ist festzustellen, daß sich Ähnliches bei allen
Synoptikern findet. Dennoch ist es wichtig, daß Matthäus und
Johannes die Atmosphäre der messianischen Debatten zur Zeit
Jesu in sehr verwandter Weise schildern. Mutatis mutandis gilt
hier Dodds Feststellung über das Joh Ev: 'we can recognize the
authentic atmosphere of early Palestinian Christianity'./58/

      Im Durchgang durch drei bedeutsame Themen: die Ich-bin-
Worte, die Sohnschaft Jesu und die messianischen Debatten, hat
sich das Urteil erhärtet, daß im Bereich der Christologie
Matthäus und Johannes weitreichende Gemeinsamkeiten besitzen.
Das ist nicht zuletzt deshalb wichtig, weil gerade die
Christologie im Vergleich Johannes/Synoptiker ein schwieriges
Problem aufgibt.

4. Zum Problem des Geistes

Bekanntlich setzt der Paraklet in Gestalt des Heiligen
Geistes nach dem Joh Ev das Werk Jesu fort. 'Der Gebrauch der
Vokabel' ist 'im NT... auf die johanneische Literatur
beschränkt' (Paraklet bedeutet soviel wie Helfer oder
Fürsprecher)/59/. Insofern ist ein reich sprachlicher Vergleich
zwischen Matthäus und Johannes nicht möglich. Doch wie steht
es, wenn wir dem Begriff des göttlichen Pneuma im Mt Ev
nachgehen?

Den Leser des Mt Ev erstaunt zunächst dessen pneumatische
Kargheit. Allerdings kennt das Mt Ev durchaus die Funktion des
Parakleten, nämlich den Beistand des Geistes in der Verfolgung:
'Es wird euch in jener Stunde gegeben werden, was ihr reden
sollt. Denn nicht ihr seid es, die da reden, sondern eures
Vaters Geist ist es, der durch euch redet' (10,19f). Dies
erinnert an Joh 15,26f, wo der heilige Geist als Paraklet
ebenfalls das Zeugnis der Jünger in der Verfolgungssituation
unterstützt. Es läßt sich weiter fragen, ob der Geist in der
Gethsemane-Szene, wo er dem schwachen Fleisch gegenübergestellt
wird, nicht ebenfalls die Funktion des Parakleten hat (vgl. Mt
26,41 mit Joh 14,16ff; 15,26ff; 16,7ff).

Vor allem aber rücken sich Matthäus und Johannes näher,
sobald man sieht, daß nach allgemeiner urchristlicher
Überzeugung der Herr und der Geist Wechselbegriffe darstellen
können (vgl. Joh 14,16 mit 14,18 und 2 Kor 3,17). Nun ist
Jesus nach Mt 28,20 'alle Tage bei euch' und nach Mt 18,20
ereignet sich dies vor allem dort, 'wo zwei oder drei
versammelt sind in meinem Namen', d.h. in der Gebetsgemeinschaft
und in der Gemeinde. Das entspricht in gewisser Weise den
Aussagen über den Parakleten im Joh Ev. wonach dieser 'bei euch
bleibt' und die Jünger nicht 'Waisen' sein läßt, ja in dieser
Aufgrabe mit Jesus selber eins ist (Joh 14,17f). Jesus und der
Paraklet sind offenbar auch da austauschbar, wo es um die
Fortsetzung der Lehre Jesu geht. Denn nach Mt 28,20 stehen die
Jünger unter dem Befehl Jesu: 'lehret sie halten alles, was ich
euch aufgetragen habe'. Andrerseits wird der Paraklet nach Joh
14,26 die Jünger 'alles lehren', und zwar ausdrücklich unter
Rückbezug auf die Worte Jesu: 'alles das, was ich euch gesagt
habe' (vgl. 14,23; 16,13). So erweist sich eine innere
Verwandtschaft der beiden Evangelien gerade unter dem oft als
schwierig empfundenen Thema des Parakleten. Abgerundet wird
dieses Ergebnis durch die Warnung vor Lästerung des Geistes
in Mt 12,31f und durch die Beobachtung, daß für Matthäus die

Taufe mit dem heiligen Geist das besondere Kennzeichen der
Jüngerschaft ist (Mt 3,11; 28,19; vgl. Joh 20,22).

5. Der Begriff des 'Zeichens'

Immer wieder hat der Begriff des 'Zeichens' im Joh Ev die
Forscher angezogen./60/ Schon ein Blick in Konkordanz und
Synopse zeigt, daß Johannes diesem Begriff mehr Raum und mehr
Bedeutung gewährt als die andern Evangelien. Auch hier kann
deshalb die Frage nur lauten: Gibt es eine Brücke, die Matthäus
und Johannes in diesem Bereich verbindet?

Zunächst berichten beide von den Zeichenforderungen, die
die Juden an Jesus gestellt haben (Mt 12,38; 16,1; Joh 2,18;
6,30)./61/ Beide sehen diese Zeichenforderungen in einem
christologischen Bezug. Denn auch bei Matthäus geht es um die
messianische Legitimation Jesu. Eine dritte Gemeinsamkeit ist
die der Forderung zugrundeliegende Auffassung, da Jesus als
Wundertäter in Frage kommt (vgl. Joh 3,2).

Aber werden die 'Zeichen' nicht im Mt Ev im Unterschied
zum Joh Ev abgewiesen? Antwort: Sie werden dort ebensowenig
generell abgewiesen wie sie hier generell bejaht werden./62/
So lehnt Jesus im Joh Ev die Mannaspeisung ab und verweist
stattdessen auf das Brot, das er selber ist (6,30ff.51ff). Im
Mt Ev lehnt er die Zeichenforderung für jetzt ab, will sie
später aber im 'Jona-Zeichen' erfüllt sehen (12,38ff; 16,1ff).
Dieses 'Jona-Zeichen' ist er selber als der Auferweckte.

Nach dem Joh Ev haben die 'Zeichen' dienende Funktion,
insofern sie zum Glauben an Jesus als den Messias und
Gottessohn führen sollen (6,26; 10,37ff; 12,37; 20,30f). Aber
eben dieselbe Funktion haben sie auch im Mt Ev. Im Kontext der
Wunderkapitel 8 und 9 ergibt sich, daß Jesus mit seinem
Wirken den 'Glauben in Israel' sucht (Mt 8,10). Ganz
eindeutig zeigt die Scheltrede an die galiläischen Städte in Mt
11,20ff, daß Jesu Wundertaten zur Umkehr führen sollten. Es
ist also kein Fehler, und wird auch nicht getadelt, wenn das
Volk in Mt 12,23 aus den Wunderheilungen auf die Messianität
Jesu schloß. Matthäus denkt hier durchaus in der Linie von
Apg 2,22, sonst hätte er die Wunder Jesu nicht so planmäßig und
programmatisch in Kap 8 und 9 zusammengefaßt. Hunters
Feststellung, 'that even in the first three Gospels Jesus'
mighty works are 'signs''/63/, ist also berechtigt. In der
wesentlichen Bedeutung des 'Zeichens' sind sich Matthäus und
Johannes durchaus einig.

6. Der Begriff des 'Brotes' und der 'Speise'
Wie viele andere Begriffe gehört der des 'Brotes' in die
Reihe der doppelsinnigen Aussagen des Joh Ev. Im selben
Zusammenhang ist uns der Begriff der 'Speise' vertraut.

Es ist typisch, daß die betreffenden Artikel des ThWNT/64/
Matthäus nur dreimal beiläufig erwähnen und jedenfalls keine
Beziehung der matthäischen Stellen zu den johanneischen
herstellen.

Aber der doppelsinnige Gebrauch: Brot und Speise als
Nahrung für das geistliche Leben, ist Matthäus keineswegs
fremd. Das zeigt z.B. die Versuchungsgeschichte. Bei der
ersten Versuchung antwortet Jesus dem Teufel mit dem Zitat aus
Dt 8,3: 'Der Mensch lebt nicht vom Brot allein, sondern von
einem jeglichen Wort, das durch den Mund Gottes geht'. Die
geistliche Bedeutung, die schon das alttestamentliche Zitat
enthält, ist hier noch schärfer herausgearbeitet, sodaß sogar
die irdische Speise entfallen kann, wenn ein Wort Gottes
vorhanden ist. Insofern wird ein Austausch von 'Brot' und
'Gotteswort' möglich. Der Schritt zu Joh 4,34 liegt nahe:
'meine Speise ist die, daß ich tue den Willen des, der mich
gesandt hat' (vgl. 4,32; 6,27). Andrerseits läßt sich zum
Offenbarungswort des Sohnes die Brücke schlagen: 'Die Worte,
die ich zu euch geredet habe, die sind Geist und sind Leben'
(Joh 6,63).

In Mt 13,33 bildet Jesus ein Gleichnis mit Hilfe des
Begriffes 'Sauerteig'. Soweit wir sehen, ist Jesus der erste,
der das Bildwort vom 'Sauerteig' im jüdischen Raum positiv
verwendet, nämlich als Ausdruck für die Wirkungskraft des
Gottesreiches./65/ Führt von da ein Weg zur Brotrede in Joh 6,
26ff? Andrerseits rückt Jesus in Mt 16,5ff die beiden
Begriffe 'Sauerteig' und 'Lehre' nahe aneinander. Dabei ist
'Sauerteig' in diesem Kontext allerdings eine Bezeichnung für
gefährliche Lehre. Die genannten Beispiele zeigen, daß beide
Evangelien mit der Assoziation: Brot/Sauerteig – Wort/Lehre –
Leben/bzw. im negativen Fall Lebenshinderung, vertraut sind.
/66/ Dem entspricht auch der innere Zusammenhang von Joh 6,27
und 6,63: Jesu Worte sind Speise, 'die da bleibt in das ewige
Leben'.

Auch in Mt 15,26f ist 'Brot' ein Bildwort für Jesu
lebenschaffendes Handeln im Wort. Ebenso ist die 'Speise'
(trophä), die der treue Knecht in Mt 24,45 austeilen soll, das

göttliche Wort, das die Gemeinde zu ihrer Rettung und zu ihrem
Dienste braucht. Wieder liegt die Verbindung zur 'Brotrede'
Jesu in Joh 6 auf der Hand.

Da Matthäus an den bisher angezogenen Stellen nur
teilweise von Markus und Lukas begleitet wird, steht er in dem
hier besprochenen Bereich Johannes wieder besonders nahe.

Die Deutung des Brotes auf den Leib Jesu, der sich im
Sühnetod hingibt, im Zusammenhang mit der Abendmahlsfeier zeigt
Jesus selbst als die Speise im tiefsten Sinne, die die Menschen
benötigen, um das Leben zu gewinnen. Hier haben wir vielleicht
die engste Beziehung zu dem 'Brot' vor uns, das uns bei
Johannes begegnet (vgl. Mt 26,26 mit Joh 6,51ff). Im Lichte
der Abendmahlsworte werden schließlich auch die
Speisungsgeschichten der Synoptiker zu Zeichen und das dortige
'Brot' zum Schlüsselbegriff, in dem sich zuletzt Jesus selber
verbirgt (vgl. Mt 14,13ff; 15,32ff mit 26,17ff).

Zwar ist sprachlich vom 'Brot' und von der 'Speise' des
Matthäus bzw. der Synoptiker noch ein Stück Weges bis zum
johanneischen 'Ich bin das Brot des Lebens' (Joh 6,35). In der
Sache jedoch sagt der johanneische Christus nichts anderes als
der Christus der Synoptiker. Von daher läßt sich vermuten, daß
Jesus in der bei allen Evangelisten anzutreffenden
Doppeldeutigkeit vom 'Brot' gesprochen hat, das er im tiefsten
Sinne des Wortes selber ist. Nicht einmal das scheint
unwahrscheinlich, daß der historische Jesus von sich gesagt
hat: 'Ich bin das Brot des Lebens'.

7. *Johannes als Ergänzung des Matthäus*
In den letzten Jahren wurde die Möglichkeit, daß Johannes
und die Synoptiker sich gelegentlich ergänzen, wieder stärker
in Betracht gezogen./67/

Die Ergänzungsfunktion, die das Joh Ev für die Synoptiker-
erklärung haben kann, demonstriert das Verhältnis von Mt 14,13
- 22 zu Joh 6,1 - 15 /68/. Dem Leser des Mt Ev ist zunächst
nicht einsichtig, weshalb Jesus nach der Speisung die Jünger
'zwang' (Mt 14,22: ἠνάγκασεν), sich so plötzlich von der Menge
zu trennen und allein auf den See hinauszufahren. Den
Schlüssel zum Verständnis bietet die johanneische Parallele 6,
14f. Aus dem 'Zeichen' der wunderbaren Speisung zieht die
Menge den richtigen Schluß, daß Jesus die messianische Gestalt
von Dt 18,15 ist./69/ Daraus folgert sie in falscher Weise

weiter, daß er die nationale messianische Erwartung eines
'Königs' erfüllen, d.h. den Kampf gegen die Römer aufnehmen
wird (vgl. Joh 11,48ff; 18,33ff). Diesem Anspruch entzieht
sich Jesus durch fluchtartige Trennung von der Menge. Von da
aus erschließt sich die Bedeutung des 'Zwingens' in Mt 14,22:
Jesus 'zwingt' die Jünger, sich vom messianischen Taumel der
Menge zu lösen, um sie vor falschen und vorschnellen Handlungen
zu bewahren.

Zu erwägen ist, ob nicht doch Mt 14,22 und Joh 6,14 einen
inneren Zusammenhang mit der rätselhaften Stelle Mt 11,12
aufweisen. Das 'an sich reißen' (harpazein) teilt jedenfalls
Mt 11,12 mit Joh 6,15. Jesus hätte dann in Mt 11,12 alle
zelotischen Versuche, das Gottesreich eigenwillig
herbeizuführen, im Auge./70/ Eine Schwierigkeit bedeutet dabei
der Ausdruck 'Tage Johannes des Täufers'. Man müßte letztere
als die ganze Epoche verstehen, die vom Alten zum Neuen Bund
hinüberleitet und deren Repräsentant der Täufer ist. Eine
solche Bedeutung bleibt jedoch unsicher.

IV. Schluß

Die Ergebnisse der obigen Untersuchung lassen sich wie
folgt zusammenfassen:

1. Das Feld der Gemeinsamkeiten zwischen Johannes und den
   Synoptikern ist beträchtlich größer, als man bis heute
   gemeinhin annimmt. Die Tatsache, daß wir gerade Matthäus
   zum Vergleich herangezogen haben, erhärtet dieses Ergebnis
   nur.

2. Es lag keineswegs in unserer Absicht, die bestehenden
   Unterschiede im Verhältnis Johannes/Synoptiker zu ignorieren
   oder zu unterschätzen. Indem wir dies deutlich
   herausstellen, ist aber ebenso deutlich darauf hinzuweisen,
   daß die genannten Unterschiede nur dann angemessen erfaßt
   werden, wenn man *zugleich* die Gemeinsamkeiten beachtet.
   Sonst gerät man in Gefahr, die Unterschiede zu *überschätzen*.

3. Gelegentlich stießen wir auf Gemeinsamkeiten, die Matthäus
   und Johannes in singulärer Weise verbinden. Dazu gehören
   u.a. Betonung und Bedeutung des Sohnestitels, die Zeichnung
   der messianischen Debatten zur Zeit Jesu, gewisse Züge bei
   der Darstellung des Geistes und eine Doppelsinnigkeit bei
   Begriffen wie 'Brot' oder 'Speise'. Es hätte jedoch den

Zweck der Studie überschritten, solchen singulären
Gemeinsamkeiten und vor allem ihren Ursachen weiter
nachzugehen./71/ Immerhin kann man die Frage aufwerfen, ob
Johannes mit Lukas oder Markus wirklich enger verbunden ist
als mit Matthäus./72/

4. Parallelen beweisen nicht die Historizität. Jedoch
erleichtert der Aufweis von Gemeinsamkeiten in geografisch,
zeitlich und theologisch verschiedenartigen Schriften, wie
im Falle des Johannes und Matthäus, die Annahme der
Historizität des gemeinsam Überlieferten. Indirekt
stärken solche Gemeinsamkeiten dann auch das Vertrauen in
solche Berichte, die entweder von Johannes oder von den
Synoptikern *allein* überliefert werden./73/ Insofern ist
eine *vorsichtige* Ergänzung aller vier Evangelien
untereinander möglich.

5. Die festgestellten Gemeinsamkeiten zwischen Johannes und
den Synoptikern erleichtern schließlich die Annahme, daß
das Joh Ev seine geistige Heimat im Judentum bzw. im
Judenchristentum hat - vorausgesetzt, daß wir wenigstens
für das Mt Ev dieselbe Annahme machen dürfen.

Anmerkungen

/1/ C. H. Dodd, *About the Gospels,* Cambridge, 1950, S. 35:
'you feel a certain strangeness when you come to the Gospel
according to John'. R. Schnackenburg, *Das Johannesevangelium,*
HThk, IV, 1. Teil, 3. Aufl., Freiburg/Basel/Wien, 1972, S. 11:
'in eine andere Welt versetzt'.
/2/ H. Bornkamm, *Luthers Vorreden zur Bibel,* Hamburg, 1967, S.
140.
/3/ E. Schrenk, *Gottesreich und Bund im älteren
Protestantismus,* BFchTh, 2. Reihe, 5.Bd., Gütersloh, 1923, S.
26.
/4/ Vgl. E. Ludwig, *Schriftverständnis und Schriftauslegung bei
Johann Albrecht Bengel,* Stuttgart, 1952, S.88, 126; ferner H.
Reiss, *Das Verständnis der Bibel bei Johann Albrecht Bengel,*
Münster, 1952, S. 58.
/5/ Nach W. G. Kümmel, *Das Neue Testament, Geschichte der
Erforschung seiner Probleme,* 2. Aufl., Freiburg/München, S. 101.
152.

/6/ A.a.O. S. 152ff.
/7/ A.a.O. S. 169ff.
/8/ Karl v. Hase, *Geschichte Jesu*, 2. Aufl., Leipzig, 1891,
S. 39.
/9/ in: *Bekenntnis zur Kirche*, Festgabe für E. Sommerlath,
Berlin, 1960, S. 33-51; vgl. Stephen S. Smalley, *John:
Evangelist and Interpreter*, Exeter, 1978, S. 10.
/10/ Vgl. neuerdings S. Schulz, *Das Evangelium nach Johannes*,
NTD, 4, Göttingen, 1972, S. 3; ferner Schnackenburg a.a.O. S.
4ff.
/11/ Vgl. hier Smalley a.a.O. S. 11. Schon C. H. Dodd sprach
von einer 'newer school of criticism' (*Historical Tradition in
the Fourth Gospel*, Cambridge, 1963, S. 5).
/12/ *The Gospel according to St. John*, 2. Aufl., London, 1978,
S. 53. Der Kommentar entstand jedoch schon ein Vierteljahr-
hundert früher, vgl. S. VIII. Vgl. auch C. H. Dodd, *Historical
Tradition in the Fourth Gospel*, Cambridge, 1963, S. 4.
/13/ *The Gospel according to John*, Cambridge, 1965, S. 4.
/14/ A.a.O. S. 13.
/15/ Smalley a.a.O. S. 38.
/16/ Smalley a.a.O. S. 12: 'here is the nucleus of the 'new
look' on John'. Vgl. schon P. Gardner-Smith, *St. John and the
Synoptic Gospels*, Cambridge, 1938; ferner C. H. Dodd,
Historical Tradition in the Fourth Gospel, Cambridge, 1963, S.
423 und 8, und den Gegenpol bei Barrett a.a.O. S. VIII. 15.
/17/ Z.B. Dodd a.a.O. S. 428; Smalley a.a.O. S. 40. 150ff.
/18/ Vgl. hier C. H. Dodd, *About the Gospels*, S. 35; Smalley
a.a.O. S. 22ff.
/19/ Vgl. C. K. Barrett a.a.O. S. 43ff; C. H. Dodd, *Historical
Tradition in the Fourth Gospel*, Cambridge, 1963, S. 428ff;
Hunter a.a.O. S. 2ff; Smalley a.a.O. S. 21.40.155ff.
/20/ So schon Irenäus (Adv. Haer. III, 1,1) und Clemens
Alexandrinus (nach H.E.VI,14,7). Allerdings ist John A.T.
Robinson der Ansicht, daß das Joh Ev 'also the alpha of the
New Testament development' darstellt, und daß das Evangelium
zwischen 30 und 70 n.Chr. allmählich zu seiner jetzigen
Gestalt heranreifte (*Redating the New Testament*, Philadelphia,
1976, S. 311); vgl. zuletzt Smalley a.a.O. S. 245.
/21/ Vgl. Irenäus Adv. Haer. III, 1,1; Clemens Alex. nach H.E.
VI, 14,5; Kanon Muratori; Origines nach H.E. VI, 25,4; Th.
Zahn, *Einleitung in das Neue Testament*, 2 Bd., Leipzig, 1899,
S. 177. 322ff; W. R. Farmer, *The Synoptic Problem*, Dillsboro,
1976.
/22/ Vgl. Barrett a.a.O. S. 42. Diese Haltung steht in einer
gewissen Spannung zu der Tatsache, daß nach altkirchlicher

Überlieferung beide Evangelisten aus Galiläa und aus dem
Zwölferkreis stammten und noch von Papias in auffallender Weise
nebeneinander gestellt werden.

/23/ Vgl. außer W. R. Farmer: R. Riesner, Wie sicher ist die
Zwei-Quellen-Theorie?, *Theologische Beiträge*, 8, 1977, S. 49-73;
J. A. T. Robinson, *Redating the New Testament*, Philadelphia,
1976, S. 86ff; H. H. Stoldt, *Geschichte und Kritik der
Markushypothese*, Göttingen, 1977; A. Schlatter, *Der Evangelist
Matthäus*, Stuttgart, 1929.
/24/ Hunter a.a.O. S. 3: alle Evangelien 'exhibit a common
outline of Jesus' ministry'.
/25/ *History and the Gospel*, 2. Aufl., London, 1964, S. 12.
/26/ A.a.O. S. 11f; vgl. Hunter a.a.O. S. 5f.
/27/ *History and the Gospel*, 2. Aufl., London, 1964, S. 58; vgl.
About the Gospels, Cambridge, 1950, S. 44.
/28/ *Historical Tradition in the Fourth Gospel*, Cambridge, 1963,
S. 432.
/29/ Von da aus kann ich H. Frankemölle zustimmen, wenn er im
Mt Ev ein 'in sich geschlossenes literarisches Kunstwerk eines
hochbegabten theologische Schriftstellers' sieht (*Jahwebund und
Kirche Christi, Studien zur Form- und Traditionsgeschichte des
Evangeliums nach Matthäus*, Inaugural - Dissertation, Münster,
1972, S. 5 - gegen K. Stendahls 'School of Matthew'!).
/30/ Betr. Mt vgl. hier P. Nepper - Christensen, *Das Matthäus-
evangelium - ein judenchristliches Evangelium?* AThD, 1,
Aarhus, 1958, S. 206.
/31/ So W. Wrede, *Das Messiasgeheimnis in den Evangelien*,
Göttingen, 1901.
/32/ Smalley a.a.O. S. 13 hält dies mit Recht als grundlegende
Gemeinsamkeit fest.
/33/ Hunter a.a.O. S. 8.
/34/ P. Stuhlmacher, *Vom Verstehen des Neuen Testaments, Grund-
risse zum Neuen Testament*, NTD, Ergänzungsreihe, Bd. 6,
Göttingen, 1979, S. 225ff, bs. S. 243. Allerdings bleiben bei
Stuhlmacher viele Positionen des Kritizismus von dieser
Erkenntnis unberührt.
/35/ Vgl. zu ἕως ἔρχομαι in Joh 21,23 das ἔρχου bzw ἔρχομαι in
Apk 22,20!
/36/ Für Matthäus ist doch wohl Palästina der Entstehungsort,
bei Johannes sprechen durchschlagende Erwägungen für Ephesus
(vgl. Hunter a.a.O. S. 1f; Smalley S. 244f. 149; anders Nepper
- Christensen a.a.O. S. 205f).
/37/ A.a.O. S. 203.
/38/ Vgl. hier Barrett a.a.O. S. 5: Der Autor des Joh Ev 'means
to write both history and theology - theological history'.

/39/ Vgl. dazu Smalley a.a.O. S. 13. Im Endeffekt kommt Smalley
zu dem Schluß: 'In the end... the difference between John and
the Synoptics is one of degree, not one of kind'.

/40/ Vgl. R. Bultmann, *Das Evangelium des Johannes*, KEK, 17.
Aufl., Göttingen, 1962, S. 167f. 260; S. Schulz a.a.O. S. 129f.
Anders z.B. E. Stauffer, *ThWNT*, II, 1935, S. 352: 'ein
Kurzschluß'.

/41/ Z.B. H. Zahrnt, *Die Sache mit Gott*, München, o.J., S.
323ff.

/42/ A.a.O. S. 343ff.

/43/ A.a.O. S. 345.

/44/ Vgl. meine Untersuchung über 'Mensch und freier Wille',
WUNT, 12, Tübingen, 1971, S. 40f.

/45/ A.a.O. S. 347.

/46/ A.a.O. S. 346.

/47/ Daß Matthäus in 26,64 das markinische ἐγώ εἰμι gestrichen
habe, kann man nur behaupten, wenn man von der m.E. unzu-
treffenden Annahme ausgeht, daß Matthäus von Markus literarisch
abhängig sei.

/48/ A.a.O. S. 342. 350.

/49/ In diese Richtung deutet Stauffer a.a.O. S. 347.

/50/ Evtl. auf dem atl. Hintergrund von Jes 41,4; 43,11; 45,21;
48,12.

/51/ Vgl. hier noch Mk 13,6.21ff; Mt 24,5ff und Stauffer a.a.O.
S. 350ff.

/52/ *ThWNT*, VIII, 1969, S. 389; vgl. den gesamten Artikel S.
364ff.

/53/ Umgekehrt Schweizer a.a.O. S. 382.

/54/ Schweizer a.a.O.

/55/ Art.: Johannesevangelium, *RGG*, 3.Bd., 1. Aufl., Tübingen,
1912, Sp. 634.

/56/ A.a.O. S. 5.

/57/ Auch C. H. Dodd rechnet damit, daß das reziproke Vater-
Sohn-Verhältnis 'was transmitted in one of the most primitive
strata of tradition', und doch sei es zugleich 'central to the
theology of the Fourth Gospel'! (*Historical Tradition in the
Fourth Gospel*, Cambridge, 1963, S. 420f).

/58/ A.a.O. S. 427. In anderem Zusammenhang spricht Hunter von
'so many signs of being written by an eyewitness' (a.a.O. S. 13
über das Joh Ev).

/59/ J.Behm, *ThWNT*, V, 1954, S. 802 und ff.

/60/ Vgl. hier K. H. Rengstorf, *ThWNT*, VII, 1964, S. 241ff.

/61/ Rengstorf ist a.a.O. S. 242 sogar der Meinung: 'Johannes
kennt auch die synoptische Überlieferung von der Forderung
eines σημεῖον an Jesus' (unter Berufung auf Joh 2,18; 6,30).

/62/ So auch Rengstorf a.a.O.

/63/ A.a.O. S. 4.
/64/ ThWNT, I, 1933, Art.: ἄρτος, S. 475f, und βρῶμα, βρῶσις
S. 640ff (Verfasser beide Male J. Behm).
/65/ Vgl. H. Windisch in ThWNT, II, 1935, S. 907f.
/66/ H. Windisch a.a.O.
/67/ Vgl. Dodd a.a.O. S. 428; Hunter a.a.O. S. 6.
/68/ Auch Dodd und Hunter verweisen a.a.O. auf dieses Beispiel,
gehen jedoch von Markus, nicht von Matthäus aus.
/69/ Vgl. G. Friedrich in ThWNT, VI, 1959, S. 847f.
/70/ Anders aber G. Schrenk in ThWNT, I, S. 608ff.
/71/ Vgl. die vorsichtige Erörterung bei Schnackenburg a.a.O.
S. 26ff, der der Sicht Dodds und Gardner-Smith's zuneigt (S.
30ff).   Vgl. auch die Kontroverse, ob Johannes Matthäus gekannt
hat, zwischen H. F. D. Sparks (bejahend, St. John's Knowledge
of Matthew: The Evidence of John 13,16 and 15,20. JThSt, NS, 3,
1952, S. 58-61) und P. Gardner-Smith (verneinend, ebd., 4, 1953,
S. 31-35).
/72/ Vgl. Schnackenburg a.a.O. S. 19: 'Spezielle Berührungen
zwischen dem Mt Ev und dem Joh Ev sind selten und geringfügig'.
/73/ Dies betont auch Smalley (a.a.O. S. 29).

John 21: Test Case for History and Redaction in the Resurrection Narratives

Grant R. Osborne
Trinity Evangelical Divinity School
Deerfield, Illinois

Whenever one deals critically with a Gospel text, there are three aspects which must be considered: its redaction, the tradition lying behind the redaction, and finally the historical nucleus lying behind the tradition./1/ Some treat these aspects as somehow mutually exclusive and try to separate them from one another. However, several recent studies have taken issue with this dichotomy and attempt to demonstrate that history, tradition, redaction and theology can co-exist on the sacred page./2/ The purpose of this paper is to test this issue by performing a redaction- and tradition-critical analysis on a key text. We will not assume that either redaction or tradition equals history but will attempt to ascertain the presence and interaction of all three in the text as well as the degree to which they overlap./3/

Furthermore, it is important to delineate clearly the meaning of redaction as it is utilized in this study. There is a great deal of ambiguity in its use today: at times it is employed strictly in its denotative sense as a technical term describing the alterations which the evangelist has made in adapting the traditions to his own purposes, while at other times it has a connotative thrust in denoting the theological purposes themselves. This latter sense is especially true of the adjective "redactional," which often is tautologous to "theological." In this study we will attempt to note such nuances, and when the point deals with the larger question of theology, we will restrict ourselves to "theological."

It is often best to center upon a difficult case when studying a controversial issue, and John 21 certainly fits this category. As is the situation with the whole of the Fourth Gospel, problems of history and redaction are particularly acute, due to the peculiar independence of this work from the so-called 'synoptic' Gospels. Moreover, chapter 21 is intimately bound up with one of the central questions regarding

John: origin and authorship. All theories regarding editorial
activity and 'stages' of composition begin here, for it has
probably been added somewhat late to the Gospel. Chapter 20
is a closely bound unity and ends with what most probably is
the intended conclusion to the Gospel, 20:30-31./4/ In spite
of the fact that manuscript evidence universally includes
Chapter 21, it seems to be extraneous, separate from chapter
20 and introduced by the phrases μετὰ ταῦτα and πάλιν; v. 14
adds that this was the 'third time' (τρίτον) that Jesus
'appeared.' While these phrases could fit the view that chapter
21 is a planned conclusion, parallel with the prologue of 1:1-18,
it is more likely that they point to a later decision to add
the section. They are all Johannine phrases (the first two
occur together in 11:7, 20:26) but the key is ταῦτα, which is
unlike John's normal precision (cf. 20:26, 'after eight days')
and links chapter 21 with the whole of chapter 20 rather than
placing chapter 21 chronologically. All of this (especially
20:30-31) points to the probability that the chapter was added
to chapter 20 at a later time. The structural unity of the
chapter and its connection with the rest of the book indicates
that it is most likely an epilogue,/5/ with a specific design
and purpose, as we hope to develop below.

The major debate with respect to the chapter as a whole,
of course, centers upon its authorship. Was it appended to the
original work by the evangelist himself or by a later redactor?
/6/ The decision depends largely upon the comparison between
this chapter and the main body of the Gospel:/7/
  1) *Similarities:*
  'Sea of Tiberias'; the characters Simon Peter, Thomas,
  Nathaniel; the beloved disciple (hereafter labelled BD)
  with Peter; ὀψάριον (vv. 6, 9, 11); the charcoal fire;
  the hesitant question (v. 12); the similarity of v. 13
  to 6:11; numbering the appearances; the name of Simon's
  father; partitive ἐκ; sheep imagery and variations in
  vv. 15-17; two-fold 'Amen' and the symbolism in v. 18;
  explanatory notes and parenthesis in v. 19; witness theme;
  reference to 'other deeds' in v. 25.

  2) *Differences:*
  ἐπί for ὑπό; φανεροῦν (v. 1); ὑπάγω plus infinitive (v. 3);
  πρωΐα for πρωΐ (v. 4); ἰσχύω for δύναμαι, and causal ἀπό
  (v. 6); οὐ μακράν for ἐγγύς (v. 8); τολμᾶν, and ἐξετάζω
  for ἐρωτάω (v. 12); πλέον for μᾶλλον (v. 15); ἐπιστρέφω
  for στρέφω (v. 20); ἕως (v. 22); ἀδελφός (v. 23). In

addition there are 28 hapax legomena to John. Few, of
course, are willing to judge on the basis of terminology
and style alone. Most agree, in fact, that the differences
(e.g. most of the 28 new terms are due to special material,
such as the fishing scene) are insufficient in themselves to
demand a separate author. The most common reasons why many
reject Johannine authorship are: (1) the clumsiness of the
transition (the evangelist would have added chapter 21 without
so difficult a transition); and (2) theories of editorial
revision, which on the basis of other evidence from the Gospel
itself demand a separate author.

The first ignores the basic structure of the Gospel itself,
where structural connection is often sacrificed because of
theological considerations. In fact, this basic lack of cohesion
has led to multiple theories of displacements, sources, and
editions. In light of this widespread lack of organization
(as we know it), it is logical to take this to be a stylistic
trait of the evangelist himself. As Lindars notes, the form
and structure are typical of John: 'a synoptic-type episode
is retold to make a particular effect....This becomes the basis
of further dialogue.'/8/ Regarding the differences he adds,
'Really important differences are not sufficiently numerous to
be decisive against Johannine authorship.'/9/ In fact, as noted
above, the transition terms may point to a later addition; they
do not demand a separate author, especially since all three are
characteristic of the evangelist.

The second is more difficult. Of course, it is quite impossible to review all the theories of editorial stages, from
Rudolf Bultmann's epochal ecclesiastical and revelational editors
to Raymond E. Brown's five stage and Rudolf Schnackenburg's
three stage composition theories, to name only a few. Such are
built upon the growing feeling among scholars that in spite of
the stylistic unity throughout the Gospel, there is at the same
time a disunity in the handling of sources. Several sections
(e.g. 1:1-18, 6:51-58, chapters 15-17, chapter 21) are seemingly
out of place. Indeed, most recent Johannine commentators have
been preoccupied with questions of source criticism./10/

We question whether any such complex theory is necessary.
Robert Kysar points out that the 'Johannine theory puzzle' still
remains when all the theories are finished. Rather than smooth-
ing out the narrative, they have created incongruities and
breaks in the narrative./11/ Might it not be better to see

such 'inconsistencies' as deliberate on the part of the evangelist rather than clumsy editing on the part of a so-called final
redactor? It is the contention of this writer that such is
indeed the case, and the exegesis in this study will attempt to
demonstrate it with regard to chapter 21. Certainly the
evangelist used sources, perhaps Mark or Luke,/12/ (although this
is greatly disputed; most today assume Johannine independence)
or some type of signs source./13/   Further, the later addition
of chapter 21 does point to 'stages' in the composition of
the Gospel. The issue is whether a series of editors revised
the Gospel.

     Finally, we would note the excellent study of B. de Solages
who has provided an extensive linguistic comparison between
John 21 and John 1-20 then between John 20 and John 1-19 and
finally between John 21 and the Gospel of Luke, examining three
things: text, vocabulary and expressions. He concludes first
that John 21 is closer to chapters 1-19 than is John 20 and second
that it is closer to the rest of the Gospel than it is to Luke.
Finally, he says, 'il n'est guère possible d'attribuer ce
chapître à une autre plume que le reste de l'évangile de Jean.'
/14/

     Our provisional conclusion is that John's work at present
can best be explained as a unity. The so-called aporias,
displaced pericopae, and theological incongruities seem to have
been deliberate on the part of the evangelist in working with
his own sources. The highly complex and disparate hypotheses
regarding several stages of redactional revision have not as
yet been proven and can be replaced with a simpler theory of
redactional activity on the part of the evangelist himself. We
believe that this may be true with chapter 21. The evidence does
not demand a separate author, and the case for unity outweighs
that for disunity. We will now see whether this is true as we
consider each section.

          Appearance to the Disciples Fishing, 21:1-14

     Tradition Study
     The numerous parallels between this and Luke 5:1-11 have
led many to posit a common origin for the two. Indeed, the
detailed resemblances between them are striking:
          1) Fishing all night but catching nothing;
          2) Command to cast the nets together with a promise
              that they would catch fish;

3)   The presence of other disciples;
4)   Obedience to the command and fulfillment of the
      promise;
5)   Peter's impulsive act and the peripheral place of
      the others in the story;
6)   Jesus as Lord;
7)   The missionary motif.

These seem so convincing to the majority of scholars that discussion today centers upon which represents the more primitive
tradition./15/ However, all has not been said regarding the
issue. There are also notable differences: most significantly,
the pericope is marked by distinctive Johannine style. But in
addition, within each similarity we find the following differences (keyed to the categories above):

1)   Seven disciples in John vs. three in Luke;
2)   The nets breaking and others called to assist in
      Luke vs. dragging the nets to shore in John;
3)   The confession of Peter in Luke vs. the BD in John;
4)   The non-recognition motif in John (v. 19);
5)   The BD in John is the central figure;
6)   Peter's swimming to shore in John;
7)   The different conclusions ('fishers of men' in Luke
      and the meal fellowship in John).

While some could be explained as redactional additions or as
separate developments of a common tradition, the differences
are sufficiently strong to compel J. N. Sanders to say, 'It is
fairly clear from the limited amount of common material that the
one narrative cannot be an edited version of the other.'/16/

This points toward another possibility, rejected by those
mentioned in footnote 15, that the two represent separate events.
While this is not commonly asserted, it cannot be dismissed
outright. Brown, for example, says that Peter could not
experience two such similar situations without recognizing
Jesus in the latter instance./17/ Yet this is inadequate and
ignores human fallibility. Peter, frustrated after a night
without success, could easily fail to note similarities between
events months (or even years) apart. As Marshall notes, the
only common feature here is the command to let down the nets,
hardly enough for Peter to draw the parallel. He states that
the traditions would naturally have influenced one another./18/
In fact, if John did know Luke's Gospel, he could easily have
consciously drawn parallels between the first 'call' and the
final 'recommissioning' of the disciples. Further, many scholars
have noted the fact that Luke's scene shows no formal signs of

a resurrection story. It is therefore probable that these are
separate traditions which reflect distinct historical incidents.
/19/

A further source-critical debate centers on Rudolf Pesch's
theory that the redactor here has combined two traditions, a
'miraculous catch of fish' legend (in vv. 2, 3, 4a, 6, 11) and
an appearance tradition (vv. 4b, 7, 8, 9, 12, 13), woven together
by the evangelist, who added vv. 1, 5, 10, 14, to unify the
whole./20/ We might contrast this with Fortna's argument that
the story as a whole was the third of the miracles in the 'signs
source.'/21/ A comparison of these two theories is highly
illuminating. The first is far too complex to be plausible,
while the other is too simplistic. For the redactor to have
combined his sources as woodenly as Pesch maintains is difficult
to accept. Brown notes three weaknesses with Pesch's theory:
1) The appearance story is truncated, for too much of it is
missing to make it coherent; in fact, part of the setting Pesch
postulates is found in the catch of fish. 2) The appearance
story is inconsistent itself, e.g. the twofold recognition in
vv. 7, 12. 3) The method of the redactor is virtually inexplicable and raises more problems than it solves./22/ In the same
way, it is unlikely that the evangelist would have incorporated
a source wholesale, as Fortna claims. The most reasonable
supposition is that John worked creatively with the basic
appearance tradition, we believe on the basis of his own theological interests.

Theological motifs
The primary value of redaction criticism is found more in
its delineation of structure and theology than in its more
speculative discussion of tradition-development and authenticity.
/23/ Our purpose here will be to discern the major themes in
this section. In chapter 21 as a whole, Schnackenburg notes five
(the latter four apply to vv. 1-14):/24/ 1) The person,
ecclesiastical purpose and fate of Peter; 2) the person and
purpose of the BD and his relationship to Peter; 3) Jesus'
continued fellowship with the disciples and the church; 4) Jesus'
work in the church through the ministry of Peter and the BD, and
5) the mission and unity of the church. The one criticism of
this is his assumption of the primacy given to Peter and the BD.
We hope to demonstrate that they also are a means to an end, and
the primary motif is ecclesiology. As chapter 20 of John's
resurrection narrative stressed soteriology (the faith-drama
of belief and recognition of the Risen One), the epilogue

stresses the church, for reasons which will be elucidated below.
The opening section sets the scene and provides the following
emphases:

1)   Recognition motif

The bridge from chapter 20 to chapter 21 is provided *via*
the recognition theme, prominent also in the Emmaus account of
Luke 24:13-35 and Mary's encounter in John 20:11-18./25/ Dodd,
in fact, calls this the central element in this pericope./26/
One of the key phrases is ἐφανέρωσεν ἑαυτόν. The verb is a
characteristic Johannine term (twenty times in his writings vs.
three in Luke and none in the other evangelists). Lindars says
that its absence in chapter 20 shows that it is not characteristic of John in a resurrection context,/27/ and Alsup argues
further that it is only found in late redactional strata and is
evidence of a later 'editorial seam.'/28/ However, these
arguments are obviated by John's constant practice of providing
a gradual unveiling of Jesus' true nature to his followers,
culminating in the resurrection itself. In I John /29/ the
term is used of Jesus' earthly ministry (1:2, 3:5) and parousia
(2:28, 3:2) and also of his life as *Heilsgeschichte*, including
his resurrection in a Johannine soteriological sense (3:8, 4:9).
In the Gospel it refers to the progressive 'revelation'/30/ of
Jesus through his works (9:3, 17:6). Hence it is reasonable for
the evangelist to use this term three times (twice in v. 1, v.
14) for the final, ultimate 'revelation' of God's 'glory' in
Jesus./31/ Therefore, the phrase is redactional: as elsewhere
in the Gospel it expresses the evangelist's reflection on the
significance of Jesus.

The similarity of this pericope to the narratives regarding
both Mary and the disciples on the Emmaus road is especially
seen in the progression of vv. 4-7. As in the other cases, the
early part stresses their failure to know Jesus. The disciples
have returned to their former occupation and are engaged in
seemingly aimless activity./32/ While some have argued that
this lack of purpose shows that this was the first appearance,
we find that extremely doubtful, since it does not take seriously
the Jerusalem appearances, which we believe were the first. At
any rate, the inadequacy of the disciples is reflected in their
failure to catch any fish, and the recognition theme follows
their success after they obey Jesus' instructions (v.6). The
message in this scene centres upon their total dependence on
Jesus, i.e. without him they can do nothing, and the connection
of the recognition motif with the successful results has ecclesiological overtones. The disciples represent the church's

encounter of Jesus' lordship as they obey his commands and
experience his blessings. This is a good example of editorial
selection: the evangelist takes the tradition and gives it
theological import by organizing the structural development of
the narrative around his theme, in this case ecclesiology.

Then follows the recognition of Jesus by the BD -- 'It is
the Lord' (v. 7, cf. 20:13, 18, where Mary progresses in her
recognition of Lordship). In chapter 20 the recognition is the
vehicle of soteriology, with faith the key to true perception
of the Risen Jesus (cf. 20:8). Here it has an ecclesiological
purpose, for the disciples who had been experiencing failure now
find prosperity via the command of the Risen Lord and thereby
come to realize his presence. A further anomaly is the hesitancy
of the disciples over saying 'Who are you?' in 21:12, which at
first glance seems out of place, since Jesus has already been
recognized as Lord in v. 7. It seems to be used theologically
to stress the fact that 'they knew it was the Lord.'/33/
Further, the exalted lordship of Jesus has now led to awe on
the part of the disciples; they 'know' not only that he is Lord
but understand that lordship entails fellowship. John has combined ecclesiology with christology. The original tradition
undoubtedly stressed the christological overtones; the disciples
experienced the glory of the Risen Lord and thereby came to
recognize his new status. John has then added further nuances
dealing with the ecclesiological implications for the disciples
and therefore the church. As a result of her participation in
the benefits which accrue from Jesus' presence, the church
experiences victory and fellowship.

  2) The BD and Peter
      So much has been written on this topic that all one can
do here is present a few highlights of current discussion. The
BD is a key to authorship (cf. 21:24 below) as well as theology
within the Gospel itself, and chapter 21 is the major source
of material in this regard. A major issue today is whether the
BD was an actual person or was merely idealized as the archetypal
disciple./34/ Most today accept as probable that he was an
actual person /35/ who nevertheless was idealized by the
evangelist (and his church, cf. 21:24). The debate, of course,
centers around his identity. Was he the Apostle himself,/36/
John Mark,/37/ Lazarus,/38/ Matthias,/39/ an anonymous figure
from the Twelve/40/ or a separate disciple whose teachings were
authoritative for the Church?/41/ This last category is attain-
ing some consensus in modern Johannine scholarship/42/ and
claims that the final evangelist used the anonymity of his

source to present his theological message. R. Alan Culpepper,
for instance, believes that the Johannine community stood in the
same relation to the BD as the BD to Jesus and Jesus to the
Father. Therefore the BD parallels the Paraclete (chapters 14-
16) in function and performs the work of the Paraclete for the
community, i.e. as the final revealer of Jesus' teachings./43/

Our question would be whether these scholars are not
correct theologically but too skeptical as to the possibility
of identifying the BD with John the Apostle. This still seems
to fit the evidence far better than the other possibilities, and
the agnosticism of many today is not warranted. On the basis
of 21:2 he was either one of the sons of Zebedee or one of the
two unnamed disciples; his presence at the Last Supper and the
Cross would also favor that. Brown argues that only John the
son of Zebedee fits the requirements: one of the Twelve, one
with a special relationship to Jesus, a close association with
Peter, and one with special memories to impart./46/

At the same time, a perusal of those passages which feature
the BD will illustrate his theological role: 1) 13:23-25, where
he intercedes for Simon Peter in asking Jesus the meaning of his
prophecy of betrayal; 2) 19:26-27, where Jesus places Mary into
his care; 3) 20:2-10, where the BD and Peter race to the tomb,
and the BD 'sees and believes'; 4) 21:7, where the BD recognizes
that the one standing on the shore 'is the Lord'; 5) 21:20-23,
where Peter is told that the BD may live to see the parousia;
6) 21:24, where the community attests to the 'true witness'
which the BD provided./45/ Several points might be noted:
First, the references all occur in the latter half of the Gospel,
i.e. the passion and resurrection sections. Second, the over-
whelming stress is on the intimacy between the BD and Jesus
('whom Jesus loved,' 'leaning on Jesus' breast'). Third, that
intimacy is connected to a revelational ministry (explicitly in
21:24 and 19:35 if that is a BD passage ; implicitly in 13:23f,
21:7). Fourth, this is connected to the relationship between
the BD and Peter. Whether there is a deliberate contrast
between these two who figure so prominently (only in 19:26-27 is
the BD seen without Peter!) has been vigorously debated.
Kragerud and Lorenzen, for instance, see a definite rivalry
between them, symbolizing conflict in the community itself./46/
However, we must wonder how this could be true in light of the
very positive picture given Peter in John, especially in
chapter 21./47/ Never is he placed in a negative light with
respect to the BD, not even in 18:15f (if that is a BD passage).
Accordingly, we theorize that both the BD and Peter have a

positive role.

        Peter is the impetuous figure, and he prepares in each one
for the role of the BD. As in 20:2-10, it is the BD who has the
insight into the true significance of the scene. Yet after he
has recognized the Lord, it is Peter who jumps into the water
to get to Jesus (v.7). This is quite similar to 20:6f, where
the BD arrives first but Peter enters the tomb. In both scenes
Peter's impetuosity is nevertheless conditioned by an obvious
love for his Master. In this scene, in fact, Peter has a greater
role (preparing for vv. 15-17), for it is he who provides the
impetus to fish, jumps in to see Jesus, and hauls the net to
shore. Yet these last two actions follow the initiative of the
BD, who alone recognizes 'the Lord' (see above). The primacy
of the BD, as elsewhere, lies in two areas: 1) witness (13:23,
19:35, 21:24) and 2) perception or faith (18:16, 20:8). The
special intimacy leads the BD to be the revelational source who
reveals the actual meaning of the scene. Peter's ministry, as
we will note in 21:15-17, is that of foundation-stone, the one
who acts in serving Jesus.

        3) *Mission Motif*
        At first glance this pericope seems to contain no mission-
ary thrust (common to group appearances--Mark 16:7, Matthew 28:
19, Luke 24:44f, John 20:21), but a strong missionary emphasis
may be embedded in the symbolism. In light of Luke 5:1-11 it
seems likely that the primitive church saw it in this way, with
the fishermen symbolizing 'fishers of men' dependent upon the
Lord for success. The great catch itself is directly applicable
to this, although the mission thrust is not nearly so evident in
this scene as it is in Luke 5. If, however, Marshall is correct
(fn. 18) when he surmises that the Lucan language influenced
John here, the missions thrust is definite.

        The recorded number of fish is highly peculiar; it corre-
sponds to no other number in Scripture, yet it is so explicit.
While it is of course possible that the evangelist includes the
figure recorded in the tradition,/48/ it also is possible that
the primitive church saw significance in the number and so
recorded it in the tradition. Thus there may be both tradition
and redaction in the number. While it seems likely that it was
historical (see fn. 48), many assert that the placement of the
scene within the larger context of the story was redactionally
motivated./49/ However, the difficulty, if not impossibility,
of ever narrowing down the possible interpretations of the figure
/50/ has led many today to say generally that in some way the

universal character and promised results of the church's
mission are depicted./51/ Others are skeptical and argue that
it should mean no more than a large catch of fish. Even here,
however, it would symbolize (in keeping with Luke 5) the success
of the church's mission.

Linguistic evidence may support such a symbolic interpretation. The term used for 'hauling in' the net and fish (ἑλκύειν,
vv. 6, 11) occurs also in 12:32, 'But I, when I am lifted up
from the earth, will draw (ἑλκύσω) all men to myself' (NIV).
Furthermore, the verb in v. 11b, 'the net was not torn'(σχίζειν),
is employed in 19:24 of the soldiers dividing Jesus' robe (a
symbol of unity?) and is related to σχίσμα, used in John (7:43,
9:16, 10:19) of the division of people over Jesus' significance.
The difference here with Luke's fish-catch (5:1-10) may be
illuminating: the latter has the net 'breaking,' while John,
possibly aware of the Lucan narrative, states that it did not
break. Schnackenburg asserts that this gives the missions
symbolism of 21:11 a wider foundation, i.e. the unity of the
church./52/

On the other hand, (1) this non-breaking of the net may be
intended to do no more than accentuate the miracle in this scene;
and (2) one must ask whether the other uses of the ἑλκύειν and
σχίζειν roots are actually parallel and whether this is a case
of drawing a false theological conclusion by equating widely
divergent semantic meanings./53/ However, as to the first
criticism, if we are correct that John knew at least the tradition behind Luke 5 then he has clearly injected a considerable
theological stress into the story. The second caution is serious
but may not undermine our thesis. The fact that ἑλκύειν is
repeated in v. 11 may provide more than merely historical
interest, especially if the catch of fish does have some theological import; moreover, in this case the semantic meanings are
parallel. The case is strongest with σχίζειν/σχίσμα but this is
a major theme in the Gospel, and we believe the criticism is more
valid for 19:24 than for this situation.

Therefore this passage may well speak of the unity of the
church in mission, a Johannine interest. Smalley/54/ connects
this mission theme with both the Johannine 'signs' theology and
his christology. John uses the 'signs' to show first 'the
manifestation of the Word to the world' (chapters 1-12) and
second 'the glorification of the Word for the world' (chapters
20-21). It therefore makes the same point as the signs in the
first twelve chapters, that 'flesh can be the carrier of spirit,'

i.e. the twofold Johannine christology--the Word (divine) incarnate in the flesh (human). Again we see that christology is central to the Johannine purpose. As is the case with the recognition theme, so mission is grounded in christology. The revelation of the Word is now symbolized as inherent in the human mission (building upon 20:21-23).

4) *Eucharistic Motif*

The meal scene (vv. 12-13) is commonly taken to be a separate scene from an appearance tradition, annexed by the redactor./55/ Several arguments are adduced: 1) the non-Johannine phraseology of v. 12; 2) editorial addition, adduced from the similarity between v. 13 and 6:11; 3) Jesus' request in v. 10 to bring some of the fish while in v. 13 breakfast is ready when they come (cf. v. 5). Therefore many conclude that vv. 12b, 14 are artificial editorial links which attempt to connect two episodes which were not originally a single event.

This indeed is a possibility and would not endanger the historical veracity of the two scenes. Virtually all the evangelists employ a thematic more than chronological arrangement of the episodes. There are certainly elements of a primitive tradition behind both scenes. However, does the narrative demand that vv. 12, 13 be a separate scene? As stated earlier, there are neither linguistic nor thematic grounds for postulating a two-source origin to this story and we wonder whether tradition-critics read more into the differences than is necessary. As Barrett notes, such aspects as 'no one dared to ask' in v. 13 (taken by some as a second 'recognition') do not provide 'indication that two stories are being combined.'/56/ The seeming contradiction between vv. 5, 10 and 13 could as easily be due to the abbreviation of the scenes and does not demand separate sources. We prefer to see the whole (vv.1-14) as a single event from the beginning. Both the fire in v. 9 and the command in v. 10 prepare for the meal scene, and the fish in v. 13 is doubtless the same fish caught (note how they are to bring fish [v. 10] even though fish are already on the fire [v. 9]). So here the disciples share in the miraculous results, and it is more likely that we have a unified scene.

Theologically, the debate centers upon a supposed liturgical or sacramental interest in the meal of vv. 12-13. The question of sacramentalism in the Fourth Gospel has been the subject of innumerable studies./57/ No definite consensus has been reached, for while more scholars than previously note

some sacramental interest (e.g. 6:51-58), so recent a commentator
as Kysar has sided with the anti-sacramental school./58/ To me
a middle position, admitting some liturgical interest, seems
most likely, for it is difficult to ignore the sacramental thrust
of 6:51-58 *et al.* Yet John characteristically accented the
theological aspect to stress the spiritual significance of the
sacraments (indeed, many crisis events of Jesus' life and
ministry, e.g. Gethsemane) and so we never see an explicit
reference to a sacrament.

With regard to the meal scene, verse 13 seems to be
patterned after 6:11 (similar wording and setting). In both,
Jesus takes the bread and distributes it to the disciples.
However, while the eucharistic flavor is pronounced in chapter
6 (especially in light of vv. 51-58), it is not so here, leading
many /59/ to deny a liturgical stress in this episode. Nevertheless, some do find sacramental indications: 1) the early
connection between the appearances and the table-fellowship of
the early church (cf. Luke 24:13-35, Acts 10:40f); and 2) the
Christian use of fish in the eucharist,/60/ although these are
certainly debatable. There are questions as to whether table
fellowship was always viewed sacramentally, and even greater
doubts as to whether fish had eucharistic significance in the
first century. It seems that the passage is devoid of any
specific eucharistic connotation (note the absence of 'broke
the bread' and 'gave thanks') but may well represent the early
'table fellowship' motif, as in the Emmaus account (cf. Luke
24:30f). As such, one may speculate that John's readers would
be reminded of Jesus' living presence with his followers in
table fellowship, and thereby perhaps in the eucharistic
fellowship as well (especially in v. 13). The major stress,
however, is upon Jesus' presence in the community fellowship.

Tradition and Redaction in 21:1-14

Our study has come to certain conclusions with regard to
the pericope: 1) it is an integrated whole and thus does not
combine two or more separate traditions; 2) there is a distinct
tradition-history, behind the episode (see further below); and
3) at the same time there is definite redaction seen in the terms
chosen and the structural development of the narrative. Bruce
Chilton (see article in this volume) and others have argued
viably that tradition-study should follow rather than precede
decisions regarding redaction, since a writer's distinct
language shows how he used his sources. However, we do not
believe that this invalidates the approach followed here, for

tradition and redaction are interdependent. One does not simply
eliminate all redactional emphases in order to arrive at the
traditional core, for often the so-called "redaction" is a para-
phrase rather than a wooden addition to the source. Therefore
we will build upon the previous discussion and present our
conclusions first in terms of tradition, then from the standpoint
of redaction.

As we consider further the tradition-history, several
indicators point to a primitive source: one of the major ones
occurs in v. 3; the disciples seem to be without a plan and
expect nothing. This is highly unlikely in a later resurrection
narrative and is quite similar to Mark's discipleship motif,
i.e. an accent on their failure./61/ Moreover, while we do not
believe that Luke 5 is the same event, the 'criterion of multiple
attestation'/62/ would still apply. The miracle of a great
catch of fish was so important to the early church that two
divergent episodes are recounted (cf. the feedings of the 4000
and 5000). Finally, of those criteria which point to a later
or non-traditional pericope,/63/ only one may apply at all to
vv. 1-14, the criterion of derivative speech/elements, i.e.
signs of later reflection or creation. However, this shows only
redaction not inauthenticity.

Our reasons for asserting that redaction in this case does
not demand an ahistorical provenance are: (1) the criteria
noted point to a primitive tradition and possibly to a basis in
history. (2) The theological stress is not restricted to those
points unique to the evangelist; the structure and indeed the very
choice of one tradition over another gives it theological import.
John's tendency to focus upon individuals in the tradition,
here the BD and Peter, is a case in point. That is likely a
personal reminiscence and therefore redaction, yet it is at the
same time authentic history. Personal reminiscence bridges the
gap between history and redaction. Further, the link via vv. 9
and 10, which some find clumsy and artificial, is a deliberate
redactional ploy to stress the connection between the miraculous
catch and the meal fellowship; and the wording of v. 13, if a
purposeful allusion back to 6:11, adds a sacramental flavor to
the episode. Finally redaction and tradition, history and
theology (note the deliberate chiasm) co-exist and supplement one
another in 21:1-14.

The Reinstatement of Peter, 21:15-17

Tradition Study
Two critical problems concern us here. First, some believe

that ὅτε οὖν ἠρίστησαν is an artificial connective and that this
scene was attached either late in the tradition development or
by the redactor himself, as evidenced in the disappearance of
the other disciples and the setting by the seashore./64/ However,
the time-note is neither vague nor clumsy and indeed is natural
to the flow of the narrative. The disciples, moreover, may
well be indicated in the τούτων (v. 15). The setting is to be
inferred from the previous context and it would be superfluous
to mention it in a dialogue scene such as this. The presence of
Peter in both scenes provides a natural connection in itself.
It is more likely that the link occurred rather early in the
development of the tradition and may well go back to the original
event. At the same time, all three (with vv. 18-19) may have
belonged to an early Peter-centered tradition which employed
rabbinic 'pearl-stringing' techniques in collecting and joining
the episodes. In this case they would have circulated independently at first. However, this latter supposition is too
speculative to be convincing, and the unity of vv. 1-17 is the
more viable solution.

Second, most agree that the pericope has a traditional
origin but question the amount of redaction employed./65/ While
the basic question-answer-response pattern may go back to the
earliest tradition, the threefold form may be redactional, for
two reasons: 1) the threefold pattern does not seem natural
and may well be a symbolic attempt to draw out and counter
the implications of the original denial scene;/66/ 2) the
stylistic variation is a Johannine characteristic/67/ which
would be highly unlikely in the original interplay between Jesus
and Peter./68/ If so, the change to a threefold pattern would
have occurred in order to correspond to Peter's threefold denial
and to accord with the legal contract which is sealed by means
of a threefold statement./69/

However, we must question whether it is necessary to
question the authenticity of the threefold form. While the
second point may support Johannine variation of language, the
first is not conclusive. It would be natural for Jesus to use
just such a technique in making Peter realize his reinstatement
and mission. In short, redaction is seen in the variation but
not necessarily in the threefold pattern./70/

Theological motifs
There are two main emphases in the language of the scene--
the love-question and the shepherd imagery--found in the question-
answer and response sections, respectively. The first involves

a complex interplay between ἀγαπᾶν and φιλεῖν. Jesus asks
ἀγαπᾶς με; in the first two and Peter responds φιλῶ σε. In the
third, Jesus reverts to Peter's φιλεῖν and Peter repeats his
previous answer. This last is accompanied by a second change,
from οἶδα in Peter's first two answers (and the first part of
the third) to γινώσκω in the second clause of the third response.
While some find theological meaning in the alteration,/71/ most
recent commentators take these to be stylistic variations.
Indeed, it is difficult to explain how the terminological switch
would be meaningful if Peter were assenting to Jesus' question
while at the same time giving that question a different definition
Thereby Jesus would finally agree to a lower definition of love
when he finally accepts Peter's usage.

Nevertheless, the answer may fall between the two poles.
The variation is stylistic in that it enables John to fit the
story into the threefold formula with less monotony, yet it
has theological force in that it indicates the comprehensiveness
of the love-relation between Jesus and Peter./72/ As we will
note below, this is also the force of the other terminological
variation, indeed, this is a major purpose in Jewish synonymous
parallelism as a whole, for it often emphasizes the comprehensiveness of the truth stated. In this passage, there are too
many terms which employ this variation to say that it is merely
stylistic; therefore we would see a theological thrust, pointing
to the universal aspect, i.e. love etc. in its totality.

The entire exchange looks back to Peter's former position.
Many see in this a restitution of Peter to his former place of
leadership:/73/
    1) They point first to πλέον τούτων (v. 15), which they
take to be masculine, 'Do you love me more than these (love me)?'
However, this bases too much on debatable grammar. There are
two other possibilities: a) 'more than (you love) these' (also
masculine);/74/ or b) 'more than (you love) these things'
(neuter)./75/ Some argue viably against b) that the phrase
would read μᾶλλον ἤ if it were neuter (cf. 3:19, 12:43) and
that the verb would be repeated in such a construction./76/
The first of the two alternatives remains quite possible and, I
believe, best fits the context. Jesus was asking Peter to leave
behind attachments to other people and follow him./77/
    2) The shepherd imagery provides better grounds for assert-
ing Peter's pre-eminence. Again we note a complex variation in
the three responses: 1) βόσκε τὰ ἀρνία μου; 2) ποίμαινε τὰ
πρόβατά μου; 3) βόσκε τὰ πρόβατά μου. As with 'love' the two

words for 'feed' translate the same Aramaic original (רעה); it is possible, indeed probable, that John wished to signify to his readers the complete activity of pastoral care, in this case feeding and tending./78/ This variation, then, refers to every aspect of pastoral activity by paralleling the 'shepherd' analogy (chapter 10) with a similar variation in the 'flock' terminology./79/ In keeping with the previous terms discussed, it accentuates the all-inclusive nature of the 'flock.'

It is certainly true on the basis of this pericope that Peter has a significant role. Several scholars (fn. 69) believe that the threefold structure is intended to lend a special solemnity and authoritative air to the proceedings. In this light we must agree with those/80/ who see here a restoration of Peter to leadership among the disciples. This, in fact, is evidence for the traditional origin of the pericope, for John characteristically elevates the BD. However, we must admit that this sense is not the central thrust of the pericope, for as in the previous pericope an ecclesiological force is predominant, and the Petrine stress is seen mainly in the subtle undertone of the dialogue.

Jesus' response becomes the focus of the whole passage. Sheehan and Brown argue that the shepherd imagery from ancient times has involved a sense of authority, here seen in Jesus as the model shepherd (building upon chapter 10)./81/ While this is true, it is not the major stress. The 'sheep' are central rather than the 'shepherd' (not explicitly mentioned at all); the emphasis thus is upon 'shepherding,' and there is more an air of responsibility than of authority. The 'shepherd' image in the early church had been applied to the office of 'pastor' (Ephesians 4:11), and it is doubtful that John's readers would have seen as much authority as some intimate. This pastoral duty is seen first in terms of obedience to Jesus' command and second in terms of love. While some/82/ emphasize 'love' as the primary accent here, the text directs that love to Jesus; 'love' for the flock is merely implied in the terms for 'tend.' 'Love' for Jesus then is fulfilled in executing the pastoral office, i.e. in 'tending' the flock. 'Love' here is vertical (i.e. to Jesus) and provides the foundation for the horizontal (i.e. Christian service). I Peter 5:2-4 builds upon this, showing that this horizontal ecclesiology is indeed the central purpose of the pericope.

Tradition and Redaction in 21:15-17

As in the case of 21:1-14, our discussion of this pericope
has noted the presence of both tradition and redaction. First,
there are few valid reasons/83/ to separate it from the previous
context and to indicate that it was added at some stage in the
transmission of the tradition. Second, there are several
criteria which point to an origin in tradition and possibly to
historical authenticity: 1) the 'criterion of "unintentional"
signs of history'--as stated above, the elevation of Peter is
below the surface of the text and is not characteristic of the
evangelist/84/ and so probably came to him from the tradition;
2) the 'criterion of multiple attestation'--if I Peter 5:2 builds
upon an independent version of this tradition, it may very well
point to a historical event/85/; at the least, it is evidence
that this was indeed a much-used tradition. Again, the negative
criteria (e.g. the 'criterion of the tendencies of the developing
tradition') point to redaction but do not truly negate the
authenticity of the pericope. These could argue against the
threefold form, but as we stated above stronger evidence exists
for the validity of this as well.

Therefore tradition is seen in the basic threefold formula
and in the question-response pattern. Redaction is evidenced in
the stylistic variation, characteristically added by the evangelist to bring out more forcefully the ecclesiological message
which he wished to convey.

The Prophecy Regarding Peter 21:18-19

Tradition Study

Most agree with Bultmann that vv. 18f are a later addition
to vv. 1-17, and this may be true. We have many examples that
the early church tended to collate various episodes and sayings
under a single head (Matthew's discourse narratives are a major
instance). However, this does not mean that this pericope is
a later creation; in fact, we would argue for a primitive tradition. As Lindars notes, 'Previous experience has shown that this
(double "Amen" formula) is often an authentic saying of Jesus.'
/86/ This is supported by the ambiguity evident in the passage
itself (see below), which shows that it went through a developing
interpretive tradition and that its true meaning is here clari-
fied by John.

Bultmann is probably also correct when he asserts that the
saying is built upon an ancient proverb, 'In youth a man is

free to go where he will; in old age a man must let himself be
taken where he does not will.'/87/ John's use of the saying
certainly shows that it was in circulation during his time.
Lindars believes that the proverb is a redaction of an original
discipleship saying 'similar to Matthew 8:18-22 = Luke 9:57-62,
where the key word is "follow" (*akolouthein*), and each of the
sayings embodies a proverb./88/ However, this is too speculative
and fails because of the ambiguity of v. 18./89/ It would mean
that the evangelist redacted it in the light of Peter's death.
The editorial aside in v. 19a provides evidence that the
evangelist accepted this as originally a prophecy of Peter's
death.

Nevertheless, the proverbial nature of the saying does not
rule out the interpretation that the imagery looks to Peter's
martyrdom, possibly his crucifixion./90/ The evangelist himself
interprets it this way (v. 19a) /91/ and the original saying
would then rework the proverb, which originally spoke of the
vicissitudes of old age. This may well have been done by the
Risen One himself, who changed the verbs in the second clause to
the future tense and added the negative in the ὅπου clause/92/
so as to apply it figuratively to Peter's death. It was probably
interpreted in the primitive church as a discipleship saying
before Peter's death (i.e. applied to believers generally rather
than to Peter specifically); to this extent Lindar's isolation
of discipleship in the saying may be correct. John evidently had
to correct a misinterpretation on the part of the early church.
The mysterious air of the saying would certainly fit the
parabolic style of the Lord, and the tradition-development
above seems indicated by the text.

Theological Motifs
The structural connection of these verses with vv. 15-17
is obvious. The pastoral ministry of Peter will conclude with
his death, and both are part of the same love-relationship with
the Lord. While some have read into this an advanced (early
catholicism) view of martyrdom, this is not necessary. Peter's
death here is viewed as a participation in Jesus' death./93/
As such, it constitutes 'glorifying God,' which looks back to
John 12:23, 15:8 (cf. I Peter 4:16, Mart Polyc. 14:3, 19:2).
This is quite in keeping with the New Testament perspective and
hardly necessitates second century views of martyrdom.

Discipleship is central throughout, seen here in Jesus'
'Follow me.' While there is a hint of literal fulfilment in
v. 20, this does not obviate the theological implications of the

command./94/ It repeats the call of the disciples in 1:43 and
is a theme encompassing nearly all the major word-pictures: the
'light' image (8:12), shepherd terminology (10:4-5, 27), and
servanthood/discipleship itself (12:26). In an important parallel
Jesus speaks of Peter 'following' him (13:36-37) in a context
obviously speaking of Jesus' death. The present imperative, then,
must include both Peter's present pastoral role (vv. 15-17)
and its future culmination in his martyrdom/95/ as 'following'
Jesus.

Tradition and Redaction in 21:18-19

The tradition behind this passage is seldom denied, for
the proverbial saying is quite obviously a primitive tradition
(criterion of 'unintentional' signs) and very likely goes back
to Jesus himself. The tradition history of the saying would be
as follows: Jesus originally gave this as a prophecy of Peter's
future death/martyrdom; this is the obvious meaning of the proverb. In the early church, however, it seems to have been
misunderstood, probably along the lines of discipleship.
Finally, John corrects the misinterpretation and takes his readers
back to Jesus' original intention. Here, then, is the extent of
the redaction. It is John alone who uses this primitive
tradition to make his point, i.e. that discipleship for Peter
meant martyrdom. Moreover, John adds this to his united tradition
in vv. 1-17, thereby further developing his central ecclesiological message.

The Prophecy Regarding the BD 21:20-23

Tradition Study

It is indeed possible that this section may have originally
been unattached to vv. 18-19, for the connection is slight (the
code-word 'follow' and Peter's turning) and the subject matter
switches to the future of the BD. However, it may also be true
that John felt no need for a formal transition and presupposed
a logical connection between them. Such would fit Johannine
style elsewhere. One cannot be certain, but we will tentatively
propose that this originally followed vv. 18-19; while the
evangelist could have added it on the basis of his own coming
demise, the transition itself and the tone of the two (Peter's
death in vv. 18-19 and the BD's here) fit together too well.

The saying itself (v. 22), like the one in v. 19, reflects
the primitive tradition. 'The very fact that the writer claims
the saying has been misunderstood makes it incredible that the
saying had been recently invented, for then it would simply have

been denied.'/96/ It probably is faithful to the tradition,
which contained vv. 21-22 while the evangelist added vv. 20,
23 from his own reminiscences and perspective. The central
emphasis is upon the twice-repeated prophecy (vv. 22, 23) which
shows it was a peculiar interest of the evangelist and was
intended to combat rumors regarding the evangelist's immortality
(see below) in light of his advanced age or illness.

Theological Motifs
The saying in v. 22, its misunderstanding in v. 23a, and
the correction in v. 23b have led to various problems:
1) BDF 373 (1) says that the conditional ἐάν in v. 22
should be understood in the classical sense, i.e. as equal to
εἰ--'if, as is expected.' In v. 23a, that is exactly how the
early church interpreted it. Peter was to die, but the BD was
to remain until the parousia. However, the evangelist in v.
23b uses the Koine sense of ἐάν--'if, as may or may not be true.'
There he states that the Lord did not intend it to be literal
prophecy.
2) Does this mean that the BD is dead at the time of this
added chapter? Most believe that it does, since it would make
little sense to argue so strongly if the BD were alive./97/
However, the wording is ambiguous and could well mean that the
BD was approaching death./98/ The wording of v. 24 supports
this, for the present participle μαρτυρῶν /99/ may indicate that
he was still alive. In fact, it would be quite proper if the
author were the BD and this reflected his uncertainty. He would
thereby intend to prepare his readers for his impending death.
3) This relates to the problem of the delay of the
parousia. The Fourth Gospel may well reflect a passage of time
since the promise of the imminent return. Its realized
eschatology is the result, with the kingdom promises applied
to the present spiritual life of the believer. Yet a realized
eschatology does not necessarily exclude a future expectation
such as is reflected here. Dodd's judgment that 'the naive
conception of Christ's Second Advent in xxi. 22 is unlike anything else in the Fourth Gospel'/100/ is certainly untrue in
light of such passages as 5:27f, 14:3f. Both realized (the
place of the believer now in the community of believers) and
final (the future place of the believer in heaven) eschatology
have a place in John./101/ This is also true of this passage.
While many have dismissed it as the work of the final redactor,
it is in keeping with the emphasis throughout the Gospel and
therefore acts very much like a summation of Johannine expectation.

4)   The final difficulty is the motive of Peter (and of
the evangelist) here. Many again see rivalry between Peter and
the BD, arguing that this reflects the later Johannine circle
when the BD's followers wished to elevate him above Peter.
They see a hint of jealousy in Peter's question (v. 21) reflected
in Jesus' curt rebuke (v. 22)./102/ However, Peter's question
need not be impudent; it could just as easily reflect an honest
interest in the welfare of the BD. The answer of Jesus in this
light has a double purpose: 1) to prepare the church for the
time, quite near, when the 'eyewitnesses' would be gone; 2) to
stress the confirmed need for discipleship./103/ One of the
major purposes for adding chpater 21 to the Gospel is undoubtedly
seen here.

Tradition and Redaction in 21:20-23
     As previously intimated we believe that 21:18-23 formed
a second block of tradition-material centering upon the deaths
of Peter and the BD. Both were misunderstood in the early church
(they may have floated independently in the oral period, similar
to vv. 1-14, 15-17) and are here connected by the evangelist,
who shows that death is part of his discipleship as well as
Peter's. The redaction in vv. 20-23, then is quite similar
to that in vv. 18-19, i.e. John's explanation with regard to
the true meaning behind the saying of Jesus. It is difficult to
ascertain how much ecclesiology there is in this section. Above
we argued that this is seen both in the symbolism of Peter and
the BD (we would see a 'reader identification' behind both
figures, fn. 103) and in the emphatic 'you follow me' (v. 22b).
Yet, this is subservient to the major theme, the impending death
of the evangelist.

The Second Conclusion 21:24-25

Tradition Study
     Those who accept these verses as Johannine/104/ argue that
they are the only ending and therefore are necessary to the
Gospel; they declare that the 'we' of v. 24 is editorial rather
than literal./105/ However, there are several problems:
1) John nowhere else changes to the first person in his Gospel
(though we might note the controversial examples in I John 1:1-5)
and 2) comparison of the style in vv. 24, 25 with 19:35 and 20:
31 may indicate an attempt to duplicate those statements.
These statements may have been added for the very reason adduced
for their authenticity, i.e. because without them there is no
conclusion. However, if chapter 21 is an epilogue, there would
be no need for such a conclusion; the evangelist would still

consider 20:30, 31 to be the proper conclusion for the Gospel.
Finally, the οὗτος in v. 24a and οἴδαμεν in v. 24b indicate
that vv. 24-25 are the imprimatur of the Johannine community,
added probably because of the anonymous nature of the Gospel.

Theological Motifs
In these verses we have an important identification between
the BD and the author. There are three ways γράψας can be taken:
1) literally, that the BD was the actual author of the Gospel
as a whole;/106/ 2) in a causative sense, 'he had these things
written,' i.e. he either dictated to an amanuensis or directed
its writing;/107/ or 3) in a remote sense, that he was the source
of the original tradition which lay behind his work./108/ The
second finds support in the causative force of John 19:19 (Pilate
'caused the words to be written' on the cross) and in Romans
15:15 (used of Tertius the amanuensis of Paul, cf. 16:22).
However, these parallels do not directly apply, and the parallel
with μαρτυρῶν would favor the view that it refers to the BD's
previous composition of the Gospel (option one above)./109/

We must now go further and question the validity of the
imprimatur. That depends largely upon the eyewitness motif
of the Gospels, stressed here in μαρτυρῶν and αὐτοῦ ἡ μαρτυρία
(note the stress on the personal pronoun in the latter instance).
There is an obvious parallel with 19:35; Bultmann believes that
both are later additions to the text./110/ However, the
significant differences between the verses provide evidence that
they are not parallel but that 21:24 imitates 19:35 (itself the
evangelist's self-witness regarding the authority of his testimony)./111/ The internal evidence adds support: there has been
an increasing tendency of late to note the basic trustworthiness
of the data in this Gospel, supported by such external evidence
as the Dead Sea Scrolls and archeological discoveries which have
undergirded the accuracy of John's historical and theological
situation in first century Palestine. Finally, the great
amount of insignificant detail and personal reminiscence in the
Fourth Gospel also support this conclusion.

There are two possible interpretations: the work is either
the work of a first-rate storyteller who knew how to weave in
authentic-sounding details, or it is evidence for an eyewitness
reflecting on his experiences. Examples of the two poles can be
found in D. E. Nineham and L. Morris: Nineham says that the
'eyewitness' motif, though early adduced for the resurrection
(I Corinthians 15:3f), is not applied to Jesus' earthly life
until later New Testament works like John and Acts; form criticism

then demonstrates that the Gospel pericopes developed apart from eyewitness testimony and are theological reflections rather than historical reminiscences./113/ Morris, on the other hand, believes that the vast amount of insignificant detail, like the time-notes, must be considered seriously as evidence for a historically accurate document./114/

The solution probably falls between the two. While archeology has led to the resolution of many of the so-called 'aporias of John, no serious student can fail to note the theological reflection in it (including Morris). There is no reason why John cannot be both historian and theologian. There is a distinct eyewitness emphasis throughout the work,/115/ and this is more than merely a theological notation. It is intended to lend credence to John's theological interpretation; there is a historical foundation behind his theological emphases, although the worth of that foundation depends upon one's estimate of the 'eyewitness' details and the validity of this motif./116/ Moreover, we do not wish to imply that it is viable to assume historicity and then to apply that a priori to each pericope. Rather, each pericope must be studied on its own merits. We believe that we have provided a strong case that here, at least, the evangelist has utilized authentic traditions.

At the same time, we must point out John's freedom to draw out the significance of his data, and the redactional nuances must be constantly considered. Event and interpretation are intertwined, and the tradition-study of these pericopes in John 21 has pointed to the strong presence of the latter. We must thereby ask whether the claim of an eyewitness behind this Gospel has any influence on its historicity. We have attempted to demonstrate that it does, indeed that it is crucial to a proper understanding of the relationship between history and theology in the Fourth Gospel. Brown argues that we must separate ourselves from 'modern historical preoccupations' and accept a basically non-historical interpretation of 'true witness' as the Paraclete-inspired reflections of the Johannine community in the Gospel./117/ However, we believe that the arguments in the preceding paragraph demonstrate the primacy of the eyewitness interpretation of the concept. On this basis the concept of a historical as well as theological imprimatur in v. 24 must stand.

Verse 25 was also added later, and its style differs from v. 24, probably because each imitates a previous statement (v. 24 = 19:35, v. 25 = 20:30)./118/ The use of such hyperbole was

quite common in ancient writing/119/ and here alludes to Jesus'
universal glory, a glory so great that 'the world itself could
not contain it.' Therefore the Gospel ends on a note of
universal glory.

Conclusion

There is a homogeneity in John's resurrection narrative,
both in chapter 20 and in the epilogue, which is not present to
quite the same degree in the synoptic accounts of the resurrection. This unity is simply a reflection of his Gospel, which is
characterized by the 'post-resurrection viewpoint' he adopts
throughout, i.e. Jesus' life and ministry proleptically anticipate
his post-resurrection 'glory.' While chapter 20, with its
soteriological thrust, is more closely connected, these same
themes can still be observed in the ecclesiological message of
chapter 21.

We have sought to show that the redactional nuances have
not obviated the historical nucleus of the pericopes and indeed
have been used to highlight the interpretation inherent in the
events themselves. In 21:1-14, for instance the interplay
between the BD and Peter, certainly a redactional stress, serves
to emphasize the ecclesiological message of the whole, i.e., the
intimate connection between recognition and mission (seen also
in the deliberate connection with the commission scene of Luke
5:1-11). The abbreviated meal scene, which has caused innumerable problems for tradition-critics, intends especially to bring
out the importance of fellowship with the living presence of the
Risen One. The stylistic variation in vv. 15-17 (and possibly
the threefold form itself) adds a special solemnity to the
universal responsibility which love for Jesus brings to one's
pastoral duties. Finally, the discipleship emphasis of vv.
18-23 shows that whether in death or life, one's primary responsibility is to 'follow' Christ. The church, when the eyewitnesses
had passed from the scene and the parousia still had not
occurred, was still responsible to follow the Lord and was
promised his living presence and power, which guarantees success
if his directives are followed (back to 21:1-11!).

In the structural development of 21:1-23, one might note
a certain chiastic order. Scholars have long discussed the
importance of chiasmus as a Johannine stylistic device./120/
Here the AB:BA would center upon the BD and Peter, with A=BD
centered passages and B=Peter-centered passages. The two BD
passages (21:1-14, 20-23) center upon his authority in recognizing

the Lord and providing authentic witness. The two Peter passages
(21:15-17, 18-19) center upon pastoral responsibility. There is
also a certain unity of development with the four as a whole, all
exhibiting ecclesiological force. The first two deal with
responsibility in mission and the basis for success while the
latter two deal with discipleship and the ultimate witness of
martyrdom. While the sections are of quite different length, it
is only vv. 1-14 which are significantly longer, and a balance
is nevertheless achieved on the thematic level.

The *Sitz im Leben* of chapter 21 is probably quite late,
especially on the basis of vv. 18-25. The probable purpose was
to make the church aware of its responsibilities in mission now
that the last of the eywitnesses was about to depart. Indeed,
in this light the imprimatur of the Johannine church is quite
necessary, for soon John would no longer be among them to attest
its genuineness personally. The christological battles are
absent from this chapter, probably not because they are over but
because they had already been discussed. The eschatological
dualism between the above and the below and between the already
and the not yet is still found with the realized eschatology in
vv. 1-14 and final eschatology in 20-23. However, one cannot on
this basis decide between the majority opinion (AD 80-90) and
that argued by Robinson and others (mid-60s)./121/ That must
be done on the basis of the Gospel as a whole.

Further, a late *Sitz im Leben* does not impugn the historica
trustworthiness of the pericopes. We have also argued throughout
that questions of this sort can often point to the redaction,
and that the tradition behind it may still be authentic. We
believe that tradition-critical criteria demonstrate the validity
of this approach for the narratives related in John 21. John
has brought out nuances from the material he used and from his
own reminiscences and applied these to the needs of his later
situation.

In summation, we have attempted to demonstrate that tradit
and redaction-critical methods do not have negative implications
for a high view of historicity with regard to the Gospel of John
or the resurrection narratives. Indeed, history and redaction
are interdependent. This paper has sought to present a cogent
defense for the reliability of the redactional elements in John
21. From the standpoint of the "burden of proof" position (see
fn. 3), it is reasonable to maintain a positive appraisal of
historical reliability regarding the traditions behind the
ecclesiological truths of John 21.

Notes

/1/ Structuralists would add a fourth, the 'deep structure'
or primordial myth behind the text. However, that is not under
consideration in this paper.

/2/ Among others, see I. H. Marshall, *Luke: Historian and
Theologian* (Grand Rapids: Zondervan, 1970), especially chapter
2; and for this study, S. S. Smalley, *John: Evangelist and
Interpreter* (Exeter: Paternoster, 1978), especially chapter 5.

/3/ On the important "burden of proof" issue, see my 'The
Evangelical and Redaction Criticism: Critique and Methodology,'
JETS, 22/4 (1979), 309-310; and R. H. Stein, 'Criteria for
Authenticity,' *Gospel Perspectives I*, ed. R. T. France and D.
Wenham (Sheffield: JSOT Press, 1980), 225-28. As we apply the
criteria for authenticity, we will be assuming this quite
different perspective, i.e. that the critic must "prove" that
the text is inauthentic rather than vice versa. I believe that
it is methodologically correct to take the gospels at their
face value, i.e. as historical documents, unless compelling
evidence forces otherwise. We will test this hypothesis in
John 21 by utilizing the widely accepted criteria of authenticity.

/4/ Raymond E. Brown, *The Gospel According to John XIII-XXI*
(Anchor Bible; Garden City, New York: Doubleday, 1971), 1078,
states further that the beatitude in v. 20 makes the narrative
of another appearance very unlikely.

/5/ See Brown, 1078-79. Rudolf Schnackenburg, *Das Johannesevangelium* II (Herders; Freiburg: Herder, 1971), 409, labels it
a redactional conclusion written for the ecclesiastical readers.

/6/ Opinion is divided. Those accepting a unified Johannine authorship are Westcott, Ruckstuhl, Cassian, Schlatter,
Plummer, Lagrange, Bernard, Kragerud, Barrett, Morris, Lindars,
Smalley. Those who do not are Boismard, Bultmann, Lightfoot,
Dodd, Marxsen, Brown, Schnackenburg, Alsup, de Jonge. In recent
years critical opinion has definitely shifted in the latter
direction.

/7/ For further discussion see Brown, pp. 1079-80;
Schnackenburg, 410-14; M. E. Boismard, 'Le chapître xxi de Saint
Jean: essai de critique littéraire,' *RB* 54 (1947), 473-501;
S. B. Cassian, 'John xxi,' *NTS* 3 (1956-57), 132-36.

/8/ Barnabas Lindars, *The Gospel of John* (New Century;
London: Oliphants, 1972), 621-22.

/9/ *Ibid.*

/10/ A good example would be Schnackenburg's exegetical
discussion of John 21. See also Smalley, *John*, 119-21.

/11/ Robert Kysar, *The Fourth Evangelist and His Gospel* (Minneapolis: Augsburg, 1975), 54. See also Don A. Carson, 'Current Source Criticism of the Fourth Gospel: Some Methodological Questions,' *JBL* 97/3 (1978), 411-29.

/12/ See C. K. Barrett, *The Gospel According to St. John* (London: SPCK, 1978), *passim*, for the view that John used Luke. C. H. Dodd, *Historical Tradition in the Fourth Gospel* (Cambridge: University Press, 1963), 366-87, posits that the connection occurred at the pre-literary stage; and Josef Blinzler, *Johannes und die Synoptiken* (Stuttgart: Katholisches Bibelwerk, 1965), 58-59, believes that John quoted Mark (and perhaps Luke) from memory.

/13/ See R. T. Fortna, *The Gospel of Signs* (SNTSMS 11; Cambridge: University Press, 1970) as well as the critiques in Kysar, 13-37 and Carson, 420-28.

/14/ Mgr. B. de Solages, *Jean et les Synoptiques* (Leiden: Brill, 1979), 234, cf. 191-235.

/15/ Those who argue for Lukan priority include Goguel, Dodd, the early Bultmann (*HST*), Benoit, Fuller and Pesch. Those who accept Johannine priority would include the later Bultmann (John commentary), Brown, Grass, Klein, Bailey.

/16/ J. N. Sanders, *The Gospel According to St. John,* ed. B. A. Mastin (London: Black, 1968), 449-50. Cf. Barrett, 578, Stephen S. Smalley, 'The Sign in John XXI,' *NTS* 20 (1974), 275-88; and I Howard Marshall, *The Gospel of Luke: A Commentary on the Greek Text* (NIGTC; Exeter: Paternoster, 1978), 200.

/17/ Brown, 1090. He takes these as a combination of the first appearances to Peter and to the Twelve (I Corinthians 15:5).

/18/ Marshall, 200.

/19/ Rudolf Pesch, *Der Reiche Fischfang Lk. 5,1-11/Jo. 21, 1-14* (*KBANT*, Dusseldorf: Patmos Verlag 1969), 126-30, argues against its historicity, but his points are based upon tradition-critical assumptions which themselves are highly disputed. The so-called 'legendary accretions' do not disprove authenticity . For a good discussion of this, see Robin Barbour, *Tradition-historical Criticism of the Gospels* (SCC 4; London: SPCK 1972)

/20/ Pesch, 53f, 148f. Schnackenburg, III 411f and Alsup, 201f, basically agree with his analysis.

/21/ Fortna, 87-94.

/22/ Brown, "John 21 and the First Appearance to Peter," *Resurrexit,* ed. E. Dhanis (Rome: Libraria Editrice Vaticana, 1974), 260.

/23/ See my article, 'Redaction Criticism,' 309f. This view is somewhat in line with the Old Testament school of 'canon

criticism,' associated especially with Brevard Childs, cf. his
Introduction to the Old Testament as Scripture (London: SCM,
1979), his most recent discussion on the primacy of the final
form over the stages for the biblical message; *contra* J. N.
Sanders, who stresses the development over the final form.

/24/ Schnackenburg, III, 408.

/25/ John Alsup, *The Post-Resurrection Appearance Stories
of the Gospel-Tradition* (London· SPCK, 1975), 211-13, believes
that they all have the same *Gattung*, i.e. a desire to restate the
church's experience of the Risen Lord in Old Testament terms.
However, these three are grouped together on dogmatic grounds
and the formal similarities are insufficient to prove common
origin.

/26/ C. H. Dodd, 'The Appearances of the Risen Christ: A
Study in Form Criticism of the Gospels,' *More New Testament
Studies* (Manchester: University Press, 1968), 109.

/27/ Lindars, 624.

/28/ Alsup, 203. Cf. Pesch, 88; Schnackenburg, III, 418.

/29/ We do not wish to assume that the Gospel and epistle
stem from a common hand. However, the similar language and
themes do point in that direction. Cf. W. G. Wilson, 'An Examination of the Linguistic Evidence Adduced against the Unity of
Authorship of the First Epistle of John and the Fourth Gospel,'
JTS 49 (1948), 147-56; Kümmel, *Introduction,* 442-45, *et al*.

/30/ See the progression from 1:3 to 2:11 and then from
3:21 to 7:4. In the Cana miracle, John editorially adds that
Jesus 'revealed his glory,' a clear post-resurrectional reflection
on the significance of the first sign, resulting in 'belief.'

/31/ Brown, 1095-96, notes correctly that 'the task of the
Baptist proclaimed in the first chapter of the Gospel has been
brought to completion in the last: Jesus has been fully revealed
to Israel, that is, to the community of believers represented
by the disciple.'

/32/ See Leon Morris, *The Gospel According to St. John*
(NIC; Grand Rapids: Eerdmans, 1971), 861.

/33/ We might note similar language about the Baptist in
1:19 and about Jesus in 8:25. Some state (e.g. Barrett):
1) Since Jesus has now been 'manifested' in a final way to his
disciples, and 2) since they now 'knew' him, such questions are
no longer necessary. However, this is unlikely and too simplistic
in light of the emphasis given to their hesitancy here.

/34/ Alv Kragerud, *Der Lieblingsjunger im Johannesevangelium*
(Oslo: Universitatsverlag, 1959) believes that the BD symbolizes
the Johannine community's prophetic activity, which was responsible for the Gospel.

/35/ Rudolf Schnackenburg, 'On the Origin of the Fourth
Gospel,' *Jesus and Man's Hope* I, ed. D. G. Buttrick (Pittsburgh
Theological Seminary, 1970), 234, argues that the constant juxtaposition of Peter with the BD demands that the latter be an
historical personage.

/36/ So recently Morris, *John*, 8-30; Smalley, *John,* 75-82;
and J. A. T. Robinson, *Redating the New Testament* (London: SCM,
1976), 28. Brown, *John*, I, xcii-xcviii, identifies the BD with
the Apostle but separates that figure from the evangelist who
used John's tradition in composing the Gospel.

/37/ Lewis Johnson, 'Who was the Beloved Disciple?', *ET*
77 (1965-66), 157-58; P. Parker, 'John and John Mark,' *JBL* 79
(1960), 97-110. While John Mark was from the priestly class,
grew up in Jerusalem, and knew Peter, he was not one of the
apostles (see further below).

/38/ F. V. Filson, 'Who was the Beloved Disciple?', *JBL*
8 (1949), 83-88; and William H. Brownlee, 'Whence the Gospel
According to John?', *John and Qumran,* ed. J. H. Charlesworth
(London: Geoffrey Chapman, 1972), pp. 191-94. J. N. Sanders,
'Those Whom Jesus Loved, St. John 11:5,' *NTS* 1 (1954-55), 29-41,
believes that Lazarus was the BD whose memoirs were edited by
John Mark, the evangelist (the 'other disciple,' 1:37f, 18:15f).
However, as Brown, x cv, notes, this would only be relevant if
the readers did not know the identity of the author. Such subtle
euphemisms would not be necessary in the Johannine circle.

/39/ E. L. Titus, 'The Identity of the Beloved Disciple,'
JBL 69 (1950), 323-28. But this has even more problems than those
above and is too speculative.

/40/ Lindars, *John*, 31-34. It is hard to understand how one
would accept one of the Twelve and yet deny John. As one of
them, he at least must be a viable candidate.

/41/ Schnackenburg, 'Origin,' 231, 239; and *Johannesevangelium*, III, 450-56; and Thorwald Lorenzen, *Der Lieblingsjunger im Johannesevangelium: Eine redaktionsgeschichtliche
Studie*(SBS 55; Stuttgart: Katholisches Bibelwerk, 1971), 74-82.

/42/ See the favorable comments of Kysar, 98-101.

/43/ R. Alan Culpepper, *The Johannine School* (SBLDS 26;
Missoula: Scholars Press, 1975), 266-69.

/44/ Brown, *John*, xcvi-xcvii. See also those listed in
fn. 38.

/45/ We omit those passages which are often connected to
the BD but do not explicitly mention him (1:41, 18:15-16; 19:35)
The latter two, especially 19:35 (with the echo of 21:24 in the
'true witness') may refer to John but may not be part of the BD
motif, since they are not part of the explicit passages.

/46/ Kragerud, 147-48, finds conflict between the

ecclesiastical hierarchy (represented by Peter) and the prophetic element (the BD); Lorenzen, 89-96, between Jewish Christianity (Peter) and the Johannine community (the BD).

/47/ See in R. E. Brown *et al.* eds., *Peter in the New Testament* (New York: Paulist, 1973), 133-47.

/48/ Morris, *John*, 866, says 'love for exactness and a readiness to supply numerical detail can be documented elsewhere in this Gospel.' Brown, *John* II, 1075-76, states that the exactness of the number stems from an emphasis on the authentic eyewitness tradition (cf. 20:7).

/49/ For similar redactional rearrangements, one need only consult a Gospel harmony and compare treatments of episodes such as the triumphal entry or the denials by Peter.

/50/ For more complete coverage, see R. M. Grant, 'One Hundred Fifty-three Large Fish (John 21:11),' *HTR* 47 (1949), 273-75; J. A. Emerton, 'The Hundred and Fifty-three Fishes in John XXI. II,' *JTS* ns IX (1958), 86-89; N. J. McEleney, '153 Great Fishes (John 21, 11)-- Gematriacal Atbash,' *Bib* 58 (1977), 411-17; Brown, 1074-76; and Lindars, 629-31.

/51/ See Smalley, 'Sign,' p. 284; and Schnackenburg, III, pp. 426-27.

/52/ Schnackenburg, III, 427.

/53/ James Barr, *The Semantics of Biblical Language* (Oxford: University Press, 1961), chapter 3.

/54/ Smalley, 'Sign,' 278-84.

/55/ See Alsup, 201; Pesch, 110f; Schnackenburg, III, 427. Smalley, 285, believes that the two scenes were already combined in the tradition.

/56/ Barrett, 582.

/57/ For an excellent survey, see Kysar, 49-59.

/58/ *Ibid*. He believes, for instance, that 6:51-58 is a later redactional insertion into a non-sacramental passage.

/59/ Sanders, 448-49; Morris, 868.

/60/ Barrett, 484; Rigaux, 243.

/61/ In fact, Brown, 1087, uses this as major evidence for his thesis that vv. 1-17 reflect the first appearance to Peter of I Corinthians 15:5.

/62/ While this is normally used of sayings, the principle would also apply to events, applicable here on the basis of our previous thesis that the language of Luke 5 influenced the nature of the John 21 episode.

/63/ See S. Westerholme, *Jesus and Scribal Authority* (Lund: Gleerup, 1978), 6-7.

/64/ See Bultmann, 711f; Grass, 82f; and Schnackenburg, III, 429. U. C. von Wahlde, 'A Redactional Technique in the Fourth

Gospel,' *CBQ* 38 (1976), 520-33, takes ὅτε οὖν to be a 'repetitive
resumptive' which returns to the tradition after a redactional
insertion (here vv. 11-14). In light of the parallel ὡς οὖν in
v. 9 (as he admits), however, his point is difficult to prove.

/65/ The presence of ἀγαπᾶν here is not Johannine. If it
were redactional, one would expect πιστεύειν. While the sheep
imagery is Johannine, it is also attached to Peter in the tradition (cf. I Peter 5:2-4). Fuller, 153, believes that the Galilean
location, the meal motif, and the Petrine imagery show evidence
of a very primitive tradition. Alsup, 62, 202n, goes so far as
to suggest that this is the lost Markan ending entailing the
appearance to Peter. Schnackenburg, III, 429-31, however, takes
it as primarily Johannine and thus redactional.

/66/ See Westcott, 377f; and Cassian, 133f.

/67/ See E. D. Freed, 'Variations in the Language and
Thought of John,' *ZNW* 55 (1964), 167-97 (especially 192-94);
and Lindars, 45.

/68/ While several Aramaic verbs mean 'I love,' there are
no Hebrew or Aramaic equivalents for ἀγαπᾶν and φιλεῖν as distinct
terms (אָהַב is translated by either in the LXX).

/69/ It was customary then to state something three times
before witnesses in order to seal a legal contract. See P.
Gaechter, 'Das dreitache "Weide meine Lammer,"' *ZTK* 69 (1947),
328-44. Schnackenburg, III, 435, calls this 'the language of
commission' which 'installs' Peter into the pastoral office.

/70/ Some might argue that we cannot separate the variation
in terms from the threefold pattern. However, Peter's obvious
frustration in the third instance would better fit a situation in
which Christ used the same terms. If there were variation originally, one would expect Peter to understand more than he does.

/71/ See Westcott, 366f; T. E. Evans, 'The Verb "Agapao"
in the Fourth Gospel,' *Studies in the Fourth Gospel*, ed. F. L.
Cross (London: Mowbray, 1957), 64-71; and C. Spicq, 'Notes
d'exégèse johannique. La charité est amour manifeste,' *RB* (1958)
358-70, take ἀγαπᾶν to be the higher form of love, while Trench,
Synonyms of the New Testament, 42f, believes that φιλεῖν is the
higher type.

/72/ Lindars, 634-35, theorizes that the two might be
present to allow for a wider range of literary allusion, cf. 15:3
where love (ἀγάπη) leads to the sacrifice of one's life for his
friends (φιλῶν). This fits the following allusion to Peter's
martyrdom and may well refer to the all-inclusive nature of the
new love-relationship.

/73/ So Benoit, 303f; Schnackenburg, III, 430. Brown and
Lindars agree but state (with Bultmann) that this is a redactiona
insertion linking this with the preceding pericope and the

'disciples' there.

/74/ See BDF, par 185 (1).

/75/ See Bernard, 704-705.

/76/ Lindars, 635; Brown, 1103f, on the grounds of Johannine style elsewhere.

/77/ N. Arvedson, in *SEA* 21 (1956), 27-29 (in Brown, 1113-14) notes a connection between this pericope and Mark 8:34 par, 'If anyone wishes to come after me, let him deny himself...' The self-denial is seen in the love question, the cross in the coming martyrdom, and the command in vv. 19,22. It is indeed possible that the application of this tradition to personal attachments (cf. Luke 14:25-27) is reflected in the question 'Do you love me more than these?' This would remove the major objection to this interpretation, that it sets up a rivalry of love between the apostles and thus has no place in the resurrection narratives.

/78/ Brown, 1105; and Schnackenburg, III, 433; *contra* Barrett, 584.

/79/ ἀρνία is clearly the reading in v. 15, but it is difficult to decide between πρόβατα and προβάτια for vv. 16-17. It seems to me that the first reading should be preferred; although some could prefer προβάτια on the basis of *difficilior lectio,* this seems to be an example of misusing the criterion, since all other evidence points the other way. προβάτια does not occur in the New Testament and it is doubtful that a scribe would introduce it here; it may have been inserted in the interest of variation.

/80/ In addition to fn. 72, see Bultmann, 713-714; Oscar Cullmann, *Peter: Disciple and Martyr,* tr. F. V. Filson, (London: SCM, 1962), 88f; Marxsen, 86-87; Cassian, 134f.

/81/ J. F. X. Sheehan, 'Feed my Lambs,' *Scr* 16 (1964), 21-27; and Brown, 1113-1114.

/82/ E. g. Spicq, Morris, Schnackenburg and Stählin.

/83/ Form critical theory often concludes that pericopes floated independently during the oral period, and therefore this connection could be discounted on an *a priori* basis. But see S. Travis, 'Form Criticism,' *New Testament Interpretation,* ed. I. H. Marshall (Exeter: Paternoster, 1977), 153-54. While various elements could have been used independently, there is no reason to doubt that these episodes were at all times connected chronologically as, for instance, the passion narrative or Mark 4:21-43.

/84/ See Brown *et al.* (fn. 49), 131-32 on John 1:40-42; 6:67-69. While Peter's portrayal is the same in John as in the synoptics, (see above) it is muted.

/85/ This is stated for the most part by those who accept
Petrine authorship of I Peter, e.g. Selwyn.

/86/ Lindars, 636. Many point out, however, that the form
could be easily imitated.

/87/ Bultmann, 713. See also Cullmann, *Peter,* 88-89.

/88/ Lindars, 636.

/89/ Brown, 1118, states, 'In our judgment, while the
redactor may be responsible for the joining of the sayings, the
sayings themselves are old, for neither lends itself easily to
the interpretation that has been given to it....Certainly, if
the statement had been fashioned in the light of Peter's death,
the wording would not have been so ambiguous.'

/90/ Bultmann, 713-714, believes that John misunderstood
the original saying as a reference to Peter's death. Most others,
however, take this to be the original thrust, though many note
that the ambiguity of the language cannot be made to assert
more than his martyrdom. A reference to crucifixion is debatable,
depending on a prior decision regarding 'stretching out your
hands,' a common ancient expression for crucifixion (Ep. Barnabas
12:4, Justin's Tryph. 90, 91 etc.). See Barrett, 585.

/91/ 'Signifying what kind of death' here is probably a
deliberate allusion to 12:33, 18:32.

/92/ It seems likely that the negative was not in the
original proverb, which said, 'in old age a man is taken where
he wishes.'

/93/ See Schnackenburg, III, 437; and Cassian, 132-133.
Peter's death may be seen as the culmination of his pastoral role.

/94/ See Wead, 40, for "double meaning" here.

/95/ For the problems surrounding Peter's death, see
Cullmann, *Peter,* 71-157. The presence of 'follow' in both the
shepherd passages and the previous prophecy of Peter's death
lends credence to the view above that John stressed the connection
between this and the 'shepherd' imagery of vv. 15-17.

/96/ Brown, 1118.

/97/ See Barrett, 485; Schnackenburg, III, 442-443 *et al.*

/98/ See Westcott, 373; Bernard, 771; Hoskyns, 668; Morris,
878f. Lindars, 640, correctly observes that the decision depends
upon one's decision regarding the BD as the evangelist. Fuller,
153, admits that the pericope 'must have been added by the
redactor' to identify 'the BD with the author of the Gospel.'

/99/ Note the deliberate contrast with the following
γραψας, which probably is intended to say that he continues to
witness but has completed his writing.

/100/ Dodd, *Interpretation,* 431. For an excellent survey of
Johannine eschatology see Kysar, 207-214.

/101/ See R. H. Gundry, '"In My Father's House are Many *Monai*" (John 14:2)', *ZNW* 58 (1967), 68-72. I disagree, however, with his contention that this 'final' sense looks to the believer's death rather than the parousia. See also Paola Ricca, *Die Eschatologie des vierten Evangeliums* (Zurich: Gotthelf, 1966), *passim*.

/102/ See Brown, 1120-1121; Bultmann, 715f; and Sanders, 458.

/103/ Note the emphatic σύ in the repetition (in v. 22b) of the phrase from v. 19. This is clearly the key phrase of vv. 18-23. Peter and the BD represent the church as a whole, and the pericope applies to the current state of the church.

/104/ Bernard, 712f; Hoskyns, 669; Sanders, 47-48. Schnackenburg, III, 446-448, believes that they are integral to the whole but that it was all written by the final redactor.

/105/ See Bernard, 713; and J. Chapman, 'We Know That His Testimony is True,' *JTS* 31 (1930), 379-387. However, as Brown notes, 1124f, this faces the objection that the writer would then refer to himself both in the third person singular (v. 24a) and the first person plural (v. 24b). For Brown 'we' represents the author of ch. 21 and the Johannine community; it is their imprimatur on the Gospel. However, C. H. Dodd has the best solution in his 'Note on John 21, 24,' *JTS* n.s. 4 (1953), 212-213, arguing for an indefinite thrust, 'as is well known' (cf. 9:31). It then refers to the community as a whole as separate from the author of the epilogue.

/106/ Westcott, 374; Lindars, 641 (who concludes that the community was wrong in their identification and that therefore a modified source-critical theory must be correct); Morris, 880.

/107/ Bernard, 713; F. M. Braun, *Jean le Théologien et son Evangile dans l'Eglise Ancienne* (Etudes Bibliques, 1959), 396f.

/108/ Bultmann, 717; Brown, 1123; Barrett, 118f.

/109/ Dodd, 'Note,' 212, says that γράψας refers mainly to vv. 20-23 and possibly to chapter 21 as a whole. However, nearly all today take it in terms of the Gospel as a whole, and this best accords with the context.

/110/ Bultmann, 678-679.

/111/ See Brown, 1127. Barrett, 588, holds open the possibility that both are glosses by the same author. Differences: the 'we know' alters 'he knows' in 19:35; 20:21 adds 'he wrote;' the BD is not explicitly mentioned in 19:35 but is only implied in ὅ ἑώρακας, which seems to look back to vv. 25f. Morris, 820-822; and Brown, 936, list the other possibilities: ἐκεῖνος may be the author but not the BD; it may refer to Jesus or God as authenticator of the eyewitness. However, it is best to take it,

in view of the context, as a reference to the BD as witness.
ἐκεῖνος is a circumlocution for 'he.' While BDF 291 and Turner,
Syntax, 46 caution against the use of this to 'prove' the
eyewitness theme, we would point out that it cannot be employed
to deny the eyewitness motif and the evidence which follows
lends credence to this view.

/112/ See R. E. Brown, 'The Problem of Historicity in John,
CBQ 24 (1962), 1-14; Smalley, *John,* 30-38, 162-190; Robinson,
Redating, 254-285, *et al*.

/113/ D. E. Nineham, 'Eyewitness Testimony and the Gospel
Tradition,' *JTS* n.s. 9 (1958), 13-25, 243-252; 11 (1960), 253-264

/114/ L. Morris, 'Was the Author of the Fourth Gospel an
Eyewitness?', *Studies in the Fourth Gospel* (Grand Rapids:
Eerdmans, 1969), 139-214.

/115/ μαρτυρέω is found 33 times in John's Gospel, ten time
in his epistles and once in the Apocalypse vs. once each in
Matthew and Luke. μαρτυρία is found fourteen times in the Gospel
seven in the epistles and nine in the Apocalypse vs. once in
Luke and three times in Mark. As in 19:35 and 21:24, this is
applied to historical events, but even more (*contra* Luke) to the
validity of the evangelist's interpretation of these events.

/116/ John certainly went to great pains to establish this,
as seen in ἀληθής, found fourteen times in the Gospel, three in
the epistles vs. once each in Matthew and Mark. R. Bultmann,
'ἀληθής,' *TDNT*, I, 238f, 245f; and Dodd, *Interpretation*, 177,
argue for a Hellenistic provenance, i.e. reality vs. appearance.
Brown, 499f; and Morris, *John*, 293-296, see a greater connection
with Old Testament views of faithfulness. A. C. Thiselton,
'Truth,' *NIDNTT*, III, 889, argues for a moderating view that
notes both aspects in John's use. Above all, we must note the
'truth' vs. 'falsehood' aspect which has special relevance for
the witness emphasis.

/117/ Brown, 1129.

/118/ This seems a better explanation than Schnackenburg's
attempt to argue that v. 25 was written by a different hand than
v. 24 (III, 448).

/119/ Cf. Qoh. 12:9f, I Macc. 9:22, Ex. Rab. 30:22, Soph.
16:8, Philo's De Post. Caini 144.

/120/ See Brown, xcccv and Xavier Léon-Dufour, 'Trois
chiasmes johanniques,'*NTS* 7 (1960-61), 249-255. Léon-Dufour
discusses 12:23-32, 6:35-40 and 5:19-30. Brown would add 13:31-
17:26 (possible only), 15:7-17, 16:16-33, 18:23-19:16a, 19:16b-
19:42.

/121/ See Robinson, *Redating*, 278-282.

The Authenticity of the Parables of Jesus

Philip Barton Payne,
Kyoto Christian Studies Center,
34 Sandan Nagamachi, Matsugasaki,
Sakyo-Ku, Kyoto, Japan 606.

Introduction

The parables, which include approximately one third of Jesus' recorded sayings, are the most distinctive form of His teaching. All together there are about fifty recorded narrative parables of Jesus in which a realistic story with plot conveys a deeper spiritual message. From a critical point of view the parables of Jesus form the bedrock of tradition about Him. There is almost unanimous agreement among scholars that the parables as recorded in the gospels are substantially authentic to Jesus. The two basic reasons for this consensus are their distinctive characteristics and their outstanding quality.

The Distinctive Characteristics of Jesus' Parables

In the OT, although there are quite a few allegories and fables (in which animals or plants speak), narrative parables are rare/1/.

There are, however, many Rabbinic parables with formal similarities to those of Jesus. Of the almost 3000 recorded Rabbinic parables, none of the extant records seem to be before the time of Jesus, and the date of their origin and original form is almost never traceable with certainty. But the continuity of משל patterns throughout the Rabbinic period in Palestine/2/ and the conservative nature of Rabbinic tradition would suggest that some of them went back in some form to Jesus' day and that parables following similar patterns were current then. Sop. 16,9 (41b) records that Hillel (shortly before Jesus' time) was fond of parables. There are several Rabbinic parables which are strikingly parallel to Jesus'/3/, and it would be safe to say that Jesus drew from and added to a common pool of Jewish wisdom, including parables.

Both Jesus' and Rabbinic parables make use of identical
introductions such as, 'I will give you a parable: To what is
this comparable? To the conduct of a king of flesh and blood
. . .'/4/. Both employ indirect reference to God/5/. They
display similar stylistic characteristics: transference of the
point of comparison (as the Kingdom being like a pearl but
expressed 'like a merchant . . .'), mention of the background
and occasion of utterance, succinct introductory and concluding
comments summarizing the application of the parable, individual
concretization rather than generalized statement, illustrations
from ordinary daily life combined with improbable situations,
apparent discontinuity, paradox, enigmatic or non-self-evident
meanings, vividness, hyperbole, direct speech, questions,
ellipsis, stereotyped expression, pleonasm, and parallelism/6/.

For both Jesus and the rabbis, parables had a teaching
function (*Cant. Rab.* 1,1,8; Mark 4:2). Clarity in the teaching
of both is aided by the use of commonly recognized OT symbols
such as: a king, judge, or father for God; sons, servants, or a
vineyard for Israel; harvest or reaping for judgment; a feast
or wedding for the Kingdom of God and its joys; and servants for
the prophets/7/.

Although paralleling Jesus' parables' freedom of form,
characteristics of style, teaching function, and use of
symbolism, the Rabbinic parables, generally speaking, are not as
vivid, realistic, or natural as those of Jesus. Furthermore,
Jesus' parables convey a distinctive message. While many
Rabbinic parables comment on puzzling Scriptures, the parables
of Jesus focus on the reign or Kingdom of God. Many of His
parables have a distinctively eschatological and messianic
character. Jesus treated the relations between God and men
more frequently and more seriously. It is generally agreed
that Jesus was sharing His own deep concerns through the
parables: His vision of reality (N. Perrin), His faith (A.
Wilder), His experience of God (E. Fuchs, J. Crossan), and His
understanding of existence (J. Kingsbury, D. Via)/8/. In
comparison, the Rabbinic parables are lacking in spiritual
depth and insight.

Typical of Jesus' parables is their implicit challenge to
their hearers to pronounce a judgment on a situation or
attitude, a judgment which will lead them to a personal
decision. This is evident in Jesus' parable introduction which
has no Rabbinic parallels, 'Which of you . . .?'/9/.

A unique characteristic of many of the parables of Jesus is the way they function as an invitation, explicit or implicit, to enter the Kingdom of God, to live under the reign of God. Sometimes the very words of the parable story echo Jesus' invitation to enter the Kingdom:

'Come!' The Great Supper (Luke 14:16-24)
    The Marriage Feast (Matt. 22:1-14)
'Be ready!' The Doorkeeper (Mark 13:33-37)
    The Men Awaiting their Master's Homecoming (Luke 12:35-38)
    The Burglar (Matt. 24:43-44; Luke 12:39-40)
    The Ten Virgins (Matt. 25:1-13)
'Rejoice with me!' The Lost Sheep (Luke 15:4-7; implicit in Matt. 18:12-14)
    The Lost Coin (Luke 15:8-10)
    The Prodigal Son (Luke 15:11-32)

Often the challenge to enter the Kingdom is implicit in the portrayal of two people or groups, one entering into the joy of the Kingdom, the other left out, as in:

    The Servant Entrusted with Supervision (Matt. 24:45-51; Luke 12:42-48)
    The Talents (Matt. 25:14-30)
    The Pounds (Luke 19:12-27)
    The Closed Door (Luke 13:24-30)
    The Rich Man and Lazarus (Luke 16:19-31)
    The Pharisee and the Publican (Luke 18:9-14)

A similar challenge is implicit in the parables which portray two situations, one representing entry into the Kingdom, the other rejection from it:

    The Sower (Mark 4:3-8; Matt. 13:3-8; Luke 8:5-8)
    The Two Houses (Matt. 7:24-27; Luke 6:47-49)
    The Tares Among the Wheat (Matt. 13:24-30)
    The Dragnet (Matt. 13:47-48)
    The Tower Builder (Luke 14:28-30)
    The King Contemplating a Campaign (Luke 14:31-32)

Some parables implicitly urge acceptance of the way of the Kingdom by picturing the consequences of rejecting it:

    The Wicked Tenants (Mark 12:1-11; Matt. 21:33-44; Luke 20:9-18)
    On the Way to the Judge (Matt. 5:25-26; Luke 12:58-59)
    The Return of the Unclean Spirit (Matt. 12:43-45; Luke 11:24-26)
    The Rich Fool (Luke 12:16-21)
    The Barren Fig Tree (Luke 13:6-9)

Still other parables by indicating that the way to the Kingdom
is open implicitly invite the hearer to enter:
>   The Treasure (Matt. 13:44)
>   The Pearl (Matt. 13:45-46)
>   The Good Employer (Matt. 29:1-16)
>   The Two Debtors (Luke 7:41-43)
>   The Friend Asked for Help at Night (Luke 11:5-8)
>   The Shrewd Steward (Luke 16:1-8)
>   The Unjust Judge (Luke 18:1-8)

The use of parables to offer or invite entry into the
Kingdom of God seems to be unique to Jesus, and as such is
evidence in favor of their authenticity. Such an offer,
intensified by the eschatological tenor of many of the parables,
presupposed Jesus' authority to invite people into God's
Kingdom. In fact, the validity of this invitation depended on
Jesus' authority to offer them entry.

Particularly striking is that Jesus' parables express
something about Himself and His activity, His role in the
Kingdom. This kind of personal involvement, the author
depicting himself in a parable, seems to be completely absent
from Rabbinic parables. The character of Jesus' involvement in
His parables is also unique. He regularly depicted Himself in
the parables through images which in the OT were used to depict
God (for examples, see appendix).

Thus, we see that the parables of Jesus exhibit features
which distinguish them from the parables of the rabbis.
Several of these features are unique to the parables of Jesus
and as such are weighty evidence for their authenticity. Taken
as a whole, the parables of Jesus form a distinctive and
original collection which stands out as the literary pinnacle
of a long tradition of Palestinian parables.

The Outstanding Quality of Jesus' Parables

The parables of Jesus are literary masterpieces. Going
beyond the position of J. Jeremias that 'the parables of Jesus
are not -- at least primarily -- literary productions'/10/,
there is now a surge of interest in the parables as literary
gems seen in the work of G. V. Jones, A. Wilder, D. Via, J. D.
Crossan, E. Jüngel, R. W. Funk, N. Perrin, S. TeSelle, and
Semeia 1, 2 and 4. Only a few scholars have played down the
parables' artistry/11/. Probably behind their comments was the

feeling that the parables were prophetic extemporary utterance.
But artistry is not incompatible with spontaneity or
functionality/12/.

The poetic artistry of Jesus' parables has become widely
recognized. This is seen in their metaphorical qualities/13/:
vivid realistic use of nature and daily life (as in the
Children in the Marketplace and the Rich Fool), use of the
unexpected twist (as in the Generous Employer and the Shrewd
Steward), thought-provoking irony (as in the Mustard Seed and
the Leaven/14/), imagination (as in the Treasure and the Pearl),
creativity (as in the Sower and the Two Houses), depth of
meaning through simplicity (as in the Lost Sheep and the Lost
Coin), irreducibility to prose/15/ (as in the Seed Growing
Secretly and the Prodigal Son), opening up new ways of seeing
life (as in the Good Samaritan and the Unforgiving Servant),
and involvement of the hearer (as in the Servant Entrusted with
Supervision and the Two Sons).

Jesus' choice of imagery and symbolism has such a
universal appeal that it could be called archetypal: seed,
planting, growth, harvest, and the depiction of such
fundamental human relationships as father and son, servant and
master. The parables reflect Jesus' insight into 'an inward
affinity between the natural order and the spiritual order'
/16/. They can open up a whole new field of perception,
thought, experience and action/17/.

The potential of Jesus' parables to create a 'language
event' has been increasingly appreciated. They created a new
possibility by communicating Jesus' offer of participation in
the Kingdom of God/18/. Sometimes this involved a shattering
of the hearer's old way of looking at the world, as in the
Good Samaritan and the Prodigal Son/19/. But they go on, as
many of Jesus' parables, to present a new way, the way of the
Kingdom. They function as a bridge offering entry to the
Kingdom, giving access to a new way of looking at and living in
the world/20/.

A further level of the event-character of Jesus' parables
is that at least some of them seem to create a new state of
affairs by offering the hearer a new possibility. The seminal
work on speech events which actualize a new situation (called
'performative utterances') is by J. L. Austin, *How to Do Things
with Words* (Oxford: Clarendon, 1962). He defines 'performative

utterances' as those which create a new state of affairs and
which require for their effective performance: a) the
appropriate authority of the speaker, b) the appropriate
situation of utterance, and c) the appropriate content of the
utterance. Austin has demonstrated that in order to actualize
what it promises, a performative utterance requires the
appropriate authority of its speaker.

The parables presuppose Jesus' authority to offer what is
announced: participation in the Kingdom, God's forgiveness or
grace, or an eschatological promise. Typical is the parable
of the Sower, which, according to many interpreters, implies
the claim that the hearers' response to Jesus' message will
determine their destiny. Accordingly, the Sower offers
fruitful life to receptive hearers of Jesus' message. This
claim and offer seem to imply that Jesus had an authority which
is Messianic or even divine/21/. By what a parable offers or
announces it may imply that Jesus had a specifically
Christological or divine self-understanding. And insofar as
the parables do offer a new possibility or announce a new
situation, their effective performance depends on Jesus'
authority.

In the light of the authority that Jesus' parables
presuppose, their literary artistry, and their unique features
distinguishing them from the parables of the rabbis, the
substantial authenticity of the parables of Jesus is beyond
reasonable doubt. They cannot be convincingly attributed to
the early church. They show the mark throughout of a creative
genius with a strong sense of personal authority, the mark of
their author, Jesus Christ.

The Authenticity of Allegorical Elements in Jesus' Parables

At one crucial point the authenticity of the parables of
Jesus has been seriously questioned, that of their
allegorical elements. This is no small exception since, as
M. D. Goulder has shown/22/, allegorical elements are found to
a greater or lesser degree in most of Jesus' parables as
recorded in the gospels. Besides allegorical elements within
the parables themselves, four of Jesus' parables are
explained point by point:
          The Sower (Mark 4:3-9, 13-20; Matt. 13:3-9, 18-23;
               Luke 8:5-8, 11-15)
          The Tares among the Wheat (Matt. 13:24-30, 37-43)

        The Dragnet (Matt. 13:47-48, 49-50)
        The Good Shepherd (John 10:1-5, 6-16, 26-28)
Another seven have interpretations which correspond closely to
the parable narrative:
        The Divided House (Mark 3:23-26; Matt. 12:25-28; Luke
            11:17-20)
        The Budding Fig Tree (Mark 13:28-29 ; Matt. 24:32-33;
            Luke 21:29-31)
        The Children in the Marketplace (Matt. 11:16-19)
        The Two Sons (Matt. 21:28-32)
        The Burglar (Matt. 24:43-44; Luke 12:39-40)
        The Unjust Judge (Luke 18:1-8)
        Childbirth (John 16:21-22)
Yet since the time A. Jülicher defended the position that the
parables of Jesus did not originally contain allegorical
elements, allegory and allegorical elements in the parables of
Jesus have been widely discredited.

        Jülicher's definition of parable came straight from
Aristotle, allowing only one point to a picture; but it must be
considered improbable that Jesus formed His parables after
Aristotle's rules. Even in classical writing the precise
distinctions of Aristotle's rhetoric were by no means always
followed. Quintilian said that allegory was popular and
understood by even simple people (*Instit. Orat.* VIII,1,51) and
the most beautiful genre of discourse is that which mixes the
qualities of similitude, allegory, and metaphor (*Instit. Orat.*
VIII,6,48-49). In fact, Jülicher contradicted his own sharp
dichotomy between authentic parable and inauthentic allegory
by an example he cited, the allegory of Ebrard, *Cheirisophos'
Reise durch Böotien*. It is interesting both for the one who
takes it as a literal description of Boetia in the year 400
B.C. and the one who recognizes it as a commentary on Bavaria
/23/.

        Jülicher's Aristotelian definition of parable turned out
to be 'une faute de méthode qui eut des conséquences
désastreuses'/24/, for as Rabbinic studies developed it became
evident that Jesus' parables are far more closely related to
the Jewish משל than the classical Greek παραβολή. Within the
Jewish משל there is no sharp distinction between parable and
allegory.

        The rabbis made no distinction in category between
comparison, common saying, parable, allegory, riddle, and

mixed form/25/. Often Rabbinic parables had only one clear
lesson, but many are 'Parabeln mit Beimischung von Allegorie'
/26/, combining significant with decorative traits, as in the
OT and other traditional Israelite literature. Their
parables exhibit a literary freedom and lack of concern for
logical consistency, unlike the approach of Aristotle.
Similarly, the parables of Jesus do not fit into Jülicher's
Aristotelian categories of pure comparison.

Concerning Jülicher's extreme position that Jesus'
parables could not have contained allegorical elements or been
given allegorizing interpretations by Him, W. Michaelis said,
'Doch, das ist ein allzu theoretisches Schema'/27/. J.
Wellhausen added, 'Das Allegorische grundsätzlich
auszuschliessen und noch damit zu prahlen, ist nicht sein'
/28/. It became more and more recognized that there were
various degrees of allegory and that a mixing of parable and
allegory was entirely appropriate in the Semitic world/29/.
A growing number of scholars have affirmed that Jesus did use
allegory/30/.

Such a sharp distinction between parable and allegory,
unfortunately, is often still made today, with allegory being
defined as though every point of the story must have a
distinct counterpart in the meaning, as though allegory cannot
be true to life, as though the relationship between story and
meaning must be artificial, or as though the meaning cannot
compose a coherent whole. Such misconceptions have led many
to think that 'pure allegory is generally discredited, even
today . . . it is for the most part sheer rubbish'/31/.

Many with Dodd claim that 'in an allegory . . . each
detail is a separate metaphor, with a significance of its
own'/32/. But even in *Pilgrim's Progress* there are many
details which seem to have no particular significance, such as
the wicket gate. Dodd calls allegory untrue to life and
follows Bultmann's statement that 'allegory does not involve
. . . transference of judgement, but is concerned with
disguising some situation in secret or fantastic forms'/33/.
D. Via alleges that allegory does not have internal
coherence and is artificially constructed, and it has
artificial internal logic. Similarly T. W. Manson regarded
allegory 'as the means for conveying correct information or
true doctrine about matters with which the story as such has
no apparent connexion [sic]'/34/. But there is no less

connection between the Slough in *Pilgrim's Progress* and
despondency than between leaven and the Kingdom, and both
depict one situation through another. Manson continued by
saying that parable, unlike allegory, 'is meant to create trust
in God and love to man by an appeal to conscience and insight'
/35/. Yet *Pilgrim's Progress*, which he had just then mentioned
as an allegory, *was* meant to create trust in God and love to
man by an appeal to conscience and insight.

These approaches to definition of allegory are far too
mechanical, in effect dismissing it as an unworthy form. I. A.
Richards' comment on hearing such descriptions of allegory was,
'Oversimplified! Artificial in the extremest degree . . . I am
sure that no one actually choosing allegory could possibly
think of it as this'/36/.

In fact, the evidence from the gospels supports the view
that Jesus used allegorical elements in His parables freely
and that allegorical features in the gospels should not be held
in automatic suspicion. The highest degree of allegory is
found, not in the latest gospels to be written, as one would
expect if the church had gradually allegorized the parables,
but rather in the earliest gospels, Mark and Matthew. Luke has
far fewer allegorical elements and the Gospel of Thomas the
least of all. The earliest evidence we have shows the parables
to contain various degrees of allegorical elements. Even
Jeremias, who is of the opinion that 'the allegorical
interpretations can be recognized as almost certainly secondary'
/37/, has to admit the 'strange result: the discourse-material
in Matthew and Luke, the Markan material, the special
Matthaean material, the gospel as we have it in Matthew, Mark,
Luke, and John, all contain allegorical interpretations, but
the Lucan special material and the Gospel of Thomas have none'
/38/.

There seems to be no solid evidence that Jesus did not use
allegorical features freely in His parables. As is common in
Rabbinic parables allegorical features added to the clarity of
the parables, helping the hearer to 'see through' to the
parable's spiritual message. Such helps are particularly
appropriate when the reality referred to is largely unknown to
the hearers, as was the Kingdom as Jesus was proclaiming it.

Conclusion

The parables as found in the gospels can be demonstrated to be substantially authentic to Jesus, including their allegorical features. These parables, with their allegorical elements, stand out as the most profound and distinctive contribution in the long history of Semitic parables. As Shakespeare to the sonnet or Basho to haiku, so Jesus is to parables.

Appendix: OT Imagery Depicting God which Jesus Applied to Himself in Parables

Image	OT passages in which this image depicts God (not exhaustive)	Parables in which Jesus applied this image to Himself
Shepherd	Gen 49:24; 2 Chr 18: 16?; Ps 23:1-6; 28:9 Ps 80:1; Isa 40:11 Jer 23:3; 31:10 Ezek 34:10-22,31 Zech 9:16; 11:7-10	The Lost Sheep Matt 18:12-14 Luke 15:4-7 The Good Shepherd John 10:1-5 The Hireling John 10:11b-13
Giver of Forgiveness	Exod 32:32; 34:7 Lev 4:20,26,31,35 Lev 5:10,13,16,18 Lev 6:7; 19:22 Num 14:18-20; 15:25-28 Num 30:5,8,12 Deut 21:8; Josh 24:19 1 Kgs 8:30-40,50 2 Chr 6:21-30,39; 7:14 Ps 25:18; 32:1-5; 78:38 Ps 85:2; 86:5; 99:8 Ps 103:3; 130:3-4 Isa 33:24; Jer 18:23 Jer 31:34; 36:3 Dan 9:9,19 Amos 7:2	The Two Debtors Luke 7:41-43 The Prodigal Son Luke 15:11-32

Appendix (continued)

Image	OT passages in which this image depicts God (not exhaustive)	Parables in which Jesus applied this image to Himself
Sower	of God's Messianic activity: Isa 61:11 Jer 31:27-28; Ezek 36:8-9 (& *Tg. Ps.-J.*) Hos 2:21-23; Zech 10:9 'planter' used of God's Messianic activity: Exod 15:17 (& *Tg. Ps.-J.* Frg.); 2 Sam 7:10 Isa 60:21 (& *Tg. Ps.-J.*; LXX?); Isa 61:3 Jer 24:6-7; 31:27-28 Jer 32:41; Ezek 17:22-23 Amos 9:15 'planter' used of God, not specifically Messianic: Num 24:6; Ps 80:8,15; Ps 94:9; 104:16; Isa 5:2,7 Jer 2:21; 11:17; 12:2 Jer 17:8?; 18:9; 24:6 Jer 42:10; 45:4	The Sower Mark 4:3-8 Matt 13:3-8 Luke 8:5-8 The Seed Growing Mark 4:26-29 The Mustard Seed Mark 4:30-32 Matt 13:31-32 Luke 13:18-19 The Tares Matt 13:24-30
Director of the Harvest	Isa 27:(3),6,12; 41:14-16 Jer 5:24; 51:53,(55) Hos 2:21-23; 6:11 Joel 3:13; and implied in Gen 8:22; Isa 4:2; 32:15 Ezek 36:30; 47:12 Zech 8:12; Mal. 4:1-3?	The Seed Growing Secretly Mark 4:26-29 The Tares Matt 13:24-30
Lord (κύριος)	one of the most common names for God in the Scriptures, either for אֲדֹנָי, for example: Gen 15:2; Ps 35:23 Isa 6:1; Mal 1:14; or for אָדוֹן, for example: Exod 23:17; Ps 8:1,9 Isa 3:1; Mal 3:1.	The Doorkeeper Mark 13:33-37 The Tares Matt 13:24-30 The Servant Entrusted with Supervision Matt 24:45-51 Luke 12:41-48

Appendix (continued)

Image	OT passages in which this image depicts God (not exhaustive)	Parables in which Jesus applied this image to Himself
Lord (continued)	Occasionally God is spoken of metaphorically as a 'lord', as in 2 Chr 18:16 and Mal 1:6. The LXX usually translates יהוה as κύριος.	The Ten Virgins 　Matt 25:1-13 The Talents 　Matt 25:14-30 Men Awaiting their 　Master's 　Homecoming 　Luke 12:35-38 The Closed Door 　Luke 13:24-30 The Pounds 　Luke 19:12-27
Bridegroom	Isa 49:18,(14-26); Isa 54:4-8; 62:4-5 Jer 2:2; 3:1-14; 31:32 Ezek 16:8-14,59-63 Ezek 23:4-5,18,35 Hos 2:1-3:1; Zeph 3:17? Ps 45:8-17 and Canticles throughout as interpreted in the Targums; implied in Isa 1:21; 50:1 Jer 2:20; 4:1; 5:7 Ezek 16:6-63; Ezek 23:2-49; Hos 4:15 Mal 2:11	The Bridegroom 　Mark 2:19-20 　Matt 9:15 　Luke 5:34-35 The Ten Virgins 　Matt 25:1-13
King	1 Sam 12:12; Ps 5:2 Ps 9:4,7-8; 10:16; 11:4 Ps 22:28; 24:7-10; 29:10 Ps 44:4; 47:2-9; 48:2 Ps 68:24; 74:12; 84:3 Ps 89:14; 93:1-2; 95:3 Ps 97:1-2; 98:6; 99:4 Ps 103:19; 145:1,11-13 Ps 149:2; Isa 6:1,5 Isa 33:17,22; 37:16 Isa 41:21; 43:15; 44:6	The Pounds 　Luke 19:12-27

Appendix (continued)

Image	OT passages in which this image depicts God (not exhaustive)	Parables in which Jesus applied this image to Himself
King (continued)	Isa 66:1; Jer 3:17 Jer 8:19; 10:7,10; 14:21 Jer 17:12; 46:18; 48:15 Jer 49:38: 51:57 Lam 5:19; Ezek 43:7; Dan 2:44; 4:3,17,25,26,32 Dan 4:34; 5:21; 6:26 Obad 21; Mic 2:13; 4:7-8 Zeph 3:15; Zech 14:9,16-17 Mal 1:14	

Notes

/1/ The major OT narrative parables are: The Ewe Lamb (2 Sam 12:1-4), The Widow's Only Remaining Son (2 Sam 14:4-20), The Soldier who Let his Captive Escape (1 Kgs 20:39-40), The Vineyard (Isa 5:1-7), The Farmer (Isa 28:24-29); The Useless Vine Wood (Ezek 15:1-5), The Cedar of Lebanon (Ezek 31:2-9).

/2/ Cf. J. Krengel, 'Mashal', *The Universal Jewish Encyclopedia* (New York: KTAV, 1967) VII, 395, 'the Palestinian teachers use such figures freely; the Babylonian teachers did so very seldom'.

/3/ Note *b. Sabb.* 153a; *y. Ber.* 2,8,5c; *Exod. Rab.* 19.5; *Num. Rab.* 13.2; *Cant. Rab.* 5:1; 8:14; *Eccl. Rab.* 3.9; 9.8; *Lam. Rab.* 3.8-9; *B. Qam.* 7.2.

/4/ R. Gamaliel, Mekilta tractate Bahodesh, quoted from J. Z. Lauterbach, *Mekilta de-Rabbi Ishmael* (Jewish Publication Society of America, 1933-35) III, 245, line 113; cf. *b. Ber.* 7b and 31b.

/5/ Cf. Str-B II, 220.

/6/ Cf. P. Fiebig, *Die Gleichnisreden Jesu im Licht der rabbinischen Gleichnisse des neutestamentlichen Zeitalters* (Tübingen: Mohr, 1912) 222-78; C. A. Bugge, *Die Haupt-Parabeln Jesu* (Giessen: Alfred Töpelmann, 1903); R. Pautrel, 'Les canons du mashal rabbinique', *RSR* 26 (1936) 45.

/7/ Cf. J. Z. Lauterbach, 'Parables', *Jewish Encyclopedia* (New York: Funk and Wagnalls, 1905) IX, 513; J. Jeremias, *The Parables of Jesus* (3d ed.; London: SCM, 1972) 88.

/8/ N. Perrin, 'The Modern Interpretation of the Parables of
Jesus and the Problem of Hermeneutics', *Int* 25 (1971) 137-38;
A. Wilder, 'The Parable of the Sower: Naïveté and Method in
Interpretation', *Semeia* 2 (1974) 134-51 and *Early Christian
Rhetoric: The Language of the Gospel* (London: SCM, 1964) 80; E.
Fuchs, *Studies of the Historical Jesus* (SBT 42; London: SCM,
1964) 35-38, 155-57; J. D. Crossan, 'The Seed Parables of
Jesus', *JBL* 92 (1973) 265; J. D. Kingsbury, 'Ernst Fuchs'
Existentialist Interpretation of the Parables', *LQ* 22 (1970)
389, 391; D. Via, *The Parables: Their Literary and Existential
Dimension* (Philadelphia: Fortress, 1967).
/9/ H. Greeven, 'Wer unter euch . . .?' *Wort und Dienst:
Jahrbuch der Theologischen Schule Bethel* (1952) 86-101; cf.
Jeremias, *Parables*, 103; G. Bornkamm, *Jesus of Nazareth*
(London: Hodder and Stoughton, 1960) 70.
/10/ Jeremias, *Parables*, 21.
/11/ Cf. A. T. Cadoux, *The Parables of Jesus. Their Art and
Use* (London: James Clark, 1930) 11, 'It is not art in the
highest form because it is harnessed for service and conflict';
Fuchs, *Historical Jesus*, 73.
/12/ Cf. E. Käsemann, 'Die Anfänge christlicher Theologie',
ZTK 57 (1960) 174 n 2; Wilder, *Early Christian Rhetoric*, 89.
/13/ For a discussion and bibliography cf. P. B. Payne,
*Metaphor as a Model for Interpretation of the Parables of Jesus
with Special Reference to the Parable of the Sower* (Ph.D.
Dissertation, Cambridge, 1975) 36-46.
/14/ Cf. R. W. Funk, 'Beyond Criticism in quest of Literacy:
The Parable of the Leaven', *Int* 25 (1971) 149-70.
/15/ Cf. Payne, *Parables*, 52-57, 86-87.
/16/ C. H. Dodd, *The Parables of the Kingdom* (London: Nisbet,
1935) 21-22; cf. J. Danten, La révélation du Christ sur Dieu
dans les paraboles', *NRT* 77 (1955) 476; C. Barry, 'The Literary
and Artistic Beauty of Christ's Parables', *CBQ* 10 (1948) 382.
/17/ Cf. Wilder, 'The Sower', 143; W. J. Harrington, 'The
Parables in Recent Study (1960-71)', *BTB* 2 (1972) 228; W. G.
Doty, 'The Parables of Jesus, Kafka, Borges and Others, with
Structural Observations', *Semeia* 2 (1974) 176.
/18/ For a bibliography cf. Payne, *Parables*, 41.
/19/ Cf. R. W. Funk, *Language, Hermeneutic, and the Word of God
God: The Problem of Language in the New Testament and
Contemporary Theology* (London: Harper and Row, 1966) 213; J. D.
Crossan, 'The Good Samaritan: Towards a Generic Definition of
Parable', *Semeia* 2 (1974) 82-112 and much of the rest of *Semeia*
2 (1974).

/20/ Cf. E. Linnemann, *Parables of Jesus: Introduction and Exposition* (London: SPCK, 1966) 22, 27; Doty, 'The Parables of Jesus, Kafka', 176-77; Via, *The Parables*, 53; Fuchs, *Historical Jesus*, 113-20.

/21/ On this understanding of the Sower cf. Payne, *Parables*, 231-34. Some details of the implicit divine claim in the parables are given in the appendix to this paper.

/22/ M. D. Goulder, 'Characteristics of the Parables in the several Gospels', *JTS* 19 (1968) 51-69.

/23/ A. Jülicher, *Die Gleichnisreden Jesu* (2d ed.; Tübingen: Mohr, 1910) I, 59-60; criticized by M. Hermaniuk, *La parabole évangélique: enquête exégétique et critique* (Louvain: Bibliotheca Alfonsiana, 1947) 47, 60-61.

/24/ Hermaniuk, *La parabole évangélique*, 44-54; cf. Payne, *Parables*, 14-15.

/25/ For a bibliography and discussion cf. Payne, *Parables*, 15,21-22.

/26/ P. Fiebig, *Altjüdische Gleichnisse und die Gleichnisse Jesu* (Tübingen: Mohr, 1904) 31-33, 42-43, 98-99; cf. the bibliography in Payne, *Parables*, 22.

/27/ W. Michaelis, *Die Gleichnisse Jesu: Eine Einführung* (Hamburg: Furche, 1956) 15.

/28/ J. Wellhausen, *Das Evangelium Marci* (Berlin: Georg Reimer, 1903) 31.

/29/ Cf. the bibliography in Payne, *Parables*, 18.

/30/ Cf. L. Fonck, *Die Parabeln des Herrn im Evangelium* (Innsbruck: Felician Rauch, 1902) 92-104; P. Fiebig, 'Jesu Gleichnisse im Licht der rabbinischen Gleichnisse', *ZNW* 13 (1912) 198-99, 203; *Die Gleichnisreden Jesu*, 252-54; A. H. M'Neile, *The Gospel According to St. Matthew* (London: Macmillan, 1915) 186, 195, 202; E. Fascher, *Die formgeschichtliche Methode* (Giessen: Alfred Töpelmann, 1924) 120; Hermaniuk, *La parabole évangélique*, 217-24; J. J. Vincent, 'The Parables of Jesus as Self-Revelation', *SE* I (TU 73; 1959) 82-86; C. E. B. Cranfield, *The Gospel According to St. Mark* (Cambridge, 1959) 111, 159, 366-68; M. Black, 'The Parables as Allegory', *BJRL* 42 (1959-60) 284; J. A. Baird, *The Justice of God in the Teaching of Jesus* (London: SCM, 1963) 27-28, 63-73; R. E. Brown, 'Parable and Allegory Reconsidered', (in *New Testament Essays*; London: Geoffrey Chapman, 1965) 254-64; C. F. D. Moule, *The Gospel According to Mark* (Cambridge, 1965) 33, 36 and 'Mark 4:1-20 Yet Once More', (in *Neotestamentica et Semitica: Studies in Honour of Matthew Black*; Edinburgh: T. & T. Clark, 1969) 109-10; V. Taylor, *The Gospel According to St Mark* (2d ed.; London: Macmillan, 1966) 249-50, 472; Via, *The*

Parables, 4-7, 13-15, 19, 24-26; F. Hauck, 'παραβολή', *TDNT* 5, 747.

/31/ G. W. H. Lampe and K. J. Woollcombe, *Essays on Typology* (SBT 22; London: SCM, 1957) 32, while primarily concerned with allegorical interpretations of Scripture rather than allegory as a literary form, this statement does reflect current opinion.

/32/ C. H. Dodd, 'The Gospel Parables,' *BJRL* 16 (1933-34) 397, 401-2; cf. *The Parables of the Kingdom*, 15, 20, 23, 126, but he is more cautious on pp. 19 and 21 and gives allegorical interpretations himself on pp. 130-31, 190-91; cf. M. Black's criticism in 'The Parables as Allegory,' 283. Also claiming that each detail of an allegory has separate significance are Via, *Parables*, 5, and D. E. Nineham, *The Gospel of St. Mark* (London: Adam & Charles Black, 1968) 129-30.

/33/ Bultmann, *Synoptic Tradition*, 198; Dodd, *The Parables of the Kingdom*, 23.

/34/ T. W. Manson, *The Sayings of Jesus* (London, SCM, 1949) 35; for further examples of misunderstanding of allegory cf. E. J. Tinsley, 'Parable, Allegory and Mysticism,' (in *Vindications: Essays on the Historical Basis of Christianity*, ed. A. Hanson; London: SCM, 1966) 153-92.

/35/ Manson, *Sayings*, 35.

/36/ In discussion with the author on Dec. 11, 1974.

/37/ Jeremias, *Parables*, 88.

/38/ Ibid. For a detailed case study note the author's article, 'The Authenticity of the Parable of the Sower and its Interpretation', in *Gospel Perspectives* I, ed. R. T. France and David Wenham (Sheffield: JSOT Press, 1980) 163-207, and his *Parables*, 146-234.

/39/ For further details cf. Payne, *Parables*, 33-34, 232-34.

Paul and the Synoptic Apocalypse

David Wenham,
Tyndale House,
36 Selwyn Gardens,
Cambridge CB3 9BA.

J. B. Orchard claimed in 1938: 'The two Epistles to the Thessalonians... are fairly bristling with verbal coincidences and reminiscences of the eschatological discourse of Christ as (severally) reported in the Synoptic Gospels, especially St Matthew'/1/. But, whether because of the weaknesses of some of his arguments or because of prejudice against his approach, including his espousal of Matthean priority, or because of both, scholars generally have been unconvinced by his claim. Thus V. P. Furnish writing thirty years later admitted only one verse in 1 and 2 Thessalonians as a sure allusion to Jesus' teaching (1 Thess 5:2), and he pronounced that 'Ultimately, nothing is going to be gained by continuing the quest for Pauline "allusions" to Jesus' teaching'/2/. The purpose of this paper is to look at some possible parallels between the Synoptic apocalyptic material (and especially the Synoptic Apocalypse) on the one hand and 1 and 2 Thessalonians on the other, and to try to judge to what extent Orchard's optimism or Furnish's pessimism on the question of their significance is justified/3/.

A 'significant' parallel for the purpose of this paper is one that suggests either direct dependence of the one tradition on the other or the use by both of them of a common Christian tradition. Parallels therefore that can reasonably be explained as due to two authors' independent acquaintance with pre-Christian Jewish apocalyptic tradition must be discounted. But that is not to say that the finding of a possible Jewish or other background for an idea occurring in two traditions automatically precludes the possibility that the two traditions may be connected: an agreement to use a Jewish or other motif in a particular way may be significant; and, especially where a number of parallels come together, a parallel that might otherwise be of no demonstrable significance will assume significance as part of a cumulative argument.

Paul's eschatological teaching in 1 and
2 Thessalonians - a 'tradition' passed on

A useful point at which to start an examination of 1 and 2
Thessalonians and the Synoptic apocalyptic material is with the
observation (a) that Paul's eschatological teaching in the
Thessalonian epistles is largely a restating of things that he
had already told the Thessalonians in his short stay with them,
and (b) that this teaching may have been received tradition.

a. It seems that teaching about the Second Coming was
central in Paul's presentation of the gospel to the
Thessalonians, since in 1 Thess 1:10 he notes that the
Thessalonians were renowned because of the way they 'turned to
God from idols, to serve a living and true God, and to wait for
his Son from heaven,.... Jesus who delivers us from the wrath
to come'. They were not only told of the fact of the Second
Coming; they were also informed about the uncertainty of its
timing; so Paul can say in 1 Thess. 5:1,2 'As to the times and
the seasons, brethren ... you yourselves know well....'. And
they were also informed about the events that must precede the
end, such as the appearance of the lawless one (2 Thess 2:5,6).

b. Paul at the end of 2 Thessalonians 2 urges his readers
to 'stand firm and hold to the traditions (παραδόσεις) which
you were taught by us, either by mouth or by letter' (2:15).
It is striking that he uses the technical term παράδοσις at
this point: although it is possible that Paul means no more
than that the Thessalonians must hold on to what he personally
has taught them, it is quite likely that he is referring to
teachings of the church which he received and passed on/4/.
And in the context of 2 Thessalonians Paul probably has in mind
particularly the teachings on the Second Coming, which he
passed on to them as a central part of the Gospel/5/.

Another piece of teaching that Paul passed on to the
Thessalonians while he was with them was that 'we were to
suffer affliction' (1 Thess 3:4); this warning may have been a
part of the eschatological tradition that he passed on. Yet
another possible reference to this tradition is 1 Thess 4:15,
'This we declare to you by the word of the Lord that we who are
alive ...', though commentators are very much divided over the
meaning of 'word of the Lord' here/6/.

Solid parallels between the eschatological teaching
of the Synoptics and of 1 and 2 Thessalonians

1.   The thief (1 Thess 4:2-4, Matt 24:43, Luke 12:39)
The least controversial parallel between Paul's
eschatology in 1 and 2 Thessalonians and the Synoptics is the
comparison of the coming of the day of the Lord to the coming
of a thief. The Synoptic reference is a Q saying, found in
Matthew's apocalyptic discourse, but elsewhere in Luke. In the
Pauline and Synoptic passages the thief reference comes in the
general context of a call to keep awake, the same Greek verb
γρηγορεῖν being used in Matt 24:42,43, Luke 12:37 and 1 Thess
5:6. The verbal parallelism between Paul and the Synoptics is
not very exact: Paul refers to the 'day of the Lord coming',
whereas Matthew and Luke refer to the 'Son of man coming'/7/;
Paul refers to the thief coming at night, something not
explicit in Luke, though clearly implied in Matthew when he
refers to the 'watch' in which the thief comes and to the
master needing to have stayed awake; in Paul it is a straight
comparison, whereas in Matthew and Luke it is a small parable.
Nevertheless, despite the verbal inexactness of the parallel,
the idea is clearly the same, and scholars seem generally
agreed that this is a genuinely significant parallel, there
being no known Jewish or other parallels/8/.

It is to be noted that this is one of the 'traditions'
that Paul passed on to the Thessalonians, of which he reminds
them in his letter. Scholars have noted that Paul's phrase
ἀκριβῶς οἴδατε ὅτι is not typically Pauline/9/; two
explanations have been given for it: (a) that Paul is echoing
the Thessalonians' own claim for themselves at this point - 'we
know accurately'; (b) that he speaks thus because he is
referring to a well-known tradition. One possibility is that
Paul is here picking up the Q introduction to the thief saying
- ἐκεῖνο (Matt; Luke τοῦτο)γινώσκετε ὅτι, the implication being
that the Thessalonians have obeyed this instruction of the
Lord/10/.

2.   The coming of the Lord from heaven
As well as teaching the Thessalonians about the timing of
the Second Coming, Paul must also have taught them about the
nature of the Coming. If we compare the four or five passages
where Paul indicates his picture of this (1 Thess 1:10, 3:13,
4:14-17, 2 Thess 1:7-10, 2:1) with the Synoptics, we find much

in common.

(a) It is a 'coming' or 'parousia' (e.g. 2 Thess 1:9, 2:1;
Matt 24:27,30 and parallels)

(b) It is a 'heavenly' event ('from heaven' in Paul; 'in
heaven' implied or stated in the Synoptics; cf. Matt 24:30,31,
Mark 13:26,27).

(c) It is 'with the clouds'. Although Jesus' coming is
described by Paul as a 'descent' from heaven, neither he nor
the Synoptists refer to Jesus arriving at the earth. The
Synoptists speak of Jesus coming with the clouds and sending
out his angels to gather the elect: the implied picture, which
is explicit in the Q passage Matt 24:40,41/Luke 17:34,35,
seems to be that the elect are lifted from the earth to the
Lord/ll/; and this is certainly the Pauline picture, since he
refers to being snatched 'with the clouds' to meet the Lord in
the air (1 Thess 4:17).

(d) It is accompanied by angels. So 2 Thess 1:7 and perhaps 1
Thess 3:13, where the ambiguous ἅγιοι may be angels/12/; also 1
Thess 4:16 speaks of the archangel's voice. In the Synoptics
see Mark 8:38 (and parallels) and in the Synoptic Apocalypse
13:27 (and parallels), where the angels are sent out to gather;
also Matt 25:31/13/.

(e) It is a glorious and mighty coming. So 2 Thess 1:7-10,
Mark 13:26 (and parallels).

(f) It is a coming in judgment on the wicked. So 2 Thess 1:7-
10. This is more implied than explicit in the Marcan
apocalypse of Mark 13 (but compare 9:38); it is explicit in
Matthew (24:30, 37-51; and 25).

(g) It is a coming to gather the elect to be with the Lord. So
1 Thess 4:14-17 (note v 14 ἄξει σὺν αὐτῷ)/14/, 2 Thess 1:10, 2:
1 (ἡμῶν ἐπισυναγωγῆς ἐπ' αὐτόν). In the Synoptics see Mark 13:
27 (and parallels. ἐπισυνάξει), and for a fuller exposition of
the idea of being in the Master's presence see the Matthean
parables of chapter 25.

(h) It is accompanied by a trumpet blast. So 1 Thess 4:16 ἐν
σάλπιγγι θεοῦ and Matt 24:31 μετὰ σάλπιγγος μεγάλης/15/.

The substantial parallelism between the two understandings
of the Second Coming seems too extensive to be accidental. It
is true that many of the motifs employed have OT or other
Jewish background (e.g. Zech 14:5, Dan 7:13); but, although it
could be argued that one or more of the motifs was used
independently by Paul and the Synoptists to describe the
Parousia, the combination of agreements makes complete
independence unlikely, and it becomes simpler to explain the

whole range of agreements as indicating common tradition of
some sort/16/.

So far as the nature and direction of the relationship
between Paul and the Synoptists goes, two provisional comments
are in order: (a) the verbal parallelism is not very impressive
with a few possible exceptions, e.g. παρουσία, ἐπισυναγωγή and
perhaps ἀπάντησις in 1 Thess 4:17 and Matt 25:6 (cf. v 1). It
is doubtful if these terms prove any direct relation between
Paul and the Synoptics; but there may have been an indirect
link in the eschatological parenesis of the Greek-speaking
church. (b) The parallelism is strongest between Paul and
Matthew, both substantially and verbally (e.g. παρουσία is only
in Matthew, not in Mark and Luke; and Matthew is the only
gospel to refer to the last trumpet blast)/17/.

3. The Sacrilegious Lawless One

As well as explaining to the Thessalonians that they
could not know the time of the Second Coming, Paul warned them
of a particular event to precede the Second Coming, namely the
coming of the 'lawless one' (2 Thessalonians 2). The parallels
between this and the Synoptic teaching about the 'desolating
sacrilege' are unmistakable.

a. The *context*: Paul gives his teaching to prevent the
Thessalonians being 'quickly shaken in mind or excited, either
by spirit or by word, or by letter purporting to be from us,
to the effect that the day of the Lord has come. Let no one
deceive you in any way ...' The Synoptic Apocalypse also
preceded the description of the desolating sacrilege with a
section warning people 'lest anyone deceive you. Many will
come in my name saying that I am (he) and will deceive many.
When you hear of wars and rumours of wars, don't get excited.
It must happen, but the end is not yet.' (Mark 13:5-7). The
exact meaning of the Markan phrase 'saying that I am' (λέγοντες
ὅτι ἐγώ εἰμι) is debated by scholars; but one, and perhaps the
best, explanation of the phrase (and of the equivalent in
Matthew) is that the reference is to deceivers who would claim
to be Jesus returned for his Second Coming/18/; in any case it
is evident that they are people proclaiming the imminent or
actual arrival of the end. The problem warned of in the
Synoptics is thus very much the same as that being faced by
Paul in Thessalonica - a problem of excessive excitement and of
deception involving the idea of an imminent Second Coming. It
is interesting that the same unusual word θροεῖσθαι is found in

Matthew/Mark and in 2 Thessalonians; there is also a close
parallel between Matthew/Mark's βλέπετε μή τις ὑμᾶς πλανήσῃ and
Paul's μή τις ὑμᾶς ἐξαπατήσῃ, though the verbs are different
and the idea is obvious enough. It is widely recognized by
commentators that the function of the whole Marcan apocalypse
was to cool down eschatological excitement, and this is also
Paul's purpose in 2 Thessalonians/19/.

b. In countering the false notions, Paul and the
Synoptists agree in describing *one major horrible event which
must precede the end*. Paul is explicit when he says that the
end will not come 'unless the rebellion comes first and the man
of lawlessness is revealed'; the Synoptists are not quite so
explicit, but in Mark 13 at least the dynamics of the chapter
seems to be that verses 5-13 describe the period before the end
when excitement is out of place and endurance is the order of
the day; but then verse 14 (ὅταν δὲ ἴδητε τὸ βδέλυγμα ....)
marks the beginning of the significant action.

Not only do Paul and the Synoptists agree that one
horrible event must precede the end, but they also seem to
agree that in some sense the horrible event will lead to the
coming (or a coming)/20/ of Christ. Thus Paul refers to the
Lord destroying the lawless one 'by the appearing of his
coming' (ἐπιφανείᾳ τῆς παρουσίας), while the Synoptics after
describing the days of the horrible event say: 'Immediately
after the distress of those days' (Matthew) or 'In those days
after that distress' (Mark) the heavenly bodies will be upset,
and 'then the sign of the Son of man will appear' (Matthew,
Mark). The exact chronological relationship between the
horrible event and the coming of the Son is not made clear in
either Paul or the Synoptics; but there at least seems to be a
connexion.

c. *The nature of the horrible event* is similar in Paul and
the Synoptics. In Paul it is an evil blasphemous person; in
the Synoptics the 'desolating sacrilege' need not be personal,
but Mark's use of the masculine ἑστηκότα suggests that he at
least saw it as such. It is in any case evidently something
horribly evil that is envisaged, and the Danielic background to
the Synoptic phrase suggests that it is a blasphemous object
or person. The Danielic background is, of course, an important
point of contact between Paul's description of the man of
lawlessness and the Synoptic desolating sacrilege: both draw on

Daniel's description of Antiochus Epiphanes and his
blasphemous actions to portray the future horrible event, Paul
using the description of Antiochus to portray the future man
of lawlessness and the Synoptists borrowing the description of
his blasphemous altar to characterize the future sacrilege.

   d. *The place of the horrible event*. Paul speaks of the
man of lawlessness sitting in 'the temple of God', and Matthew
and Mark of the desolating sacrilege standing 'in the holy
place' (Matthew), 'where it ought not' (Mark cryptically). The
point of contact here is obvious enough, whether we take the
references by Paul and the Synoptists literally or somehow
metaphorically/21/. The agreement may be partly explicable via
the Danielic background, though Daniel does not speak of
Antiochus as sitting in the temple, so that Paul's description
of the lawless one in terms that fit the Synoptic sacrilege
better is of interest/22/.

   e. *The accompanying deceptive signs and wonders*. Having
described the lawless one and having in fact described his
destruction, Paul says that his coming will be with Satanic
power and with 'pretended signs and wonders (σημείοις καὶ
τέρασιν ψεύδους) and with wicked deceit for those who are to
perish'. It is not said that he himself performs these signs
and wonders, though this could be supposed. Matthew and Mark
after their description of the desolating sacrilege and of the
awful suffering that will go with it (and after a reference to
the ending of those terrible days) go on to warn of false
prophets and false Christs arising, who 'will do signs and
wonders (σημεῖα καὶ τέρατα) to mislead, if possible, the elect.'
The exact chronological relationship of this deceptive assault
to the previously described events connected with the desolating
sacrilege is not clear in the Synoptics, though the τότε of
Matt 24:23/Mark 13:21, can very plausibly be taken to mean that
it is an accompaniment of the events. But whatever the answer
to that and despite the differences between Paul and the
Synoptists (e.g. Mark 13:21 has no parallel in 2 Thessalonians),
the coincidence in the positioning of a reference to deceivers
cannot easily be dismissed as accidental/23/.

   The different points of similarity between Paul's and the
Synoptists' description of the horrible crisis to precede the
end are considerable and strongly suggest that their
traditions are in some way related/24/. The agreement is much
more in substance than in wording. The most striking verbal

agreements are θροεῖσθαι and σημεῖα καὶ τέρατα; and of these
the latter is such a common phrase that it cannot be taken to
prove a literary connexion or a significant connexion at the
Greek stage of tradition. The former is more striking, and may
suggest some contact at the level of Greek tradition; but it is
certainly insufficient to prove that Paul and the Synoptists
are drawing primarily or to a significant extent on a common
Greek tradition. Even though the verbal parallelism is slight,
the substantial parallelism is remarkably extensive, and it
includes parallelism of structure as well as of ideas: Paul's
teaching in 2 Thess 2:1-12 runs roughly parallel to much of the
first part of the Synoptic Apocalypse (from Mark 13:5-22).

So far as Paul's relationship with the different gospels
is concerned, there is little evidence of similarity to Luke,
much more to Matthew and Mark. We noted two respects in which
he may be thought closest to Mark (and not Matthew), the most
interesting of these being their agreement in referring to the
horror as personal/25/. In two respects (in addition to the
use of παρουσία) Paul has possible contacts with Matthew (and
not Mark): his reference to the ἐπιφανεία of the Lord's
parousia is rather remotely similar to Matthew's verse 27
ὥσπερ γὰρ ἡ ἀστραπὴ ... φαίνεται ... οὕτως ἔσται ἡ παρουσία
(cf. also v 30 φανήσεται τὸ σημεῖον); much more interesting is
his agreement with Matthew in the use of the word ἀνομία. The
word is quite common in both Matthew and Paul/26/, so that
their use of the term in their eschatological teaching could
be explained as coincidence. However, Matthew's verse 12 καὶ
διὰ τὸ πληθυνθῆναι τὴν ἀνομίαν ψυγήσεται ἡ ἀγάπη τῶν πολλῶν
is reminiscent not only of Paul's title ὁ ἄνθρωπος τῆς ἀνομίας,
but also of his expression ἡ ἀποστασία, if this is taken to
mean 'apostasy' (also 2 Thess 2:3). If Matthew saw the setting
up of the desolating sacrilege as the supreme example of the
'multiplication of lawlessness' as may be inferred from οὖν in
his verse 15 and other considerations/27/, then the coincidence
with Paul's idea is the more striking/28/.

Summary of argument so far
In beginning an examination of the possible parallels
between Paul and the Synoptic apocalyptic material, I have
deliberately chosen three examples that seem strong evidence
for a significant link between Paul and the Synoptics - the
thief saying, the description of the coming, and the
description of the preceding horror. The evidence, when put
together, seems conclusively to indicate some common

tradition. Even from the evidence so far examined, the links between 1 and 2 Thessalonians and the Synoptic tradition have seemed quite extensive: much of the Synoptic teaching about events before the end (Mark 13:5-23) is paralleled in 2 Thessalonians 2, the description of the Parousia itself (Mark 13:26,27) is paralleled, and the teaching about the uncertainty of the time and the need to watch (Mark 13:32-36, Matthew 24:42-44) has a parallel (1 Thess 5:1-6).

As to the nature and direction of the links, this is far less obvious. There is little to suggest a direct link, either literary or in Greek oral tradition, though a few phrases may have been drawn from a common Greek tradition of eschatological exhortation. So far as the different gospels go, the links are stronger with Matthew than either Mark or Luke (the thief saying, of course, not appearing at all in Mark), though there are one or two links particularly with Mark.

Other parallels

Having made out the case for a significant link between the traditions of Paul and the Synoptists, we can proceed to examine further passages where there may be a connexion.

4. Luke 21:34-36
a. Luke 21:34,35 related to 1 Thess 5:3
In the same passage where Paul compares the coming of the day of the Lord to the coming of a thief in the night we find what are probably the most striking verbal links between Paul and the Synoptists in the sections we are considering. In Luke 21:34,35 the Lord warns of being weighed down by carousing, drunkenness (μέθη) and worldly cares, καὶ ἐπιστῇ ἐφ' ὑμᾶς αἰφνίδιος ἡ ἡμέρα ἐκείνη ὡς παγίς. ἐπεισελεύσεται γὰρ ἐπὶ πάντας ... ἀγρυπνεῖτε δὲ .... ἵνα κατισχύσητε ἐκφυγεῖν. In 1 Thess 5:3, having spoken of the coming of the ἡμέρα κυρίου, Paul says ὅταν λέγωσιν· εἰρήνη καὶ ἀσφάλεια, τότε αἰφνίδιος αὐτοῖς ἐφίσταται ὄλεθρος ὥσπερ ἡ ὠδὶν τῇ ἐν γαστρὶ ἐχούσῃ, καὶ οὐ μὴ ἐκφύγωσιν. He goes on to urge γρηγορῶμεν καὶ νήφωμεν and contrasts those who sleep and get drunk (μεθύουσιν).

This is a strong case of substantial and verbal parallelism: αἰφνίδιος occurs only in these two places in the NT. ἐφιστάναι, though common in Luke/Acts, occurs only three

times in Paul (the two others being in the Pastorals), and
ἐκφεύγειν occurs only twice in Paul and three times in Luke/
Acts. In addition to these very striking parallels, there are
other less remarkable parallels, including the references in
both Paul and Luke to 'the day' of the Lord, to drunkenness,
and to the need to be awake. Also we note how in the sentence
regarding the sudden coming of judgment day Paul's αὐτοῖς
corresponds to Luke's ἐφ' ὑμᾶς and his ὥσπερ ἡ ὠδῖν to Luke's ὡς
παγίς. All these verbal and structural parallels, together
with the agreement in meaning, make it very probable that there
is a common tradition here/29/.

   b. The differences point to Lukan originality
   The similarity between the Pauline and Lukan tradition is
especially close, where Luke has ἐπιστῇ ἐφ' ὑμᾶς αἰφνίδιος ἡ
ἡμέρα ἐκείνη ὡς παγίς and Paul has .... τότε αἰφνίδιος αὐτοῖς
ἐφίσταται ὄλεθρος ὥσπερ ἡ ὠδῖν τῇ ἐν γαστρὶ ἐχούσῃ. There are
however, two substantial differences, an examination of which
confirms the idea of a common tradition, but also throws light
on the history of the tradition: (1) Paul has ὄλεθρος for
Luke's ἡ ἡμέρα ἐκείνη. The difference here in sense is slight:
Paul in the immediately preceding verse has referred to the
'day of the Lord', and so the coming of the ὄλεθρος is the
coming of that day. As for whether the Lukan or the Pauline
wording is original, it is possible that Luke put 'that day'
for 'destruction' to fit his context and perhaps under the
influence of Mark 13:30; but it is probably simpler to suggest
that, having just referred to the 'day of the Lord' in the
previous saying, Paul substitutes ὄλεθρος (a term he uses
elsewhere) for a further reference to 'the day' for the sake of
variation. Either way, there is no difficulty in postulating
one form of words behind the two traditions.
   (2) Paul has ὥσπερ ἡ ὠδῖν ... for Luke's ὡς παγίς. The
variation in this case may seem more surprising, but there are
in fact several possible explanations. L. Hartman, following
earlier writers, has proposed an explanation of this difference
on the basis of Hebrew/Aramaic, since in Hebrew and Aramaic
the word חבל/חבלא (with slightly different pointings) can mean
either 'rope' (hence 'trap') or 'birth-pangs'; the suggestion
is therefore that we have a translation variant here in Paul
and Luke/30/.
   This idea has some plausibility. Although חבל is not the
most obvious Hebrew/Aramaic word for 'trap', Greek παγίς, it is
sometimes used with that sense (e.g. Job 18:10, Ps 119:61, 139:
5, Prov 5:22); and it is possible that an original כחבל might
have been understood by one translator to mean 'like a rope/

trap' and by another to mean 'like pangs'. The idea of sudden
trouble would be conveyed by both translations. Interestingly,
we find a similar sort of variation in translation with the
Hebrew phrase חבלי מות שאול, this being taken in the LXX to
mean 'the pangs of death', but by modern commentators as 'the
cords of death'/31/. Even more remarkably, the Hebrew phrase
may be taken both ways in neighbouring contexts in the Hymn
Scroll of Qumran ('pangs' 1 QH 3:7f., 'cords' 3.28)/32/.

But, although the idea is possible, it loses a lot of its
attraction when it is realised that the difference between Paul
and Luke may also be well explained on the basis cf a common
Greek text. In the first place, it may be noted that the two
terms ὠδίν and παγίς are not completely unconnected, even in
the LXX: both are found in OT eschatological contexts that
describe the day of the Lord (e.g. Isa 13:6,7; 24:17), and in
Ps 18:6 LXX the two words are found in close parallelism. So
even without the hypothesis of a Semitic original, it is
possible to conceive of a New Testament writer substituting the
one term for the other.

But secondly and more specifically it may be plausibly
argued that the Lukan form of the saying 'like a snare' is the
original text and that Paul has changed this to 'like pangs'
/33/. In favour of this is (1) the fact that two of the ideas
present in 1 Thessalonians 5 and Luke 21, the idea of the
unexpectedness of the day of the Lord and the thought of
'escaping', both fit slightly better with the Lukan 'snare' than
the Pauline 'pangs', and (2) that the Pauline alteration of
Luke can be well explained from Isa 13:6,7 'Wait, for the day
of the Lord is near; as destruction from the Almighty it will
come ... Pangs and agony will seize him; they will be in
anguish like a woman in travail'. This OT passage on the day
of the Lord was of obvious relevance to NT eschatology: verses
9,10 of the same chapter are echoed in Matt 24:29 (and
parallels; cf. Rev 6:12), and several possible links may be
shown with 1 Thessalonians 5: (a) Paul's use of ὄλεθρος, where
Luke has ἡ ἡμέρα ἐκείνη, may, we suggested, have been for the
sake of variation; but his particular choice of word may be
explained from Isa 13:6, 'the day of the Lord is near; as
destruction from the Almighty it will come' (though the LXX on
this occasion does not translate שׁד with ὄλεθρος). (b) The
reference to pangs and the 'woman with child' obviously
connect the two passages, though Paul speaks of a 'woman with
child' and the onset of labour whereas Isaiah speaks of a

'woman giving birth' and the experience of labour.   (c) Paul's
reference to people saying 'peace and security' when judgment
comes has been linked by commentators with Jer 6:14.
Interestingly Jer 6:14 is followed in 6:24-26 by a passage
portraying judgment in terms very similar to Isa 13.   It seems
possible that Paul (or his tradition) has been influenced by
these two related OT traditions/34/.

Since such a plausible explanation of the divergence
between Luke 21 and 1 Thessalonians 5 is possible on the basis
of the Greek text, and since several of the other vocabulary
links between Luke 21 and 1 Thessalonians suggest a connexion
at the level of Greek tradition, the hypothesis of a Semitic
original becomes unnecessary, though still not impossible.   But
with or without a Semitic original/35/, our investigations have
made the idea of a common tradition here the more plausible and
have pointed to the Lukan form of the tradition being the
earlier form and to Paul (or his tradition) having modified it
/36/.

One further phenomenon that would be accounted for by this
explanation is the unPauline style of 1 Thess 5:3.   Best,
following Lightfoot, notes (i) the impersonal λέγωσιν, (ii)
εἰρήνη in the sense of security, and (iii) the unusual words
ἀσφάλεια, αἰφνίδιος, ἐφιστάναι/37/.   Most of these untypical
features may be explained from the postulated underlying
tradition, also attested in Luke, or from the OT passages,
whose influence has been detected in Paul's version of the
tradition.

c. Luke 21:36 related to Ephesians 6
As well as echoing 1 Thessalonians 5, Luke 21:34-6 also
echoes Ephesians 6.   Thus Luke 21:36 reads ἀγρυπνεῖτε δὲ ἐν
παντὶ καιρῷ δεόμενοι ἵνα κατισχύσητε ἐκφυγεῖν ταῦτα πάντα τὰ
μέλλοντα γίνεσθαι καὶ σταθῆναι ἔμπροσθεν τοῦ υἱοῦ τοῦ
ἀνθρώπου.   In Ephesians 6 Paul calls his readers to take the
armour of God πρὸς τὸ δύνασθαι ὑμᾶς στῆναι ... (v 11).   Paul
goes on ἵνα δυνηθῆτε ἀντιστῆναι ἐν τῇ ἡμέρᾳ τῇ πονηρᾷ καὶ
ἅπαντα κατεργασάμενοι στῆναι· στῆτε οὖν (vv 13,14a).   He
continues a few verses later διὰ πάσης προσευχῆς καὶ δεήσεως
προσευχόμενοι ἐν παντὶ καιρῷ καὶ εἰς αὐτὸ ἀγρυπνοῦντες ἐν
πάσῃ προσκαρτερήσει καὶ δεήσει (v 18)/38/.

The parallels here are less striking than those between 1
Thessalonians 5 and Luke 21, especially when it is recalled

that exhortations to 'stand' and to 'pray always' are found
quite often in Paul's writings and may have been a common part
of the Early Church's parenesis/39/. However, the close
similarity of wording in Luke 21 and Ephesians 6, notably in the
use of ἀγρυπνεῖν (found only here in Paul) does suggest some
specific link between the traditions, not just that they both
drew on the general stock of early Christian parenesis; none of
Paul's other injunctions to 'stand', 'to watch' or 'to pray'
come so close to Luke 21.

     Against this conclusion it might be argued that one of the
key words in common, to 'stand', is used differently in the two
contexts - in Luke 21 of 'standing' in divine judgment, in
Eph 6 of 'standing' in battle. But this point should not be
given too much weight: both in Luke 21 and Ephesians 6 the
picture is of getting through a dangerous situation (from the
devil and the evil day in Ephesians, from coming events in
Luke), and the final 'standing' after the battle referred to at
the end of Eph 6:13 is not dissimilar to the 'standing' before
the Son of man in Luke 21. One possibility is that Paul has
incorporated a traditional, non-military exhortation to 'stand'
into the context of the warfare metaphor, thereby giving it
military overtones. In favour of this may be (a) the fact that
non-military exhortations to stand are found elsewhere in Paul
in contexts that could be related to Ephesians 6/40/; (b) the
multiplication of references to 'standing' in Eph 6:11-14
(twice 'being able to stand'). This repetitiousness could be
partly explained if Paul is working with a traditional
'standing' motif, which he elaborates in verse 12 and then
again in the description of the armour in verses 14-18. It is
interesting that the description of the armour is immediately
followed by a slightly repetitious call to unceasing prayer,
being paralleled in Luke 21:36. Is Paul here reverting to his
tradition, having wandered from it? If so we have, as with 1
Thessalonians 5, a significant connexion between a Lukan and
Pauline tradition, Paul's version showing most signs of
modification/41/.

     d. The connexion between Luke 21:34,35 and 21:36
     Even if the last suggestions about Ephesians 6 are too
speculative to build on, we still have come to the probable
conclusions (a) that the exhortation of Luke 21:34,35 is
related to 1 Thessalonians 5, and (b) that the exhortation of
Luke 21:36 is related to Ephesians 6. The two Lukan
exhortations form a pair, one being the negative exhortation to

get rid of evil 'lest ....', the other being the positive
encouragement to prayer and faithfulness 'so that .....'. We
are reminded of similar balancing exhortations in the epistles.
Luke's particular combination of sayings might be judged
secondary in the light of the Pauline parallels; but, since
there is some reason to think Luke's form of the sayings more
primitive than Paul's, it is quite possible that his ordering
of them is also primitive/42/.

This suggestion receives rather striking support from the
observation that, quite apart from their relationship to Luke
21, 1 Thessalonians 5 and Ephesians 6 seem to be related to
each other, and also to Romans 13 (another eschatological
passage with some similarity to Luke 21)/43/. These three
Pauline passages all have a call to 'wakefulness' and an
injunction to don the Christian armour/44/, and it can be
reasonably argued that Paul is drawing in all three passages
on an early catechetical tradition, a tradition that was
originally strongly eschatological, but which in Ephesians has
lost some of its eschatological flavour (though not all of its
eschatological vocabulary, e.g. ἀγρυπνεῖν, also the reference
to standing 'in the evil day'). The internal Pauline evidence
by itself may be considered by some insufficient to establish
the case for this sort of catechetical tradition; but when Luke
21:34-36 with its clear links with two of the three passages
and possible links with the third is considered and also the
probability that Luke 21:34,35 is primitive material, then the
cumulative case is strong, and the possibility that all Luke
21:34-36 is based on primitive tradition becomes a
probability/45/.

e. An eschatological discourse of Jesus?
The combination of different interlocking observations in
the previous discussion makes it reasonable to conclude, not
only that Luke 21:34-36 contains early traditions - a
relatively sure conclusion - but also that the Lukan verses and
various Pauline passages are based on an early collection of
eschatological exhortation. Could this collection originally
have been part of an eschatological discourse of Jesus? In
favour of this is (1) Luke's evidence. We have concluded that
Luke is working with early traditions at this point, and so his
positioning of the material must be taken seriously. (2) Real
or supposed dominical origin would explain how the saying
became a regular part of early Christian catechesis used by
Paul and others. (3) The sort of eschatological parenesis that,

according to the earlier argument, lies behind Luke 21:34-6 and
1 Thess 5:3-8 (and the other Pauline passages) makes good sense
following some reference to the Second Coming. It may not be
accidental that Paul agrees with Luke in placing the section
after a description of the Second Coming. (4) It has been
argued that much of Paul's other eschatological teaching in 1
and 2 Thessalonians, including the section immediately
preceding in 1 and 2 Thessalonians, has significant parallels
in the Synoptic Apocalypse. (5) There are several small verbal
connexions between the Lukan verses and the Marcan ending to
the apocalyptic discourse, notably ἀγρυπνεῖν, ἐξαίφνης/
αἰφνίδιος, and perhaps βλέπετε (cf. Luke's προσέχετε). Since
there is reason to think that Luke found ἀγρυπνεῖν and
αἰφνίδιος in his non-Marcan source, and since neither term is
Marcan - e.g. we might expect Mark's usual γρηγορεῖν - the
simple explanation of these links is that Mark also knew the
pre-Lukan ending of the discourse/46/. (6) There is one link
with the Matthean ending of the apocalyptic discourse, since
Matthew (though not Luke) has the thief saying towards the end
of the apocalyptic discourse in a position parallel to Luke 21:
34-36/47/.

   All this evidence does not add up to proof of anything;
but at least there is a real possibility that Paul knew a form
of the eschatological discourse that included the Lukan material
of 21:34-6, and also perhaps the thief saying. If that
possibility is contemplated, then interesting further questions
arise about the possible relationship of that ending to the
endings of Matthew and Mark. We have seen some reason to think
that Mark may have known the Lukan form. So far as Matthew is
concerned, several commentators have noted the similarity of
the ideas in Matt 24:37-41 and 1 Thess 5:3. There could be
something in this, even though we have seen possible reason to
link the Pauline verses with Jer 6:14/48/; but such
speculations cannot be pursued here/49/.

   ## 5. *The persecution teaching*
   Paul's concern over the sufferings of the Thessalonians is
very clear in his letter. But he explains in 1 Thess 3:3:
'You yourselves know that this is to be our lot. For when we
were with you, we told you beforehand that we were to suffer
affliction (θλίβεσθαι), as it has come to pass, and as you know.'
He doesn't here explain why they are suffering but in 2 Thess
1:4-7 he picks up the idea of the Thessalonians' sufferings,
referring to 'your endurance (ὑπομονῆς) and faith in all your

persecutions and afflictions (θλίψεσιν) which you are enduring.
This is evidence of the righteous judgment of God, that you may
be made worthy (καταξιοῦσθαι)/50/ of the kingdom of God, for
which you are suffering - since God deems it just to repay with
affliction (θλῖψιν) those who afflict you (θλίβουσιν), and to
grant rest with us to you who are afflicted (θλιβομένοις).' We
note here (a) the prominence of the words θλῖψις/θλίβεσθαι (not
uncommon elsewhere in Paul, but especially frequent in 2
Corinthians and in 1 and 2 Thessalonians); (b) the fact that
Paul explains their sufferings eschatologically as something
necessary that will lead to vindication at the last day of the
kingdom/51/, not in terms of sharing the sufferings of Christ.

The argument for connecting this teaching with the
Synoptic Apocalypse is as follows: (a) the Synoptic Apocalypse
contains a substantial warning of the persecutions and
sufferings that Jesus' followers will face (Mark 13:9-20 and
parallels), and the word θλῖψις is an important one in the
Markan and Matthean versions of the chapter, although it must
be said that in Mark the word is used in connexion with the
setting up of the desolating sacrilege and the sufferings that
that will involve (including for the elect); only in Matthew is
it used in the preceding section describing the sufferings of
the disciples (24:9).   (b) The suffering is not explained in
the Synoptics, but the promise is clear that 'he who endures
to the end will be saved' (Matthew/Mark, similarly Luke). This
thought is not far removed from Paul's explanation that the
Thessalonians' endurance and faith are evidence that they are
being made worthy for the 'kingdom of God' and that God is
going to reward them on judgment day. It is possible that
Paul's argument here finds its explanation in the fact that
Paul had already taught them the traditions found in the
Synoptic Apocalypse (though it must be admitted that the idea
of suffering leading to vindication is a common enough
apocalyptic theme). (c) Paul specifically says that he taught
them about suffering while he was with them. There is strong
evidence showing that other parts of his eschatological
teaching, which he passed on to the Thessalonians, are
significantly parallel to the Synoptic Apocalypse. So it seems
quite probable that this eschatological teaching about
suffering was part and parcel with the other teaching and that
the parallelism with the Synoptics is not accidental/52/.

So far as the nature and direction of the links are
concerned, it must be said that the links are not verbally

close. θλῖψις is a common word, not found however in Luke here
/53/. There is a parallel between Mark 13:23 προείρηκα ὑμῖν
πάντα and 1 Thess 3:4 προελέγομεν ὑμῖν ...., but not in
significantly parallel contexts. The word ὑπομονή is found in
Luke 21:19 (and the verb ὑπομένειν in Mark 13:13, Matt 24:13)
and in 2 Thess 1:4. But none of these parallels are
sufficient to prove very close connexion. So far as the links
with particular gospels are concerned, Matthew puts the word
θλῖψις in the section on persecution, and Luke has a few
verbal links. But none of this points clearly in one
direction.

6. *The Jews' persecuting activities*
a. 1 Thess 2:14-16 parallel to Matt 23:29-38
The possible parallel in this case is not with the
Synoptic Apocalypse itself, but with the Q section immediately
preceding it in Matthew's gospel, i.e. Matt 23:29-38/54/.
Orchard notes four words in common ἀποκτείνειν, προφήτης,
(ἐκ)διώκειν, (ἀνα)πληροῦν, and thinks it remarkable to find all
the four words together in two passages. More substantially he
notes a common thread of thought and similar development:
(i) Paul speaks of the Jews ἡμᾶς ἐκδιωξάντων (1 Thess 2:15);
and in Matt 23:24 Jesus says διώξετε ἀπὸ πόλεως εἰς πόλιν;
(ii) 1 Thess 2:16 εἰς τὸ ἀναπληρῶσαι αὐτῶν τὰς ἁμαρτίας
πάντοτε parallels Matt 23:32 ὑμεῖς πληρώσατε τὸ μέτρον τῶν
πατέρων; (iii) 1 Thess 2:15 τῶν καὶ τὸν κύριον ἀποκτεινάντων
Ἰησοῦν καὶ τοὺς προφήτας parallels Matt 23:34,37 (Jerusalem)
ἀποκτείνουσα τοὺς προφήτας; (iv) 1 Thess 2:16 ἔφθασεν δὲ ἐπ'
αὐτοὺς ἡ ὀργὴ εἰς τέλος parallels Matt 23:36 ἥξει ταῦτα πάντα
ἐπὶ τὴν γενεὰν ταύτην, v 38 ἰδοὺ ἀφίεται ὑμῖν ὁ οἶκος ὑμῶν ...

Although these parallels are not all very close and need
not be regarded as significant, it is impressive how much of 1
Thess 2:15,16 can be paralleled in Matt 23:29-38 (or even in
the shorter 23:32-36). Were the Lukan wording of the Q
passage to be preferred in Luke 11:49 ἀποστελῶ εἰς αὐτοὺς
προφήτας καὶ ἀποστόλους, καὶ ἐξ αὐτῶν ἀποκτενοῦσιν καὶ
διώξουσιν ...., this would give an even closer parallel to
Paul's τῶν..ἀποκτεινάντων...τοὺς προφήτας καὶ ἡμᾶς ἐκδιωξάντων
... But it is only Matthew who has the reference to 'filling
up your fathers' measure', which is perhaps the most
distinctive parallel to 1 Thessalonians 2 'to fill up their
sins'/55/.

b. An explanation of oddities in 1 Thess 2:14-16
In favour of seeing significance in the parallelism
between 1 Thessalonians 2 and Matthew 23, apart from the
overlap of language and ideas, is the slight oddity of Paul's
references in 1 Thess 2:14,15. E. Best discusses, in the
first place, why Paul picks on the churches of Judea as an
example when writing to Thessalonica/56/. This is quite
simply explained, if there is reason to think that Paul is here
using the tradition that is also found in Matt 23:29-38.

Similarly, in verse 15, where Best and others are
mystified by the unparalleled violence of the accusation
against the Jews, if Paul is here quoting, then much of his
vehement language may be explicable. So may the unusual use
of ἀποκτείνειν in connexion with the death of Jesus, since
this hypothesis must presuppose that Paul added the reference
to 'the Lord Jesus' to the original simple reference to the
killing of 'the prophets'/57/.

A final point at which the hypothesis of a common
tradition may help is in the difficult Pauline phrase
ἔφθασεν δὲ ἐπ' αὐτοὺς ἡ ὀργὴ εἰς τέλος. We cannot go into the
numerous difficult questions surrounding this verse; but one
possible interpretation is that ἔφθασεν refers to something
future (probably imminently future)/58/, since it is
difficult to see what past event Paul could mean with the very
serious ἡ ὀργὴ εἰς τέλος, a phrase with a definitely
eschatological ring about it/59/. Best, who takes this view,
suggests that Paul's knowledge of the sins of the Jews
together with his beliefs about the end-time led him to the
logical conclusion that final disaster was about to descend on
the Jewish people, but he denies that Paul had the fall of
Jerusalem in mind. If, however, as Best himself accepts, Paul
had access to something like the Q tradition at this point,
then there is no need to look further for the explanation of
Paul's thought, since the thought of judgment descending on
the Jews is part and parcel of it. As for how Paul understood
this imminent judgment, he may well have understood it, as
Matthew did, of the destruction of Jerusalem; this is likely if
Paul knew the Q tradition and if Matthew has retained the Q
sequence with the lament over Jerusalem immediately following.
Although Luke has a different sequence, he probably took the
Q prophecy of judgment in the same way as Matthew; and it is
interesting, if not significant, that in his description of
the fall of Jerusalem in 21:23 he speaks of ὀργὴ τῷ λαῷ τούτῳ

in words reminiscent of 1 Thess 2:11/60/.

Conclusions

Our examination of parallels between Paul's eschatological teaching and that found in the Synoptics is almost completed. There are a number of other words, ideas or phrases common to 1 and 2 Thessalonians and the Synoptic Apocalypse/61/; but none of these parallels are sufficiently close to add much or anything to our case for a significant connexion between Paul's and the Synoptic traditions.   Even without further evidence, however, our study has brought us to various important conclusions:

1.   Our first conclusion is that there is considerable significant overlap between the eschatological traditions that Paul passed on to the Thessalonians/62/ and the eschatological traditions preserved in the Synoptics, especially in the Synoptic Apocalypse.   (A very considerable proportion of the material found in the main body of the Synoptic Apocalypse has possible or probable parallels in 1 and 2 Thessalonians).   All the evidence for this thesis is not of equal weight; but there are sufficient solid arguments upon which to base the case, and then to justify the inclusion in a cumulative argument of some less certain, though still plausible, points.

2.   Paul's traditions have links with all three gospels, or (in conventional source critical terms) with Mark, Q, M and L.   Interestingly his closest links seem to be with Matthew or M, though they are hardly sufficient to prove Orchard's thesis of literary dependence; but there is also one striking link with L material in Luke 21:34,35 (and just possibly in Luke 21: 23,4), which suggests that Luke, while using Mark (or, on the Griesbach hypothesis, Matthew) also had a non-Marcan source available.

3.   Paul's links with the Synoptics are not just at the level of individual sayings; there is also some evidence of common sequences of sayings, notably in 2 Thessalonians 2, probably also in 1 Thessalonians 4 and 5.

4.   Establishing links between Paul's teaching and the Synoptics is not the same thing as proving that the traditions antedate Paul.   It could be that in some or all cases the Synoptists are dependent on Paul, i.e. that he is the originator of the traditions/63/.   We have, however, seen

(a) that Paul in the Thessalonian epistles is restating
traditions that he passed on to the Thessalonians and that he
may well have received these traditions from others; (b) that
at several points Paul seems to be drawing on earlier
traditions (e.g. 1 Thess 2:16-16, 5:3), traditions that are
preserved in the Synoptic apocalyptic material. It is
reasonable to suppose that this is also the case elsewhere,
where his traditions overlap with the Synoptics.

5. There was one possible trace of evidence to suggest
that the material in common between Paul and the Synoptics had
an Aramaic/Hebrew base/64/. But, although the level of verbal
similarity between Paul and the Synoptics was often such as
would be compatible with this hypothesis, the evidence in that
particular case did not demand it; and some of the evidence
clearly suggested a link at the Greek stage of tradition.

6. To conclude that there were early eschatological
traditions behind 1 and 2 Thessalonians and the Synoptics
leaves the question of the nature and arrangement of those
traditions unsolved. We have no grounds to conclude that Paul
knew the traditions of Matthew 23 in the context of Matthew
24, 25, just because he uses both in his eschatologically
flavoured epistles; Luke after all puts them in a different
context. However, there is, as we have seen, some evidence
that Paul knew some of the material in the Synoptic sort of
order. In particular there is reason to believe that there
was a pre-Pauline account of the coming of the abomination/
lawless one followed by the victorious coming of the Son of
man, this being the core of the Synoptic discourse; there is
also a possibility that Paul knew a hortatory ending to the
discourse, including the saying about the day coming suddenly
and perhaps the thief saying. If he did, then this points to
Luke and Matthew also having known a non-Marcan discourse
ending.

7. Even if the common Pauline/Synoptic traditions are
pre-Pauline, this is not the same as saying that they were
thought to derive from Jesus. Although that question takes us
slightly beyond the immediate scope of our paper, it may be
worth observing: (a) that Matthew, Luke and perhaps Mark each
have different points of agreement with Paul in material which
they ascribe to Jesus; they may, then, be seen as three
independent witnesses to Paul's use of dominical traditions/65/.
(b) If the argument that Paul in 1 and 2 Thessalonians was

passing on tradition that he received and that he regarded as
authoritative is correct, then we are evidently dealing with
a very primitive authoritative tradition.   (c) We know that
Paul recognized the authority of Jesus' teaching, though his
explicit references to it are few; whether he would have
regarded other tradition (e.g. prophetic tradition) as being of
fundamental importance is at least doubtful.   (d) If our
suggested explanation of 1 Thess 4:15 is correct/66/, then this is
evidence that Paul regarded this particular piece of teaching
as dominical (in the sense of deriving from the earthly Jesus).

Quite apart from the question of authenticity, the findings of
our paper, if they are justified, are of considerable
importance, not least in that they suggest that the
distinctively Matthean and Lukan elements in the Synoptic
triple tradition should not be as quickly dismissed as is often
done.   We may indeed say that our conclusions, if valid,
enlarge the Synoptic problem in a significant way, since Paul
is seen to be our earliest witness to the Synoptic Apocalypse
and his evidence must be brought in when the different
Synoptic accounts are compared.

Notes

/1/   'Thessalonians and the Synoptic Gospels', *Biblica* 19
(1938) 19.   For more recent statements of a similar position
see L. Hartman, *Prophecy Interpreted* (Uppsala: Gleerup, 1966)
178-205, and G. H. Waterman 'The Sources of Paul's Teaching
on the Second Coming of Christ in 1 and 2 Thessalonians', *JETS*
18 (1975) 105-113.
/2/   *Theology and Ethics in Paul* (Nashville: Abingdon, 1968)
59.   A similar position is taken by R. Pesch, *Naherwartungen:
Tradition und Redaktion in Markus 13* (Düsseldorf: Patmos 1968),
e.g. pp. 214,215.
/3/   In this paper I am using the terms 'apocalyptic'/
'apocalypse' in the common rather loose way; whether all or
any of the material being considered should strictly be so
described is debatable.   I am also taking for granted the
Pauline authorship of 1 and 2 Thessalonians.
/4/   Compare the use of παραδιδόναι in 1 Cor 11:23; cf. 11:2,
15:1-3.   Cf. R. Schippers, *NovT* 8 (1966) 224.
/5/   The context would suggest this; compare vv 5,6 with v 15.
Also note the verbal echo of v 2 in v 15.   On the other hand,
the 'tradition' in 3:6 seems ethical and not specifically
eschatological tradition (cf. 3:10).

/6/   In this case Paul does not say that the Thessalonians
already know what he is saying; possibly he assumes it.   On
this verse and on the teaching about suffering see further
below, note /17/.

/7/   But Matthew's immediately preceding οὐκ οἴδατε ποίᾳ ἡμέρᾳ
ὁ κύριος ὑμῶν ἔρχεται comes quite near to the Pauline wording,
as Orchard observes (Biblica 19, p. 25).   Matthew does not
actually refer to the 'day' coming - contra Orchard.

/8/   The 'thief' usage does have parallels elsewhere in the NT
and in early Christian tradition.   See 2 Pet 3:10, Rev 3:3,
16:15; also Gos.Thom. 21 and maybe Did. 16:1.   In all these
contexts there is an accompanying call to keep awake (only
implied in 2 Peter), but the parallels do not give us certain
clues about the original wording and subsequent development of
the 'thief' tradition.   All the NT passages, except the Q
passage, have a simple comparison ὡς κλέπτης, not a parable as
in Q; but Gos.Thom. 21 also has a parable.   2 Peter agrees with
Paul in comparing the coming of the day, rather than the coming
of the Lord, with the thief's arrival; but Revelation sides
with Q in this.   The wording of Rev 3:3 has certain
resemblances to Matthew's (a conditional clause and the
subsequent reference to not knowing the hour), as does Gos.
Thom. 21.   On the other hand, Rev 15:15 with its μακάριος ὁ
γρηγορῶν has links with Luke 12:37,38.

      We may be content for the present to note E. Best's
conclusion in his Commentary on the First and Second Epistles
to the Thessalonians (London: Black, 1972) 205 that Paul's
wording could be a simplification of the Q parabolic form
(avoiding the distasteful comparison of Jesus with a thief); or
that the Q parable could be an expansion of some simpler
comparison of the Lord's coming with the coming of a thief.
See also R. J. Bauckham's argument about 'deparabolization' in
NTS 23 (1977) 162-176.

/9/   The use of οἴδα with an adverb is not usual in Paul.
Hartman (Prophecy, 197) compares Paul's quite frequent use of
the interrogative 'Do you not know..?', but this is not quite
the same as the usage here.

/10/ Some have compared Paul's opening phrase preceding the
thief analogy, περὶ δὲ τῶν χρόνων καὶ τῶν καιρῶν, with Matthew/
Mark's περὶ δὲ τῆς ἡμέρας ἐκείνης καὶ ὥρας (in Matthew also
preceding the thief analogy) and with what is sometimes
regarded as Luke's equivalent verse, Acts 1:7 οὐχ ὑμῶν ἐστιν
γνῶναι χρόνους ἢ καιροὺς.   Although a connexion cannot be
completely ruled out, we note against the idea (a) that περὶ δέ
+ genitive is a very normal Pauline introduction to a section,

(b) that χρόνοι καὶ καιροι is a common OT phrase.

/11/ Following the earlier reference to the angels gathering the elect, the 'taking' in Matt 24:40,41 is more likely the taking to salvation than a taking away to judgment.

/12/ As in Zech 14:5; cf. Best, *Thessalonians*, 152,3. Contrast Paul's usage of ἅγιοι to refer to believers elsewhere, including 2 Thess 1:10.

/13/ Orchard (*Biblica* 19, p. 32) suggests that Paul's somewhat unusual phrase in 2 Thess 1:7 μετ᾽ ἀγγέλων δυνάμεως αὐτοῦ echoes the Synoptic μετὰ δυνάμεως καὶ δόξης πολλῆς καὶ ἀποστελεῖ τοὺς ἀγγέλους αὐτοῦ (Matt 24:30,31); Best (*Thessalonians* 258) and B. Rigaux (*Epitres aux Thessaloniciens* [Paris: Gabalda, 1956] 627) explain it as meaning - angels which belong to his power.

/14/ Hartman (*Prophecy*, 186) connects this phrase with Dan 7: 13, 'and they brought him (the one like a son of man) before him' (the Ancient of Days). He appears not to notice the link with 2 Thess 2:1 and Matt 24:31/Mark 13:27.

/15/ In addition to these points Waterman (*JETS* 18, p. 109) finds also a parallel reference to 'the survivors' in 1 Thess 4:15,17 and Matt 24:13 (and parallels), and he compares the eschatological idea of salvation in 1 Thess 5:8 and Matt 24:13 (p. 111).

/16/ Contra Pesch, *Naherwartungen*, 214,5.

/17/ Although in the preceding section we have drawn on 1 Thess 4:15-17, it is not essential for this study to decide on the meaning of λόγῳ κυρίου. But it may be worth observing that several elements in verse 16,17 may be traditional material (e.g. the Lord's descent, the angels and trumpet, the rapture and probably the κέλευσμα; so P. Nepper-Christensen, *ST* 19 (1965) 145). The major element not under suspicion of being traditional is the point about the respective positions of the living and the dead. Since this point was the crucial one for Paul's argument, it might be argued that the 'word of the Lord' must have been a word of Christian prophecy about this, not the traditional but irrelevant description of the Parousia. But (a) if the received traditional description of the Parousia (e.g. the trumpet etc.) was irrelevant to Paul's point, why does he bother to bring it in? (b) We know that Paul could speak about received traditions as a 'command of the Lord' (1 Cor 7:25, cf. 7:10,12; 11:23). In view of these two points it seems at least as likely that the 'word' here is the traditional description of the Parousia and that the application of that tradition to the Thessalonians' problem is Paul's exegesis of it (not dissimilar from some of his OT exegesis).

If a Synoptic saying was the basis of Paul's exegesis, the most likely candidate would seem to be Mark 13:27 (and parallels). Faced with the Thessalonians' problem, Paul might well have argued that this strong statement about the gathering in of the elect from the ends of the earth to the ends of heaven implied the gathering in of the Christian dead. In support of this note: (1) Paul's reference to the 'word of the Lord' leads on from a reference to God bringing the Christian dead with Jesus (ἄξει σὺν αὐτῷ); compare Mark 13:27 ἐπισυνάξει τοὺς ἐκλεκτοὺς and 2 Thess 2:1 ἡμῶν ἐπισυναγωγῆς ἐπ' αὐτόν. (2) It is presumably the same trumpet that announces the angelic gathering of the elect in Matt 24:31 and the resurrection of the dead in 1 Thess 4:16, 1 Cor 15:52, Did. 16:6. Whether Matthew or the others preserve the earlier tradition, we may see here confirmatory evidence that the gathering of the elect and the resurrection of the dead were closely associated (cf. also M. D. Goulder, *Midrash and Lection in Matthew* [London: SPCK, 1974] 147, on the Danielic background).

If Paul is using the sort of tradition we have suggested, then he is expounding it freely rather than quoting it verbatim, not only because the Thessalonians probably knew the saying in question, but also because the saying did not contain an explicit reference to the resurrection - hence the Thessalonians' problem. For a possibly parallel free quotation see Rom 14:14, too quickly dismissed by Best, *Thessalonians* 191.

/18/ So J. Lambrecht, *Die Redaktion der Markus-Apokalypse* (Rome: Pontifical Institute, 1967), 96-100, who argues that the combination of the two phrases ἐπὶ τῷ ὀνόματί μου and λέγοντες ὅτι ἐγώ εἰμι demands this interpretation.

/19/ There are differences: in the Synoptics the excitement seems caused by wars, persecutions and other events; in 2 Thessalonians the immediate cause seems to have been some sort of misunderstanding or distortion of Paul's teaching (though this misunderstanding might have been encouraged by the sort of things referred to in the Synoptics).

/20/ It is arguable that the coming in the Synoptics is not the final coming of Christ on the last day; so J. M. Kik, *Matthew Twenty-Four An Exposition* (Swengel: Bible Truth Depot, 1948), and others. Whether it is or not, the parallelism between the Synoptics and 2 Thessalonians remains.

/21/ The Synoptic 'holy place' or 'where it ought not' could be either the city of Jerusalem or the temple; in the light of

the Danielic background the latter may be more likely.
/22/ The Roman general Pompey defiled the temple by his
presence; and the emperor Caligula threatened to have his
statue set up there.
/23/ Note the possible important parallel in Revelation 13,
where the description of the blasphemous beast is followed by a
description of another beast (identified in Rev 19:20 as the
ψευδοπροφήτης) performing signs to deceive men into believing
in the first beast. In Did. 16:4 the κοσμοπλάνος himself does
σημεῖα καὶ τέρατα.
/24/ The alternative view that we have in 2 Thessalonians and
the Synoptics two separate events described in closely parallel
ways is possible, but less simple; we would still want to say
that the similarity of description was deliberate, the one
event being described in terms of the other.
/25/ Their agreement, together with the occurrence of the
personal Antichrist concept in other early traditions, e.g. 1
John, Revelation, the Didache, could suggest that this is a
primitive concept, which Matthew has altered, perhaps under the
influence of Daniel. On the other hand, Matthew's neuter,
though easier grammatically, is perhaps the more difficult
concept (certainly if he was writing after AD70 about AD70);
and Mark's masculine looks like the Greek writer's
interpretative hand. So it is possible that the concept has
been made personal in the Marcan and Pauline traditions,
perhaps in the light of the Caligula crisis of AD40. Yet
another possibility is that the personal Antichrist and the
impersonal temple sacrilege are equally primitive ideas, which
though distinct are closely related via Daniel and have to an
extent been assimilated to each other in Mark (hence his
masculine participle) and in Paul (hence his reference to
sitting in the temple).
/26/ It is also found elsewhere, e.g. in 1 John (e.g. 3:4), a
book having various interesting connexions with the Pauline and
Synoptic eschatological traditions.
/27/ See my article 'A Note on Matthew 24:10-12', TB 31 (1980)
155-162, where I note among other things that ἀνομία is used in
the LXX where we might expect βδέλυγμα.
/28/ Orchard's suggestion (Biblica 19, p. 34) that there may
be significance in the occurrence together of the three words
ἀνομία, ἀγάπη and σώζειν both in Matt 24:12,13 and 2 Thess 2:
7-10 seems speculative, since they are not used in the same
way. Equally unpersuasive is his connecting of 2 Thess 2:7 ἕως
ἐκ μέσου γένηται with Matt 24:34 ἕως ἂν πάντα ταῦτα γένηται
(pp. 40-2), even though the construction may be untypical of
Paul.

/29/ The punctuation found in some MSS ὡς παγίς γὰρ ἐπελεύσεται
... would give a slightly poorer parallelism. Another textual
variant καταξιώθητε for κατισχύσητε would give a new verbal link
with the Thessalonian epistles (2 Thess 1:5); κατισχύσητε could
be explained as a simplification, and perhaps assimilation in
sense to Eph 5:11; but cf. Luke 20:35 and I. H. Marshall, *The
Gospel of Luke* (Exeter: Paternoster, 1978) 783.

/30/ Hartman, *Prophecy*, 192.

/31/ Ps 18:5,6, the parallel 2 Sam 22:6, and Ps 116:3. Cf.
Acts 2:24, regarded by C. C. Torrey as a NT example of a
mistranslation of חבל (*Composition and Date of Acts* [Cambridge:
CUP, 1916] 28,29); but on this see M. Wilcox, *The Semitisms of
Acts* (Oxford: OUP, 1965) 46-48. Although some of Wilcox's
arguments lack cogency, it is possible that Psalms 18 and 116
were testimonia passages.

/32/ Translators and commentators are not unanimous on 3:28,
some taking it there as 'pangs'. If 'cords' is correct, then
we apparently have a deliberate play on the two senses of the
word in the scroll (so K. G. Kuhn, *Konkordanz zu den
Qumrantexten* [Göttingen: Vandenhoeck and Ruprecht, 1960] 67).
It is not impossible that the same is true of the LXX and of
Acts 2:24: thus, when the translators of the Hebrew phrase
opted for the rendering 'pangs', this may not have been an
accidental misunderstanding, but a deliberate play on an
ambiguity; and even though the one word is used, the other
meaning may not have been forgotten by the translator. This
could perhaps be suggested by the use of verbs such as
περιέχειν, περικυκλοῦν, λύειν with the noun ὠδίν, though for
λύειν see Job 35:2 LXX.

/33/ The opposite possibility cannot be excluded: Luke could
have altered the Pauline wording in order to avoid the
eschatologically loaded ὠδίν (cf. his omission of Mark 13:8,
though there is some doubt as to whether ὠδίν in 1
Thessalonians 5 is being used with eschatological overtones cf.
Pesch, *Naherwartungen*, 215), choosing instead another term with
good OT background (cf. Isa 24:17). However, the balance of
the argument seems to point the other way.

/34/ I am indebted to Dr R. J. Bauckham for drawing my
attention to the possible importance of these OT texts, as well
as for other useful comments on my paper.

/35/ If an original חבל does lie behind the two texts, the
case for the originality of the Lukan form is even stronger:
(a) because Luke's 'like a snare' translates directly into an
ambiguous Aramaic/Hebrew (e.g. כחבל), whereas Paul's 'like
pangs on a woman with child' does not; (b) because the sense

'trap' is not a very prominent meaning for חבל, so that it is
probably easier to conceive of an evolution from 'trap' to
'pangs' than vice versa. Furthermore ὠδίν is arguably the
more familiar eschatological term.
/36/ If it is thought that Paul and Luke are here using a
tradition purporting to come from Jesus, then it is not
surprising that Paul would feel more free to modify the wording
in his free allusion than Luke in his direct citation.
/37/ *Thessalonians*, 207.
/38/ I am assuming the basic Paulinicity of Ephesians, though
the argument might stand even without that assumption.
/39/ The similarity is less if καταξιωθητε is read in Luke
21:36 rather than κατισχύσητε. See note /29/ above.
/40/ E.g. 1 Cor 15:13 combines the call to 'stand' with a call
to wakefulness - cf. Luke 21:36 - and with a call to strength -
cf. Eph 6:10,18; 2 Thess 2:15 has a call to stand followed by a
call to prayer (3:1) rather similar to Eph 6:18,19.
/41/ R. P. Martin's suggestion that Luke had a hand in the
writing of Ephesians might account for the links between Luke
and Ephesians, but not for the links between Luke, Ephesians 6
and other parts of Paul that we are going to note. (*New
Testament Foundations* 2 [Exeter: Paternoster, 1978] 230-3).
Some of the links he notes between Luke and Ephesians might be
explained by our theory of a common tradition: he notes, e.g.,
'girding up the loins' in Luke 12:35, Eph 6:14, conceivably
another case of the Ephesians context giving military
connotations to a non-military metaphor.
/42/ If the exhortation form of Luke 21:34,35 is primitive, it
seems likely that there would have been a balancing positive
exhortation. If there was, then it is simpler to suppose that
Luke has retained it (in his verse 36) than to suppose that he
displaced it with a substitute saying.
/43/ Compare Rom 13:11,12 with Luke 21:28,31; 13:13 with Luke
21:24.
/44/ The parallels are the more striking if we include with
Ephesians 6 the talk of light/dark in Eph 5:8-21. Note too the
parallel between 1 Thess 5:16 and Eph 6:18 in the call to
unceasing prayer; cf. Luke 21:36.
/45/ That is not to say that Luke has not rephrased the
tradition to some extent.
     If this primitive tradition existed, then it may be
possible to trace other elements in the Thessalonian epistles
back to it. Note that the reference to 'standing' and
'praying' in 2 Thess 2:15, 3:1 comes in a context rather
similar to 1 Thess 5:9,10; is Paul echoing the one tradition in

both contexts (cf. 1 Thess 3:8)?

The only plausible alternative explanation of the parallels between Luke and the different Pauline passages would seem to be to explain that there was in the early church a · widely known and frequently used stock of parenetic sayings, and that similar combinations of sayings in different parts of the NT are only to be expected. But (a) in this case the considerable meshwork of links between Luke 21, 1 Thessalonians 5, Ephesians 5,6 and Romans 13 makes the explanation unlikely. (b) There is no likelihood of the sayings in question having floated in splendid isolation at any period in their transmission; they must have been collected and combined together in various ways from very early (indeed from the beginning). We would expect such early combinations to be reflected in the NT. (c) The fact that in both the sayings of 21:34-6 Luke hits on a form closely related to the Pauline tradition, though apparently more primitive, is well explained if Luke has drawn both from one source.

What may be slightly problematic for our hypothesis is the absence from Luke of several of the motifs that unite the three Pauline passages, i.e. the light/dark, put on/off and armour motifs. But this may be explained either as the result of Luke's selectivity or perhaps preferably as the result of development of the tradition into the Pauline form. In favour of this is (i) the evidence for the primitiveness of Luke's form of the sayings; (ii) the Pauline put on/off and armour motifs sound more like church parenesis than the Lukan sayings (but a dominical saying may lie behind the light/dark motif; cf. John 12:35, Eph 5:8, 1 Thess 5:3,4); (iii) it is possible to see how the suggested development could have occurred: Paul's put on/off motif is not very far removed from Luke's call 'not to be weighed down' by drunkenness etc. (cf. Heb 12:1), nor the light/dark saying from Luke's call to wakefulness before the 'day' of the Lord.

/46/ Mark has mixed it with the parable of the watching servants, a parable separately attested in Luke 12:36-8 (cf. Matt 25:1-13).

/47/ It is notable that the 'thief' tradition is linked in Luke to the parable of the watching servants and that that parable is put at the end of the apocalyptic discourse by Mark; this fascinating web of interconnections deserves further exploration.

/48/ If Luke 17:22-37 (and even 18:1ff.) is an independent non-Marcan version of the Synoptic Apocalypse, then Luke 21: 34-36 could be parallel to Luke 17:26-18:1ff. (note the call to prayer).

/49/ Dr R. J. Bauckham has suggested to me that the Lukan
tradition of 21:34-6 might be connected with the tradition
reflected in Rev 3:10, Herm.Sim. 23:4. See his article in *JTS*
25 (1974) 27-40, where his discussion of the 'great distress'
opens up interesting possibilities; the influence of this idea
might be detected not only in Luke 21:35,36, Rev 3:10, 7:14
and perhaps in Matt 24:21, but also in Luke 21:23 (note the
agreement with Matt 24:21, and the possibility of linking Luke
21:23,24 and 21:36) and even in 1 Thess 3:7,8 (note the ἀνάγκη,
θλῖψις, πίστις and στήκειν).

/50/ For the textual variant see note /29/ above.

/51/ Cf. Phil 1:28 as a possible parallel.

/52/ It is possible that some of the Marcan section about the
disciples' sufferings in 13:9-13 is not in its original context
in its Marcan position; it may have originally belonged in a
'Q' mission discourse (cf. Matt 10:17-22; Luke 12:11,12).
But it is still probable that there was teaching in the
apocalyptic discourse about the disciples undergoing θλῖψις,
hence the Marcan positioning of the material.

/53/ On the other hand Luke's equivalent words in 21:23 ἀνάγκη
and ὀργή both have parallels in the Thessalonian epistles.

/54/ Cf. Orchard, *Biblica* 19, pp. 20-3, R. Schippers *NovT* 8,
pp. 230-4.

/55/ Paul's particular choice of wording may have been
influenced by Gen 15:16. The relevant Matthean phrase is often
regarded as secondary, being absent from Luke; but it is
possible that in some respects Luke is secondary in this Q
passage.

/56/ Best, *Thessalonians*, 113-120.

/57/ The aorist ἐκδιωξάντων is not very hard to explain after
the preceding ἀποκτεινάντων and if Paul is thinking of his past
experiences in Judea. As for the aorist ἀναπληρῶσαι
πάντοτε, could this be somehow explicable if Paul is here
incorporating traditional material into the context and/or if
πάντοτε is taken with κωλυόντων?

/58/ Whether the verb will bear the meaning 'to be just about
to happen' is debatable. But even if it is insisted that it
means 'to have just arrived' - and other Pauline usage in Rom
9:31, Phil 3:15 might support this - it may perhaps be possible
to keep a future tense by appealing to the prophetic use of a
past tense. Cf. Jude 14.

/59/ The simplest translation of the phrase would be 'but
retribution (has) reached them'. But what can be meant by this,
unless we resort to the textually unsupported speculation that

the phrase is a post-Pauline gloss reflecting the events of AD
70? Perhaps the best suggestion is that the ὀργή is divine
rejection of the Jews such as is described in Romans 11 (cf.
Rigaux, *Thessaloniciens* 455). But the ὀργή is described here
in a way that probably suggests a drastic divine response to
the Jews' misdeeds, when they are filled up, not a continuing
spiritual state of affairs. If Paul is referring to an
imminent eschatological judgment, he probably does not mean the
end of all things, but a particular judgment on the Jews (ἐπ'
αὐτούς), after which the Gentile mission (just mentioned - as
hindered by the Jews) may go on.

/60/ It is tempting to try to exploit the 1 Thessalonians/
Synoptic link in the interpretation of εἰς τέλος in 1 Thess
5:16, since the same phrase occurs in the Synoptic verse about
enduring εἰς τέλος. One possibility is to take εἰς τέλος in
both places to mean 'until the end'; this would bring 1 Thess
2:16 into line with several other NT passages that speak of a
period prior to the end of judgment on the Jews and of Gentile
mission (Rom 11:25, Luke 21:24, if it is correctly taken of
Gentile mission, and perhaps Rev 11:2-4 on the trampling of
Jerusalem and the two witnesses), and could be supported by the
fact that the phrase is immediately preceded in 1 Thess 2:16 by
a reference to the Gentile mission. (It is possible that the
Matthew/Mark form of the apocalyptic discourse with its
reference to judgment on the Jews and preaching to the Gentiles
lies behind not only Luke 21:24, but the other passages as well,
including 1 Thess 2:16. This might, incidentally, support
the interpretation of the 'restrainer' in 2 Thessalonians 2 as
the preacher/preaching of the gospel.) On the other hand, εἰς
τέλος might be taken adverbially 'finally', 'utterly', both in
Matthew/Mark and in 1 Thessalonians 2; this seems to be the
sense of the parallel to Paul's phrase in T.Levi 6:11 and is
perhaps the best sense in Matthew/Mark. But clearly the fact
that the Synoptic phrase may be taken in these two quite
different ways means that the link between 1 Thessalonians 5
and the Synoptics is of little use in determining the meaning of
the Pauline phrase, and in any case the respective uses of the
phrase in the two contexts are so different as to make any
argument for or from the link extremely hazardous.

/61/ E.g. ἡ ἡμέρα ἐκείνη, βασιλεία (of the future kingdom),
εἰς ἀπάντησιν (but this is a common Septuagintal phrase). The
'shout' at the bridegroom's coming in Matthew's parable of the
virgins has been compared to the Pauline 'word of command'.

/62/ There are possible hints of Paul's eschatological teaching
elsewhere in his letters, e.g. Romans 13, 1 Cor 7:26,31, 15:52.

/63/ So M. D. Goulder (*Midrash*, 427-9) arguing for Matthew's
use of Paul.

/64/ The בַל case. It is tempting, but even less convincing,
to note the Semitic superlative use of the divine name and
then to argue that Paul's ἐν σάλπιγγι θεοῦ and Matthew's μετὰ
σάλπιγγος μεγάλης may be alternative renderings of a common
original.

/65/ We might add the evidence of John, if his 12:35,36 is
correctly linked with 1 Thess 5:3,4 and Eph 5:8. See J. A. T.
Robinson, *Jesus and His Coming* (London: SCM, 1957) 115,116.
Compare his general approach in that book with his more recent
Redating of the New Testament (London: SCM, 1976), e.g. pp. 97,
105,106. Although he continues to hold that Paul and the
evangelists have moved away from Jesus' eschatological
understanding, he thinks that the agreements between Paul and
the Synoptics (or Matthew at least) can be explained via a very
early tradition of the 'words of the Lord', probably 'the first
formulated statement of "the gospel" used by the apostles,
teachers and prophets'. For a major discussion of early
Christian catechetical forms, including many of the texts
discussed in my paper, see E. G. Selwyn *The First Epistle of St
Peter* (London: Macmillan, 1946) 365-466.

/66/ See note /17/ above.